The Royal Domain
in the Bailliage
of Rouen

Joseph R. Strayer

The Royal Domain
in the Bailliage
of Rouen

Revised Edition & Appendix

VARIORUM
London 1976

The Royal Domain in the Bailliage of Rouen
first published 1936 by Princeton University Press
Revised and augmented edition Variorum 1976
by arrangement with Princeton University Press

ISBN 0 902089 88 9

Published in Great Britain by *Variorum Reprints*
                            21a Pembridge Mews London W11 3EQ

Printed in Great Britain by   *Kingprint Ltd*
                            Richmond Surrey TW9 4PD

VARIORUM M10

TABLE OF CONTENTS

PREFACE

Since the publication of this book in 1936, a number of documents have been discovered that give additional information about the value and composition of the royal domain in the *bailliage* of Rouen. The most important of these are grants of portions of the domain to Enguerran de Marigny (printed by Jean Favier in his *Cartulaire d'Enguerran de Marigny*), an account rendered by the viscount of Auge in 1312 (printed by Robert Fawtier in the *Comptes Royaux*, II, nos. 17359[19] ff.), and a survey of the county of Beaumont-le-Roger which I analyzed in an article in *Speculum* in 1951. The relationship of these documents to the 1261 survey of the domain which is transcribed in this book is discussed in the essays now reprinted in the Appendix.

The appearance of a new edition has made it possible to correct some mistakes and to clarify some statements. The most important changes are in the sections of the Introduction dealing with prices and measures of grain. Four photographs of pages of the manuscript have been added in order to demonstrate the way in which the scribe organized his material. The Index has been expanded to include subject headings in addition to the entries for names and places.

Once more I must thank those who have aided me in this work over many years. The grant of a Sheldon Fellowship by Harvard University gave me my first opportunity to become acquainted with Norman documents. The late M. Labrosse, Director of the Municipal Library of Rouen, made it possible for me to secure photostats of the 1261 survey of the domain. Princeton University not only supported the original publication, but gave me repeated grants for work in French archives. Finally, I should like to thank Mrs. Eileen Turner, editor of Variorum Reprints, for encouraging me to prepare a new edition of a work that has long been out of print.

This book is dedicated to the memory of Professor Dana Carleton Munro of Princeton, to whom I owe my first interest in medieval history.

J. R. STRAYER

Princeton,
June 1975

THE ROYAL DOMAIN IN THE BAILLIAGE OF ROUEN

BY

JOSEPH REESE STRAYER

1936

PRINCETON: PRINCETON UNIVERSITY PRESS

TABLE OF CONTENTS

INTRODUCTION

I

DESCRIPTION OF THE MANUSCRIPT

Ms. 2665 (formerly Martainville Y 94) of the Bibliothèque Municipale de Rouen is described in the official catalogue as an "Etat du domaine royal dans les vicomtés de Rouen, du Pont-Audemer, de Bernay, du pays d'Auge, et du Pont-de-l'Arche."[1] Since the entire *bailliage* of Rouen was included in these viscounties[2] we may abbreviate the title somewhat and say that the manuscript is a description of the royal domain[3] in the *bailliage* of Rouen.

The manuscript is parchment in a good state of preservation. There are 231 folios, most of them measuring 217 by 156 millimeters. The manuscript has been foliated twice. The first foliation began on folio 3, which was marked folio 1; in the second foliation this error was corrected and some attempt was made to strike out the earlier numbers.

The manuscript is written in French, and is all in the same hand—good, clear thirteenth century writing. With one or two exceptions there is only one column to a page. Ordinarily the pages are not crowded, the margins are generous, and there is plenty of space between the lines. The one difficulty in reading the manuscript lies in the fact that the c's and t's of the scribe are interchangeable. This may have caused some errors in transcribing proper names which could not be identified from other sources.

Abbreviations are not overly numerous, and are of the usual sort. They have been expanded without comment, except when they involved proper names which could not be otherwise identified, or when the sign of abbreviation itself was not clear. In such cases the expansion has been indicated by brackets. There are a few words for which the scribe had several spellings (e.g. *verge, vergie, vergee*). When such words were abbreviated it seemed best to leave them as they were, since any expansion would suggest that the scribe preferred that spelling.

---

[1] *Catalogue Général des Mss. des Bibliothèques Publiques de France. Departements II. Rouen*, (Paris, 1888), p. 22.

[2] J. R. Strayer, *The Administration of Normandy under Saint Louis*, (Cambridge, 1932), p. 9.

[3] "Royal domain" in a somewhat restricted sense. *cf. below*, p. 11.

Marginal notes are frequent in the manuscript. They all appear to be in the same hand as the body of the work, and indicate the nature of the items opposite which they are placed. For example, the marginal note "mesure" means that the area of the lands described in that paragraph has been measured and not estimated. "Rentes" means that the revenue in question comes from manorial dues, boon labor, customary offerings at Christmas and Easter, rather than from the lease of land. "Comtée par sey" probably means that the item thus marked was listed separately in the *bailli's* account rather than lumped under some general heading. The other marginal notes are self-explanatory, except for a peculiar sign (a cross in a circle) which I have reproduced as an asterisk. This indicates the omission of a word or a numeral in the text. Apparently the scribe was unable to complete some of his entries with the information which he had available, and he made these marks to enable him to find the blanks when new information came in.

The scribe tried to indicate the proper grouping of items by a somewhat elaborate system of marginal lines. It seemed impossible to reproduce these lines, but an attempt has been made to preserve his arrangement by the use of spaces and indentations. With the exception of these lines, nothing has been intentionally omitted.

II

DATE

The exact date at which the manuscript was written cannot be determined. At the very beginning of the record a lease is mentioned as still in effect which we know from other sources was terminated in 1261.[1] There are several indications that the record is describing conditions as of the year 1260.[2] Yet allusions to events in 1262 and 1263 are fairly common[3] and there is one reference to an agreement made at Christmas 1265.[4]

There is nothing surprising in these discrepancies. The manuscript contains a great deal of detailed information which could not have been compiled rapidly, especially under medieval conditions. If the work

---

[1] fol. 3, note 1. *cf.* fol. 9v, which must have been written before 1263.

[2] fols. 58v, 85v, 105v, 206. None of the royal charters whose effects can be identified in the manuscripts are later than 1260, and those drawn up in 1258 and 1259 are very close in language and arrangement to the descriptions given in our record. *cf.* notes on fols. 74, 172, 185v.

[3] fols. 25v, 204v (1262); fols. 10, 26 (1263).

[4] fol. 96. *cf.* fol. 174, a reference to Easter 1264.

were planned in 1261, the *bailli* would naturally ask for reports of conditions in the year 1260, the last complete accounting period. But the first reports would not come in until the end of 1261, and a few laggards would still be working on their returns in 1265. The men who were slow in handing in their reports might well include more recent information. Moreover our scribe was able to correct some of the older reports from his own knowledge, since he was often present when leases of the royal domain were made.[5] The form of the manuscript makes it clear that it was written slowly, and that the scribe left plenty of space for additions and corrections.[6]

It seems probable, then, that the compilation of material for the record was begun in 1261, and that the scribe began copying the material soon after that date. He cannot have finished his work before Christmas 1265. He must have completed his task by 1270, since he has no knowledge of leases made early in the reign of Philip III.[7] Thus all the work on the document was done in the decade 1261-1270, and probably in the six years 1261-1266.

III

Author, Purpose, Method of Composition

The actual writer of our document was probably a clerk of the staff of the *bailli* of Rouen. He is constantly referring to the administrative activities in which he took part: "nos devons avoir conseil sur l'aide," "icele superficie fu ballie a iceli en nostre voie quant nous aliom a Caem a l'eschiquier de Pasques en l'an LX," "une piece de terre que nos n'avons pas en escris," "nous feismes a Colin Espec une somme de 93 l. 14 s. 6 d. d'iceste ferme," "nous devons descomter et descomterons por le visconte de Pont de l'Arche 33 s. por les aumosnes et les fieuz trop comtez."[1] He was obviously a man with a great deal of experience and ability. He was able to arrange a mass of details in an orderly and systematic way. His work is clear and well organized. There are only a few items which are not in their proper place, only a few passages which are difficult to understand. He was an accurate copyist; his work stands up well when tested by contemporary documents dealing with the same matters. Yet this man, capable and intelligent though he was, was not even chief clerk

---

[5] fols. 105v, 174.
[6] *cf.* p. 8.
[7] *cf.* notes, fols. 8, 185v, leases made in 1271.

---

[1] fols. 13v, 105v, 171v, 174, 207.

of the *bailliage*. The chief clerk at this time was Master Richard du Fay, an important and powerful personage who was more a lieutenant of the *bailli* than a clerk.[2] Master Richard is frequently mentioned in the earlier part of the manuscript,[3] but always in the third person. It seems impossible to identify him with the author of the document.

There is, of course, the possibility that the *bailli* himself dictated the work. The references to administrative work given above would fit the *bailli* as well as his clerks, since he was responsible for all such activity. The document was certainly drawn up by the *bailli's* orders, and he was probably responsible for its general plan. That he did any more than this is extremely doubtful. He had no time for detailed labor on such a report, for the thirteenth century *bailli* was a very busy man. The mere business of holding his circuit of assizes kept him moving about the *bailliage* so constantly[4] that steady work, such as was necessary for this record, was almost impossible. And of all the thirteenth century *baillis*, Julien de Peronne, who was *bailli* of Rouen at the time that this manuscript was written, was one of the busiest.[5] He stood high in royal favor, and as a consequence, many extra tasks were added to his ordinary duties. As a matter of fact, he was so busy that he could not even hold all his assizes in person, and he frequently delegated his judicial authority to Master Richard du Fay.

Thus we may assume that while Julien de Peronne and Richard du Fay planned the work, they left the execution of it to some subordinate clerk. The fact that the ordinary clerical staff of a *bailliage* was capable of doing such work as this, shows how the administrative services had developed during the reign of Saint Louis. There was no longer a shortage of trained, efficient administrators; the technique and traditions of the bureaucracy were already established. All the *bailli* had to do was to ask for a report, his subordinates would gather the necessary information, and one of them would put it into usable shape. We are already a long way from the unspecialized, record-poor government of Philip Augustus.

The reasons for making a revised list of holdings in the *bailliage* of Rouen are fairly obvious. Saint or sinner, a thirteenth century king was always in need of money. Louis IX was no exception to this rule, and he

---

[2] Strayer, *Administration of Normandy*, p. 98.
[3] fols. 5, 8, 9, 11, 15, 30, 46.
[4] Strayer, *Administration of Normandy*, pp. 20-1.
[5] *cf.* Delisle's account of his career in *H.F.*, XXIV, p. *103. Julien was *bailli* of Rouen 1261-1272.

was grateful to any official who could increase his income by legitimate means. The *baillis* were constantly trying to get more money for the king by reclaiming forgotten royal rights and possessions. The *Olim* are full of cases testifying to this activity. Julien de Peronne was an exceptionally able *bailli*, as is shown by the fact that he held the richest *bailliage* of the richest province of the kingdom for eleven years. Julien went about the business of increasing the royal income more methodically than some of his colleagues. He probably planned a general survey of his *bailliage*, soon after he arrived in Rouen in 1261, with the double purpose of restoring everything to the domain which belonged there, and making as much money as possible from rights and properties already in the domain. The results of this survey had to be recorded. They might have been added as insertions and corrections in the old lists[6] of royal property, but this would have made the old records almost illegible in places. Moreover there was a general tendency during the reign of Saint Louis to improve the form of financial documents, and Julien's survey certainly afforded an opportunity to revise old records which may have been badly arranged. Most important of all, Julien and his clerks had done a good job. The revenue from the *bailliage* had been increased by 2421 l., if we may trust our scribe's addition,[7] and Julien naturally wanted credit for this accomplishment. So, in recording the results of the survey, he had the scribe make marginal notes calling attention to property which had been recovered,[8] and careful summaries at the end of each subdivision showing how much the king's income in that district had increased.[9] In fact, the scribe became so interested in showing the increase in income, that he completely neglected to give the total income for any large division, or for the *bailliage* itself. This emphasis on the increase in income indicates that Julien expected some of his superiors to see the record. Certainly if this document were ever shown to the king or to high officials of the *curia regis* it must have impressed them. It

---

[6] Descriptions of the domain must have existed before this document was drawn up, cf. fol. 32v, "La mare du parc n'estoit pas es roules"; fol. 171v, "une piece de terre que nos n'avons pas en escris"; fol. 198v, "n'estoit pas es roules."

[7] This total is given on fol. 205. It agrees very closely with the total obtained by adding the increases in revenues reported for each viscounty (given on fols. 39v, 98, 156v, 204v, 231). The totals for viscounties can be checked only in the case of Pont-Audemer; elsewhere the scribe forgot to give a total for each sergeanty. In Pont-Audemer the scribe's total is within 6 l. of the total obtained by adding the totals for the sergeanties.

[8] fols. 8, 9, 17v, 23, 27, 27v, 29, etc.

[9] fol. 12v, "Iceste ferme creist selonc ballie et a ballier de XX lb."; fol. 13v, "La serganterie de Pavellye creist de XXVII lb. V s."; fol. 156v, "La viscomté de Bernay creist de VI.C.XII lb., XIX s."

is conceivable that it may have aided Julien in gaining such honors as his nomination to the Council of Regency in 1270.[10]

This revision of the records was based on complete and accurate information. Investigators, probably clerks of the *bailli* and of the viscounts, were sent out to inquire as to the location and value of royal property. It seems clear that the work in each district was done by different men, since, while the general form of report remains the same, there are minor differences in organization. For example, the report for Pont de l'Arche is badly arranged in comparison with the report for Bernay. These investigators obtained most of their information by means of the sworn inquest. Men of each district had to give, under oath, a description of royal property in that district, and an estimate as to its value. This is shown by the fact that for many farms there is an estimate of area marked "jurée."[11] In one case, in which a priest was accused of encroaching on royal land, the names of the jurors are given;[12] elsewhere, the record usually is content to report that "on dit."[13] It is possible that these investigators also accumulated information in private conversations; for example, the recovery of a piece of property at Neuville is due to a statement by one man.[14]

These inquests, accurate enough when it came to indicating rents, work-services, and the location of land, were not so useful in determining exact areas. So the tremendous task of measuring, foot by foot, the scattered lands of the domain was undertaken. This work was going on while the scribe was writing the report. He left a space for the actual measurement of the land of each farm, to come after the sworn estimate, and in many cases the space remained blank.[15] When it was filled in, the measurement almost always showed an increase over the estimate. For example, the inquests reported four farms as having an area of 73, 25, 40, and 131 acres respectively; measurement gave those same farms areas of 79 acres, 3 virgates, 14 *perches*; 29 acres, 1 virgate; 50 acres, 2 virgates, 19 *perches*; and 149 acres, 2 virgates, 35 *perches*.[16] It is

---

[10] *Gallia Christiana* XI, 98.

[11] fols. 10v, 26, 26v, 29, 31, etc. The clearest case is fol. 228v, "somme selonc cen que eles sont estimées des jureors XVI.C.IIII.XX.X lb. XVII s. VIII d."

[12] fol. 133. "Etienne, prestre des Mostiers Hubert, tient VIII acres de terre que il a porpris et ajostée a son aumosne, . . . et cen seit Guillaume de Friardel, . . ." (14 other names). A.N., K. 1201, no. 4 may be an original inquest, see p. 61.

[13] fols. 48, 49v, 90, 171v, etc.

[14] fol. 23. "Ricart Bordon dit que issi est."

[15] fols. 66, 72, 106v, 118v, 119v, etc.

[16] fols. 30, 53v, 87, 91v.

easy to see how important the work of measurement was in increasing the revenue from the domain, since the land was farmed at so many shillings the acre. The names of some of the men who did the work of measuring have survived, but there is nothing to show whether they were clerks or laymen, permanent or temporary officials.[17]

The author was not entirely dependent on information supplied by investigators and surveyors. As we have seen, he often had the estimate of the area of a farm written down before the report of the surveyors reached him, and that estimate was not always based on an inquest. He must have used the records of the *bailliage* in such cases, and there is evidence to show that he frequently copied, or rather translated, old documents. There are the references to the rolls and documents of the *bailliage*.[18] There are frequent slips into Latin,[19] which would indicate that the scribe was writing with Latin documents in front of him, which he occasionally forgot to translate into French. These documents must have been taken from the archives of the *bailliage*, for it seems improbable that the evidence given by the jurors was laboriously translated into Latin, only to be put back into French when the report reached headquarters. There are occasional sentences in which essential words are omitted.[20] Some of these omissions may be due to carelessness or lack of information, but on two occasions there is no doubt that the gap was left intentionally, and that the information necessary to fill it was in the archives of the *bailliage*. In each case the scribe omitted a rather rare word, which he may have found difficult to understand or to translate.[21] Very probably some of the other omissions were caused by similar difficulties in reading old documents.

Apparently none of these documents which our author used have survived. We have many royal charters describing perpetual farms of the domain, and some of these charters give almost a Latin equivalent of portions of our text. Yet the correspondence is never perfect, the descriptions are often fuller in our record than in the charters, and the arrangement and grouping of the items is not quite the same.[22] It seems probable

---

[17] fols. 43, 43v, 45, measure of Vincent; fol. 47v, measure of Gautier; fol. 142, measure of Odart.

[18] *cf.* above, p. 5.

[19] fols. 26v, 32, 51v, 152, 155, 217v, 219v.

[20] fols. 6v, 52v, 132v, 165, 185, 212v.

[21] *cf.* fols. 185 and 212v and notes. The words omitted were "scallate" and "subtrabum." Curiously enough Leopold Delisle, like our scribe, had difficulty in reading the word "scallate."

[22] *cf.* fols. 172, 185v, and notes.

that the clerks who drew up the charters and the scribe who composed
our manuscript used a common source, perhaps older descriptions of the
domain which have been lost.

Even though the scribe was constantly receiving new information
while he was writing, he was able to keep his record neat and orderly.
He arranged the manuscript so that information which came in late
could be inserted in the proper place without crowding. The spaces left
for recording the results of measurements of land-area have already been
discussed. The scribe also left half, or a quarter of a folio blank from
time to time,[23] so that newly discovered possessions or new leases could
be entered under the farms to which they belonged. At the end of each
viscounty he left several blank folios, which could be used for material
reported too late to be classified by sergeanties and farms. Some of these
end folios were filled with descriptions of miscellaneous, scattered pieces
of the domain;[24] others remained blank.[25] These precautions were effective; there are few erasures, and few corrections.

IV

THE ROYAL DOMAIN

A. TERRITORIAL DIVISIONS

The *bailliage* of Rouen had been formed by uniting the older and
smaller *bailliages* of Rouen, Pont-Audemer, and Bonneville.[1] As a result of this union, the city of Rouen was not in the center of the *bailliage*,
but was in its northeastern corner. The bulk of the *bailliage* lay west of
the Seine, in what is now the department of the Eure. In terms of modern administrative units, the *bailliage* included the following districts:

In the Department of the Seine Inférieure—the cantons of Rouen,
Darnetal, Boos, Maromme, Grand Couronne, Elbeuf, and parts of the
cantons of Duclair, Pavilly, Tôtes, Bellencombre and Clères.

In the Department of the Eure—the arrondissements of Pont-Audemer, Bernay (without the canton of Broglie), Louviers (without the
canton of Gaillon), and the canton of Fleury-sur-Andelle.

In the Department of the Calvados—the cantons of Honfleur, Blangy,

---

[23] e.g., fols. 5, 8, 11, 12v.

[24] fols. 98, 98v, 99, 99v, 156v, 205, 206, 206v.

[25] fols. 42, 42v, 100, 100v, 157, 157v, 206v.

---

[1] Strayer, *Administration of Normandy*, p. 8.

Pont-l'Evêque, Orbec, and parts of the cantons of Lisieux II, Dozulé, Cambremer and Livarot.

In the Department of the Orne—parts of the cantons of Gacé and Vimoutiers.

The *bailliage* was divided into five viscounties—Rouen, Pont-Audemer, Bernay, Auge, and Pont-de-l'Arche. The viscounty of Rouen included the cantons of the Seine-Inférieure mentioned above, plus the canton of Fleury (Eure). The viscounty of Pont-Audemer included all of the present arrondissement of that name (except the southern parts of the cantons of Cormeilles and St. Georges-du-Vièvre), and in addition the eastern parts of the cantons of Beaumont and Brionne, and a few places just across the Calvados border in the cantons of Honfleur and Pont-l'Evêque. The viscounty of Bernay covered the arrondissement of Bernay (except for the canton of Broglie and the parts of Beaumont and Brionne which were in Pont-Audemer), the southern parts of the cantons of Cormeilles and St. Georges, the canton of Orbec and the eastern parts of the cantons of Blangy, Lisieux II, and Livarot in the Calvados, and the small district in the Orne mentioned above. The viscounty of Auge took in the cantons of Honfleur, Dozulé, Pont-l'Evêque and parts of the cantons of Blangy and Cambremer in the Calvados. The viscounty of Pont-de-l'Arche corresponded fairly closely to the arrondissement of Louviers, without the canton of Gaillon.

Each viscounty was divided into sergeanties. It is exceedingly difficult to determine the boundaries of these units. The domain was scattered, and there were long gaps between one farm and another in most sergeanties, gaps in which the boundary line might turn in any direction. Moreover, some of these sergeanties seem to be relics of ancient administrative divisions. For example, the sergeanties of the Roumois and La Londe are probably remnants of old Angevin *bailliages*. These old administrative units never had had very logical boundaries, and when they were whittled down into sergeanties their frontier became even more irrational. Finally, lands newly added to the royal domain had to be fitted into old sergeanties without much regard for geography.

As a result, the sergeanties are exceedingly irregular in shape, and give the impression of being put together by accident. The town from which the sergeanty takes its name may be ten or fifteen miles from the region in which the bulk of the royal possessions in that sergeanty lie. For these reasons, no attempt has been made to give boundaries of the sergeanties. Instead, I have simply listed the chief towns and villages of each sergeanty.

Sergeanty of Rouen—Rouen.

Sergeanty of Pavilly—Pavilly, Sierville, Limésy, Mesnil-Panneville.

Sergeanty of Cailly—Cailly, la Rue-St.-Pierre, Mont-Gaille, Colmare, St. Germain-sous-Cailly.

Sergeanty of Pont-St.-Pierre—Pont-St.-Pierre, Pîtres, Romilli, Amfreville-sous-les-Monts, la Neuville-Champ-d'Oisel, Périers-sur-Andelle.

Sergeanty of St. Victor—Claville-Motteville, Vassonville, Etampuis, Grigneuseville, Cottévrard.

Sergeanty of Couronne—Grand Couronne, Sotteville-les-Rouen, Moulineaux, Grand Quevilly, Cléon, le Port-Saint-Ouen, Amfreville-la-Mivoie, Tourville-la-Rivière, Oissel.

Sergeanty of Saint-Georges—Hautot-sur-Seine, Canteleu, Villers-Ecalles, Ambourville, le Mesnil, Maremme, Montigny, Sahurs, Déville-les-Rouen.

Sergeanty of Brionne—Beaumont-le-Roger, Combon, Launay, Beaumontel, Barc, Brionne, Serquigny, Nassandres.

Sergeanty of Montfort—Montfort, Appeville, Brestot, Glos-sur-Rille, Routot, Rougemoutiers.

Sergeanty of Roumois—Thierreville, Honguemare, Ecaquelon, Barneville, Bourneville, la-Haye-de-Routot, Bourg-Achard, St. Ouen de Touberville, Hauville, Corneville-sur-Risle, Colletot.

Sergeanty of Quillebeuf—Saint-Thurien, St.-Mards-de-Blacarville, Quillebeuf.

Sergeanty of Epaignes—Saint-Paul-sur-Risle, Campigny, Saint-Germain, Epaignes.

Sergeanty of Le Mesnil—Foulbec, Boulleville, Martainville, Ablon (Calvados), Fiquefleur-Equainville, Beuzeville, Berville, Pont-Audemer, Quetteville (Calvados), Conteville.

Sergeanty of La Londe—Bourgthéroulde, part of the commune of Brionne, Berville-en-Roumois, Boisset-le-Chatel.

Sergeanty of (Bernay)[2]—Drucourt, Saint-Vincent-du-Boulay, Saint-Martin-du-Thilleul, Bournainville, Faverolles, Duranville, Le Theil-Nolent, Menneval, Campfleur, Le Favril, Plasnes, Freneuse-sur-Rille, Franqueville.

Sergeanty of Gacé—Le Sap, Orville, Canapville, Croisilles, Coulmer.

Sergeanty of Orbec—Orbec, Orbiquet, Saint-Martin-de-Bienfaite, La Folletière-Abenon, Meulles, Cerqueux, Les Moutiers-Hubert, Notre-Dame-de-Courson, Livarot, Lisores, Pretreville, La Chapelle-Yvon, Pontchardon (Orne), Avernes-Saint-Gourgon (Orne), Ticheville (Orne).

Sergeanty of Cormeilles—Glos (Calvados), Cordebugle, Marolles, Moyaux, Fontaine-la-Louvet (Eure), Le-Pin-en-Lieuvin.

---

[2] The name of the first sergeanty under the viscounty of Bernay was omitted by the scribe. It seems likely that it was a sergeanty of Bernay. The omission would be accounted for by the repetition.

Sergeanty of   Ouche —Saint-Lambert (Beaumesnil), Corneville-la-Fouquetière, Epinay, Le-Noyer-en-Ouche.

Sergeanty of Lieurey—Lieurey, Saint-Jean-de-la-Lequeraye.

VISCOUNTY OF AUGE

Sergeanty Sus la Mer—Darnetal, Branville, Angerville, Cresseveuille, Cricqueville-en-Auge, Beuzeval, Dive, Grangues, Villers-sur-Mer, St. Pierre-Azif, Blonville-sur-Mer, Bénerville, Auberville.

Sergeanty of Beuvron—Pont-l'Evêque, Beaumont-en-Auge, Clarbec, Drubec, Co-quainvilliers, Saint-Hymer, Le Torquêne, Le Ham, Goustranville-Saint-Clair.

Sergeanty of Bonneville—Saint-André-d'Hebertot, Les Authieux-sur-Calonne, Canapville, Englesqueville, Trouville, Tourville, Touques, Saint-Martin-aux-Chartrains, Bonneville, Equemauville.

Sergeanty of [3]—Grandouet, Crèvecour, Manerbe, Hotot-en-Auge, Glanville.

Sergeanty of Honfleur—Pennedepie, Fourneville, Barneville-la-Bertran, Honfleur, Le Theil.

VISCOUNTY OF PONT DE L'ARCHE

Sergeanty of Vauvray.[4]

Sergeanty of Pont-de-l'Arche—Pont-de-l'Arche, Igoville, Elbeuf, Le Thuit-Anger, Martot, Le Thuit-Signol, Saint-Amand-des-Hautes-Terres, Vraiville.

Sergeanty of Vaudreuil—Le Vaudreuil, Saint-Pierre de Vauvray, Portejoie, Ecque-tot, Léri, Poses, Pinterville, Montaure, Ecrosville, La Haye-Malherbe, les Damps.

Sergeanty of Crasville—Mandeville, Damneville, Quatremare, Surville, Hectomare, Surtauville, Daubeuf-la-Campagne.

Sergeanty of Le Neubourg—Tourville-la-Campagne, Saint-Ouen-de-Pontcheuil, La Pyle, Crosville-la-Vielle, Crestot, Ivile.

B. VALUE OF THE DOMAIN

Our manuscript does not give a complete description of the domain, in the broad sense of the word. It gives practically no information about certain important classes of royal rights and possessions. There is nothing about fiefs held of the king, or rights of high justice, and little about the forests or rights of patronage and *garde* in churches and monasteries. Such omissions seem to have been determined by two principles. The author is interested only in the parts of the domain which produce a fairly regular annual income, and can be farmed to private individuals. Fiefs produced revenue only on the extraordinary occasions when aid or relief was collected, and so the king's income from military fiefs could not be counted as part of the regular revenue of the *bailliage*. Income

---

[3] The name of this sergeanty was omitted by the scribe. It is small and scattered, and has no real center, so it is impossible to guess its name.

[4] This heading was probably a mistake; at least the scribe listed nothing under it, and passed immediately to the Sergeanty of Pont de l'Arche. Vauvray is later listed in the sergeanty of Vaudreuil.

from rights of high justice was stable enough, in spite of minor fluctuations, so that it might have been farmed, but it was contrary to royal policy to surrender such rights to private individuals. A large part of the king's authority and prestige was based on the excellent quality of his justice, and he could not run the risk of allowing it to be administered for private profit by unskilled men. There was no hesitation, however, in farming out the right of low justice over peasants.[5] Most forest revenue was too intermittent to be included in a list of the regular revenues of a *bailliage*. The great cuttings of timber produced large sums from time to time, but it was impossible to count on money from this source every year. Moreover, the forests had their own administration, which kept independent accounts.[6] There were, however, some regular revenues from the forests. There were payments for the privilege of gathering wood or pasturing animals in the forest, payments by *hôtes* for their lands in forest clearings, payments by charcoal burners, smiths, tile-makers and other artisans who worked in the forests.[7] These payments were made annually and were included in our record. Income from the exercise of the king's rights over the Church was intermittent, and it would have been against both royal and ecclesiastical policy to farm such rights. In a few cases our scribe included the right to present to a church in the description of a farm,[8] but this was not his regular practice.

With these exceptions, the record is surprisingly complete. Everything which could produce a regular income was included. Minute and purely formal rents were carefully recorded, and were probably collected with equal care. For example, a horseshoe worth twopence, a penny loaf of bread, a penny bunch of garlic, a pair of threepenny gloves, an arrowhead worth twopence[9] are all included in our record. The Norman administration had lost none of its thrift since the days when officials of Henry II saved chestnut sacks.[10] In the same way, every scrap of land which the king could claim was leased, and its value, however slight, recorded.[11] Even in the great farms, where the scribe was dealing in hundreds of pounds, he never forgot the items which produced only pence and shillings.

---

[5] fols. 82v, 86v, 92, 93v, etc.

[6] Strayer, *Administration of Normandy*, pp. 43, 73.

[7] fols. 32v-35v, 39v-41v. Descriptions of such payments in the forests of Rouvray and Roumare.

[8] fols. 153v, 159v, 171v.

[9] fols. 92, 182v, 88v, 18, 44v.

[10] C. H. Haskins, *Norman Institutions*, (Cambridge, 1918), p. 191.

[11] fol. 71, "la terre Baboin, VI d."; fol. 97v, "la terre Guillaume Pelous, II s. VIII d."; fol. 149, "la terre Rogier Belot, X d."

The royal domain of the *bailliage* of Rouen, even in the restricted sense in which it is used in our manuscript, produced very large sums for the king. The table given below will give some idea of its importance, and also of the relative value of different sections of the *bailliage*. These figures should not be taken too literally, since our scribe was more interested in potential income than in actual revenue. Undoubtedly some of the sums due could not be collected, and some of the things listed had to be farmed at less than their real value. Moreover, in the descriptions of some of the large farms, there is a certain amount of confusion. It is difficult to determine just what items are included in the grand totals and what items must be added in separately. In deciding such questions, many minor errors may have been made.

It is possible to check the accuracy of my figures in the viscounty of Pont-de-l'Arche, where the scribe gave grand totals for the whole viscounty. According to my addition, the potential income from Pont-de-l'Arche was 1824 l. This agrees fairly closely with the scribe's statement that the jurors estimated the value of the viscounty at 1741 l.,[12] since measurement of the land and competitive bidding for farms increased the value of some portions of the viscounty above the estimated values. But the *bailli* was able to farm out only 1643 l.[13] of these revenues, and it is likely that it was difficult to collect the remainder. Thus in the viscounty of Pont-de-l'Arche the actual revenue was, at the worst, only 10% less than the potential revenue.

POTENTIAL INCOME FROM THE ROYAL DOMAIN OF THE BAILLIAGE OF ROUEN

VISCOUNTY OF ROUEN

	l.	s.	d.
Sergeanty of Rouen	1914	18	2
Viscounty of the water	2615		
Sergeanty of Pavilly	185	1	4
Sergeanty of Cailly	716	10	7
Sergeanty of Pont-Saint-Pierre	543	8	2
Sergeanty of Saint-Victor	642	9	11
Sergeanty of Couronne	290	6	10
Sergeanty of Saint-Georges	318	19	

---

[12] fol. 228v. The value of everything in the viscounty to this point, according to the jurors' estimate, was 1690 l. To this should be added the total value of the new farms described on fols. 230v and 231, which was 51 l. This gives the sum of 1741 l. mentioned above.

[13] fol. 228v. "La somme de toutes les choses devant dites selonc le bail au ballif 1592 l." To this should be added the 51 l. for new farms mentioned in note 12, which gives 1643 l.

	l.	s.	d.
No sergeanty given	196	14	

Total for the viscounty of Rouen, 7423 l. 8 s.

VISCOUNTY OF PONT-AUDEMER

	l.	s.	d.
Sergeanty of Brionne	1758	9	
Sergeanty of Montfort	1047	19	11
Sergeanty of Romois	1001	17	7
Sergeanty of Quillebeuf	92	13	6
Sergeanty of Epaignes	158	19	1
Sergeanty of Le Mesnil	1231	4	1
Sergeanty of La Londe	440	4	
No sergeanty given	127	19	

Total for the viscounty of Pont-Audemer, 5859 l. 6s. 2 d.

VISCOUNTY OF BERNAY

	l.	s.	d.
Sergeanty of [Bernay]	959	16	5
Sergeanty of Gacé	524	9	8
Sergeanty of Orbec	1435	10	7
Sergeanty of Cormeilles	365	10	6
Sergeanty of Ouche	143	1	10
Sergeanty of Lieurey	44	13	
No sergeanty given	3	7	

Total for the viscounty of Bernay, 3476 l. 9 s.

VISCOUNTY OF AUGE

	l.	s.	d.
Sergeanty Sus la Mer	1369	19	2
Sergeanty of Beuvron	401	5	6
Sergeanty of Bonneville	460		2
Sergeanty of ———	269	14	1
Sergeanty of Honfleur	240	18	
No sergeanty given	6		

Total for the viscounty of Auge, 2747 l. 16 s. 11 d.

VISCOUNTY OF PONT-DE-L'ARCHE

	l.	s.	d.
Sergeanty of Pont-de-l'Arche	441	13	6
Sergeanty of Vaudreuil	620	17	3
Sergeanty of Crasville	327	12	8
Sergeanty of Le Neubourg	434	15	4

Total for the viscounty of Pont-de-l'Arche 1824 l. 18 s. 9 d.

Grand total for the *bailliage* of Rouen, 21,331 l. 18 s. 10 d.

Grand total without the viscounty of the water,[14] 18,716 l. 18 s. 10 d.

---

[14] This is probably a safer figure to use, for our scribe's description of the viscounty of the water is very incomplete; for example, he gives no figures for the income from the duties on wine. *H.F.* XXI, 255, in 1238 the viscounty of the water yielded 5900 l.

It is rather difficult to compare this total with the total income from the *bailliage* of Rouen as given in other documents. No other record is based on the same principles as ours; they all include a great deal of intermittent, irregular revenue. We have a summary of Norman revenue for the term of Easter 1230,[15] which includes sums owed from previous years, and income from the forests and from the administration of justice. If these sums and the income from the viscounty of the water, are eliminated the total gross income from Rouen-Pont-Audemer-Bonneville was 5746 l. This would mean a yearly revenue of something more than 11,492 l., since Easter payments were apt to be smaller than those of Michaelmas. Many farmers paid only one-third of what they owed at Easter, and made their heavy payment in the fall.[16] We have another summary of Norman revenue for the Easter term, 1238.[17] Eliminating the same sort of items, we obtain a total of 7083 l. for Rouen-Pont-Audemer-Bonneville, or a revenue of something more than 14,088 l. for the year. While both these totals may be a little low, it is perfectly clear that royal income from Normandy was increasing steadily.[18] If individual items from the list of 1238 be compared with the same items in our record, an increase may frequently be noted. Thus a *vivarium* worth only 10 l. a year in 1238, brought in 45 l. a year in 1260; the market of Beuzeville produced 150 l. in 1238, and 250 l. in 1260; and the land of Guillaume Bardol increased in value from 8 l. to 21 l. in the same length of time.[19] Such individual increases make it quite possible that income from the domain of Rouen increased from fourteen or fifteen thousand pounds in 1238, to eighteen thousand pounds in 1260.

The towns, and especially the town of Rouen, were the most valuable single units of the domain. Each town had to pay customs on goods which were brought within its walls for sale, and these levies, with payments for market-stalls and market-places brought in very large sums. Tolls were less productive. Altogether the revenue from the towns, amounted to 8423 l., or 39% of the total revenue of 21,331 l. If the income from the viscounty of the water had been fully reported, this percentage would have been even greater. Half of the town revenue was produced by the city of Rouen. If Rouen is eliminated town revenue is only 28% of the revenue of the other viscounties.

Curiously enough, the king made very little out of the real estate

---

[15] *H.F.*, XXIV, *preuves* no. 89.
[16] fol. 207. All farms of Pont-de-l'Arche pay one-third at Easter.
[17] *H.F.*, XXI, 255-256.
[18] Strayer, *Administration of Normandy*, p. 43.
[19] fols. 3, 85v, 186v.

(other than that used for markets) which he owned in the towns. In the country, on the other hand, by far the largest amount of revenue came from leases of land. Old ducal levies, such as *bernage*,[20] had been preserved, but they yielded comparatively small sums. Payments for usages in the forest, such as *pasturage*,[21] *herbage*,[22] *ramage*,[23] or *bigrage*[24] were not much more productive. The old manorial dues, such as *cens*, payments of grain and offerings of fowl, eggs, and bread at Christmas and Easter were somewhat more valuable, but leasing the demesne land of the manor usually brought in much more money. The number of *corvées* on most estates had been so reduced that they contributed little to the income of the *bailliage*. In most cases the only *corvées* which had survived were those requiring two to four days' plowing and harrowing a year.[25] In some places other services were required, but these services were valued at a very low figure.[26] Mills were very valuable,[27] but other seigneurial monopolies, such as ovens, were farmed for small sums.[28]

Altogether, it is perfectly clear that the development of commerce and the increased use of money were breaking down the old manorial system. Labor-services and rents payable in kind had been useful to a lord who had to derive most of the necessities of life from his estate. They had no great value to a lord who wanted money, who could buy whatever he needed in open market. The men who leased portions of the royal domain often paid more than the estimated value of the land, but they seldom paid more than the estimated value of services or rents in kind. By the thirteenth century, Normandy was a thickly settled country in which land was dear and labor cheap; it was a rich country in which trade in agricultural products was well developed. For these reasons, the king made a great deal of money from taxes on commerce and leases of land, and very little from labor-services and payments in kind by the peasants.

---

[20] fols. 13, 83, 178v, 192v, etc. *Graverie* is mentioned on fol. 9; *l'aide le comte* on fols. 25, 144v.

[21] fols. 34v, 39, 44, 63, etc.

[22] fols. 11v, 17, 22v, 41, etc.

[23] fol. 40v. A payment for the right to collect fallen wood.

[24] fol. 97. A payment for the right to collect wild honey.

[25] fols. 10, 12, 27, 38, 53, etc. The *corvées* on the great meadows of Bonneville are an exception to this statement; they had real value. *cf.* fols. 189, 191, 191v.

[26] fol. 12v, a day's work worth 6 d.; fol. 18v, a day's work worth 4 d.; fol. 27v, a day's sowing worth 4 d.

[27] fol. 85v, mill of Beuzeville worth 60 l. a year; fol. 103, mill of Ouilly worth 100 l. a year.

[28] fol. 134, two ovens worth 6 l.; fol. 159v, an oven for 2 l.; fol. 167v, an oven for 25 s.

C. ORIGIN OF THE DOMAIN

In the reign of St. Louis, the king was the greatest landed proprietor in the *bailliage* of Rouen. This had not been true in the past, and was not to be true in the future. The Angevin dukes had saved very little arable land for themselves. They were able to draw all the revenue they needed from other sources, notably the forests and the towns. It is amazing to see how few of the manors mentioned in this document were part of the domain before the conquest. The fourteenth century French kings could depend on taxes, tolls, and rights of one kind and another for their income. They found it unnecessary to retain actual possession of the soil, and sold, or gave away, most of their Norman estates. But in the reign of St. Louis, the king's increasing need for money had not yet been met by the development of the taxing power. He had to make the most of his position as landlord, because he could not yet make enough money from his position as king. As we have seen, more than half of the revenues listed in this document came from the king's country estates.

The growth of the ruler's landed possessions began under Philip Augustus. He added little in the way of profitable rights of suzerainty, control of important towns,[29] or forest possessions; the Angevin dukes had acquired almost everything of this sort which was worth having. But Philip did confiscate the possessions of those nobles who adhered to John, and this put a great many country estates in his hands. Scores of nobles remained loyal to John, for fear of losing their English lands, which were more valuable than their Norman possessions. Philip's officials were very strict in deciding what constituted adherence to John. A journey to England, even after the actual fighting had ceased, was enough to ruin a man.[30] This strict interpretation of the law increased the number of confiscated estates. It is no exaggeration to say that the great majority of royal holdings listed in this manuscript, outside the forests and the towns, were acquired as a result of the conquest.

The lands confiscated by Philip did not all fall into the royal domain immediately. His government was not yet well enough organized to undertake the task of administering hundreds of rural estates. Moreover, he had to reward the Norman nobles who had deserted John, and his own followers who had aided in the conquest.[31] Therefore, he granted

---

[29] He did acquire Pont-Saint-Pierre, (*cf.* fol. 20). The towns of the Meulan family (Brionne, Beaumont-le-Roger, Pont-Audemer) had been taken over by John, but he might have restored them after his reconciliation with the count of Meulan. Philip's victory made the confiscation irrevocable. (*cf.* Stapleton, II, CXCVIII *ff.*)

[30] *Quer. Nor.*, nos. 41, 62, 79, 84, 278, etc. *cf.* fols. 44, 79v, 82v, 86v, 182v.

[31] *M.A.N.*, 2ᵉs., V, 155 *ff.*

the confiscated estates freely to his supporters in Normandy. In spite of this he retained much of the property which he had seized, and the part which he alienated began to return to the domain after his death. Many estates which Philip had granted to his followers are listed in our manuscript as royal possessions.[32] Either a remarkable number of these men died without heirs, or else Louis VIII and Louis IX were inclined to put pressure on Philip's favorites to make them surrender their holdings. We know that Cadoc, a former *bailli*, was held in prison until he had surrendered everything which Philip had given him,[33] and lesser men may have been treated in the same way. Philip had not been too particular about the character of his servants, as long as they got results, and it is quite likely that his protégés were out of favor in the more virtuous times of Blanche and St. Louis.

The lands of the domain increased almost as rapidly after 1226 as before. England and France were still officially at war, and estates could still be forfeited because the holder visited England, or because an heir happened to be living in England when the succession passed to him. St. Louis acquired the great estates of the Marshals in this way. Richard Marshal, the Norman representative of the family, died without direct descendants, and the government refused to allow his lands to pass to English relatives.[34] This action was taken, although the Marshals had been more successful than any other family in remaining in the good graces of the rulers of both countries. Louis also acquired a number of estates through failure of heirs, or by direct bequest. For example, the last holder of the barony of Le Sap left her possessions to the king.[35]

Louis made the most of his opportunities. Unlike his grandfather, unlike most medieval kings, he kept almost all the land which fell to him. He granted very little of it as fiefs. The need now was not for political or military support, but for money. Louis had more and better administrative officials than Philip had had; they were capable of of dealing with the problems of making a profit out of scattered rural holdings. They perfected the technique of farming the domain[36] and so assured the king a steady income with a minimum of administrative expense. The success of this policy probably had much to do with the unwillingness of the king to alienate any land.

---

[32] *cf.* notes on fols. 20, 21, 25v, 31, 36, etc.

[33] *H.F.,* XXIV, p. *130; *Cart. Nor.,* nos. 363-366.

[34] *Quer. Nor.,* no. 327; *cf.* fol. 125.

[35] *Quer. Nor.,* no. 328; *cf.* fol. 118.

[36] *cf.* pp. 20-21.

This unwillingness to give up any part of the domain was hard to over-come. Louis IX was certainly sincere when he protested that he wanted to keep nothing which was not his. He had a real desire to right the wrongs done by his officials when he ordered the great investigation which produced the *Querimoniae*. Yet, to judge by the results shown in this manuscript, it was very easy to convince the king that his officials had been right in confiscating property, and it was very difficult to persuade him or his advisors to surrender anything which had once entered the domain. There are fifteen clear references in our manuscript to posses-sions which were claimed by private individuals in the *Querimoniae*.[37] In eleven cases no satisfaction was given the claimants, and the property remained in the king's hand. In one case the land was still in the king's hand when our record was written, but the scribe admitted that there was some doubt about its status.[38] In two cases a compromise was made; the claimants received something, although less than they had asked.[39] Only once was the claim satisfied in full.[40] It is probably true, as Petit-Dutaillis has suggested,[41] that many of the Norman complaints were entirely un-justified. Nevertheless, it seems doubtful that so large a proportion were utterly extravagant or unreasonable. Frequently, as in the cases involving confiscation because of a voyage to England, the government could justify its action only by a very narrow interpretation of the law. It seems that we have here one more proof of how early the royal administra-tion developed the bureaucratic spirit, the feeling that in doubtful cases the government must always win, that the official is always right, and the private individual always wrong. Even Louis IX could not keep his officials from being more royalist than the king. It was to their interest, as much as his, to make the government strong and wealthy. If Louis intimated that he attached great value to the lands of the domain his administrators would strive to increase them in every possible way, and they would be very reluctant to surrender land to any claimant, how-ever good his case.

---

[37] fols. 43v, 44, 65, 79v, 80, 80v, 81, 82v, 86v, 89v, 125, 131v, 182v, 196v, 199.
[38] fol. 125.
[39] fols. 81, 131v.
[40] fol. 43v.
[41] C. Petit-Dutaillis, "Querimoniae Normannorum," *Essays Presented to Professor Tout,* (Manchester, 1925).

V

Collection of Revenue from the Domain

It appears clearly in our document that the king wanted money rather
than produce, from his possessions, but the domain yielded very little
money directly. Even in the towns, some tolls were payable in kind,
and in the country the whole manorial system was designed to yield
agricultural products. Moreover, in spite of the increased number of
royal officials, there were still not enough of them to collect the king's
revenues directly, even in the towns. The great problems of the royal
administration were to collect all that was owed the king from the in-
numerable, scattered possessions of the domain, and to insure collection
of money, instead of a mass of food-stuffs. The first step was to assign a
money value to everything, land,[1] labor-services, payments in kind, and
rights of one kind and another. Then, with the money value of each
part of the domain known, it could be leased to private persons. In this
way the problem of collecting and marketing the products of the domain
was transferred to private individuals. All that the royal officials had to
do was to collect money twice a year from the leasors of the domain.

As far as possible everything was farmed, with the exception of rights
which conveyed too much political power, such as high justice, lordship
of fiefs, and patronage. Customs and market-rights, mills and ovens, land
and manorial dues could all be leased. The government farmed the
domain in as large units as possible; it preferred to lease a whole manor,
or all the customs in a town to one man, rather than to divide them
among several bidders.[2] The larger the farms, the easier the problem of
administration became. For the same reason, the government seems to
have favored perpetual leases—that is, leases which never expired as long
as the stipulated payments were made. Though the thirteenth century
was a century of rising prices[3] the change was gradual. There was an
illusion of economic stability, and in these circumstances the perpetual
lease seemed a very good idea. The perpetual leases seem to have been
made at just as high rates as the temporary ones. They assured the king
a steady revenue, whatever happened. The king might take a heavy
loss on property which had been leased temporarily if he could not farm
it again promptly on the expiration of the old lease. A temporary lease

---

[1] Very rarely the value of land is expressed in measures of grain, rather than in
money, cf. fols. 46v, and 197v.

[2] A small lease was sometimes subordinated to a large one of later date, that is, the
first leasor paid his rent to the second leasor rather than to the king. Cf. fol. 172.

[3] cf. pp. 24 ff.

might expire in a bad year, and the property would have to be let at less than its real value.[4] No one saw any dangers in the perpetual farm to offset these advantages, especially as the perpetual farm often resulted in nothing more than a long-term lease. There are many cases in our manuscript where a so-called "perpetual" farm was lost after ten or twenty years.[5]

If the government could not lease estates or its rights in towns as a unit, it would break them up into smaller and smaller sections until at last it found a bidder. This subdivision at times went rather far; we have farms of less than an acre of land.[6] Yet in the end it was effective; most of the domain was farmed, and royal officials had to administer very little of it directly.

Farms, whether temporary or permanent, were assigned by competitive bidding, although there probably was no formal auction. We have several cases in which the names of two or three bidders for a farm are given,[7] and in each case it seems clear that some time elapsed between one bid and the next. If the whole thing had been done in a few minutes, the scribe would not have bothered to record the first bids, but if each bid seemed final for a month or two, until a higher one was made, he would naturally write them down. Once a perpetual farm had been assigned, and approved by the proper authority, the holder was safe from competition. The holders of temporary farms, however, must have been quite worried as their leases drew near the expiration date. A few tried to protect themselves by getting the government to promise that they would not lose their holdings unless the new bid were distinctly higher than the price they were paying,[8] but this arrangement seems to have been rare. On the other hand, the holder of a temporary lease probably was not required to pledge part of his property as security that he would pay the rent due. Such security was regularly required of the holders of perpetual leases[9] and if they failed to make the payments which they owed, they lost not only their lease but also the property which they had pledged.[10]

---

[4] e.g. fol. 85v. The market of Beuzeville had to be farmed for 250 l. in 1260, although its value was estimated at 270 l.

[5] fol. 26, a farm made in 1263 (n.s.) forfeited by 1281; fol. 185v, a farm made in 1259 surrendered before 1270. cf. B.N., Ms. fr. 25993, no. 193. Most of the farms of Auge had been revised by 1312. See appendix, pp. 269-270.

[6] fols. 189v, 190 contain nine leases of less than an acre. Most of Pont de l'Arche was divided into small farms.

[7] fols. 17v, 45, 54, 58, 204v, 210.

[8] fol. 146. The new bidder must go 8 l. above the old price. In this particular case the clause was of no avail, for a new bidder was willing to make the increase.

[9] e.g. fols. 10, 11, 21v, 28, etc.

[10] *Cart. Nor.*, no. 981.

The actual arrangements for most of the leases seem to have been made by the clerks of the *bailli* or the viscount. We know that Master Richard du Fay made leases,[11] and our scribe seems to have acted in a similar capacity.[12] Occasionally a lease is mentioned as having been made by a viscount,[13] which is not surprising since viscounts had many financial duties. Perpetual leases had to be approved by the king's council, since they involved the writing of a royal charter.[14] In practice, this approval was probably given by those members of the king's council who sat in the Exchequer. Our scribe frequently mentions the consent of the Exchequer, or the fact that a farm was made at the Exchequer,[15] but he never speaks of the *curia* at Paris. It seems logical to assume that the Exchequer reviewed important leases of the domain, since it reviewed the financial operations of the *baillis*.[16]

The procedure regarding temporary leases is not so clear. As late as the reign of Philip IV, many of them seem to have been purely oral conventions, made without issuing any documents.[17] Such arrangements were probably made by subordinates, and may not have required the consent of any higher official. Other temporary leases were made in writing,[18] but there is no proof that they had to be accepted by the exchequer, or even the *bailli*, although it was probably customary to obtain the latter's approval.

The fact that the farms of the domain ranged in value from a few shillings to thousands of pounds, and included all sorts of rights, products, and properties, meant that every class of the population was able and anxious to bid for them. The most remarkable thing in the whole document is the absence of a class of professional farmers of the domain. No person, and stranger still, no corporation, held two important farms. Farms were usually taken by people who lived quite close to them, and these people might be of any class—higher and lower clergy, barons and knights, bourgeois and peasants. A monastery wished to round out its

---

[11] fols. 5, 8, 9, 11, 15, 17v.

[12] fols. 105v, 174.

[13] fols. 44v, 50v, 58v, 66, 85v, etc.

[14] e.g. *Cart. Nor.*, nos. 604, 608, 610, 614, etc.

[15] fols. 5, 10, 11, 20v, 26, etc.

[16] Strayer, *Administration of Normandy*, p. 39.

[17] E. Perrot, *Arresta Communia*, (Caen, 1910), no. 91. The fact that our scribe is careful to note whether "letres" have been issued proves that they were not yet required in all cases.

[18] fols. 219, 219v, 220, record leases of small areas for which "letres" were issued. These farms seem temporary, since the farmers give no security.

holdings in a district, so it farmed all the royal rights there.[19] A noble wished to enlarge his estate; he took over the royal lands which lay near his manor.[20] A bourgeois wished a country home; he rented it from the king.[21] Even the peasants were able to enlarge their little holdings by leasing parts of the domain. In one case, a priest took the farm in the name of the village;[22] elsewhere, the community took the farm in its own right.[23] Frequently a group of men joined together to lease land,[24] and there were dozens of peasants who were able to take land as individuals and pay rather high prices for it out of their own resources. There was even a curious type of farm in which labor-services were leased to the men who owed the services,[25] thus, in effect, commuting the services for a regular money payment.

As remarkable as the wide distribution of farms among men of all classes, is the fact that most farms were made for more than the estimated value of the property.[26] This was especially true of farms of country estates; it was more difficult to increase the annual payments for farms of town properties and rights. Apparently land was a very desirable investment in thirteenth century Normandy.

The participation of all classes in farming the domain, and the prices paid for farms testify to the prosperity of Normandy at this time. Apparently there were plenty of people, in all classes, who had money, or found it easy to get money which they could invest in farming the royal domain. There seems to have been a good market for agricultural products, and very active local commerce all over the *bailliage*. This was enough to insure some profit to the farmers of the domain, unless they met with unusual misfortunes.

VI

PRICES

Our record gives valuable information about rental value of land, commodity prices, and wages for day labor. In many cases we have not only the estimated value of these things, but the actual price at which they

---

[19] fol. 73. Jumièges, which held most of Quillebeuf, farms the king's property there.
[20] fol. 218. Renaud Trossebout, knight, takes land near his manor.
[21] fol. 19v and note 3.
[22] fol. 11.
[23] fol. 231, farms taken by the men of La Haye-Malherbe, Montoire, and Crasville.
[24] fols. 17, 26v, 31, 166.
[25] fols. 12, 31v.
[26] The estimated values themselves were fairly high, at least as compared with values of the same type of property around 1200. *cf.* pp. 24 *ff.*

were farmed. It is sometimes possible to compare these prices with those of earlier years listed by Delisle.[1] Generally speaking, wherever the sources make such comparison possible, there seems to have been an increase in prices between 1200 and 1266.

Land

Arable land naturally varied greatly in value. The estimated price for a year's lease of an acre ran from 1 to 38 s., depending on the region. Land was actually leased for sums ranging from 4 s. to 39 s. per acre per year. These extremes were rare, but there was a great deal of land leased for 20 s. or more per acre (fols. 45, 54, 91v, 101, 101v, 104, 104v, 106, 106v, 111v, 113v, etc.), and very little was granted for less than 10 s. an acre. Out of 77 leases selected at random, the mean price for an acre of land was 16 s. The most valuable land was found in the sergeanties of Montfort and La Londe, at Drucourt in the viscounty of Bernay, at Honfleur in Auge, and, above all, in the viscounty of Pont-de-l'Arche. Here the average price per acre was well above 20 s., and in the sergeanty of Le Neubourg, there were 79 acres which were farmed at an average price of more than 30 s. an acre (fols. 223v-224v). The poorest land seems to have been in the sergeanties of Pavilly, Cailly, Epaignes, Le Mesnil, Gacé, Orbec, Sus la Mer, and Beuvron, where there was much land valued at 10 s. or less an acre. Elsewhere the price fluctuated between 10 and 20 s. an acre.

Earlier records give few figures which can be compared with these, since the lease of land for a fixed sum of money per acre was rather rare before the reign of St. Louis. Land of La Trinité de Caen, c. 1190, was worth, at the most, 1 setier of oats an acre. At prevailing prices, the setier was worth from 2 to 4 s.[2] In 1210, 58 acres of good land at Cressi were worth 4 s. an acre.[3] In 1225, 60 acres at Ricardiville, were farmed for 6 s. an acre.[4] If these prices are typical, the value of land increased greatly during the reign of St. Louis.

Meadows

Normandy was a well watered country, and meadowland was not as valuable in proportion to plough-land as it was elsewhere. The

---

[1] Delisle, *Etude sur la condition de la classe agricole en Normandie*, (Evreux, 1851), Chap. xx.

[2] Delisle, *op. cit.*, pp. 576, 590.

[3] *ibid.*, p. 577.

[4] *Cart. Nor.*, no. 345.

estimated value of meadows runs from 10 to 40 s. an acre. Meadows were actually farmed for sums ranging from 14 to 40 s. an acre. Farms of meadow land for 30 s. or more an acre were not rare (fols. 32, 36, 39, 43, 102, 162, 195), and the average price paid was over 20 s. an acre.

Enclosures

There was little enclosed land in the *bailliage* of Rouen. What there was, was estimated at 10 to 40 s. an acre. Most of it was valued at 20 s. an acre or more (fols. 26v, 37, 65, 75, 106v, 119v, etc.).

Waste Land

Waste land was useful for pasture, and so had considerable value. Its value was estimated at 1 to 9 s. an acre, with the usual price 4 to 6 s. an acre. Some of it was farmed for 6 to 8 s. an acre (fols. 26, 102v, 217v).

Wood-land

Wood-land seems to have been somewhat more valuable than waste. Even though it was forbidden to cut timber, the holder could collect dead wood, as well as use it for pasture. The average price of wood-land was about 10 s. an acre (fols. 17v, 27, 67v, 79v, 122, 130v, 142, etc.).

Grain

It is difficult to determine the value of grain, since the measures used were not the same in all parts of the *bailliage*. Moreover, in some districts the measure for oats was either larger or smaller than the measure for wheat. Roughly speaking, west of the Seine and near the borders of the *bailliage* of Caen, measures were larger and therefore prices were higher.

There are more entries for oats than for any other grain. In the viscounty of Rouen the most common price was 6s. a *setier* (fols. 9, 13, 14, 15v, 16, 23, 25, 25v, 30), though in few cases it was valued at 5s. (fols. 8v, 9v, [this is specifically said to be small measure], 13, 16). On the other hand, farmers bid up the price to 7s. in one case and to 8s. in another (fols. 14, 21v).

In the viscounty of Pont-Audemer the *setier* of oats was usually valued at 4s. (fols. 56, 58v, 61v, 64, 68v, 84, 86, 87, 91v, 93v, 95v), or 5s. (fols. 44, 46v, 52v, 59v, 62v, 92v) but on two occasions it is said that a small measure was used (fol. 52v, fol. 61v). In the viscounty of Bernay all but two entries give 6s. as the estimated value of a *setier* of oats (fols. 102v, 108, 109v, 114v, 115v, etc). The viscounty of Auge is almost equally divided between a valuation of 5s. (fols. 148, 159v, 161, 169v, 171v, 178, 188, 204) and 6s. (fols. 161v, 174, 175v, 180v, 184v, 194, 199v, 200v, 201) with the higher valuations concentrated in an area where a large measure was used. One farmer bid up the price to 8s. the *setier* (fol. 205). The few entries for Pont de l'Arche are all 6s. (fols. 209v, 212v, 217, 223v).

Thus for the *bailliage* as a whole, 6s. a *setier* was the most common value for oats.

There are fewer entries for wheat. In the viscounty of Rouen the value was given as 12s. a *setier* (fols. 4, 15v, 23v, 25), with one exception at 10s., although the farmer bid it up to 12s. (fols. 28, 28v). In Pont-Audemer prices were higher; 14s. was common (fols. 44, 46v, 47, 49v, 84v, 92v, 95v); 15s. and 16s. each occur once (fols. 54v, 84), and 20s. three times in the Bonneville region where a large measure was used (fols. 50, 64v, 72v). In Bernay the price was 16s. a *setier* (fols. 120v, 130, 133v, 137, 140v, 142v) with two exceptions at 12s. (fols. 107, 145). For the latter of these we know that a small measure was used. In Auge there were two valuations at 15s. (fols. 166v, 178) and five at 16s. (fols. 173, 185, 188, 201, 204); in Pont de l'Arche three at 12s. (fols. 209v, 216v, 217) and one at 14s. (fol. 223). Overall, the prevailing value given for a *setier* of wheat was 12s. in the viscounties of Rouen and Pont de l'Arche, 14s. or more in Pont-Audemer (with a peak of 20s. near Bonneville) and 16s. in Bernay and Auge.

Barley is not mentioned often enough to establish local differences in prices. It was valued at 6s. a *setier* in Rouen, Pont-Audemer, and Bernay (fols. 9, 25v, 28, 61v, 86, 86v, 107, 109v, 114v), and 7s. in Rouen and Bernay (fols. 14, 112), at 8s. in Pont-Audemer (fols. 54v, 58v, 59, 84, 96) and at 10s. near Bonneville, where the large measure was used (fol. 72v). But it should be noted that one farmer near Rouen bid the price of a *setier* of barley up to 8s. (fol. 28v) so that its real value was probably above the mean of 6 or 7s.

Even allowing for differences in the measures used, these prices are higher than those which were current at the end of the twelfth century. In the period 1180-1200, the price of the *setier* of oats averaged about 3s., and only occasionally went as high as 6s.[5] The price of wheat was more variable, as usual, but the *setier* was often valued at only 9 or 10s.[6]

---

[5] Delisle, *Etude sur la condition de la classe agricole en Normandie*, pp. 589 *ff*.
[6] *ibid.*

Fowl and Eggs

Capons were usually valued at 6 d. apiece (fols. 15v, 16, 19v, 21v, 32, 39v, 52, 216), less often at 5 d. (fols. 10, 105v, 126). Hens were 4 d. apiece (fols. 15v, 16, 21v, 52). Geese were valued at 10 d. apiece in the viscounties of Rouen and Pont-Audemer (fols. 47v, 55, 59v, 64v, 72, 82, 92), and at 8 d. in the viscounties of Bernay and Auge (fols. 110, 112, 115v, 136v, 156, 163, 182, 188). Eggs were uniformly estimated at 10 for a penny (fols. 8v, 10, 12, 19v, 21v, 32, 105v, 216). In the period 1180-1220, capons were valued at 4 d. apiece,[7] and hens at 3 or 3½ d. apiece.[8]

Sheep

Sheep were valued at 4 or 5 s. apiece (fols. 14, 15v, 16, 22), and lambs at 12 d. (fols. 55, 86, 95v, 185, 216) or, occasionally, 18 d. (fols. 21, 107). Between 1180 and 1200, sheep were valued at a shilling apiece, and lambs at 9 or 10 d. apiece.[9]

Other Articles of Food

The loaf of bread is valued at 1 or 2 d. (fols. 182v, 214v), pears 100 for a shilling (fol. 137), eels at about 5 d. apiece (fol. 160v), salt at 3 s. a *somme* (fols. 171v, 175v, 180), pepper at 2 s. a pound[10] (fols. 18, 21, 29, 30v), onions and garlic 300 for a shilling (fol. 37).

Beverages

A gallon of wine is valued at 1 s. (fols. 92v, 95v) and a *muid* at 16 s. (fol. 25v). The *muid* of cider is said to be worth 10 s. (fol. 188).

Manufactured Articles

We have considerable information about the price of iron-work. Horseshoes were 2 d. apiece (fols. 92, 196, 201v), spurs 8 d. (fols. 130v, 138v),[11] knives 6 d. (fols. 140v, 196), arrowheads 2 d. (fols. 44v, 67v), a plowshare 20 d. (fol. 129v). The iron-work for a plow was valued at 4 s. (fol. 196), the wheels of a plow at 12 d. (fol. 137). A *somme* of charcoal was worth 3 s. (fol. 30v). Gloves were 3 d. (fols. 18, 203).

---

[7] Delisle, *Etude sur la condition de la classe agricole en Normandie*, pp. 611, 613, 614.

[8] *ibid.*, pp. 612, 613.

[9] *ibid.*, pp. 611, 612.

[10] It was farmed at times for 2 s. 6 d. a pound, fols. 21v, 37v.

[11] Silver spurs were 2 s., and gilded spurs 2 or 3 s., fols. 48, 122, 178.

Wages

The wages paid for voluntary labor were probably higher than the value ascribed to the same sort of labor performed as a *corvée*. Peasants performing a *corvée* undoubtedly did less work than they did when they were working for their own profit. For this reason, the figures given below should be used with caution in estimating the value of labor in the thirteenth century.

The most valuable services were those rendered by men who had horses and plows or carts. A day's plowing was usually considered worth 15 or 16 d. (fols. 10, 12, 27, 56v, 63v, 72v, 76, 103, 131) though in parts of the viscounty of Pont-Audemer, it was valued at only a shilling (fols. 53, 66), and in parts of the viscounty of Bernay at 18 d. or 2 s. (fols. 119, 122v, 124v, 151v, 153v). Harrowing was almost always valued at 6 d. a day (fols. 10, 12, 27v, 53, 62v, 105v, 131). Carting was worth 1 to 2 shillings a day, depending on the distance to be covered or the season in which it was due (fols. 10v, 12, 27v, 34, 92). An ordinary day's work in the fields was worth 4 to 6 d.; services connected with harvesting were usually worth more than sowing (fols. 12v, 18v, 27v, 58v, 148, 151v, 153v).

VII

Measures

Land was measured in *perches*, virgates, and acres. Ordinarily there were 40 *perches* to the virgate, and 4 virgates to the acre (fols. 112, 114, 117, 148, 154v, 158).[1] The length of the *perche* is given only once (fol. 32). Here it is 22 feet, but this length was probably mentioned because it was abnormal. It seems probable that the longer *perche* of 25 feet was used, since this was known as the royal *perche*.[2]

Grain was measured in bushels, quarters, *mines*, *setiers*, and *muids*. The relations between these different measures were not constant, and two measures of the same name were not always of the same capacity. There were 12 bushels to the *setier* at Beaumont-le-Roger, and in the Roumois (fols. 44, 64v), only 9 bushels to the *setier* at Saint-Clair-d'Arcey near Bernay (fol. 107), 15 bushels to the *setier* in the forest of Beaumont (fol. 44) and 16 bushels to the *setier* in the sergeanties of Beuvron and Honfleur (fols. 181v, 204). There were bushels, *mines*,

---

[1] Exceptions are fol. 71v, 30 *perches* to a virgate; fol. 76, 46 *perches* to a virgate. These figures might be due to errors in copying.

[2] Delisle, *Etude sur la condition de la classe agricole en Normandie*, p. 532.

and *setiers* "a la petite mesure", and "a grant mesure" (fols. 8v, 10, 34v, 86). There was heaping measure (fol. 13), full measure (fols. 93v, 112, 197v), and level measure (fol. 84v). Each district had its own standard. Our manuscript mentions the measures of Rouen, Beaumont-le-Roger, Bonneville, "Bitone," Robert Bertran, and Saint-Pierre-sur-Dive (fols. 32, 44, 72v, 107, 145, 197v).

The *setier* is the measure most frequently used by our scribe. It has no constant relation to the bushel, as was shown above. Its value in regard to other measures is more stable; ordinarily 2 *mines* make a *setier* and 12 *setiers* make a *muid*. Fourteenth century royal officials tried to work out tables for bringing the different measures used in France to a common value — the *setier* or the *muid* of Paris. They did not cover Normandy very thoroughly, but one can derive the following tables from their work.

Measures of oats[3]

    Vernon — 12 *setiers* = 17 *setiers*, 1 *mine* of Paris

    Andely — 12 *setiers* = 15 *setiers*, 1 *mine* of Paris

    Rouen — 12 *setiers* = 16 *setiers* of Paris

    Caudebec — 12 *setiers* = 17 *setiers* of Paris

    Beaumont-en-Auge — 12 *setiers* = 17 *setiers* of Paris

    Caen — 12 *setiers* = 12 *setiers*, 1 *mine* of Paris.

Measures of wheat[4]

    Andely and Rouen, as above

    Vernon — 12 *setiers* = 15 *setiers*, 1 *mine* of Paris

    Caen — 12 *setiers* = 22 *setiers* of Paris

    Harfleur — 1 *muid* (12 *setiers*) = 18 *setiers* of Paris.

These tables fit well with the prices established in section VI. The Rouen-Andely measures differ so little (by 1/32) that one would expect prices in the viscounties of Rouen and Pont de l'Arche to be about the same.[5] The large measure of Beaumont-en-Auge probably is reflected in the higher prices around Bonneville, which is near Beaumont, and perhaps in the generally high price for wheat in the viscounty of Auge. The very large measure used for wheat in Caen may also have been used in parts of the viscounties in Auge and Bernay, which would help to explain high prices in both districts. Note that the Caen measure for oats is a small measure,

[3] J. Petit, *Essai de restitution des plus anciens mémoriaux de la Chambre des Comptes* (Paris, 1899), pp. 146-147

[4] *Ibid.*, pp. 143-144.

[5] R. Fawtier, *Comptes royaux* II (Paris, 1954), nos. 24601-24603, in 1299 the Rouen-Andely ratio is the same as the one given in the table, but the Vernon measure seems a little smaller.

and while wheat valuations are much higher in the two viscounties nearest Caen, oats in these areas remain at the Rouen level. The measures used in Caudebec (-en-Caux) and Harfleur had no influence on the viscounty of Rouen.

Salt had its own measures, the *asquet* and the *somme*. Usually there were 4 *asquets* to a *somme* (fol. 176).

VIII

AGRICULTURAL METHODS

Agriculture was still dominated by the manorial system, though it was possible, and even desirable, to use other methods. Enclosures were rare in this *bailliage;* most of the king's holdings lay in open fields of the old type.[1] No effort seems to have been made to concentrate the king's land in one or two fields. Usually it was divided fairly evenly among all the fields of the village.

Arable land seems to have been used to produce grain almost exclusively. Flax is mentioned occasionally,[2] and apples were an important crop in the viscounty of Auge,[3] but grain was the most valuable product even in the regions where these other things were grown. Judging by the frequency with which they were mentioned, oats and wheat were the staple grains. Barley is listed only about half as often as oats, and other grains have no importance.[4]

It seems probable that the three-field system was generally used in the *bailliage*. Horses, rather than oxen, were used for plowing, a practice which usually indicates the three-field system. In addition, there are definite references to winter and spring sowings in the viscounty of Pont de l' Arche.[5]

The typical list of *corvées* states that plowing is due twice a year and harrowing twice a year. Our scribe seemed to assume that the work would be done with horses. He recognized the fact that many peasants had no horses, for he was careful to note that some services could not be required if the men who owed them lacked horses.[6] Since many peasants had no draft animals, much cultivation must have been done by hand.

---

[1] These fields were usually called "camps," or "coutures." In the viscounty of Auge, the Scandinavian word "delle" was used (fols. 177v, 186, 197v).

[2] fols. 12v, 78v, 112.

[3] fols. 163, 185v, 188, 196, 199v, 201.

[4] fol. 32, rye is mentioned.

[5] fols. 214, 215, 215v.

[6] fols. 12, 27v, 68, 82.

Fertilizer, usually manure,[7] was used whenever it was available, but few fields had the benefit of such treatment.

Every peasant kept hens, but geese seem to have been less common, and ducks are never mentioned. The frequent occurrence of payments for pannage shows that most households had pigs.[8] Sheep, while not rare, appear less frequently, and cows are seldom mentioned.[9] As was noted above, many peasants had no horses. Often only four or five men on a manor possessed these animals.

Saint Louis encouraged the use of forest land for agriculture, and there are many references in our manuscript to land which had been recently cleared.[10] These clearings amounted to hundreds of acres, and attracted numerous settlers. While the men living in the forest clearings formed village communities,[11] they were not subject to all the restrictions of the manorial system. There was little or no demesne land in the clearings, and as a result *corvées* were rare. The settlers in the forest paid low rents for their land, and possessed more food-animals than the ordinary peasant. If their land proved fertile, they were in a very favorable position.

---

[7] fols. 12, 76, 156, 175v, 197.

[8] fols. 4v, 15, 41v, 56v, etc.

[9] fols. 9v, 34, 62v. For additional references to sheep, *cf.* p. 27.

[10] fols. 33, 40, 57, 154, and especially fols. 207-215v, 229-231.

[11] fols. 213v, 231.

List of Abbreviations

Cart. Nor.—L. Delisle, *Cartulaire normand* (Caen, 1852, *M. A. N.*, 2e série, VI).

Delisle-Berger—*Recueil des Actes de Henri II* . . . *concernant les provinces françaises* (Paris, 1909-1916).

Ech.—L. Delisle, *Recueil de jugements de l'Echiquier* (Paris, 1864).

Eude Rigaud—T. Bonnin, *Registrum visitationum archiepiscopi Rotomagensis* (Paris, 1852).

H.F.—*Recueil des Historiens des Gaules et de la France* (Paris, 1738-).

M. A. N.—*Memoires de la Société des Antiquaires de Normandie* (Caen, 1824-).

Olim—E. Beuguot, *Les Olim* (Paris, 1846).

Quer. Nor.—*H.F.*, XXIV, *Querimoniae Normannorum*.

Stapleton—T. Stapleton, *Magni Rotuli Scaccarii Normanniae sub Regibus Angliae* (London, 1840-1844).

fol. 3

CI COMMENCHE LA VISCOMTÉ DE ROEM

La Serganterie de Roem

comté
par sey

Le vivier de souz Sainte Katerine, XIII lb.—baillie a l'archevesque de Roem por XLV lb.[1]—et creist de XXXII lb.

L'aioue de Roem, VIII.XX lb.

La terre as foulons, XX lb.

La terre au comte de Leucestre, XL lb. } Le maire et la ville la tienent.[2]

comté
par sey

Le cay de Saint Emont, XII lb.—perpetuel.[3]

Le molin Bernart Commin,[4] C s.—perpetuel—comté par sey a Pasques.

Por le sel de Roem vendu por tout l'an en fieu, LXVI s.

La teneure Aalart, IX lb. du cens—perpetuel.

Anvers Roem en menus cens, CX lb.—perpetuel.

Une nef d 'Ylande—un timpre de martres ou X lb.—perpetuel.[5]

---

[1] *H.F.*, XXI, 255. This vivarium brought in only 5 l. at Ascension, 1238 (probably 10 l. for the whole year). *Cart. Nor.*, nos. 619, 670, 671, 688. This lease to the archbishop was made in 1259, and was cancelled in 1261, as part of an exchange of property between St. Louis and the archbishop, by which the Convent of the Emmurées was established. In 1262 the king included the "vivarium de Martinvilla" in a great farm of royal property to the commune of Rouen.

[2] *Cart. Nor.*, no. 330. Louis VIII grants the burgesses of Rouen the fuller's earth in Roumare for 20 l. a year; *ibid.*, no. 647, the town made 65 l. from this earth in 1259. *ibid.*, no. 291, the land of the earl of Leicester was granted to the commune in 1220, at an annual rent of 40 l. *ibid.*, no. 647, the commune gained 5 l. from the fief of the earl of Leicester in 1259.

[3] *H.F.*, XXI, 255. This lease was made at least as early as 1238, since it is mentioned in the Easter roll of that year.

[4] Delisle, *Ech.*, no. 474. In 1231 the Exchequer maintained the rights of the burgesses of Rouen to 'placita de terra Bernardi Comin, sicut rex haberet." Stapleton, I, 79; Delisle-Berger, I, 412, II, 88, 209; Bernard Commin appears as a citizen of Rouen in several acts of the time of Henry II.

[5] Ch. de Beaurepaire, *De la vicomté de l'eau de Rouen*, (Paris-Rouen, 1856), p. 299. The late thirteenth century *coutumier* of the viscounty records: "La nef qui vient de Hybernie doit a la Visconté de l'Eaue de Rouen XX s., et au chastel de Rouen I timbre de martines, ou X livres de tornois, mès que serement soit avant feit des marchaans qu'il ne pourent trouver a vendre le dit timbre ès parties de Ybernie ou la nef fut carchie. . . ."

Les hales as couroiers, II.C. lb. por tout.

La hale a gros drapiers por la metie de la hale, CXII lb. X s.

L'autre metie d'icele hale, IIII.XX.XVI lb.

fol. 3v Les hales as raiers por la metie de la hale, LXXVI lb. X s., ne ne tienent pas toute la metie.

Item la metie d'icele hale por les estranges drapiers, VIII.XX.X. lb.

La hale as drapiers qui vendent bureaulz de Bernay, LXIIII lb. por la metie de la hale.

Por V poostiaulz d'icele hale, XL lb.

La hale as filandiers por la portion que il tienent, XXIX lb. XII s. VI d.

La hale as suors por tout, XXVI lb. X s.

La hale au ble por tout, V.C lb.

La hale a la lainne.

La costume du caage et des estaulz non louez, C s.

La hale ballie as cordoaniers, IIII.XX.X lb. ⎤ eles ne nos estoient pas

De lescamge de la Vielle Tour, XVI lb.[1] ⎦   dites

      L'en doit enquere des hales desus dites.

comtées par eles cinc poises de sel qui valent aucune foiz—X lb.

fol. 4 La ferme de la terre de Hionville, XXV lb., n'est pas baillie.

    Robert Piquet, demie acre de terre, I setier de forment, XII s., II gelines.

    Guillaume Orenge, por III vergies de terre.

    Les heirs Guibert, I verg., I mine de forment.

    Ricart Masceline por demie acre de terre, I setier de forment.

    Raoul Masceline V verg., I somme de forment, I some d'orge.

    Clarembosc de la Posterne, X s. por le fieu.

    Ricart Orenge, II s., I capon.

    Ricart Quesdieu, II s., I capon.

    Guillaume Tostain, II s., I capon.

    Enmeline des Haies, XVI s. por la piece de terre.

    Thomas des Haies, et Enmeline, et Gillebert du Pont, III capons.

    Les heirs Raoul des Haies, III capons.

    Lucas Filloil, I capon, II s. et le campart de demie acre, IIII s.

    Le jardin de la mare, XX s.

    Item X acres de pré, I verg. meins, valent XX lb.

        Somme XXVII lb. XIIII s. VIII d.

---

[1] *Cart. Nor.*, no. 688. The market of the Vielle-Tour was farmed to the commune in 1262.

fol. 4v La porcherie de Roem, L s., ou X pors de V s. por le porc.[1]

De chascune porcherie eu tenz de pasnage a autre tenz, XXV s.

Robert Huart, X pors en la serganterie de saint Jeure, laquele tient Symon Fromont.

Rogier le Fiselier, tout autant et ileques.

Nichole de Baudesac, tout autretant et ileques.

Jehan de Bosc Essart, tout autant et ileques.

Guillaume Basin, tout autant et ileques.

Thommas le Clerc, tout autant et ileques.

Guillaume Bouvet, et ses parchonniers, tout autant et ileques.

Guerout le Boqueron, tout autant et ileques.

Rogier Lestout, tout autant en la serganterie de Kally.

Guillaume Basile, tout autant en la serganterie de Coronne.

Somme por chasque porc XLV d.—XIIII lb. XII s. VI d.

fol. 5
comtée
par sey
Anvers saint Jame[1] prez de Roem doivent III hommes de lor fieu I mui d'avoine de rente, par Ricart du Fay[2] est ballie a Gefroy du Val Mesnil por IIII lb. X s., se il plest as maistres.

comtée
par sey
La ferme de la terre Ricart le Mareschal, XVI lb.[3]

Le cens menu anvers Yonville.

Perronnele Gombosc, III s.

Robert de Buesemoncel, XIIII s.

Perres de la Fonteinne, IIII s., III gelines.

Perres et Guillaume Quevalet, XII s.

Ricart Felinges, V d.

Nichole Mabile, III s. V d.

---

[1] Stapleton, I, 99. In 1180 there were eight or eight and one-half *porcariae* in the forest of Roumare, which would correspond to the eight in the sergeanty of Saint Jeure listed here, and one in the forest of Rouvray, which corresponds to the one in the sergeanty of Coronne. These nine brought in 93 pigs (Rouvray 13, the others 10 each), worth 14 l. 2 s. 11 d. after a tithe was paid. There is no trace of the *porcaria* in the sergeanty of Cailly at this time.

[1] Saint-Jacques-sur-Darnétal, Seine-Inférieure, a. Rouen, c. Darnétal.

[2] See above, p. 4.

[3] *Quer. Nor.*, no. 327. Richard Marshal, who had at first saved the family holdings in Normandy, eventually forfeited them by his death in England. See fols. 125, 212. *H.F.*, XXI, 255, the land of Richard Marshal in Rouen brought in 9 l. for one-half the year 1238.

Guillaume Perier, VIII s.

Maheut Dorgeil, XIIII d. et I geline.

Jehan Botton, XIIII d., I geline, et I fes de jargueil.

Maheut Charhardie, XIIII d., I geline, et I fes de jargeil.

fol. 5v
Guillaume Dorgeust et Guillaume Vivien, XXXI d., I geline de jargeil. [*sic.*]

Guillaume Vivien, XXXI d., I geline, I fes de jargeil.

Raoul Botton, XXXI d., I geline, I fes de jargeil.

Guillaume Herouarst, XIIII d., I geline, I fes de jargeil.

Raoul Botton tout autant, et du camp Rogier as Saz, VIII s., et une livre de poivre.

En la couture Poigniant, I acre de terre, IIII s.

En icele couture, demie acre de terre, II s. II d., et sus la granche II s. VI d.

Clarembosc le Rouz, XIIII s. II d.

Anvers Aubevoie, Symon Heridel, XIIII d.

Jehan le Pastor, XIIII d.

La fille au capelier, XIIII d.

Emengart la Borsiere, XIIII d.

Jehan du Bosc, XIIII d.

Orenge, XXIII d.

Pieres le Petit, XXIII d. por Hue de la Porte.

Ricart de la Commune, XXIII d.

Por le camp du Pardon, Hue de la Porte et Maheut la Grosse, VI s. III d.

Lucas le fils Jehan, VII s. II d.

Anvers Aubervoie, Mahieu Hateleu, XIIII d.

Nichole Lebarnier, IIII d. ob.

fol. 6
Thehart le Macon, IIII d. ob.

Hue le Rouz, V d.—Julian du Valet, XIIII d. Du fieu Guillaume Lovel que Hue le Boulengier tient, VII s.

Du fieu que Nichole Lebarvier tient—XIIII d. Dedenz la ville de Roem, Raoul de Conches, XIIII d.

Robert le Petit Seignor, IX s.

Nichole de Cotevrart, IX s.

Le prestre de Saint Guedart, II s.

Lucas Valentine, XX s. et II.C de parmeins.[1]

---

[1] Parmein, or permaine, a kind of apple, still cultivated in Normandy, according to Delisle. *cf.* Delisle, *Etude sur la Condition de la Classe Agricole*, p. 500 for another rent in permaines in Rouen.

En la meson Toroude, XVIII s.

En la meson Silvestre Tessart, VIII.C parmeins.

Nigaise de Carville,[2] L s., I livre de poivre.

Maheut la Grosse, V s., I lb. de poivre.

Garnier le Genne Roy, XXV lb., I lb. de poivre.

Clarembosc le Rouz, VIII s.—du traict des poissons XV s. et une breme; du cimetiere as Ivieulz V s.

Anvers la porte Giffart, XIIII d.

Raoul Vapail,[3] I lb. de poivre en la meson Rad. le Drapier.

Phelippe le Gall[ois], II lb. de poivre.

Ricart de la Fonteinne, XIIII d.

Jehan Burellion, XII s.

fol. 6v

Item Hue Gatel, VI s. VI d. et une livre de poivre.

Somme XVI lb. XII s. VI d.

et creist iceste serganterie de XXVII lb.

La viscomté de l'Aioue de Roem

Les parties des muiz qui sont deuz en la dite viscomté.[1]

Caudi vini doit XXI d. de la muiance—se il soit costumier XVI d. La pipe de vin. II s VI d.—se il est costumier XVI d. Un tonniau de vin III s. VI d.—se il est costumier XVI d. Un tresel de vin IIII s.—se il est costumier XVI d. Un tonniau de Rocele V s.—se il est costumier XVI d.

* Item de chascune nef

* Item de chascune tonne

fol. 7

Les fermiers de l'aioue de la viscomté de Roem

---

[2] *Cart. Nor.*, no. 647, note 50. The Carville were one of the leading families of Rouen. A Nicaise de Carville was mayor of Rouen in 1229-1230, and 1237-1238.

[3] *H.F.*, XXIII, 252. "Radulfus Wapaille" was lord of La Vaupellière (c. Maromme) before 1229. *cf.* fol. 7v.

---

[1] This is a very incomplete account of the duties on wine. See the complete list in Beaurepaire, pp. 291 *ff.* Our scribe probably did not finish the list because duties on wine could be collected directly and were not one of the seven great farms (see p. 38).

Por le fes du tenz Mahieu le Gros,[1] III.C.XXV lb.

Por IIII piez et la porte d'outre le pont, VIII.XX lb.[2]

Por les estaulz et la porte de Caulz et de Biauveiz, IIII.C.L lb.

Por la porte du port Homfrey, por la porte de Saint Vivian et
la lainne non lanée, por le fil et la viscomté Darnestal, VI.XX
lb.

Por la muiance d'Oissel, L lb.

Por tanure et escueles, X lb.

Les menues boistes de la viscomté, XV.C lb.

Les fieuz et les aumosnes ileques.[3]

Por le molin—a l'archevesque de Roem, M lb. par an.[4]

Por les freres de Grant Mont, II.C lb.[5]

Por la Sale a Puceles, II.C lb.[6]

---

[1] Stapleton, I, cxlvi; Cart. Nor., no. 50. A Mathieu le Gros was mayor of Rouen in 1195 and 1199.

Eude Rigaud, p. 113. Another Mathieu le Gros had led some of the rioters of 1250; he had to seek absolution, and pledges for his good conduct were given by prominent citizens of Rouen.

[2] Ch. de Beaurepaire, De la vicomté de l'eau de Rouen, p. 282. The Coutumier of the viscounty, written between 1269 and 1292, divides the viscounty into seven farms. Three, the "ferme des Estaus," the "ferme de la Prevosté de Darnestal," and the "ferme des IIII Piez" are identical with ones given here. Two others, the "ferme des Peaus engravellées" and the "ferme de Chanvre" are perhaps summed up above as "tanure et escueles." The other two, the "ferme de la Caherie" and the "ferme du Grant Poiz et du Petit," cannot be distinguished above. ibid., p. 424, receipts of the viscounty for Easter 1301 give "de minuta boista, VI.C.VIII l. II s. . . . de firmis traditis, pro medietate, III.C.IIII.XX.XVIII. l. X s." Remembering that at Easter only half the year's income was accounted for, these figures agree fairly well with those given above.

[3] Lists of fixed charges on the viscounty of the water of Rouen may be found in Stapleton, I, 70, 154; II, 304, for the years 1180, 1195, 1198; in Cart. Nor., nos. 210, 211, c. 1210; and in Beaurepaire, op. cit., pp. 316 ff., between 1269-1292; ibid., pp. 423 ff., for the years 1301, 1304, 1305, etc. There is considerable agreement among all of them; very seldom was a rent on the viscounty surrendered, though new ones were constantly added.

[4] Cart. Nor., no. 210. This sum was paid regularly soon after the conquest but the reasons for the payment are obscure. In the original agreement by which Richard gave the mills to the archbishop in exchange for Gaillon, (M.A.N., 2ᵉs., V, 89), no such payment is stipulated. Gaillon proved to be more profitable than the mills, since the archbishop paid 4000 l. to have the exchange reversed in 1262 (Cart. Nor., no. 685).

[5] Cart. Nor., no. 224. A document of doubtful authenticity records a confirmation of this rent by Philip Augustus in 1212. There must have been some basis for the charter, since in 1273 Parlement forced the bailli of Rouen to pay this rent (Olim, I, 938).

[6] Stapleton, I, cxlvi. This home for female lepers was established and given 200 l. annually on the viscounty by Henry II in 1183.

Por les moinnes du Bec Helloin, C lb.[7]

Por les chanoines de Biauleu, C lb.[1]

Por II provendes de Saint Marie de Roem, XXX lb.[2]

Por la capele du chastel le—Roy, VIII s.[3]

Por Jehan du Moncel, chevalier, X lb.[4]

Por les chanoines du Mont as Malades, LXX lb.[5]

Item, a iceulz VI s. VIII d. por VI setiers de vin a la Saint Martin.[5]

Item, a icelz LX s. por III.M de harenz.[5]

Por le segrestein du Pré, XLVI s.[6]

Por Bertin du Chastel, X lb.[7]

Por Gefrey du Val Richier, XL lb.[8]

Por les chanoines de la Magd[alene] de Roem, L lb.[9]

Por mons. Adan de Maretot, XXVII lb. VII s. VI d.[7]

Por mons. Rad. Vapail, IX lb. II s. VI d.[10]

Por les malades de Chartres, X lb.[11]

Por le Temple, XX lb.[12]

Por les besanz de Sainte Marie.

---

[7] Delisle-Berger, II, 109. Henry II gave Bec this rent in 1178; *Cart. Nor.*, no. 545. Saint Louis confirmed it in 1256.

---

[1] Beaurepaire, *op. cit.*, p. 52. This rent was originally given to Pierre de Préaux by John. He gave it to Beaulieu, with John's consent.

[2] *ibid.*, p. 49. These prebends were established by Richard.

[3] Stapleton, I, 70. This provision goes back at least to 1180.

[4] *M. A. N.*, 2ᵉ série, V, 157. This rent was granted by Philip Augustus in 1221.

[5] Beaurepaire, *op. cit.*, p. 46. These rents were granted by Henry II.

[6] Stapleton, I, 70. In 1180 the sacristan received 4 l. 8 s. "ad missas cantandas."

[7] Beaurepaire, *op. cit.*, p. 45, suggests that Bertin was jailer of the castle, since he received approximately the same salary given the jailer in the twelfth century rolls. This is an obvious slip; it was the *porter* who received 9l. 2s. 6d. The *jailer* received 27l. 7s. 6d., exactly the sum received by Adam de Maretot in this list. It seems likely that Adam held the jailership, perhaps as a fief. The identification of Bertin as porter is much less certain. He was a prominent citizen of Rouen (*cf.* Eude Rigaud, p. 127).

[8] *Cart. Nor.*, no. 647, note 11. Several members of this family were named Geoffroi; all were prominent in the affairs of the commune. This rent probably goes back to the first Geoffroi, who lived before 1200, since it is listed in *Cart. Nor.*, no. 210, a document drawn up shortly after the conquest.

[9] Stapleton, I, cxlvii. This rent was granted by Richard.

[10] *H. F.*, XXIII, 252. "Radulfus Wapaille" was lord of La Vaupellière (c. Maromme) before 1229. *cf.* fol. 6.

[11] Stapleton, I, 70. The lepers of Chartres received this rent in 1180, "per cartam Regis."

[12] *ibid.* The Templars received this sum in 1180, probably as the result of a grant by Henry II shortly before.

Por Saint Oein, LXX s.
Por Saint Lo de Roem, VI s.[13]
Por Saint Candre, VI s.
Por la moesum de Vernon, VII.XX.X lb.[14]
Por l'aioue de Roem, XXIIII lb.[15]

fol. 8
N'estoient
pas en
ferme

Anvers Borneville son II acres de terre par mesure et de cen le—Roy ne n'avoit riens—baillies a Guillaume Tempeste par Ricart du Fay, l'acre por XII s.

Item I isle en mie Seinne que l'en apele le Blanc du Sablon, baillie est a Tebaut du Chastel[1] por XX s.

Comté
par sey

Un jardin[2] que le Roy achata por les freres menors, valut le fruict en l'an de grace LIX, VII lb.

fol. 8v

Veci la Serganterie de Pavellye[1]

En iceste serganterie Guillaume de Amanville, XX s.,   } a la Saint
    Thomas Malassis, XXV s., Rogier Helluel, XXV s., } Michel sont
    Raoul de Brametot, XVIII d., II capons.   } deus por lor
                                          } vavass[ories]

Comté
par sey

L'abbé de Saint Wandrille, C s. por le conrey—perpetuel.

La terre Thomas de Gueteville IIII lb.—perpetuel.

La ferme de la terre d'Anqueteuville,[2] XLV s.—par ces parties.
    Une masure continant I acre, III verg., por V mines d'avoine, valent XII s. VI d.
    Item I acre et demie por V mines et demie a la petite mesure, valent XIIII s.

---

[13] Beaurepaire, *op. cit.*, p. 47. This sum was granted by Henry II to buy pepper to season game which they received from the royal forest.

[14] *Cart. Nor.*, no. 210. 100 l. "pro modiatione Vernonis" were paid shortly after the conquest.

[15] Stapleton, I, 71, roll of 1180, "Pro aquagio Sequane quod Hug. de Cresseio habet ad custodiam turris Roth., XXXV l." *ibid.*, I, 154; II, 304, this revenue is regularly assigned to the keeper of the tower. *ibid.*, I, XCIX, according to Stapleton "aquagium" was a payment made by fishermen for the right to fish in the river.

[1] *Olim*, I, 638. "Theobaldus de Castello, civis Rothomagensis . . ."; *cf.* fol. 58.

[2] *Cart. Nor.*, no. 807. In 1271 this garden was given as a perpetual farm to Pierre Blondel, for 7 l. a year.

[1] Pavilly, Seine-Inférieure, a. Rouen.

[2] Ancretieville-l'Esneval, Seine-Inférieure, a. Yvetot, c. Yerville.

Item XXII capons et I geline, XII s. IIII d., o une corvée de
I cheval, vaut VI s.

Item C oeus valent X d.

fol. 9 Le cens ileques, XIX s. IIII d.

Gillebert le Fevre fist ileques I meson sanz mandement. La
superficie est nostre.

Item sont ileques I acre et demie de bois—n'estoit pas en ferme.
Ballie a Jehan de Bordeville, l'acre por XXIIII s., par
Ricart du Fay.

La graverie de Seherville,[1] IIII lb.—perpetuel.

N'estoient
pas
en ferme Sont ileques VII acres de terre—Ballies par Ricart du Fay a Pierres de
Gros Fay, l'acre por IX s.

La ferme de Lymisi[2] LXX lb.

Anvers Limisi et Sierville IIII.XX.XVI acres, chascune acre
III m[ines] et demie d'orge, valent X s. VI d.

fol. 9v Es cens, XV lb.

*En moute anvers Yerville,[1] est ileques la mote s[eiche], XXVIII
mines et demie de forment, vaut la mine VI s.

Eu moulin de Sasinbec[2] IIII moez et demie de ble, valent XIII
lb. X s. franchement a la main le—Roy, mes le Roy met la
metie a refaire le molin.

*Anvers Yerville est la mote.

Item sont ileques II acres de bois de noviau vendues. Ballies par
Ricart du Fay a Robert Avelin, l'acre por XX s.

La ville de Sideville[3] de VII ans en VII ans XXX s., ou plus
selonc cen que il ont plusors fies ouailles por un pasturage.
Paié fu icest pasturage deraien en l'an de grace MCCLVI
a la feste saint Michel.

fol. 10 Guillaume Tempeste prist chascune acre de terre de Lymisi por XII s.,
et le molin por XXI lb., denier por denier, la mine d'avoine por III s.,
le capon por V d., oeus X por I d.

Les preeres des carues por XX s.

La justice et les reliez por XL s., et mist iceli Guillaume en

[1] Sierville, a. Rouen, c. Clères.
[2] Limésy, Seine-Inférieure, a. Rouen, c. Pavilly.

[1] Yerville, Seine-Inférieure, a. Yvetot.
[2] Vallée de Saffonbec(?), Seine-Inférieure, a. Rouen, c. Pavilly.
[3] Cideville, Seine-Inférieure, a. Yvetot, c. Yerville.

contreplege sa terre de Lymesi en l'an de grace MCCLXIII, a l'eschiquier de Pasques.

Anvers Yerville,[1] XVIII mines d'avoine de rente a la petite mesure, vault la mine II s. VI d.

Anvers Limesy, II mines d'avoine a cele mesure.
Item, ileques LXXII capons et o chascun capon I d.

Anvers Hyerville,[1] LVII capons et o le capon I d.
Item, ileques IIII poucins.
Item, anvers Lymesi VII.C oeus et o X oeus I d.

Anvers Hyerville[1] III.C.IIII.XX oeus, et o X oeus I d.
Les preeres de XXXI carues II foiz en l'an, vaut la iornée XVI d.
Item, tout autant d'erches, vaut la iornée VI d.

fol. 10v

Item XIX jornées d'ommes en aoust, vaut la iornée XII d.
Item chascun aiant quarete doit I iornée en aoust et sont XXXII quaretes, vaut la iornée II s.
Somme CIIII lb. XII s.

La ferme de la terre de Hardouville[1] vaut XX lb.
Sont ileques XXXIIII acres de terre arables en ces leuz—
Anvers Boocort, X acres, vaut l'acre VIII s.

Jurée

En iceli camp, entre II voies, V acres, vaut l'acre IX s.
En camp du pré, VIII acres, estimée l'acre a X s.
En camp souz l'iglise vers le val, VI acres, l'acre VIII s.
En val Raoul VI acres, l'acre III s.

Mesure

fol. 11

Raoul le prestre de Hardoville prist les terres devant dites au mestier des hommes de Hardoville por XVIII lb.
Item, est ileques I clos que l'en apele le leu le comte, vaut IIII s.
Item, est ileques I acre et demie de bois, vaut XII s.
} par Ric.du Fay
Raoul le prestre de Hardoville prist por lui et por son frere chascune acre de pasturage et de bois por VIII s. et le remanant de la ferme qui n'estoit pas ballie por VII lb. VI s. IIII d. et mistrent en contreplege

---

[1] Yerville, Seine-Inférieure, a. Yvetot.

---

[1] Hardouville, Seine-Inférieure, a. Rouen, c. Pavilly, cne. Mesnil-Panneville. *H.F.*, XXIII, 615. At Hardouville three-fourths of a knight's fee was in the king's hand after the conquest.

tout lor heritage que il ont a Pavelly, en l'an de grace MLXIII a l'eschiquier de Pasques.

fol. 11v

Item, est ileques le manage, estimé a XV s.

Item, est ileques l'erbage en V acres de bois, estimé XIIII s.

Item, sont ileques I pestiz par la reson desquelz le—Roy a de III anz en III anz une ouaille de chascun aiant ouailles et est estimée ceste rente a VIII s. par an.

Item sont ileques XLVII capons et o chascun capon I d.

Rentes

Item, sont ileques V vavassors, sont estimez les services d'icelz a C s. Ices vavassors est remis le service que il devoient, item, le capon o le denier que il devoient, les preeres des carues et d'erches et le cariage des gerbes en aoust que il devoient, a chascun por L s. a paier de chascun d'an en an.

En menu cenz XI s.

Item son ileques III hommes qui doivent II iornées a I quarete, estimée a II s. VI d.

Ices III hommes doivent o III chevalz aler anvers Dyepe a harenz une fieie en l'an.

fol. 12

Item, iceulz III hommes doivent porter le ble au seignor quant le seignor voudra, de Hardoville anvers Pavilly, et le fienz porter as camz II foiz en l'an, estimé chascun service a IIII s.

Ices III hommes, c'est assavoir Jehan Esgagnie, Guillaume Burel, et Guillaume Bagot reperierent les services que il devoient chascun por VI s. d'anuel rente.

n'est pas ballie

Item, XIIII mines d'avoine et I mine d'orge.

Item, chascune carue estant eu fieu doit II iornées de carue et II d'erche et sont VIII carues, estimée chascune carue a XV d. Chascun qui a cheval doit iornées d'erche, estimées les iornées a VI s.

Rentes

Item, sont ileques les reliez estimez a V s.

Item, est ileques la meson qui devient au Roy par deffaute d'eir, vaut IIII s.

Item, IIII.XX.X oeus et o X oeus I d., valent XVIII d.

Item, chascun vavassor qui a cheval doit amener I quaretée de garbes en aoust, estimée la iornée a XVIII d.

fol. 12v

Item, uns sont en la ville qui doivent tasser une jornée et sont V, vaut la iornée VI d.

Item, le fermier de Hardoville li quart a cheval a un conree sus Pierres de Brechi, vaut VI s.

Guillaume de Roquelon doit trouver a la dame de Hardoville

palefrey et chape quant le seignor de Hardoville et la dame iront por prendre le conrey.

Item, iceli Guillaume de Roquelon doit tenir les ples de Hardoville et de cen tient le grant fieu.

Item, sont ileques III hommes qui doivent coedre le lin I fiec en l'an et neteer la granche.

> Somme XL lb.—Ballie est a iceulz sicomme desus est dit.
>
> Iceste ferme creist selonc ballie et a ballier de XX lb.

fol. 13

Le bernage de Pavelly L s. en ces parties:

> Anvers Pavelly XXVIII mines d'avoine,[1] vaut la mine III s. foulée et renplie.
>
> Anvers le Mesnil sus Pavelly[2] IIII mines d'avoine a celi pris.
>
> Anvers Anqueteville IIII mines d'avoine a cel pris et I geline.
>
> Somme CVIII s.

La ferme de la terre Robert le Moine IIII lb.

> Sont ileques XV mines d'avoine, vaut la mine II s. VI d.
>
> Item, o les dites XV mines XV d. Item III capons, III d. Item XL oeus, III d.
>
> Item, sont ileques XVIII acres de terre, estimée l'acre VII s.
>
> Somme VIII lb. VII s. VI d.
>
> > Ballie est a Guillaume le Fevre du Val Martin[3] por IX lb. perpetuel, et creist de C s.

fol. 13v

En la ville de Saint Martin as Arbres[1] est une ferme de la terre Guillaume des Estables que nos avons allors.

> La serganterie de Pavellye creist de XXVII lb. V s.

Veci la Serganterie de Kally[2]

comtée
par sey

mema.

La ferme de Kally VI.C lb.[3]

> Anvers la Fresneie en deniers XXXV lb.

memoire de la taille de la Fresneie qui vaut LXVI s. VIII d.

---

[1] Stapleton, I, 78. In 1180 the accounts give "XXVIII min. avene de bernagio de Paveilleio. . . ."

[2] Mesnil de Fer, Seine-Inférieure, a. Rouen, c. Pavilly.

[3] Valmartin, Seine-Inférieure, a. Rouen, c. Clères, cne. La Houssaye-Berenger.

---

[1] Saint-Martin-aux-Arbres, Seine-Inférieure, a. Yvetot, c. Yerville.

[2] Cailly, Seine-Inférieure, a. Rouen, c. Clères.

[3] H.F., XXI, 255. The land of Cailly brought in 300 l. at Ascension 1238, probably 600 l. for the whole year.

que le fermier de Gornay prıst par Ricart du Fay.

Nos devons avoir conseil sus l'aide de la fille marier.

fol. 14 La taille de la Ferté, C.X s.

Item, ileques XIII.XX capons.

Les regarz ileques, XL s. en deniers.

Item, II moutons, VIIIs. Ballie a Vincent de Chevreville por X s.

Item, LXIIII mines d'orge, IX lb. XII s. A iceli por III s. VI d. la mine.

Item, XLVII mines d'avene, VII lb. XII d. A iceli la mine por III s. VI d.

Item, ileques la costume en deniers, XXX s.

Item, ileques X acres de terre, por tout XXX s.; par mesure XXXVIII acres III verg. XVI perches.

Item, ileques XL acres a celi pris.

Item, ileques le campart de IX.XX mines d'avoine, XXVII lb., a celui Vincent, la mine por III s. VI d.

Item, les services de quarier et de tasser.

Item, anvers la Fresneie a I miniere a fein, vaut par an VIII lb.

Item, ileques II.M de tuile de rente, valent XX s.

Item, le cens ileques X s.

Item, les corvées des carues—I herche, valent XL s.

n'est
pas
ballie
Item, ileques XII mines d'avene, l'estraim et la paille, por tout LX s.

Les regarz a Pasques, LIIII s.—n'est pas ballie.

fol. 14v Vincent devant dit prıst la taille de la Fresneie, les ventes, les services de quarier et de tasser, et les corvées des carues, tout por X lb.

Item, ileques XII mines d'avene, l'estraim et la paille por C s.

Item, les regarz a pasques por LIIII s.

Somme de tout VI.XX.VIII lb. VIII s. VI d.

Ices choses devant dites sont ballies au dit Vincent de Chevreville—Iceli meesmes les esples et les reliez des vilains por LX s.

Somme CXII lb. VIII s. VI d., sans les regarz et sanz les XII mines d'avene et l'estraim et la paille.

fol. 15 Item, au bois de Kally XIIII moez d'avoine por terres fieufées, perpetuel, valent L lb. XII s. Baillie la mine por III s. VI d.

Item, ileques por le fieu du Quesney, XX s.

Item, ileques XXXVII capons et XII s. de la costume.

Le fieu au Croisie, XIIII s.

Les esples et les reliez, C s.

Pierres Andreu por le service de querre les caretes au castel, IIII s.—Ices choses sont ballies a Jehan, seignor de Preaulz, por LXIII lb.[1]

Item, la metie du pasnage des porz jesans sus la terre de Kally qui vent en la forest de Saint Oein, vaut XL s.

> L'abbé de Saint Oein prist la metie du pasnage. Item, XII mines d'avoine en la granche de Saint Oein, l'estraim et la paille, la place entre les hales et la fossete, le petit jardin. Item la mote, le four et l'usage des quaretes en la forest por LX lb. o II pichiers de vin—il ont lor letres.[2]

fol. 15v

Anvers la Haie Gungor,[1] XII mines de mesteil, IIII s. por la mine, valent XLVIII s.

Anvers le Borc Saint Pierre, LX mines d'orge, IX lb.

par R. du Fay

Item, ileques XII mines d'orge, par Ricart du Fay.

Item, ileques VI mines de forment, XXXVI s.

Item, ileques VIII.XX et une mine d'avoine, XXIIII lb. III s.

Item, ileques VII capons, valent III s. VI d.

Item, ileques XXXVI gelines, XII s.

Item, ileques XVIII moutons, valent LXXII s.

Les regarz ileques, LXI s. II d.

par R. du Fay

Item, anvers Cally, II capons.

Item, a la Rue Saint Pierre,[2] le gardin, III galopins, vaut VIII s.

Item, anvers Bouquerel, II acres de pasturage, valent por tout V s.

Item, la haie de Bouquerel, demie vergie, vaut II s.

n'est pas ballie

Anvers Petreville, XII mines d'avene.

Item, ileques X acres de terre, XL s.

Anvers la fosse Basire, VII acres. Gefroy de Maudestor et Gau-

---

[1] *H.F.*, XXIII, 772. Jean de Préaulz owed three knights in 1272.

[2] *Cart. Nor.*, no. 604. In 1258 the monastery of St. Ouen took as a perpetual farm for 60 l., "medietatem pasnagii porcorum, jacentium in terra de Calli; 12 minas avene cum palea et stramine quas percipiebamus in grangia de Calli; plateam sitam inter halam et fossatum de Cailli; parvum jardinum, manerium predicti loci . . . cum . . . fossatis, furnum, usuarium quadrigarum in foresta de Serveisons, et duos potos vini debitos in quolibet adventu nostro Rothomagi."

[1] La Haye-Gonor, Seine-Inférieure, a. Rouen, c. Clères, cne. Bosc-Guerard-Saint-Adrien.

[2] La Rue St. Pierre, Seine-Inférieure, a. Rouen, c. Clères.

tier le Meteer pristrent l'acre por V s. Item, prist les services
que il devoit por IIII s. Item, ileques autres IIII acres, Robert
le Carons prist l'acre por IX s.

fol. 16

Anvers Mongoile,[1] XLVIII mines d'avoine, VII lb IIII s.

Anvers Colimare,[2] VII.XX mines tant d'orge quant d'avoine,
valent XXI lb.

Item, V boiss, de forment, VII s.

Item, XXXI capon, XV s. VI d.

Item, XVI gelines, V s. IIII d.

Item, XIIII moutons et demi, LVIII s.

Anvers Mongoille, XXII gelines, VII s. IIII d.

Item, ileques IIII capons, II s.

Anvers Colemare, III acres et demie de terre, valent XII s.—
Ricart Brunel prist l'acre por IIII s. VI d.

fol. 16v

Anvers Saint Germain,[1] VI mines d'avoine, XVIII s.

Anvers Kally en la granche de Saint Oein, XII mines d'avene,
XXXVI s.

Item, ileques le fourrage et la paille, LX s. Ballie est sicomme
desus est dit.

Anvers Cally, en rentes en deniers, L lb.

Item, ileques XXXV capons, XVII s. VI d.

La prevosté de Kally, LI lb.—par ces parties.
En cens des masures, XIII lb.
La costume du denier et de la maalle, XVIII lb.
Les foires ileques, IIII lb.
Le jardin le—Roy, le vivier, et le pré, X lb. Ballie o le
molin si comme dedenz est dit.

fol. 17

Item, l'autre jardin et demie acre de terre, XXX s.
Les herbages ileques, IIII lb.
Le fermier ileques, III pichiers de vin.

Item, ileques VIII.XX acres de terre, estimées LVI lb.

Mesure

Par mesure, VII.XX.XVIII acres et demie—Bailies a Renaut
Foucheri, a Rogier de Flosquet, a Guillaume Daufin, a Guillaume Piquet, a Raoul Biau Filz, a Anquetil de Braquetuit,
a Nichole le filz Pierres, a Jehan dit l'Asne, a Guillaume

---

[1] Mont-Gaille, Seine-Inférieure, a. Rouen, c. Clères.
[2] Colmare, Seine-Inférieure, a. Rouen, c. Clères.

[1] St. Germain-sous-Cailly, Seine Inférieure, a. Rouen, c. Clères.

Hermer et a Hue Tirel l'acre por VIII s.

Renaut Foucheri en a XVI acres par sey.

Anvers le Houlleis est une piece de terre contenant III verg., vaut VIII s., par Ricart du Fay.

Item, la fame Thomas de Holebest doit VI d. de rente, ne unques ne les pai apar XV anz.

Item, le seignor de Lintot[1] anvers Lillebonne[2] doit au seignor de Kally un esprevier sor por un fieu.

Anvers Cally est I bosc qui est apelé le Bosc des Haies, contient VIII acres, par mesure IX acres, et la terre atoche audit bois contient VII acres.—Ballie a Estace le Monnier, a Gefroy et a Pierres de Maudestors, chascune acre por X s. Item, la superficie du bosc, c'est assavoir chascune acre por C s. Thomas Hellebot encheri et prist l'acre por VI lb. X s.

*   ileques C lb.

II peires et demie d'esperons, V s.

Item, VII peire de ganz, XXI d.

Item, III livres de poivre, VI s.

Item, II livres de cire, III s.
Por XXI carue ileques, C s. } ne sont pas ballies

Por V oues, V s.

Le molin ileques, XV lb.
Item, l'autre molin, XL lb.
Item, l'autre molin, XVIII lb. } Mons. Nichole de Saint Germain[1] prist ices molins, le vivier, le pré, et le jardin joste le pré por C lb. C s.—enprez uns encherissemenz.

Les esples de Kally, X lb.
Le fosse, un jardin tient, IIII s.
Le fosse entre le castel et les hales, XX s. } Ballie a l'abbé de Saint Oein si comme est devant dit.

Pierres Safadin, demie capon.

Item, est ileques un usage en la forest a l'abbé de Saint Oein a III quaretes lequel la dame avoit—Ballie a l'abbé de Saint Oein sicomme desus est dit.

---

[1] Lintot, Seine-Inférieure, a. Le Havre, c. Bolbec.

[2] Lillebonne, Seine-Inférieure, a. Le Havre.

---

[1] Delisle, Ech., no. 813. "Nicholaus de Sancto Germano," knight, attended the Exchequer in 1258.

Item sont ileques IX jornées de saclage, vaut la iornée IIII d.
Toz les homes du fieu doivent le tassage eu castel—Ballie a
Thomas Hellebot.
Somme V.C.IIII.XX lb. LXXVI s. I d.
Iceste ferme creist selonc ballie et a ballier de CXVIII lb.
XI s.

fol. 19

La ferme de la terre de Quevron,[1] LIIII s.—Les parties sont cestes
Sont ileques III acres de terre, vaut l'acre IIII s.
Item une acre de pré, vaut X s.
Les cens, XXXVI s.—Ballie a Jehan de Maukency[2] por LXX s.
et creist de XVI s.
Somme IIII lb. VI s.
La serganterie de Kally creist de LXXIX lb. VIII s.
XI d.

fol. 19v

Veci la serganterie du Pont Saint Pierre[1]

La ferme de Franqueville,[2] XX lb.
Le cens de Franqueville, CXIII s. II d.
Item IIII.XX.VI capons et demi, valent XLIII s. III d.
Item, XII.C. oeus, XXII oeus meins, valent X s. IIII d.
*Le jardin ileques
Item, ileques XXIII acres de terre, valent VII lb. III s.
Item, ileques les corvées, XXX s.
Les reliez ileques, V s.
Somme, XVII lb. IIII s. VII d.
Pierres Blondel[3] prist ensemble o le jardin por XXV lb.,

---

[1] Crevon, Seine-Inférieure, a. Rouen, c. Buchy, cne. Blainville-Crevon.
[2] H.F., XXIII, 243, 772. Jean de Mauquenchy, knight, was patron of the church of
Cordelleville, in the deanery of Cailly. He held one knight's fee in 1272. ibid., 707, 242.
The family of Mauquenchy were lords of Blainville, and patrons of the churches of Crevon
and Blainville.

---

[1] Pont-Saint-Pierre, Eure, a. Les Andelys, c. Fleury-sur-Andelle.
[2] Saint-Pierre-de-Franqueville (or perhaps Notre-Dame de Franqueville) Seine-Infèrieure,
a. Rouen, c. Boos.
[3] Olim, I, 355. Pierre Blondel was a citizen of Rouen, and at one time had farmed
the viscounty of the water with Guillaume de Croisset and Nicolas de Senort. In February 1260, Eude Rigaud records that he ate "in manerio Petri Blondel, burgensis Rothomagensis, apud Franquevillam," so this farm had probably been made before that time (Eude
Rigaud, p. 358). Cart. Nor., no. 807. In 1271 he took for 7 l. as a perpetual farm, a garden
at Rouen, (cf. fol. 8) near the "porta de Goufrai." He gave as security his houses near
the same gate.

sanz le superficie du jardin.

Guillaume du Valmesnil l'encheri de LX s.

Somme XXVIII lb.

La ferme de la terre nostre seignor le Roy du Pont Seint Pierre[1]—
XVI.XX lb.

La prevosté du Pont Saint Pierre, et de Pistres,[2] et de Romigni,[3] et le
campart de Pistres—IIII.XX lb. XL s., par ces parties—

Anvers Pistres est une meson du Roy et I acre de terre.

La costume du denier et de la maalle, XXXII lb.

Le havage, XIIII lb.

L'aiage de la pesquerie, VII lb.

Les estaulz as taneors, VI lb.

Les hales as quaretes au pain, LX s.

Les hales as merciers, LX s.

La costume de la lainne, IIII lb.

La costume des poissons et des ruques, IIII lb.

La costume desus semainne, XX s.

La prevosté de Romeli, XXX s.

La prevosté et le campart de Pistres, LXX s.

La justice ileques, C s.

Le fenestrage, X s.

Item, un molin vaut LX lb.[1] ⎤ Ballie a Rogier de Sartiaux
Le molin de Romelli, XV lb.[1] ⎦   por IIII.XX.XV lb.

Item, est ileques I acre de pré, vaut XXX s.[1]

---

[1] *Cart. Nor.*, no. 98. This had once been held by the earls of Leicester and was
granted to Albert de Hangest in 1204 by Philip Augustus. *H.F.*, XXI, 255. At Ascension
1238, the land of Pont-Saint-Pierre was reckoned as bringing in 200 l. for the term,
or 400 l. a year.

Cart. Nor., no. 976. An inquest on the value of Pont-Saint-Pierre, in 1281, reported:
"Costuma denariorum et oboli, cum costuma hale quadrigarum, et cum costuma septi-
mane mercenariorum, lanarum, piscium et ruscarum, valet per annum 40 libras. Hava-
gium 16 libras. Aquagium 8 libras. Stalla tanatorum 7 libras. Hala drapariorum 25 s.
Masura Oudardi de Pistris, cum duabus pechiis terre 40 solidos. Campipars, prepositura,
palagium, corveie et fenestragium de Pistris, 100 solidos. Prepositura de Romillie 15 s."
This was part of the land given Hervé de Léon in exchange for his castles (*cf. Cart.
Nor.*, 973, 974).

[2] Pitres, Eure, a. Louviers, c. Pont de l'Arche.

[3] Romilli-sur-Andelle, Eure, a. Les Andelis, c. Fleury.

---

[1] *Cart. Nor.*, no. 976. "1 acra prati, valet 20 solidos. Burgagium et census Pontis
Sancti Petri et molendinum ad Secures 100 s. . . . Acelina la Torte, pro 3 masuris,
40 s. . . . Unum molendinum apud Romille, . . . valet per annum 12 libras. Item,
unum molendinum apud Pontem Sancti Petri . . . valet per annum 78 libras.

Alain desouz Saint Pierre, V s.

Deniers por le bois, V s.

Le borgage et le cenz ileques, LXVI s.[1]

Le fieu au chevalier de Pittres por le service de cheval, XX s.

Anvers le Point Saint Pierre sont III masures qui furent Asceline la Torte[1]—Pierres Poostel les prist, se il plest as maistres, por XL s.

In ma.[2]

Item sont ileques III verg. de terre.

Item, memoire de la quarte partie du fieu de hauberc joste Erneville[3] du quel menbre le seignor de Preaulz out la garde por XX anz, vaut par an XX lb.

Ricart le Rouge doit II s. de rente.

Pierres le Damoisel demie livre de poivre.

fol. 21

La ferme du Plesseiz Nichole,[1] LX lb., par ces parties.

Le cens ileques, VIII lb. XII s.

Uns gorz, VI lb.

Item, XIII acres, I verg. meinz, de terre, vaut l'acre XX s.

Item, ileques XXVI acres, l'acre XIII s.

Item, ileques VI acres, l'acre VIII s.

Item, IIII acres esquelz le—Roy a la metie, estimé a LXX s.

Les parties

Item, II lb. de poivre, valent IIII s.

Item, XLV capons Item, III.C.LX oeus.

Item, XVIII hostiez, chascun doit I pain et I d.

Item, VII s. d'autre cens.

Item, de chascune carue, III corvées, valent XI s. III d.

Item, XIIII mines d'avoine.

Item, por le campart de IIII mines de ble commun.

Item, uns hommes sont qui doivent coedre les verges a rapareller les gorz. Item, un aignel vaut XVIII d.

Le Priour du Mont de II. Amanz prist en la ferme desus dite chascune acre de terre por XX s. Les gorz en Seinne/ por VIII lb., chascune

fol. 21v

acre de campart por IIII s., denier por denier, capon por VI d., gelines por IIII d. et poucins ensement, oues X por I d., la livre de

---

[1] See note on preceding page.

[2] This note seems to be in a different hand. It is out of place; it should call attention to the next entry.

[3] Renneville, Eure, a. Les Andelis, c. Fleury.

---

[1] Le Plessis-Nicole, Eure, a. Les Andelys, c. Fleury, cne. Amfreville-sous-les-Monts.

Cart. Nor., no. 1085. This land had once belonged to Margaret de "Tooniaco" and was granted to Raoul de Boulogne by Philip Augustus in 1206.

poivre por II s. VI d., la mine d'avoine por IIII s., les reliez et les services por XL s., les corvées des carues non pas appresagies, un aignel por XVIII d. Item, il prist chascune acre de bois sanz le superficie por XVII s.—Et mist XX lb. d'anuel rente en contreplege sus la terre de Honville, et enprez l'encheri dedenz Pentecoste de C s.

fol. 22

Le molin de Saint Victor, LXX lb.—Ballie a l'abbé de Saint Victor por IIII.XX lb. C s.

La hart as poissons, XL s.[1]

Anvers Noeve Ville,[2] IIII.XX.X masures, chascune masure vaut IIII s., II gelines.

Chascun feu desdites masures par chascune, XII d. Vaut IIII lb. X s.

Anvers Meningrim,[3] XIII mines d'avoine, valent XXXV s.

Anvers le Mesnil Raoul,[4] XL mines d'avoine, C s.

Item L gelines, II setiers de forment, II setiers d'avoine por la court de Saint Amant.

Item II moutons, valent X s.; II formages, VI d.

fol. 22v

Anvers Franqueville XL mines d'avoine, valent C s.

Item . . L gelines.

Et por l'erbage, XXV s.

Anvers le Hamel du Bosc VIII m[ines] d'avoine, valent VIII s.; et VIII gelines.

Anvers le Mesnil Raoul, a Franqueville et au Hamel du Bosc IIII.C oeus.

Item en iceles meismes villes por tortiaulz de Noel, XXV s.

La prevosté de Noeue Ville, XL s.

Les monz souz Saint Pierre, VII s.[1]

fol. 23

Les cenz de Pittres, XXXVIII lb.[1]

Les gorz des aioues, XXV s.

Item, II sieges a molins foulerez.

---

[1] *Cart. Nor.*, no. 976. "La hart au poisson, 40 s."

[2] La-Neuville-Champ-d'Oisel, Seine-Inférieure, a. Rouen, c. Boos.
Cart. Nor., no. 976. "Masure et census de Novaville, solutis elemosinis, 23 libras et 8 solidos," 1281.

[3] Le Mesnil-Grain, Seine-Inférieure, a. Rouen, c. Boos.

[4] Le Mesnil-Raoult, Seine-Inférieure, a. Rouen, c. Boos.

---

[1] *Cart. Nor.*, no. 976. "Montes supra Pontem Sancti Petri, 2 solidos et 6 denarios."

---

[1] *Cart. Nor.*, no. 976. "Census de Pistris, solutis elemosinis, 10 libras, 14s., et 5 denarios."

Item, l'avoine de chievres anvers Ville Noeve, VI setiers valent XXXVI s.

N'estoit pas en ferme

A Noeve Ville de Cante Oisel[2] est une masure laquele Jehan Biausire tient, laquele fu d'un bastart qui s'en ala sanz heir, vaut XXX s.

Guillaume Normant, frere du bastart, balla por XXV s. a lui et por V s. au—Roy. Ricart Bordon dit que issi est.

Somme XVIII.XX.XVI lb. XIIII s. X d.

Et creist iceste ferme selonc ballie et a ballier de IIII.XX.XVI lb. IIII d.

fol. 23v
comtée
par sey

La ferme du Mesnil Amis de Osonville,[1] laquele maistre Ricart de Torny[2] tint, vaut XII lb.

Les terres arables XIII acres, par mesure XV acres LXVII perches, vaut l'acre VII s.

Item, le campart en III acres de terre, vaut VIII s.

les parties

Le cens ileques, XXIII s. IX d. et III pictes.

Item, sont ileques VI mines et II sytereins[3] fru[ment], vaut la mine VI s.

Item, est ileques I jardin estimé a XL s. Item, ileques XIIII capons.

fol. 24

Icele ferme devant dite est baillie a Pierres du Parrey, chevalier, por XV lb. X s. VI d., et mist en contreplege C soudées de sa terre. Ballie sanz le maneir et creist de LXIX s. VI d.

Somme de tout, comté le maneir, XVI lb.

Item est ileques le maneir atouche au jardin

Icest maneir est ballie au devant dit chevalier por X s. VI d. en tele maniere que se la superficie vaille LX s. remaindra a iceli, se il vaut plus donra plus, selonc l'estimation des biens.

fol. 24v

La ferme de la terre de Periers[1] VI. lb.

Sont ileques VII acres de terre, estimée l'acre a VIII s.

---

[2] La-Neuville-Champ-d'Oisel, Seine-Inférieure, a. Rouen, c. Boos.

---

[1] Auzouville-sur-Ry, Seine-Inférieure, a. Rouen, c. Darnétal.

[2] *H.F.*, XXIII, 281. Master Richard de Torny, canon of Sainte-Marie-la-Ronde, held the living of Baons-le-comte (Seine-Inférieure, a. Yvetot, c. Yerville); Eude Rigaud, p. 795, he died shortly before the fall of 1257.

[3] Probably for "boisseau sisterens," a bushel which equalled one-sixth of a *mine*.

---

[1] Périers-sur-Andelle, Eure, a. Les Andelis, c. Fleury-sur-Andelle.

Item, une acre anvers Erneville, estimée a VIII s.
Item, une acre de pré, estimée a X s.
Le cens ileques, XXXIII s.
Item VI capons, II d., XL oeus.
Item le campart de IX acres de terre, XXX s.
Les ventes et les reliez.
Somme VII lb. VI d.

fol. 25

Du fieu Restout, X s.
Romain Bonaide, II s.
Jehan de la Roonde, XVIII s.
Thommas Lesuor, X s. VI d. } a la Saint Michiel
Estiene Poostel, XL s.
De la terre au Beart, V s.
Du fieu vassal, XII s.

Anvers Saint Gille de III anz en III anz LX s., a la feste Saint Michiel, et sont apelées l'aide le comte.

La prevosté du Pont Saint Pierre, XX lb.
Le campart XXII acres de terre, et sont estimées a LXX s.
Une acre de pré elquel le—Rey a la metie du premier falcage o le campart de la plus haute partie, X s.

parties

Le cens ileuques, VIII s. VI d.
Item, VIII mines d'aveine foulées—et VIII min[es] et demie qui valent XI m[ines], vaut chascune mine III s. La somme LVIII s. VI d.
Item II mines de forment, valent XII s.
Item VIII gelines, la costume du boissiau et des estaulz, VI lb.

fol. 25v

Le cens et le montenage, X s. VIII d.
Le faucage, X s.
Les pors de la ville por estoublage, V s.
La some XV lb. VI s. X d.

Item, est ileuques une meson assise entre la meson Pierres du Creus et la meson Ricart Huue, laquele meson Guillaume dit Auflaon a pris por L s. tor. d'anuel rente, en tel maniere que il doit metre en amende de la dite meson XX lb., en l'an de grace M.CC.LXII au jor de diemence devant la feste Saint Vincent———
Item, en la prevosté du Pont Saint Pierre est une meson baillie a Henri Leclerc por C s., laquele fu monseignor Jehan de Biaumont, laquele est louée as II anz XIII lb.

La ferme Mahieu de Caumucel, XXXV lb.[1]

Sunt ileuques XXXV acres de terre, vaut l'acre VII s.

Item, ileuques VIII acres de pré, vaut l'acre XX s.

Le cens ileques, IIII lb. IIII s. VI d.

Item, XIIII mines d'aveine, vaut la mine, III s.

Item, VII boiss. quarteniers de forment, valent X s.

Item, le campart XIIII mines d'orge, vaut la mine III s.

Item, I mieu de vin, vaut XVI s. Item, VI capons. Item, VII gelines et LXV oes.

La some XXX lb. V s. IIII d.

Item, est en la ferme devant dite un bosc continent entor XV acres.

Jehan le prevost de Frenose prist chascune acre sanz le superficie por VIII s., en tel maniere que chascune acre poet estre encherie de VI d. juques a la Pasque et doit faire la metie de la paie a l'eschiquier de la Saint Michel et l'autre metie a l'eschiquier de Pasques enssuiant, en l'an M.CC.LXII eu meis de jenvier.[1]—

La Sergenterie de Saint Victor[2]

Anvers Claville[3] IIII lb. Le cens sur le terre de Claville perpetuel.

La ferme de la terre Rogier de Mortemer[4] III.C.IIII.XX lb.

Sunt ileuques XVII.XX et I acres de terre en ces parties

---

[1] H.F., XXIII, 613. "Mahi de Chaumontel" held land by grant of the king in the *bailliage* of Rouen as late as the end of the reign of Philip Augustus.

[1] Cart. Nor., no. 982. In 1281 this farm was seized by the king as a result of repeated defaults by John. It was regranted to St. Ouen for 55 l. a year, plus 100 l. for John's arrears and "pro introitu." The farm is described as "31 acras terre arabilis, 8 acras et 1 virgatam pratorum, 13 acras et dimidiam bosci, 4 libras, 4 solidos, 6 denarios censuales, 14 minas avene, campipartem quam habebamus ibidem, 7 boissellos annuos quarteniers frumenti, 1 annuum modium vini, 6 capones, 7 galinas, 65 ova. . . ."

[2] Saint-Victor l'Abbaye, Seine-Inférieure, a. Dieppe, c. Tôtes.

[3] Claville-Motteville (?), Seine-Inférieure, a. Rouen, c. Clères.

[4] M.A.N., 2e s., V, 156. Roger Mortemer lost this land at the time of the conquest. He adhered to John (Stapleton, II, cxx *ff*.).

En gastines VIII.XX.XV acres, vaut l'acre III s., sunt ileques
par mesure VII.XX.XII acres.

Guillaume Tibermont en prist V acres joste Robert Vandin,
l'acre por VII s.

Renaut Lebraceor prist demie acre de terre qui fu trouvée par
mesure joste le V acres du devant dit Guillaume et la prist
por IIII s. eu jor de mercredi devant la feste Saint Jehan
en l'an M.CC.LXII.

Jurée

Ricart Trove, par mesure VIII acres et demie et X perches eu
camp des Buors por VII s. l'acre, por LX s. tout, et mist en
contreplege XX s. de rente que il a envers Fresnay sus Garin
de Maisi.

Guillaume Tessel X acres X perches eu Val du Prée montant
au chemin et vaut l'acre IIII s. VI d.

L'abbé de Saint Victor a le remanent por IIII s. l'acre et sunt
ileques VIII.XX.VI acres.

Item, ileques LIIII acres, par mesure LX acres et demie et
XXXI perches, vaut l'acre VI s.

fol. 26v

Guillame du Peior, G. son filz, Robert Fouques, Hue de Lulli,
Robert Pilate, et Hue Safare ont pris des devant dites acres
de terre por chascune acre IX s. La somme XXVII lb. VI d.

Item, ileuques XXXVII acres, et vaut l'acre VI s., et sunt par
mesure XLIIII acres I verg. Guillaume Leconte prist d'icele
terre l'acre por VIII s. VI d. et acompaigna ovecques lui
Pierres du Bosc, Raoul Fourre, et Rogier Berte.

Envers Wasonville[1] XL acres et creit de III acres et demie
XXIII perches, vaut l'acre IIII s. Guillaume Baudoin prist
l'acre por VI s., valent XIIII lb. XVI s. X d., et est assavoir
por ceste terre et por autres choses que il prist dedenz sanz
une masure, et out nen ses letres e obliga touz ses biens.

Envers Ogerville XXIII acres, vaut l'acre VII s., et sunt par
mesure XXVII acres III vergiees—Guillaume Hardi, Gautier l'Abbé, et Guillaume Ysabel pristrent l'acre por VIII s.
quite au—Rey. Item, iceli les corvées lesqueles les dites terres
devoient por XX s. par an, c'est assavoir des carues et des
herces et de tasser et de quarier les garbes.

Non est
tradit.

Envers Biaumont[2] XII acres, vaut l'acre IIII s.

Envers Saint Victor a I jardin o la mote contient IIII acres,

---

[1] Vassonville, Seine-Inférieure, a. Dieppe, c. Tôtes.
[2] Beaumont-le-Harenz, Seine-Inférieure, a. Dieppe, c. Bellencombre.

Jurée

fol. 27

non est
tradit.

n'estoient
pas en
ferme

fol. 27v

N'estoit
en
ferme

valent CXV s. Item, II petites mesonceles sont ileques joste le mostier; sont ballies a l'abbé por X s. Iceli—abbé les prist por VI lb.

Envers le Petit Quesnot[3] a I jardin, vaut XXIII s. IIII d.

Rogier Berte prist le devant dit jardin por XXXII s. et le bosc du jardin sus la terre por IIII lb. X s., sanz le tiers et le dangier.

Envers Lulli[1] I jardin, vaut VI s.

Item, une piece de pré continente II acres et I vergie de pré valent por tout XVIII s. Ballie a Rogier Lemaistre tout por XXII s. VI d.

Envers Frunntmare II acres, autant par ⎫ Ascelin
mesure, vaut l'acre V s.   ⎪ Manevin
Eu camp de la vastine tout autant, par ⎬ encheri l'acre
mesure II acres, vaut l'acre V s.   ⎭ de VI d.

Item, II autres masures jost la hale au ble, vaut V s.—l'abbé de Saint Victor les prist por XVI s.

Item, au Petit Quesne[2] X corvées de carues II foiz en l'an et sont ballies a Guillaume Cornes, a Rogier Berte, a Pierres du Bosc et a Pierres Leece, prestre, chascune jornée por XV d.

Marc tendra sa ferme par tout le terme qui creit de LXXII lb. III s. VIII d., et de ices LXXII lb. III s. VIII d. comtera por la metie a chascun eschiquier et d'icele metie paiera a chascun eschiquier XVIII lb. XIII d.

*Le bosc de Estampuis[3] en III campz, XII acres, par mesure XXXII acres et XXXVII perches. Guillaume du Perier le genne prist la terre por X s. sanz le superficie.

Le bosc qui est apelé Dutelaie, sunt ileques par mesure XXIII acres et demie. Marc prist l'acre por X s. sanz le superficie. Marc prist le bosc sus la terre por XVI lb., mes il nen paera fors XI lb. et prendron les C s. demoranz sus le fermier.

Envers Saint Victor une masure es fossez le—Rey. Baillie a Guillaume le Mercier et a Rogier son frere por V s.

Item, envers Wasonville demie acre et XXX perches de bois. Baillie a Guillaume Baudoin sanz le superficie por X s., et valent les superficies LX s., et out letres et obliga touz ses biens.

---

[3] Le Petit Quesnay, Seine-Inférieure, a. Dieppe, c. Tôtes, cne. Bracquetuit.

---

[1] Loeuilly, Seine-Inférieure, a. Dieppe, c. Tôtes, cne. Etampuis.
[2] Le Petit Quesnay (?), cf. fol. 26v.
[3] Etampuis, Seine-Inférieure, a. Dieppe, c. Tôtes.

Le cenz ileuques XL lb. XVI s. II d., por les estalz XXX s. Baillie a—l'abbé, le cenz et les estaulz.

Item, sunt ileques les corvées de LV carues II foiz en l'an, vaut la iornée XV d.—Ballie—a l'abbé de Saint Victor por C s.

Item, sunt ileques XXII vavassories, chascune doit II iornées d'erche, estimée la iornée a VI d., et une quarete se il a cheval, autrement non, vaut II s. Item, sunt ileques V hommes, chascun doit II iornées a semer, vaut la iornée IIII d. Item, sunt ileques VIII hommes, chascun doit I iornée a tasser, vaut la iornée VIII d.—Ballie—a l'abbé de Saint Victor por XVIII s.

Item, sunt ileuques XII vavassors, chascun qui a quarete doit I jornée a quarier les garbes au seignor en aoust, vaut la iornée II[1] s.—Ballie audit—abbé por XXIIII s.

Item, est ileques la costume du marchie, comtées les foires, valt XI.XX.XIIII lb.—Ballie—a l'abbé de Saint Victor por XIII.XX lb.

Item la terre de Pleies,[1] eu quel leu sunt XXX acres de terre. Ballie fu par Guillaume de Cambremer,[2] l'acre II s., vaut l'acre XII s.

Item, la terre du Petit Quesney en icele ferme.

Item, des massoors qui sunt XVIII, qui ne sunt feufez, doivent service a cheval.

Item, de la terre Pierres Lecavelier laquele fu ballie par le—visconte por LX s., vaut XX lb.

Envers Wasonville a I jardin qui contient I acre, et un pré eu quel sunt environ III vergies, vaut tout XVIII s.—Ballie a Guillaume Baudoin por XXV s., out ses letres et obliga toz ses biens.

Item, ileques VII.XX.XVIII capons. Item, VII gelines et demie. Item, CX oes XI d. et o les chapons XIII s. II d. Item, VI ovees, valent VI s.

Item, sunt ileques XI mines et demie de forment, V s. por la mine et XXVIII mines d'orge, III s. por la mine, et LXXIIII mines et demie de avene, valt la mine II s.

---

[1] This figure is doubtful; it looks as if the scribe had written IIII and then partially erased the first two letters.

[1] Le Plix, Seine-Inférieure, a. Dieppe, c. Bellencombre, cne. Grigneuzeville.

[2] Guillaume de Cambremer was clerk to the great *bailli*, Jean des Vignes, who governed both Rouen and Caen from 1228 to 1244. Guillaume was more active in Caen; cf. my *Administration of Normandy*, p. 99.

Envers Saint Agnien VI lb. de rente, les esples C s.—Ballie a l'abbé/ de Saint Victor, prist la mine de forment por VI s., la mine d'orge por IIII s., la mine d'avene por III s., les esples X lb.

> Ices choses lesqueles sunt dedenz ballies sunt o les bois qui ne sunt ischi.

Envers Saint Victor II capons et demie, I mine et demie d'orge, I setier d'avene. Item, III bordages, valent XVIII d., le fes a la lainne XXX s., la quarete a esprover les chevaus XXX s.

Item, a Estempuis a I piece de terre, vaut l'acre X s. et une livre et demie de poivre. Item, la terre laquel est apelée le pré Galet, vaut VIII s.

Item, envers Saint Agnien sunt les pessages des ouaille en gastine, XXV s. Item, sunt ileques CII borgages, valent L s., et sunt ices borgages balliez—a l'abbé por L s.

Item,—l'abbé prist le campart de XLVI acres de terre, l'acre por III s.

Item, le campart envers Lulli et aillors por IIII.XX.XIII acres de terre. A l'abbé de Saint Victor est baillie le campart de XL acres por VI lb. Raoul Safare X acres et demie lesqueles il tenoit a campart et les prist por VI mines de mesteil, vaut la mine V s. Guillaume Feret VII acres a campart por III mines de mesteil et II d'orge et a letres et obliga touz ses biens. Item, sunt ileques XXV mines d'orge et autant d'aveine, valent CX s. Ballies audit—abbé.

Item, ileques I livre et demie de poivre vaut III s.—Ballie a l'abbé.

Envers Biaumont III acres de bois. Item, II acres XXXVI perches par mesure, vaut l'acre VI s.

Item, ileuques XX acres de terre et XXXV perches, prist l'acre por V s. VI d.; Raoul du Mont Bernart en a XVII acres por lui et por Hue de Costes, l'acre por V s. VI d.

L'abbé de Saint Victor doit III simenealz, III galons de vin, III pieces de poisson, III troites d'oeus, et sunt deues ices choses III fiees en l'an, et III flaons a Pasques.

Touz les hommes du fieu devent de III anz en III anz

Un jardin—ballie—a l'abbé por X s.

> La some de totes les fermes ballies et a ballier V.C.XXIX lb. VI s. XI d.

La ferme de la terre de Coteinart[1] LVI lb., comtée par lie.

Eu camp de la pierre, VII acres, vaut l'acre VII s.

Souz Saint Martin,[2] I acre I vergiee, l'acre VII s.

Eu val souz la buscaille, II acres et demie, a celui priez.

Sus le camp Rogier Passem[er] V verges, a cel meismes priez.

Eu cam Ysaac, V verg., a celui priez.

En la fosse Dame Ame, I acre et demie, a celi priez.

Au puis de Druelle,[1] V verg., par iceli priez.

Vers le Grant Mesnil,[2] II acres et demie, a celi priez.

Eu camp de Becotel, IIII acres et demie, par celi priez.

Eu frique de Salicoses, I acre et demie, a celi priez.

En l'autre camp vers le Grant Mesnil, III verg., a celi priez.

En la fosse as vavassors, III acres, par celi priez.

Eu camp au Borc, V verg., a celi priez.

Es fossez Odeline, V verg., a celi priez.

Eu val des granches I acre et demie, a celi priez.

Eu camp de Petiho, VII acres, a celi priez.

Eu camp des Miniers, II acres et demie, a. p.

Eu fieu Coutant, V acres, vaut l'acre V s.

Eu val des Corveies, VIII acres et demie, a celi priez.

En la rue du mostier, III acres, a. p.

Suz le camp Durant Mellin, IIII acres, a. p.

Eu val Ober II acres, par celi priez.

Eu fric du Mont Aug[ier], acre et demie.

A Busques en meschin, I acre, a. p.

Sus le camp Gautier Maunorri, I acre, a. p.

Sus la croiz Jehennet, V verg., a. p.

Eu fricue de la Sablonerie, II acres, au pries pardevant.

Eu Val de l'Essart, II acres et demie, et vaut l'acre VII s.

Au Hoc, demie vergiee a celui priez.

La somme LXXIII acres, par mesure LXXIX acres, III verg., XIIII perches.

Rogier Passem[er] prist les terres devant dites, chascune acre por VIII s.

Item, iceli meismes prist les corveies ileques et VIII herches por C s.

---

[1] Cottévrard, Seine-Inférieure, a. Dieppe, c. Bellencombre.
[2] Saint-Martin-Osmonville (?), Seine-Inférieure, a. Neufchâtel, c. Saint Saëns.

---

[1] Dreule, near Cottévrard.
[2] Grosmesnil, near Cottévrard.

et croist selonc cen que ele est ballie et a ballier XXI lb. IIII s. VII d. et a ses letres.

La somme selonc les letres XXXVI lb. XVIII s.

Item, en la ferme devant dite est I clos, vaut III s., ne n'estoit pas a ferme, par—Ricart du Fay.

Le cens ileques, XXXII lb.

Les corvées ileques, IIII lb. X s., VIII herches, IIII s., et les prist Rogier Passem[er] sicomme est desus dit.

Item, LIIII capons, et L d., et VI gelines.

Item, CL oeus, II d.

Item, XXVI mines d'avoine, vaut la mine III s.

La costume forainne XXV s. Les esples ileques XV s.

Item, VI livres de poivre, valent XII s. Item, est ileques une mote.

La somme des rentes desus dites LXVII lb. XII s., I d.

Rogier Passem[er] prist les rentes desus dites por XLV lb., des queuz il paiera LX s.—a l'abbé de Jumeges se il sont deues et tout ne soient il deues si paiera il XLV lb.

La ferme du lengnage de Roem, vaut XXI lb.

Sunt ileques VI.XX et X chevauz, chascun doit une somme de carbon en l'an, valt la somme III s.

La costume du lengnage qui vienent en chevauz et en quaretes IIII lb. X s.

Item, quant aucunz citeeinz de Roem ou autres et les buches lor sont données et le loage de chevau o mener les buches qui lor est deu vaut XV s. par an.

La somme XXIIII lb. XV s.

La ferme de la terre Estiene Lepeintor XL s., comté est par sey.

Iceste sergenterie creist de IIII.XX.X lb. III d.

La Sergenterie de Coronne[1]

La ferme Thommas d'Orgeus XXVIII lb.[2]

Sont ileques XXXI acre de pré et demie et XI perches, valt l'acre XIII s.

---

[1] Grand Couronne, Seine-Inférieure, a. Rouen.

[2] *H.F.*, XXIII, 613. "Thomas d'Orchouse" held land under Philip Augustus at Coronne "de dono regis." A.N., K 1201, no. 4, a 13th c. inquest on this farm by 3 knights and 9 men gives 22 acres of meadow valued at 13 s. an acre but farmed for 14 s., and 24½ acres of land at 3 s.

Rentes

fol. 30v

parties

fol. 31

Jurée

Item ileques LXIIII acres de terre par mesure, vaut l'acre II s. VI d.

Maistre Guillaume le Carpentier de Coronne[1] et Maistre Jehan Baudri, Robert de Cleom, Guillaume de Cleon, Rogier le Suor, Guillaume Sauchor, Rogier le Fevre et Ricart le Boef ont pris les prez devant diz, c'est assavoir l'acre por XIIII s. et les terres devant dites l'acre por III s.

Envers Petite Coronne[3] VIII acres et demie et XI perches et demie de pré, valt l'acre XV s.
Item, ileques demie acre et VI perches et demie de terre, valt III s.

Clement le Forestier et Gillebert Gascom pristrent l'acre por XX s., et demie acre ileques por III s.—Nos devons avoir le fein de II acres —Et chiet de la somme des terres IX acres LX perches et les queles sont piecha ballies a metie, nequedent que aucunnes sont ballies par greignor priez.

Le campart ileques LX s. en LXX acres de terre sicomme nen dit.
Parties vienent.

Item, ileques VII feuz vilainz, valt chascun XXXV s. VIII d.
    Les parties de chascun fieu sont cestes.
        Chascun fieu doit I somme d'avoine, valt X s.
        Item por l'acre de terre laborée, V s.
        Item, I iornée de fauqueure, valt XVIII d.

parties

        En deniers XVI d. Item, V gelines. Item, le carriage et le fenage en XXI acres de pré; icest service est estimé VI s.
        Item, XX garbes d'orge, et tout autant de seigle, estimé a X s.
        Item, XX oeus, II d. Item, chascun qui a son porc doit I d. d'estoublage.
        Des services devant diz se delivrent ices, c'est assavoir— Jehen le Prevost por son service XLIII s. Jehen le Canu XLIII s. Jehen le Sesnes XLIII s.; Robert le Fanier, Thomas le Forestier, Jehan Baudri, Colete la Bolengiere, chascun d'ices ont pris lor service que il devoient por XLIII s.

[3] Petit Couronne, Seine-Inférieure, a. Rouen, c. Grand Couronne.

Les heirs Nichole le Feron, por I esperons II s.

Ricart le Doulz et ses parchonniers I jornée de fenage, valt VI d.

Fromont le Gay I alose, vaut XII d.

Le cenz menu XXXIX s. VIII d. Item, VIII gelines, XXXII d.

Item, XII capons, estimez a VI s.

Guillaume le Carpentier, une petite masure, III s.

Item, I acre et demie de pré et XI perches, valt l'acre XIIII s., et la prist Guillaume Barbe por XIIII s. l'acre.

Item, XXX oeus, valent III d.

Item, vers Petite Coronne III setiers tam d'orge quam de seigle a la mesure de Roen, valent XVIII s., que Ricart Godefrey doit.

La masure Calot XVIII d. Icest ferme creist de XXXIX lb. XVII s. VII d.

El molin Vincent de Goi II m[ines] d'orge.

Envers les Molineaulz[1] II acres et demie de pré et XXIX perches, valent LX s. et iceulz des Moliniaulz doivent fener et fauquier, valt V s. Robert de Combon prist tout por LXXV s.

Vers Saint Estiene[2] IIII acres de pré et demie et XIX perches, valent C s.

Robert de Combon prist l'acre por XXXVII s.

La somme de tout XI lb. XVI s. VII d.

La ferme des prez Conpaignon IX lb.—comtée est par sey.

Sont ileques VI acres et demie et XXVI perches a la perche XXII pies.

Item, les fossez, I acre et demie et LXX perches, valent XL s.

Item, ileques III acres de maresc. Item, en la mare du parc entor II acres de terre.

Baillie a Lambert de Soteville por XXII lb. X s. VI d. et creist de XIII lb. X s. VI d.

La ferme de la mote Compaignon, LX s.

Lambert de Soteville la prist por IIII lb., et creist de XX s.

Item, sont ileques III verg. de pré, estimées a XXX s.

Item, IIII acres qui sont dites les mares, valt l'acre X s.

La mare du parc n'estoit pas es roules—Ballie audit Lambert de Soteville por L s., sicomme desus est dit.

---

[1] Moulineaux, Seine-Inférieure, a. Rouen, c. Grand Couronne.

[2] Saint-Etienne-du-Rouvray, Seine-Inférieure, a. Rouen, c. Sotteville-les-Rouen.

Le cens des alneiz,[1] XXVII lb., comté par sey, perpetuel.

Le cens Raoul Poitel vaut LX s., XX oeus, II capons, perpetuel.

Le cens des prez souz les Mouliniaulz, VI lb. II s. VI d.—comtée en somme des parprestures par dedenz.

Comté par eulz

Les parprestures de la forest de Rouveray, XXII lb. III s.[2]

Ices choses sont deues au—Rey envers Corone la petit—comtée par elz.

Jehan d'Yssie, XXXVI s.

Jehan de Compiegne, XXI s.	a Tafen, VIII s. VI d.
Robert de Meulent, LVI s.	a Pierres de Coronne, VIII s. VI d.
Les freres du Temple, V s.	a Counitre, XVII s. III d.
Robert le Torneor, II s. VI d.	a Robert Romain, X s. VI d.
Pierres le Buc, IIII s. VI d.	a Jehan Mascelin, XVIII d.
Pierres le Cerier, III s. IIII d.	a Rad. le Fevre, XVIII d.
Robilliart, IIII s.	a Ricart le Moingne, IX d.
Jehen le Prevost, VIII s. IX d.	a Gillebert de la Haie, VI s.
Jehan Canu, VIII d.	a Alexandre le Ceu, III s.
Jehan le Forestier, XII d.	a Robert Macecrier, III s. IX d.
Canu le Fevre, II s.	a Ricarde, II s.
	a Le Sesne, IIII s. IX d.
Michel le Bouc, XII d.	a Robert le Clerc, II s.
Ricart Ober, VI d.	a Robert le Tue, XII d.
Jehan Blondel, XII d.	a Lebeicu, VII s. IIII d.
Robert Hamel, XVIII d.	a Hebert le Suor, XVIII d.
Piquenot, XVIII d.	a Guillaume Reborz, II s. VI d.
Perres de Corone, XXXIII s. V d.	a Perres Coullie, V s. IX d.
Mascelin Pithache, IIII d. ob.	a Bertin de la Fonteinne, V s. IX d.
Rad. Alberi, VI d.	a Rad. Hunost, IX d.
Guillaume Huart, III s. V d.	a Guillaume Goomout, VI s.
Lerot, IX d.	a Mascelin, III s. V d.
Laurenz de la Vaquerie, XVI s. III d.	a Rad. Anselee, XI s. VI d.

fol. 33

---

[1] Le Grand Aunay, and Le Petit Aunay, Seine-Inférieure, a. Rouen, c. Grand Couronne, near Petit Couronne.

[2] Stapleton, I, 167. In 1195 the purprestures "a ponte Roth. usque ad Molinellos" brought in 17 l., 8s., 10 d.

Ricart au Mont, XI s. V d. a Anquetin, XIIII s. VI d.
Jehen Baba, V s.   a Malotru, III s. I d.
Alexandre Feret, II s. IX d. a Jehanet Dalli, II s. III d.
Renaut de Poissy, IIII d.
Romain Daliden, IX d.
Nichole Morin, VI s.

fol. 33v Ices choses sont deues a nostre seignor le—Rey envers les Mouliniaus.
Le prestre de Saint Jaque, II s.
Durant Reborz, XII seetes ferées enpenées de pennes d'aigle, et XXXIII d.

a Nichole Goobout, VI s. III d.
Rad. le Prevost, XV s. III d. ob. a Rad. de Rootot, XIII s. II d.
Les malades XIII s. II d. ob.   a Robert Poret, XVIII d.
Musehier, X s. IX d.   a Robert de Bosc, XIII s. VI d.
Flamenc, XXIIII s.   a Berengier, VI s. II d. ob.
Le seignor de Harecort, III s. a La Baarde, XIIII s. VI d.
Le moine de Sain Nicholas, a Gillebert de Hotot, XVIII d.
   IX d.   par essart.
Jehan Ober, VIII s. III d.
Jehan Morel, XV d.   La somme XXX lb. IX s.
   II d. ob.

Perres Caum, XV d.
Biset, VII s. VI d.
Quatre hommes, III s. IX d.
Pierres Piquart, VI s. X d.   Item, ileques sont contées VI
Guillaume Boudart, X s. IX d.   lb. II s. VI d. por les
Laurenz Letelier, III d.   cenz des prez des Mol-
Robert Gefrey, XXIII s. IX d.   iniaus si comme desus
Item, ileques, XIX s. VI d., et   est dit.
   XVIII d.
Almauri de Biau Puiz, XIX s.
   VI d.
Robert Goobout, VII s.

fol. 34 Envers Saint Gile LXXVII feuz—por chascun VIII d.; LI f[euz], IIII d.
Envers Cleon[1] LXIII feus—chascun feu—une mine d'avene a la petite mesure, XIIII gelines por lotoueur et VIII carr[ues].

---

[1] Cléon, Seine-Inférieure, a. Rouen, c. Elbeuf.

Envers Grant Coronne[2] gelines, desqueles les serganz en ont II, por chascune vache VI d., valt VI s. Item, XVII iornées de carues, valent XVII s. et une tuilerie, XXIIII s.

Envers Petite Coronne[2] por chascune vache alante en la forest, VI d., valt IIII lb.

Envers le Grant Quevillie[3] por chascune vache ensement, VI d., valt VII s. Por chascune carue I iornée, vaut XII s. Item, est ileques le fouage, vaut XII s. Item, chascun qui va a la feugiere, une oee, valt XII s. Item, VII gelines.

Envers Petit Quevilli[3] por chascun feu—II boiss. de seigle a la mesure de Roem valt LX boiss. Por les iornées de quatre carues IIII s. L'abbé du Bec I sextier de forment valt XII s. Item, VII gelines.

Envers Soteville[4] por chascun feu—I mine d'avene a la grant mesure et XI carues et VIII potiers—chascun doit V s.

fol. 34v

Envers Ermentruville[1] chascune vache II s., por chascune ouaille IIII d., valt XX lb.

Envers Saint Estiene[2] por chascun foier de XXX feuz, I mine d'avene a la petite mensure. Monseignor Gervaise, chevalier, I sextier de forment a la grant mesure. —L'abbé de Saint Wandrille, VI mines de forment. Item, sont ileques XXII carues, chascune doit I iornée. Item, XI masures et demie, chascune doit I gelline. Item, est ileques le tuilier, valt XX s. Item, chascune vache qui va en la forest por chascun meis I d. de fevrier jusques a juing, vaut IIII lb. X s. Item, le pasturage et de Roncevoi valt VI lb.

Envers le port de Saint Oein[3] chascun feu aiant la costume en la forest, I mine d'aveine a la petite mesure, et sont XL foiers.

Envers le Beiquet[4] chascun feu aiant costume, I mine d'avene a cele mesure, et sont XII feuz.

Envers la Poterie[5] chascun feu costumier, I mine a cele mesure, et sont VII feuz.

---

[2] Grand Couronne, Seine-Inférieure, a. Rouen; Petit Coronne, *ibid*.

[3] Le Grand-Quevilly, Seine-Inférieure, a. Rouen, c. Grand-Couronne; Le Petit Quevilly, *ibid*.

[4] Sotteville-les-Rouen, Seine-Inférieure, a. Rouen.

---

[1] "Ermentrudi Villa," a suburb of Rouen across the Seine, now called Saint-Sever.

[2] Saint-Etienne-du-Rouvray, Seine-Inférieure, a. Rouen, c. Sotteville.

[3] Le Port-Saint-Ouen, Seine-Inférieure, a. Rouen, c. Boos.

[4] Le Becquet, Seine-Inférieure, a. Rouen, c. Boos, near Saint Crespin.

[5] La Poterie, Seine-Inférieure, a. Rouen, c. Boos, near Amfreville-la-Mi-Voie.

Envers Oufroville[6] XXII foiers, valent XXII mines d'avene a cele mesure.

Envers Lescure[7] XVIII foiers, valent XVIII mines d'avene a cele mesure.

Envers Aieue Plot[8] I foier aiant costume, valt I mine d'aveine.

fol. 35 En la paroisse de Torville[1] por LVII foiers, LVII mines d'avoine.

Envers Oissel[2] sont IIII.XX foiers, chascun doit XII d. por le fouage. L'abbé de Fescamp I somme d'aveine et tot autant de forment. Item, XVIII gelines, ou por la geline VI d. Item, XIIII carues. Item, I mine de bran . . valt III s.

Item le fieu au comte de Meullent envers Oissel, eu quel feu sont deues au seignor mappe, escueles, estraim en la cambre au seignor et mener ou envoier en batel de Oyssel juques au port de Heulebeu.[3] Item, por chascune vache ileques V d., vaut IIII lb.

Envers Oyssel por la fouchiere, C s.

Envers Orival sont carrieres, valent XL s.

Chascun fevre resident es dites villes doit V s., I coignie ou XVIII d., et sont ileques XI fevres.

Por chascun festage ou la livrée esdites villes.

Les bochiers de Roem doivent el ior de Pasques I iambe de boef ou X s., item, les chars d'un mouton a l'Ascenciom, valt VIII s. De ices choses ne nen comte pas. Le castelain de Rupe prist ices choses.[4]

fol. 35v Ices choses prist le verdier.

De—l'abbé de Fescamp, I setier d'avene, et I setier de forment.

De Cleon, XIIII gelines.

De l'erbage parti, X s.

Les carues de Cleon, d'Oissel, de Saint Estiene, de Soteville, de Petit Kevilly, de Grant Quevilly et de Grant Corone.

Les oees de Grant Quevilly, de Feucherie, et de Londes.

Por chascune perche en la forest, I d.

---

[6] Amfreville-la-Mi-Voie, Seine-Inférieure, a. Rouen, c. Boos.

[7] L'Escure, Seine-Inférieure, a. Rouen, c. Boos.

[8] Eauplet, a suburb of Rouen on the right bank.

---

[1] Tourville-la-Rivière, Seine-Inférieure, a. Rouen, c. Elbeuf.

[2] Oissel, Seine-Inférieure, a. Rouen, c. Sotteville.

[3] Elbeuf, Seine-Inférieure, a. Rouen.

[4] On the line following this the scribe wrote "la somme" and then partially erased it. On the next line he began "Laj" and then stopped.

Chascun jour de diemenche I vitecoc ou V mauviz de chascun oiseloor.

Item de V serganz fiefez, de chascun VI gelines a Noel. Item, de chascun I setier de vin et VI denrées de pain.

Item, de II serganz de Coronne iceles redevances et I frique de bacom ou V s. Item, la flour de demie mine de forment.

La somme des eissues sanz Soteville CVI lb. X s.

La ferme de Ronverai IX lb. VI d.

Iceste serganterie creist de XXIII lb. XVI s. VII d.

fol. 36

La sergenterie de Saint Jeure[1]

La ferme de la terre Girart du Marc,[2] vaut XI.XX lb.

Envers Hotot[3] XIIII acres et demie et VIII perches de pré, valt l'acre XV s.

Ices cancelliers ont autres III parties de chascun por VI lb. VII s. il doit VI lb. XIII s., quar Nichole de Loseree prist por XXXII s. et I masure por VI s. Item, iceli le fenage et le tassement des prez, l'acre por III s.

Envers Bapaumes[4] VII acres de pré, valt l'acre XXX s.

Eu pré de Home III acres et demie.

Eu pré de Sensue V vergees, VIII perches et demie.

parties   Eu pré la metie de II acres et demie, XXVII perches.

Eu pré de III verges sont III verges et XVIII perches.

Thommas Sodemon, Gaifrey de Daieville les pristrent por XXXV s. l'acre.

La somme XIIII lb. s. VI d.

Item, ileques III molins, valent VI.XX lb.

Envers Warfaut I molin estimé a XV lb.——Monseignor Robert des Vuiz[5] le prist por XVIII lb. et a letres et met en contreplege C s. de rente.

---

[1] Saint-Georges (now Saint-Martin) de-Boscherville, Seine-Inférieure, a. Rouen, c. Duclair.

[2] *H.F.*, XXIII, 613. "Girardus de Marc" held land near Rouen by virtue of a grant made by Philip II.

[3] Hautot-sur-Seine, Seine-Inférieure, a. Rouen, c. Grand-Couronne.

[4] Bapaume, Seine-Inférieure, a. Rouen, c. Maronne, cne. Canteleu.

[5] *H.F.*, XXIII, 252. Robert, lord of "Les Vez" (Les Vieux, Seine-Inférieure, a. Rouen, c. Duclair, cne. Saint Paër), presented a priest to the church of Les Vieux not earlier than 1245.

fol. 36v

Item en la—viscomté du Pont Audemer XV lb. de laquels ces parties sont teles.

Est ileques demie acre de terre, vaut VIII s.

Item, V acres de terre donnée au t[er]ers, valent XXX s. por tout au Runge Houz.

La moute ileques, XII s.; a la haie de Saint Michiel por moute XXXV s.

parties

Item, XIIII boiss, d'avoine, valent V s. X d.

Envers Fouteincourt por moute, XII s.

Item ileques por le cenz, XIII lb., XIIII d.

Envers Hotot, VII lb. VII s. IIII d.

Item, ileques I acre de terre envers le viez fosse, valt VI s.

Item, ileques I masure, qui vaut III s.

Item, ileques VI.C.LX oeuz. Item, II capons, VI gelines, II d.

Item, une livre de poivre.

Item I piece de vingne qui contient III acres, estimé a LX s.

Envers le Quesne le—Roy II acres de terre, vaut l'acre VI s. Guillaume Durant prist l'acre por VII s.

Le cenz—A Noel de nostre seignor, XVII s.

Item, celz de Hotot doivent la vingne vendanger.

Envers Hotot II masures continentes I acre, valt VI s.

Herveu Bordel a I des II masures por VI s. et I capon.

Nichole de Loseroie[1] prist l'autre por VI s.

fol. 37

Envers Bapaumes I acre de pasture, estimé a VIII s.

Item, demie acre, laquele Rogier Bovet tient por VI s.

Item, I jardin continant I vergée, valt VIII s.—Rogier Bovet prist por XXVIII s., quite au—Rey.

Item, IX lb. III s., le cenz a la Saint Michiel et a Noel.

Item, IIII.C et L oeuz, valent XLV d.

Item, V gelines et capon. Item I livre et demie de poivre, valt IIII s.

Item, XVIII.C aulz et oignons, valent VI s.

Item, I vergie laquele Jehen de Fresnes tient, estimé a III s.

Item, il devent curer le bief.

La somme II.C.IIII lb. IIII s. XI d.

N'est pas en ferme

Pierre du Bosc, Guillaume Sorcraist, III vergies de pré joste le pré maien et ne sont pas en ferme.

---

[1] *cf.* fol. 36.

La ferme de la terre de Villiers,[1] por' tout X lb., perpetuel, comtée est par sey.

Le molin Chambellenc, XI lb. X s., perpetuel.

Les prez du Val du Fenil,[2] IIII lb., perpetuel.

fol. 37v

La ferme de la terre Guillaume de Roues VII lb.

    Sont ileques XI acres de terre, vaut l'acre IIII s., par mesure XV acres et demie, XXVI perches.

    Le cenz ileques, LVI s. Item XXX capons et XX d.

    Item, V livres de poivre, valent X s.

    Item I acre de terre a campart, vaut XVIII d.

        La somme VI lb. VIII s. II d.

Gilles de Loure prist la devant dite ferme, l'acre por VI s., la livre de poivre por II s. VI d., l'acre du campart por II s., le capon por VI d. et autres rentes a la value.

        La somme selonc la mesure IX lb. VI d.

La ferme de la terre de Auborville[1] vaut XVI lb.

    Envers le Natai I acre de pré, XXVI s.

    Eu camp de Lande Marete I acre, XIIII s.

    Eu camp de Manequet I acre et demie de terre, valt VI s. Jehan Alains prist l'acre por VIII s.

    Souz la Vigne Mote II acres, par mesure III acres XV perches meinz, valt l'acre VIII s. Gautier de la Mare prist l'acre por X s.

fol. 38

    Item, ioste iceli camp I acre et I vergie, valt l'acre VIII s.

    Souz la Vigne Mauduit, I acre en III pieches, a celi pries.

    Envers le Noef Dors, II acre, l'acre X s.

    Eu camp qui est apele le pré de la mare, IIII acres, IX s. l'acre.

    Envers le port de Lille,[1] I acre, IX s.

    Eu clos I acre et demie et V perches, VIII s. l'acre. Evrart de Lisle prist tout por XVIII s.

---

[1] Villers-Escalles, Seine-Inférieure, a. Rouen, c. Duclair. Gautier le Chambellan held land there, *H.F.*, XXIII, 252.

[2] Delisle-Berger, II, 105. Henry I granted his meadows of "Valle Fenili" to Bec in 1122. They seem to be in, or near, the forest of Roumare.

Val au Phénix (?), Seine-Inférieure, a. Rouen, c. Duclair.

---

[1] Ambourville, Seine-Inférieure, a. Rouen, c. Duclair. Delisle-Berger, II, 105. Henry I had held at least part of Ambourville as early as 1120.

---

[1] Port d'Yville (?), Seine-Inférieure, a. Rouen, c. Duclair.

Eu camp de Landemare, I acre VIII s.

En la paroisse d'Auborville, XXXIII acres, valt l'acre XVIII d. Symont Fromont prist tout por IIII lb. X s.

Item, sont II clausages en la Vigne Mote et de Mauduit continanz III acres, estimées a LX s. et sont par mesure III acres I vergie. Gautier de la Mare les prist por IIII lb.

Le cenz en deniers, LXI s.

Item, ileques LX capons, XXX gelines, o les capons XLV d.

Item, VII.C et XX oeuz, valent V s. XI d., et en deniers V s.

Item, sont ileques V carues, II foiz en l'an, valent X s.

Item, chascun aiant cheval doit I hercie et sont ileques autres cures ou seurvices.

fol. 38v

Item, les heirs Robert de Roem tienent I acre de terre a campart. Ballie est a iceulz por II souz de rente, perpetuel.

Ricart du Mostier, demie acre de terre a campart.

La somme de la ferme devant dite XX lb. III s. III d.

Et croist icele ferme selonc baillie et a ballier de IX lb. III s. III d.

La ferme de la terre Jehan Bordet X lb.

Eu camp Coques, III acres, l'acre VIII s.

Eu camp d'entre les II villes, IIII acres, l'acre X s.

Eu camp Terri, VI acres, I vergie, vaut l'acre VII s.

Le cens en deniers, LXXII s.

Item, XII capons, XI gelines et XIX d.

Item II.C oeus et o X oeus I d.

La somme IX lb. XIIII s. IIII d.

La ferme de la terre laquele fu Trossebout[1] XXIII lb.

fol. 39

Eu val de la mare V acres, valt l'acre VIII s., paié la rente.

Envers Conniheut[2] du fieu au Despensier, III acres valt l'acre X s.

Envers le Cluis, II acres, vaut l'acre VI s.—Ballie—a l'abbé de Jumeges sicomme dedenz est dit.

En la paroisse de Saint Jeure, VI acres de pré, estimée l'acre a XX s. Rad. de la Riviere[3] prist l'acre por XXV s.

Envers Bapaumes III acres et demie, valt l'acre XXV s. Durant Faiel prist l'acre por XXX s.

---

[1] cf. below, fol. 218.

[2] Conihout-de-Jumièges, Seine-Inférieure, a. Rouen, c. Duclair or Conihout-du-Mesnil.

[3] Cart. Nor., 903. "Radulfus de Ripparia" had holdings in the parish of St. Martin de Bocherville in 1277.

Item, les rentes en deniers, LXXV s. II d.
Item, XXXVI capons et III.C.LIIII oeus.
Le cens envers Conniheut, VI s.

Ballie est au devant dit—abbé sicomme dedenz est dit.

Envers le Cluis est I campart estimé a IIII setiers d'orge, vaut le setier VI s. Totes ices choses pardesus ballies et a ballíer sont—a l'abbé de Jumeges por XIIII lb.
Item, ileques I pasturage estimé a III s.
Le cens envers Bapaumes, XIIII s.

La somme XXI lb. XII s. IX d.
Iceste ferme creist de IIII lb. XII s.

fol. 39v

La ferme de la terre de Villiers[1] XL s.
Le cens ileques, XXVII s.
Item XXXV capons, valent XVII s. VI d.
Item, mil oeus, valent VIII s. IX d.
La somme LIII s. III d.

Les parprestures de Romare valent XI lb., nos n'avons pas les parties, deue est la diesme et comté par sey.
La tuilerie de Romare XV lb.
Envers Marromme[2] I acre de terre laquele Renaut Fermen tient et doit III s.
Gefrey Bouchart ileques I acre, valt III s.
Robert Clarice I vergie IX d.

Icest serganterie creist de XI lb. IIII s. VI d.
La some de tote la—visconté de Roem III.C.LXIIII lb. XV s. III d.

L'avoine de la Londe, XVIII muiz, por tout XXXV lb., comté est par sey.

fol. 40

La terre laquele fu Bacon, por tout a la feste Saint Michiel, XXIIII s.
De un fosse qui fu Ogier, III s.
La terre Guillaume le Clerc, XXIIII s.
La terre Engerran de Marromme, XX s.[1]
Monseignor Robert du Gue, demie livre de poivre.

Tout a la Saint Michiel

---

[1] Villers-Escalles, Seine-Inférieure, a. Rouen, c. Duclair.
[2] Maromme, Seine-Inférieure, a. Rouen.

[1] Stapleton, II, 416. In the roll of 1198 we find "XX so. de terra Enguelardi de Maromme fug. pro latrocinio."

comtée
par sey
La terre Pierres de Claville, XIIII lb.—comtée par sey.

Les issues de la forest de Romare, ballies sont por VI.XX.XV lb.

Envers Villiers, XII s. en deniers.

Envers Varenguierville,[2] XI s.

Romare, XLVI s.

Marrome, XX s.

Henonville,[3] VI s.

Montigni,[4] XVIII d. et X s. d'erbage.

Bapaumes,[5] III s. Le fieu du Temple envers Croisset,[6] V s.

fol. 40v
Le fieu Robert Bertran de Croisset,[1] X s.

Cantelou[2] VI s. Le fieu a l'abbé de Saint Jeure, XX s.

Le feu Jehan Guedon, VII s.

Le fieu Estiene Bordet,[3] XXIII s.

Le fieu Fouquet de Villiers, XX s.

Le fieu Michiel de Saint Sanson, XX s.

Le fieu mons. Robert Bertran envers Sahurs,[4] XVII s.

Le fieu de Lisle, III s. IIII d.

Le fieu a la Robillarde, XII d., I capon.

Le fieu Guillaume Lorp, VII s.

Renout de la Campaigne III s. por la costume du foage.

Jehan Leharel por icele costume III s.

Ricart de Sahurs por icele costume III s.

Le prevost de Croissel por icele costume III s.

*Le fieu Lambert por la costume de   V s.

Jehan le Normant, XII d. du ramage.

Jehan le Hericie, XII d. du ramage.

Aubin, XII d. por icen.

---

[2] Saint-Pierre-de-Varengeville, Seine-Inférieure, a. Rouen, c. Duclair.

[3] Hénouville, Seine-Inférieure, a. Rouen, c. Duclair.

[4] Montigny, Seine-Inférieure, a. Rouen, c. Maromme. Delisle-Berger, II, 189. William the Conqueror had held land in Montigny.

[5] Bapaume, *ibid.*

[6] Croisset, *ibid.*, cne. Canteleu.

---

[1] *H.F.*, XXIII, 608, 618, 634. The barony of the Bertrans was one of the largest fiefs left in Normandy after the conquest. The name Robert was traditional in the family, and it is impossible to say which Robert Bertran is meant here.

[2] Canteleu, Seine-Inférieure, a. Rouen, c. Maromme.

[3] Delisle-Berger, I, 412. A "Stephanus Bordet" acted as a witness for the abbot of Saint-Georges in an accord reached at the court of Henry II, *c.* 1167.

[4] Sahurs, Seine-Inférieure, a. Rouen, c. Grand-Couronne.

Robert le Corbout por icen XII d.

    La somme XIII lb. X s. IIII d.

Veci les rentes et la value des jarbes

    Envers Warengerville,[1] VIII. XX garbes, II sommes d'avene, IIII gelines, XL oeus.

    Envers Saint Jeure, XXX garbes, VI gelines.

    Envers Montigni, XXX gerbes.

    A la riviere de Sahurs, VI.XX garbes.

    Le fieu Guillaume Sequebout, II sommes d'avoine.

    Robert le Comte, I mine d'orge.

    Jehan Foilliet, I mine d'orge.

    Hurtaut, I mine d'orge.

    Robert le Boulengier, I mine d'orge.

    Le fieu Jehan de la Boche, III mines d'orge.

    Le fieu Guillaume de Saint Sanson, II mines d'orge.

    Le fieu Phelippe de la Court, I mine d'orge.

    Le fieu Espouse, I mine d'orge.

    Envers Cantelou, LX garbes, IX mines d'avoine, et IIII gelines.

    Envers Croisset, IX.XX garbes, XXV gelines, por la geline V d.

    Envers Marrome, CX garbes por l'erbage, les tortiaulz et le foage XX s.

    Envers Deaiville[2] por le foage, de l'erbage, et des tortiaulz XX s.

    L'erbage du fieu le comte de Augi, III s.

    Envers Sahurs VII capons, II gelines; de l'erbage, du f[oage] et des tor[tiaulz] XX s.

    Envers la Riviere, VI.XX oeus.

    Envers Croisset por l'erbage, fo[age], et tor[tiaulz], XX s.

Le fermier qui tient la forest receit les rentes devant dites.

Item, il a la metie des amendes de la forest, sanz hestre, sanz quesne verte, et sanz sauvagine.

Item, il a le sec bosc fors l'usage des genz du pais.

Item, il a touz les cas escheus par vent, sauvé la costume du pais et le chaable le—Rey.

Item, il a les coupiaulz de la forest que le—Roy fait sceer.

Item, se le—Roy doit a aucun mesrien il a les copiaulz que les carpentiers lessent.

---

[1] Saint-Pierre-de-Varengeville (?).

[2] Déville-les-Rouen, Seine-Inférieure, a. Rouen, c. Maromme.

Item, se ileques soit quariere—Ballie est par le fermier . . .

Item, se le cendrier soit ileques—Ballie est par iceli.

Item, se le pasnage soit ileques il a la metie ariere del pasnage.

Item, a le—Roy seetes por le parc forain.

Item, chascun batel a clouz qui hante la forest doit II s. par an.

Item, le carruage entor la forest, valt XX s. par an.

Item, de chascune rei a videcos, IIII d., et tout autant au pincons et
(fols. 42 and les teuliers doivent chascun I denier.
42v are
blank) Envers Saint Jeure a I teulerie, baillée par le—visconte se le Roy veut
sostenier la por C s. Ele n'estoit pas contée en ferme ne au—Rey.

fol. 43 ICI COMMANCHE LA VISCONTÉ DU PONT AUDEMER

La sergenterie de Briorne[1]

La prevosté de Biaumont le Rogier[2] XII.C lb.—comtée est par sey.

Ices choses qui n'estoient pas a ferme et des queles nen ne comtout pas
Eu marcie de Biaumont une petite place, valt II s. Ballie est
au visconte por II s.
Item, les fossez qui sont apelez liece, I acre et demie et VIII
perches—Ballie l'acre a Michiel du Bosc Rogier por XVI s.
Item, eu camp Compil V acres et XXI perche—Ballies a Renout
Malebranque, l'acre por XX s.

La prevosté de Combon[3] et la moute XLIII lb., contée la costume du
denier et de la maaille de Combon.

Les ples annuelz, XXX s.

La prevosté de Launey,[4] L s.

Le vinages ileques XIIII lb.

Le guerbage du pain et des gelines de la forest, XVII lb.

Le parc, V acres et les prez, V acres, valent XVI lb., sanz le bosc sus
la terre—Ballie au priour de Biaumont, chascune acre por XL s. et
sanz le bosc sus terre.[5]

Et sont ileques XXVIII acres par la mesure de Vincent.

Item I petit isle devant les baies escriptes dedenz qui contient

---

[1] Brionne, Eure, a. Bernay.

[2] Beaumont-le-Roger, Eure, a. Bernay. Stapleton, II, cc. This town was part of the
Meulan holdings. The count of Meulan played fast and loose with both John and Philip;
as a result, both kings issued orders of confiscation against his lands.

[3] Combon, Eure, a. Bernay, c. Beaumont-le-Roger.

[4] Launai, Eure, a. Bernay, c. Beaumont-le-Roger.

[5] *cf.* note on fol. 43v.

XLVIII perches par mesure. Baillie est a icelui[1] au priez XL s. por l'acre.

Item la vigne joste le chastel por LX s.[1]

Les prez le—Rey des Noviaulz Molins[2] XXI acres, le priez de l'acre XX s. Baillies sont a Jehen Guiart, a Rogier de Preaulz et a Robert le Galois o les services qui sont deuz as prez, c'est assavoir fener et auner, et en ceste maniere chascune acre por XX s. et sont ileques par mesure XXII acres et IIII perches de Vincent.

La moute seiche de Biaumont XV lb., en apres la prengnent le—Prior de Biaumont, et une autre tierce partie, c'est assavoir por C s.[3]

L'estoublage, VI lb.

Le molin tannerez, LX s.

Les pesqueries de Rille, XL lb.[4]

Les aloages de molins, LX s. et cen est que les banniers du molin ne poent aillors moudre mes ne d'aillors—le pain a lor user querre ou achater for de la mouture du molin, et que a chen repairent donnent aloage.

Le cens de Touzseinz, LX s., il creist et descreist selonc le nombre habitanz mes le chier cenz remaint,

Le cenz de Saint Martin, IIII s.

Le cenz de Saint Remi, XXVII lb.

Le dangier de la quarriere quant a fouir, X lb.

Les capons de Noel, X lb.

Les amendes de la forest de Biaumont por la partie le—Rey, XII lb.

Les ples de la ville de Biaumont, X lb.

Les pasturages de la forest, L s.

Les releveies ileques, LX s.

Les preeres des carues feaulz, LX s. et sont XVII.

Le chastel de la Lune,[1] IIII.XX lb.

Les services de III chevauz, VI lb.

---

[1] *Cart. Nor.*, 608. In 1259 St. Louis gave La Trinité de Beaumont-le-Roger, as a perpetual farm, for 59 l. 10 s. a year "parvam insulam de vivario continente 48 perticas, prata et alnetum de prato nostro Bellimontis Rogeri, . . . que prata, alnetum et aqua continent 28 acras . . . vineas nostras sitas juxta castrum Bellimontis Rogeri. . . ."

For the vineyard, *cf.* Delisle, *Etude sur la Condition de la Classe Agricole,* p. 436.

[2] Les Neuf-Moulins, Eure, a. Bernay, c. Beaumont, cne. Beaumontel.

[3] Does this refer to the rent claimed by Renaud de Botemont, *Quer. Nor.,* no. 274? Renaud claimed that his grandfather had been given a rent of 100 s. on the mills of Beaumont and that Philip Augustus had wrongfully refused to pay it.

[4] *cf.* note 2 on fol. 44.

---

[1] Châtel-la-Lune, Eure, a. Bernay, c. Beaumesnil.

Le soucage, XIIII lb.

Un fevre, XII fers a chevau o les clouz.

Les heirs Robert du Barc, les fers d'une charue de II piez de I chevau de la partie devant et les fers de I jument, valent X s.

La costume du denier et de la maaille, VI.XX lb.

Le havage, XXXIII lb.[2]

Les avoines de la forest de rente, XVII muiz IX setiers a la mesure de la forest, qui tele est que el setier sont XV boiss. en comun. La mesure de la ville sont XII boiss., et en tele maniere l'avoine de la forest vaut XXII moez IIII setiers et I quartier a la mesure de la ville, vaut le moe LX s.

Item sont en la forest XXX videcos de rente, valent V s.

A la Hermereie I setier de forment de XIIII s., et IIII oees, valent II s.

Robert Foucheri por les oblations le—comte, V s.

Item, sont ileques II livres de poivre, II s.

fol. 44v Item, VI setiers d'avoine de rente laquele doit le praier por unes redevances lesqueles il a es prez. Cen n'estoit pas a ferme ne n'est baillie.

Memoire que Ricart le Galois doit IIII capons de rente et de arrerage de XV anz.

Les heirs Jehan le Masuier, II fers a saete, IIII d.

Item, est ileques le petit isle devant les baies, XXV s.—Ballie au priour de Biaumont sicomme desus est dit eudevant foillet.[1]

Item I autre petit jardin, II s.

Item, l'autre, qui est apelé le pommier Morin, III s.—Baillie a Gefrei Cauchere por IIII s.

Item, est ileques la vingne joste le chastel, vaut LX s.[1]

Ballie au priour de Biaumont sicomme est dit pardevant.

Item, le jardin le—Roy ioste Saint Martin, XX s.—Maistre Henri Gambart prist la partie le—Roy en jardin por XXV s.

N'estoit pas en ferme Item, eu marcie est une petite place, II s.—Baillie a Jehen Guiart par le visconte por II s.

Item, le pré le prael ioste le camp Fromont, III s.—Ballie a Ricart le Galeis por V s.

---

[2] *Quer. Nor.*, no. 278. Pierre de Cracouville, knight, claims that the *havage* of Beaumont, the custom of the fisheries of Pont-Audemer and various lands in and about Beaumont were wrongfully confiscated by the *bailli* Cadoc (*c.* 1209); officially because Pierre's father went to England without license, actually because he refused Cadoc a falcon which he coveted.

---

[1] *cf.* note, fol. 43v.

II molins en estanc
Le molin de la fosse }V. C. lb.
Le molin Guion

Les fossez qui sont apelez liece, I acre et demie et VIII perches par
mesure. Eulz n'estoient a ferme ne n'estoient apresagies.—Ballies a
Michiel du Bosc Rogier et a son fuilz de la terre Girart du Moncel
jusques a la croiz Galeiz, chascune acre por XVI s. et est ileques I
acre et demie et VIII perches, par mesure de Vincent.

Item, eu campil, V acres ioste le Noef Bourc, vaut l'acre XX s. Eles
n'estoient pas en aucune ferme.—Ballies a Renout Malebranque,
chascune acre por XX s., et sont ileques V acres par mesure.

Les terres arables anvers Biaumont Ville,[1] LXXIII acres et XXVIII
perches. Anvers la Rouge Fosse[2] XXXV acres des quelz de II terriers
les parties sont continues en IIII leus dedanz escriptes, et est estimée
chascune acre l'une par l'autre XIIII s.—C'est assavoir en la costure
du Sevel XXV acres et demie et LX perches par Vincent.

Vechi le bail des dites terres, premierement a

Ricart le Galoiz, VII acres et demie, le priez de l'acre XXII s.
Item, iceli prist demie acre de terre eu buc de la cousture de la
peire por XI s. et ne nos estoit pas dit.
Guillaume Gambart, IIII acres, le priez de l'acre XXIII s.
quar il encheri sus Ricart le Galoiz.

Guillaume Doule, V verges, l'acre por XXIII s., quar il encheri
sur Ro. Legaleis.
Raoul Doule, II acres et III verges, l'acre por XXIII s., en-
sement il encheri.
Maistre Ricart Tornarst, II acres, le priez de l'acre XXII s.
Berthelemeu Ledrapier, I acre, le priez de l'acre XXII s.
Robert Legranchier, I acre, XXII s.
Robert Lesergant, I acre et demie vergie, a celi priez.
Iniorran de Marrome, VII vergees, le priez de l'acre XXII s.
Nichole Billioc, III acres, a celi priez.
Esmont Flori, demie acre por XI s.

Item, en la costure de la Rouge Fosse XXX acres et demie et XX
perches

Michiel du Bosc Rogier, IIII acres, le priez de l'acre XXII s.

---

[1] Beaumont-la-Ville, Eure, a. Bernay, c. Beaumont.
[2] La Rouge Fosse, *ibid.*

Renaut de Tiron, III acres, le priez de l'acre XXII s.

Guillaume Gambert, I acre et demie vergee, a celi priez.

Pierres du Bosc Rogier, IIII acres, le priez de l'acre XXII s.

Giefrei le Cauchieres, V acres et I verg., a celi priez.

Raoul Formentin, III acres, a celi priez.

Arnoulf Guerost, III acres, a celi priez.

Robert de Genestai, demie acre, a celi priez.

Phelippe as Den[iers], III verges et demie, a celi priez.

Crespin le Barbier, demie acre, a celi priez—Et encore sunt IIII acres I verg. et demie a ballier.

fol. 46
Ices choses lesqueles sont baillies en ceste ferme sanz terres que en tel maniere commenchent les terres arables valent selonc nostre baille—IIII.XX.IIII lb. X s. III d. Ricart du Fay fina por ces fermiers de XLV lb. et en tel maniere a nos remaingnent de la crescence a ore a comter XXXIX lb. XI s. III d.—et le fermier tendra sa ferme aussi comme devant.

En la costure de Marnieres XX acres et demie et IIII perches

Guillaume Serorge en a VII verg., le priez de l'acre XXII s.

Item, ileques demie acre et IIII perches, a celi priez.

Maistre Ricart Tornarst, VII acres, a celi priez.

Berthelemeu Ledrapier, II acres et demie, a celi priez.

Henri Ledrapier, III acres et demie, a celi priez.

Jusques ici durent les terres et les seignories
Robert Maugoire, VII verg., a celi priez.

Guillaume Novel, II acres, le priez de l'acre XXIII s.

En la costure du Val Tellie XXXII acres, XXVIII perches.

Michiel du Bosc Rogier, IIII acres, le priez de l'acre XXII s.

Alixandre de Tanai, III verg., lesqueles il avoit encheri, le priez de l'acre XXIII s.

fol. 46v
Item, en iceli leu iceli, I acre pour XXII s.

Jehan Masquefer, II acres et III vergies, le priez de l'acre XXII s.

Item, iceli, V vergies, a celi priez.

Maistre Ricart Tornart, III acres, le priez de l'acre XXII s.

Imorran de Marrome, IIII acres, par celi priez.

Rogier Brundos, I acre et demie, a celi priez.

Rogier de Tanay, I acre et demie, a celi priez.

Jehan de Pierre Lee, II acres et demie, a celi priez.

Crestian des Monz, I acre, a celi priez.

Tierri Pootel, I acre, a celi priez.

Sedile, et Michiel Iniorran son filz, I vergee, le priez de l'acre XXII s.

Robert Legranchier, I acre por XXII s.

Anfrei Begon, II acres et demie, le priez de l'acre XXII s.

Raoul du Fosse, II acres, a celi priez.

Alixandre Ribost, II acres et XXVIII perches, a celi priez.

Vechi terres fieufées

Envers Barc,[1] la Roge Fosse, et anvers Vetigni[2] II.C.LX.VI acres et I vergie fiefées, des queles chascune doit I mine de forment et tout autant d'avoine; la mine de forment valt VII s. et la mine d'avoine II s. VI d.

fol. 47 Les bordages anvers Biaumont Ville, XV acres fiefées en cele maniere.

Le fieu Laurens, XIIII acres fiefées en cele semblable maniere.

N'est pas en ferme Item, anvers Biaumont le sergant de la ville doit I besant sicomme l'en dit, ne n'estoient pas comté en somme, et valt VII s. VI d.

La ferme de Biaumont creist selonc cen que ele estoit estimée et selonc ices choses lesqueles baillies—IX.XX lb. CXIX s. II d., et por iceles qui n'estoient pas en ferme VI lb. XIIII s. IX d.

Computer par se Item por la garenne Jehan de Gaillon, XIII lb., de la voie qui maine du Noefborc au Mont le Rogier vers le chastel de la Lune.[1]

        La somme XII.C.IIII.XX.XIX lb. V s., sanz cestes qui n'estoient de ferme.

Item les superficies du bois du parc. Ballies a Rogier de Preaulz por II.C lb. Un autre pour XI.XX lb.

fol. 47v La ferme Loqueri de la Cambre LX s.

        Les terres, I acre vaut XIIII s.

        Le campart de V acres de terre, le priez de l'acre por le campart IIII s.

        Item ileques la metie de V verges de pré, vaut por tout VIII s.

        Le cens ileques, XI s. Item IIII capons et demie, et o les capons IIII d. ob.

        Item II oees, valent XX d. Item LX oeuz et VI d.

---

[1] Barc, Eure, a. Bernay, c. Beaumont.

[2] Vetigny, Eure, a. Bernay, c. Beaumont, cne. Barc.

---

[1] *Cart. Nor.*, nos. 1002, 1003. Ysabel de Grolai took this warren in 1282 for her son Jean (who seems later to have been called Jean de Gaillon), for 13 l. tur. a year.

Item III boiss. de forment et les III parties de I boiss, le priez du setier XIIII s. Item I setier d'avoine VI s. Item, demi quartier de mouton XII d. Item demie quarteron de bres XII d. Item, I quartier d'orge II s.

Item, por l'acre et demie de terre, laquele tient Robert le Maior, demie boiss. de bres, valt IIII d., et II boiss. et demi d'avoine, valent XII d., et por le mouton de la vente et de la iustice—
La somme LXXIIII s.

La ferme de la prevosté de Briorne XVII.XX.X lb.[1]

Les prez des Allieries IX acres, par tout IX lb.—Ballies au priour du Parc de Harecourt por XXVIII s. chascune acre et sont ileques IX acres et LXIIII perches pa[sic] la mesure de Gautier.[2]

Les prez du vivier VI acres, por tout XIII lb.—Baillies a mons. Ricart de Briorne,[3] chascune acre por XLIIII s., et sont ileques V acres III vergiees et XXIIII perches par Gautier, sanz le pré le fevre.

fol. 48
Ne n'en
comtout
pas en
ferme

Item, ileques le pré Guillaume le Fevre, I acre XXV perches —Ballie a iceli Guillaume por L s. tout.

Ricart Pivot por le prael, II s.

Ricart Huart por la masure, X s.

Le heirs Guillaume le Pertol, V s.

La pesquerie et l'aieue, XLI lb.

Item, III livres de poivre, valent VI s., nen ne dit pas qui les doit.

Uns esperons dorez, III s.

Robert dit Larchevesque por la moute, XII d. et ob.

Berthelemeu Huart, VI d.

Le forbir d'une espée ou d'un hiaume, XII d.

Ricart de Briorne, chevalier, por I auven II besanz, valent XIIII s.

Ices choses remaignent au—Roy quites.

---

[1] Stapleton, II, cxcix. Brionne had been given by John to Richard d'Harcourt. Philip allowed the Harcourts to keep only 1/3 of it, (cf. fol. 48) since it had been part of the Meulan lands, which he confiscated.

[2] This may refer to Master Gautier de Tornam, who measured some essarts in Bort c. 1230 (cf. Cart. Nor., no. 1144).

[3] H.F., XXIII, 771. Richard de Brionne served as a knight for the abbot of Bernay in the army of Foix, 1272.

Es parties dedanz escriptes a le—seignor de Harecourt[1] la tierce partie
Envers Briorne II molins, valent por tout CL lb.

La costume des coriers, XX lb.

La costume de IIII piez, LX lb.

La costume as drapiers et as telandiers, XXXVI lb.

La costume du lin et de la canvre, VI lb.

La costume des ruques et des peletiers, X lb.

La costume de la laine, XXXII lb.

fol. 48v
La costume des fers et des fus, IIII lb.

Le pavage du Pont d'Autou[1] et de la Cambre, XXIII lb.

Le pavage de la Riviere de Tibouville,[2] XX lb.

La costume de Lacendre et de Sarquini,[3] XXIII lb.

Le tour du marché, LXXVIII lb.

Le seignor de la Bosseie por le fieu, XII d.

Ricart de Briorne, chevalier, II capons.

Le fieu a—l'abbé du Bec, X s.

Le fieu au seignor de Tibouville,[2] por la costume de ses hommes,
X s.

Les hommes au priour de Saint Lau, por icen, VIII s.

Ricart de Briorne, por icen, V s.

Guillaume le Moigne et Rad. son frere, por icen, XII d.

Le fieu de Bigarz,[4] X s. VI d.

Le fieu de Harecourt,[5] VIII s.

Le fieu Rogier, IIII s.

Le fieu du Val,[6] IIII s.

Le fieu Guillaume Croc, X s., et I setier de forment.

Le bordage des alleus, XXXVIII s.

Le—Rey a ileques les ples et la justice.

La somme XVIII.XX.XVII lb. VII s. quite au—Roy.

fol. 49
La devant dite ferme croist selonc baillie et a ballier
XXXI lb. IX s. VI d.—Et por le pré au fevre,
XLV s., que nos avons gaagni.

---

[1] The Harcourts were one of the great families of Normandy, cf. Stapleton, II, clxvii, cc ff.

[1] Pont-Authou, Eure., a. Pont-Audemer, c. Montfort-sur-Risle.

[2] La Riviere-Thibouville, Eure, a. Bernay, c. Beaumont-le-Roger, cne. Nassandres. H.F., XXIII, 713. The king has two "hospites" in the fief of Thibouville.

[3] Serquigny, Eure, a. Bernay, c. Bernay; Nassandres (?), Eure, a. Bernay, c. Beaumont.

[4] Bigards, Eure, a. Bernay, c. Beaumont, cne. Nassandres.

[5] Harcourt, Eure, a. Bernay, c. Brionne.

[6] Le Val, Eure, a. Bernay, c. Beaumont, cne. Nassandres.

La ferme de la terre Loquet de Briorne XXXV s.

> Les terres eu camp Loquet, I acre, vaut XVIII s.
> Eu camp de Morceri, demie acre, VIII s.
> Eu camp du Goulet de Mommale, demie acre, valt VI s.
> Item, ileques I vergee, vaut III s.
> En l'angle du Callioel, demie vergie, XII d.
> A la haie Flamingni por tout, XVIII d.
> Item la place Loquete, XII d. de rente—Iceste ferme est baillie
> a Rogier Vesin por XLV s., et creist de X s.

Rogier du Quesnoi por la moele as couteaulz, III s.
Nichole le Fevre por une moele a fevre, V s.   } feod.
Mahieu le Fevre por une moele a fevre, V s.
Guillaume Moisson, I livre de poivre.
Estiene Vincent, II s. de rente.

fol. 49v La ferme de la terre de Waqueville et du Val[1] LVII lb.

> Sont ileques XLI setier de forment, le priez du setier XIIII s.
> Item, XXIX setiers et I mine d'avene, le priez du setier VI s.
> Les prez, mes il ne dit pas combien. Les pesqueries et le cens X lb.
> Le molin du Val por la quarte partie le—Rey, XV lb.
> Le cens et le pasturage eu Val, X lb.
> Item, II acres de terre, por tout L s.—Baillie est a mons. Jehan
> de Harecort[2] por IIII.XX lb et creist iceste de XXIII lb.
> La somme LXXV lb. XII d.

Por la terre de Bigarz[3] I livre de poivre, III s.

La terre Rogier Harenc, LX s., et est enquis—

> La somme de la crescence de tote la serganterie XI.
> XX.XVII lb. VI s. VIII d., et por iceles qui n'estoient
> pas en ferme VIII lb. XVI s. IX d.

fol. 50   La sergenterie de Montfort[1]

---

[1] Le Val, Eure, a. Bernay, c. Beaumont, cne. Nassandres.
[2] *cf.* fol. 33v, note.
[3] Bigards, Eure, a. Bernay, c. Beaumont, cne. Nassandres.

---

[1] Montfort-sur-Risle, Eure, a. Pont-Audemer. Stapleton, I, cxviii, Henry II seized Montfort in 1161 and added it to his domain.

La prevosté de Montfort XIII.XX lb.

　　Les prez de Montfort IX acres en I tenant, le priez de l'acre XVI s.

　　Les foires de la Saint Symon et Saint Jude, XII lb.

　　Les foires de la Saint Jehan, por la metie le—Roy C s.

　　La moute seique, XX lb.

　　Le cens menu por tout, VI lb.

　　Por les corniex, XLII s.

　　La costume forainne, L s.

　　La costume du vinage, XII lb.

　　Le molin tannerez, VI lb.

　　III molins, VIII.XX lb.

　　Robert de Montfort, II s. VI d.

　　Robert Pelet, I mine de forment, vaut X s.

　　Symon le Roy, II s. VI d. de I iardin.

　　Robert Pelet, II s. VI d.

fol. 50v

Guillaume de sus le pont prist le buc du fosse devant le molin ioste sa meson, et contient sis perches, por IIII s.

N'estoit en ferme

Item, est ileques I piece de terre continente XIX perches en lonc et XL piez en le.—Ballie est au prestre de Montfort por V s.

Item, estoient ileques les parprestures lesqueles Thomas Pelet et Robert le Blanc tenoient; icelz les pristrent por IX s.

La ferme de la terre de Roondemare[1] et des Planez,[2] II.C.XIII lb.

　　Ices choses lesqueles sont en ceste ferme ballies valent XXXVI lb. XXI d.

　　Le remanant est baillie par le visconte por IX.XX lb.

　　　　La somme II.C.XVI lb. XXI d.

　　Eu camp de Braetot[3] X acres et demie et I vergie, le priez de l'acre XIII s. et est baillie a—Guillaume du Quesney, l'acre por XVI s.

　　Eu camp Osb[ert] VII acres et I verg., le priez de l'acre XIII s. —Ballie est a Nichole Groart et a Hervi le Mande, l'acre por XVII s.

---

[1] Rondemare, Eure, a. Pont-Audemer, c. Montfort-sur-Risle, cne. Appeville.

[2] Les Planets, *ibid.*

[3] Brestot (?), Eure, a. Pont-Audemer, c. Montfort.

En la costure de Geneherost X acres et demie, le priez de l'acre
   X s. et est ballie a Rogier Bucart, et prist l'acre por XIIII s.

Eu camp du val III acres et I vergie, le priez de l'acre X s.—
   Ballie tout a Guillaume Boulli por XLIII s. III d.

En la grant costure XXVI acres et demie, le priez de l'acre
   XII s. Ballie a Robert a la Teste X acres que il prist d'iceles
   por XVI s. vers la Caene, et mist en contreplege III acres de
   sa terre assise eu camp des mares en l'an de grace M.CC.LXI
   eu jor de joedi apres la feste Saint Estiene en aoust.

Rogier du Mont prist le remanant por XV s. l'acre—et mist en
   contraplege II acres et demie que il a envers Lestanbres, vers
   le Quesnay[1] et vers la Quaene.

En la costure souz le iardin de Roondemare II acres, le priez
   de l'acre XII s.

In En icele costure X acres, le priez de l'acre VI s.

Envers le bosc Herost eu camp de Londes, sont ileques XI acres
   et demie, vaut l'acre XVI s.

En la fosse de la Pomeroie III acres et XX perches, le priez
   de l'acre XVI s.

En la haie Cocun, sont ileques II acres et demie, le priez de
   l'acre XVI s.

Joste la terre Rolant Gomont, demie acre et III perches, valt
   VIII s.

En la corte piece demie acre, vaut VIII s.

Eu camp qui est apelé ensement le camp Gasti, sus le iardin, VII
   acres, le priez de l'acre XII s.

Eu camp qui est apelé le camp Gautier des Monz IIII acres,
   valt l'acre X s.

Es valz de la forest XIII acres et demie, ne ne ni soloit avoir
   que XII acres, desqueles III en valent por tout XXXVI s.
   Robert de la Londe prist l'acre por XV s. Des autres IX acres
   vaut l'acre IIII s., et sunt ibi X acres et demie p[ar]
   m[esure]. Item, Robert de la Londe prist l'acre por V s. VI
   d., exceptez en III qui valent XXXVI s.

Eu camp de l'Espine Mossue II acres, le priez de l'acre IIII s.
   et sont ileques IIII acres.

Eu camp au Vergees I vergie et demie, por tout VI s.

---

[1] Le Quesnay, Eure, a. Pont-Audemer, c. Montfort, near Brestot.

Eu camp des Londelz V acres XLII perches.
Eu clos Normant III verges.
Eu camp Piquart I acre et III verg.   vaut l'acre XII s.
Eu camp Duredent IIII acres.
Eu camp a la Morele I acre et demie.

Le jardin de Roondemare IIII acres, por tout XL s. Estoient ileques le quart plusors fiees lesqueles furent comtées et cen soit le viscomte. Robert de la Londe prist l'acre por XV s.

Au Planez[1] en la paroisse de Catelions VII acres, por tout VIII lb., et sont ileques VI acres, XIIII perches par mesure. Jehen du Fou prist l'acre por XXV s.

Eu terrier des Planez par mesure XXVI acres III verg. et XVIII perches, le priez de l'acre XI s.

Eu leu qui est dit les prez des Planez, sont ileques II acres et XII perches, le priez de l'acre VI s. Thommas Biset prist l'acre por VIII s.

Item le clos de Tornoie, demie verge, por tout III s., et l'en dit que ileques fu le siege du molin. Guillaume Migniot prist por VI s., sanz le siege du molin.

Le cens ileques, XX lb.

Les III molins o la pesquerie et la moute seiche, C lb.

Item, IIII.XX capons, valent XL s.

Item XL gelines, la geline IIII d.

Item IIII.C oeus et o X oeus I d.

Item, VIII setiers d'avoine, et sont VIII boiss. le setier, le priez du setier Vs. L'en dit que II moez sunt ileques.

Les residences ileques, XX s.

Item, est ileques I fou, valt XX s.

Les preeres des carues II fois en l'an, XX s., qui a cheval il doit herce.

Item, sont ileques XXIIII fieuz, lesquelz doivent fouir la glebe et metre en la nef a rapareillier la calcie du molin.

Le cens des Planez, XL s.

Capons, XX; gelines, II.

En oeus et en deniers, III s. II d.

*Item I   de sel, vaut XII d.

Le pasnage ileques, X s.

---

[1] Les Planets, Eure, a. Pont-Audemer, c. Montfort, cne. Appeville.

Un potier X s.
Releveies et justice.

Item, le clos du don Hue, lequel n'estoit pas en somme, vaut V s. Baillie est a Thommas Musart por IX s.

Les esclusages de Montfort, ne sont pas ore en aucune ferme, valent

Item, une forfaicture, laquele est apelée Robert de Montfort. Ballie fu par un sergant, vaut IIII setiers de forment.

Item, le roullage du chastel de Montfort, LX s. de III anz en III anz.

Item, anvers Croville[1] LX s. de III anz en III anz par cen meesmes.

Item, I feu des Houles est eslongnié du—Roy, doit estre de la seignorie le—Roy; l'en lesoit par le visconte du Pont Audemer.

La somme II.C.XII lb. XVIII s. IXd- et creist iceste somme de XXII lb. XVIII s. II d. selonc baillie et estimé.

La ferme de la terre Ricart Descaquelon XIII lb. Ballie est a Jehan du Buc por XVIII lb.

Les terres crescent, l'encressement vaut XL s., il doit issi por la ferme XX lb.

Iceste ferme creist de VII lb.

En la costure des espines VIII acres, l'acre XII s.

Sus le maneir a la dame de Wiquetot VI acres, l'acre XII s.

Joste la cousture de Wiquetot II acres, a celi pris.

Joste la forest, IX acres en pasturage, l'acre VI s.

Somme XXV acres.

Par mesure XXIX acres et I verg.

La quarte partie d'un molin, LXX s.

En capons, en deniers, et en oeus, XLVI s. V d.

Item, XVIII boiss. d'avoine, valent XI s., II d. mainz, et III boiss. d'orge, II s.

La preere d'une carue II foiz en l'an, II s.; d'une herce XII d.

La somme XVIII lb. XVIII s. selon la jurée.

La ferme de la terre de Rootot[1] XVII.XX.X lb.

L'abbé du Bec prist ices terres ballies et a baillier a rencherissant iceles sus Guillaume de Rootot qui avoit pris iceles, l'acre por XX s., et le dit—abbé le prist por XXI s.

[1] Croville, Eure, a. Pont-Audemer, c. Montfort, cne. Glos-sur-Rille.

[1] Routot, Eure, a. Pont-Audemer.

En la costure fosse de la Griose, VII acres et demie, l'acre XVIII s.

En la costure vers l'arbre, XX acres acel pris.

En la costure du Hamel au Pie Fort, par mesure XVIII acres, le pris de l'acre XVI s.

Jurée

En la costure souz le Buc, sont ileques XXVI acres a cel pris. Guillaume du Bosc prist X acre, l'acre por XIX s.

Raoul Pinchon prist V acres pardevers lui, l'acre por XX s.

En la costure du Val Tremble,[1] XIIII acres XVIII perches, a cel pris.

En la costure Pelete, V acres III verg.

En la costure sont VII acres, V acres et I verg.

En la terre Symon de Longuemare, III acres XIIII perches.

Item I acre de la metie Ricart Legablier.

fol. 54v

Devant l'uis Raoul du Hamel, III verges.

Devant la meson Pierres Savon, III verg. X perches.

Eu camp Tirart, demie acre.

En la costure devant l'uis Ferache, XI acres.

En travers Symon de Longue Mare, II acres.

Eu camp Bauquier, I acre XXVIII perches.

Au Rouge Mostier,[1] I acre XII perches, de la moiteerie Mahieu Legablier.

Le forment de ceste ferme, avene, orge, et oeus et capons, XLVIII lb.

Item, le campart de IIII.XX.IX acres, oees comtées o les campars, vaut l'acre du campart III s. VI d.—tant en eust eu Ricart. La somme XV lb. XI s. VI d.

Sont ileques II setiers et pleine mine de forment, le pris du setier XV s., cinc moez et VIII setiers d'avoine, le pris du moe XLVIII s.

Rentes
fol. 55

Item, VII setiers d'orge, II boiss. meinz, le pris du setier VIII s.

Item, VIII oees, le pris de l'oie X d.

Item, VI.XX.VIII capons, et o chascun capon I d.

Une mappe, vaut VII s.

VI formages, valunt XII d.

Por oeus et por deniers, X s.

---

[1] le Tremblai, Eure, a. Pont-Audemer, c. Routot, near Rougemontiers.

[1] Rougemontiers, Eure, a. Pont-Audemer, c. Routot.

Un aignel, vaut XII d.
Un esprevier, II s.

Le cens ileques, XXIII lb.
La costume du ble, XL lb.
Une livre de poivre, II s.
La costume de la leinne, X lb.
La costume a coroiez et a peletiers, XVI lb.
La costume a merciers, LXX s.
Les salniers et loinctiers, LXX s.
Les foires ileques, VIII lb.
La costume as drapiers, VIII lb.
La costume des ruques, L s.
La roage ileques, L s.
La costume de IIII pies, LXII lb. VIII s.
Les hales ileques, XXXIX lb.
Le pavage ileques, XXX lb.
Guillaume du Bosc, XII s. por une masure de Rootot, laquele
   valoit XVIII d.
Les rel. et justices.

Iceste ferme creist selonc ballie et a ballier de
   XXXVIII lb. IX s. X d.
La somme III.C.XLIX lb. XII s. VIII d.

fol. 55v

La ferme de la terre de Toqueville LVII lb.—valt encore par le bail
   au viscomte LX lb.
Eu plain de Torville, IIII acres, l'acre XVI s.
Ileques LXVI acres, le pris de l'acres XVI s.—meillor est eu
   val vers le mostier de Touqueville.

Jurée premiere

fol. 56

Eu camp devant la meson Thommas de Touqueville, III verg.
Joste la meson Godart, III verg. X perches.
Joste la costure—a l'abbé de Jumeges, I acre LXII perches.
Joste la meson Guillaume Legrant, demie acre.
Joste la meson Ricart du Mostier, demie acre et XI perches.
Joste la terre Biauvilain, demie acre XX perches.
Eu camp Berte, demie acre LX perches.
Eu camp des jardins de Coisi, III acres XXVI perches.
Eu camp Cauches, III acres et demie.
En la grant costure, LIII acres et demie.

Mesure

Eu camp joste Fag[er]non, IX acres.

La somme LXXIIII acres et demie, XXIX perches.[1]

Raoul Fag[er]non prist I acre en somme de ses terres et II acres au lonc chemin, l'acre por XXI s.

Guillaume Fag[er]non le remanant, c'est assavoir V acres, l'acre por XXII s.

Jehan de Toqueville, III acres entre son gardin et le gardin de la cort, l'acre por XXI s.

Ricart Torode, eu camp au Fevre, II acres, l'acre por XX s.

Rad. Borg[er]gnon, eu camp au Cauces, III acres et demie, l'acre por XXII s.

Ricart Maigne et Climent de Faug[er]non et Robert Couvet l'acre por XXII s.

Jehan Torode, II acres et demie, LX perches, l'acre por XXIIII s.

Guillaume Legrant, demie acre IX s.

fol. 56v

L'aveine VIII setiers, le pris du setier IIII s.

Item, XVII boiss. de mesteil, vaut le boiss. XII d.

Item, XVIII boiss. d'orge, le boiss. VIII d.

Item, LX capons et LX d., IIII gelines, II d.

Rentes

Item V. C. XXX oeus, et III s.

Le cenz en deniers, VI lb. XIIII s. VIII d.

Les preeres de V carues II foiz en l'an, valt la iornée XVI d.

Item, XII herces, XII s.

Reliez et justices.

Le pasnage in la forest a l'abbé de Fescamp.

Item, un fou, X s.

La somme LXX lb. X s. VI d.

Iceste ferme creist selonc baillie et a ballier XXIII lb.

La terre laquele fu Aub[ert] le Lou, I acre, vaut XX s.

La terre Morel de Lorteil, I verge, VI s.

Por les rentes du Vievre por tout, LX s.—n'est pas perpetuel.

La terre Robert de Montfort, XII s., perpetuel.

fol. 57

Une parpresture, XII s., perpetuel.

La terre Tiebaut Lepetit, XVII s. en la main le—Roy est.

Le forestage de Montfort, LXX lb.

---

[1] This sum gives 160 *perches* to the acre, or 40 *perches* to the *vergée.*

Comtée
par sey

Les parprestures de Montfort, III.C acres I acre—Comtées par eles.
En apres—l'abbé de Corneville et ses moines pristrent XLVI acres.
Les hommes de Montfort, LXI acres.
Icels de Breetot,[1] XV acres.
L'enmosnier du Bec, XL acres.
Le priour de la capele, XIII acres.

La somme de tote la serganterie de Montfort LX lb. VII s. II d.

Le bosc des gastines de Montfort sus terre—n'est pas vendu.
Icestes parprestures dont ballies por LXXV lb. mes enapres l'en descomta XV lb.

Sanz Rootot XXXII lb. XVIII s. IIII d.

fol. 57v

La serganterie de Romois

La ferme de la terre de Tierreville[1] laquele est apelee Mallioc.[2] Le fieu au Cheirre. La terre au Tornoor. Le fieu de Hotonne. Le feu de Fresnes[3] que l'en apele la Pipe. La terre Ernaut du Bois.[4] La terre d'iceli a Wateville. La terre de la Boissiere[5] et Guillaume de B[er]neville VII.XX.XVIII lb.

Tierreville

La terre qui fu Henry de Mallioc en la costure de Tierreville, XIIII acres, valt l'acre X s.
Eu camp du Val Raoul, XII acres, le pris de l'acre VIII s.
Eu camp du Re, II acres, l'acre X s.

Jurée

Eu camp Fosse, II acres, aceli pris.
En la Valeie du Puis et de Gloz,[6] II acres, por tout XV s.

---

[1] Brestot, Eure, a. Pont-Audemer, c. Montfort-sur-Risle.

---

[1] Thierville, Eure, a. Pont-Audemer, c. Montfort-sur-Risle.

[2] Le Maillot, cne. Thierville.

[3] Les Fresnes, Eure, a. Pont-Audemer, c. Routot, cne. Honguemare.

[4] Stapleton I, 101. The king obtained 49 l., 19 s., 4 d. from the land of "Ernaldi de Bosco" in the Roumois in 1180. *Cart. Nor.*, nos. 71, 775, 790, 1220. There was an "Ernaldus de Bosco," one of the chief tenants of the earl of Leicester, whose lands were confiscated at the time of the conquest. His principal holdings, however, seem to have been near Rugles.

[5] la Boissière (?), Eure, a. Pont-Audemer, c. Bourgtheroulde, cne. Bosguérard-de-Marcouville.

[6] Glos-sur-Risle, Eure, a. Pont-Audemer, c. Montfort.

fol. 58

A Maupertuis,[1] II acres, et au bosc—a l'abbé II acres, por tout XXVI s.

En Longue Val II acres, au Re III acres, eu camp Fosse II acres, por tout XLII s.

Au bosc—a l'abbé, V verges, por tout XII s.

Eu val du Puis, I acre, IX s.

Dariere le maneir, XV acres d'erbage, le pris de l'acre III s.

La somme LX acres I vergée.

II fermes de Tierreville et d'Escaquelon[2] baillies a Thiebaut du Castel[3] por IIII.XX lb., et doit metre XX lb. de rente en contreplege, et doit avoir le rel[iez] et la justice—La justice du Bec li rencheri de IIII lb.

Ices choses lesqueles sont en la ferme de Tierreville et d'Escaquelon et en tel maniere sont ballies—a l'abbé du Bec por IIII.XX.IIII lb. et doit avoir li rel[iez] et la justice. La ferme de Tierreville creist por l'encressement des terres X lb. XVI s. La ferme d'Escaquelon creist por l'encrement des terres VI lb.

Et en tel maniere valent ices II fermes C lb. XVI s.

fol. 58v

En la ferme de Tierreville crescent les terres de XXX acres, III verg. et XXVIII perches et vaut l'acre VII s.

La somme X lb. XVI s.

Rentes

Le cens, VI lb. VI s.; avene, XV setiers, IX boiss., le pris du setier IIII s.; orge, IX setiers XI boiss., le pris du setier VIII s.

Capons, LXI; et XXV gelines; VII.C.XXX oeus; I oue; XVIII jornées en aoust, vaut la iornée IIII d.; et un masage.

Iceste parties de la ferme de Tierreville est ballie par le viscomte pour LXX lb., non pas en perpetue mes a ferme en l'an LX.

Esqua-
quelon

La terre d'iceli Henri anvers Escaquelon

En la costure du Genestel, V acres et demie, por tout LX s.

Eu camp de la Croiz, II acres et demie. Eu camp de la Corte Piece, II acres. Eu camp de la Briche, I acre et demie. Icestes III pieces, por tot, C s.

Jurée

Item, en la Corte Piece, I acre et demie; au jardin Morieut, I acre et demie.

---

[1] La Mare-Pitri (?), Eure, a. Pont-Audemer, c. Montfort, cne. Thierville.
[2] Ecaquelon, Eure, a. Pont-Audemer, c. Montfort-sur-Risle.
[3] *cf.* fol. 8.

Eu camp du Buquet, I acre et demie et I verg. Eu camp du gardin, V verg., lesqueles sont ballies por LVII s.

Item, la fame Thommas Durant, I acre et demie, vaut XVIII s.

Rogier Phellippe, IIII acres en marleis et demie, por tout XXV s.

Eu camp de Tierreville, II acres, por tout XXI s.

Envers les Fretez, VII acres, por tout XXXVII s.

La somme XXXII acres et demie.

Ices terres creissent de XII acres I vergie et VI perches, qui valent VI lb., pour l'acre IX s. IX d.

Une mine de forment, vaut VI s. Item, IIII setiers III boiss. d'avene. VIII setiers, V boiss. d'orge, le pris du setier VIII s.

Rentes

Les preeres de II carues et tout autant d'erches II foiz en l'an. Une oue X d. VI pains et X jornées en aoust. XXXII capons, XIII gelines, CXVII s. en deniers et en cens et III.C. IIII.XX.X oeus.

Anvers Churre, VIII acres a la Borserie, le pris de l'acre XV s.

Le pasturage ileques entor V acres, por tout XV s.

Item sont ileques XXIII boiss. de forment, valent por tout XXIIII s.

Le fieu
au
Churre

L'avoine ileques XIII setiers, le pris du setier V s. Capons XXXV et XXXV d. Le campart, por tout VII lb. Le cens ileques, IIII lb. XIX s. Le moutonnage, por tout III s. Item VII oees, vaut l'oie X d. Item, XII gelines et XII d.

Item, IIII.C.LXX oeus, et o X oeus I d.

Iceste ferme est baillie a Ricart Lecambelier tout por XXVIII lb. VIII s., et por toute la crescence. Ices terres cressent de I acre de terre. Item, le pasturage creist IIII acres.

Mons. Rogier de la Haie tient la premiere ferme por XXIX lb., et a letres, et mist en contreplege X lb. de rente sus son feu du Quesney[1] en la paroisse de la haie Saint Michiel.

La terre
au Tornoor

En la ferme devant dite, sont ileques III acres de terre, et demie acre de jardin, le pris de l'acre XV s. Ballie a Ricart Davot por IIII lb. XII s.

N'estoit
pas en
ferme

L'abbé de Saint Wandrille doit toz les anz I pellice au viscomte du Pont Audemer.

---

[1] Le Quesney (?), Eure, a. Bernay, c. Brionne, cne. Malleville-sur-le-Bec:

Le fieu de Hotonne

    Eu fieu Bernart, VIII acres, le pris de l'acre X s.

    Eu fieu Noel, VIII acres, a cel pris.

    Item, ileques entor les tailleis, IIII acres, a cel pris.

    Item, ileques IIII acres, a celi pris.

Jurée   Item, IIII autres acres, a cel pris.

    Eu camp a la Seulee, acre, a cel pris.

    A la coste Ribout, I acre, a cel pris.

    Item, en iceli meisme territor[re?], XII acres, le pris de l'acre
      VI s.

    L'erbage du talleis, IIII acres, valent por tout X s.

la par mesure   Par la mesure XXXV acres, XIIII acres de pasturage, V acres
      de bois.

Rentes   Le cens en deniers, VI lb. Item, XXXVI capons et demi et
      XXVI d. Item, XIII.XX et V oeus, et o X oeus I d. II
      preeres de carue II foiz en l'an, vaut la iornée XII d.

Ices choses, les queles sont en la ferme de Hotonne, baillies a Gefrey du
Fay por XXXIII lb. por la cresc[ence] et por tout.[1]

Le fieu des Fresnes.

    Anvers les Fresnes, eu camp au fevre, VIII acres, le pris de
      l'acre XV s.

    Raoul Pasquet prist l'acre por XVIII s., et sont a ball[ier] les
      rentes.

        La somme XXXV lb. XI s.

    Item, idem Rad. prist les rentes por XX s. III d.

        La somme de tout XXXVI lb. XI s. III d.

    En la costure, VII verg., le pris de l'acre XV s.

    Envers la haie du Val Belot, III verg., a cel pris.

    En somme de la costure, I acre et demie, a cel pris.

Jurée   Anvers Mareville, III acres, a cel pris.

    Prez la meson Jehan Oein, I acre, a cel pris.

    Entor les Fresnes, VII acres, a cel pris.

    En summo d'iceles terres, V acres I verg., a cel pris.

    Aus Muteriaus, demie acre, a cel pris.

    Anvers les Gres, IIII acres, a cel pris.

    Sus le chemin du Hamel, II acres, a cel pris.

---

[1] This account of the lease was crowded in the right-hand margin, apparently some time after the rest of the page was written.

fol. 61

Eu camp au fevre, et eu camp de II acres, VIII acres et demie.

En la costure de Fresnes, entor la mote, XIX acres.

Eu camp ioste la meson Jehan Oen, III verg.

Mesure

A la Mareville, III acres.

A la haie du Val Beloc, I acre.

En la costure, III acres.

Eu camp des Gres, IIII acres.

En la vergee sus le chemin, I verg.

La somme de la mesure XXXIX acres et demie.

Le cens en deniers, XIII s. Item, IX capons, IX d.

Item, VI.XX oeus, et XII d.

Ernaut[1]
du Bosc

Eu camp de Wateville, sont ileques VI acres, XLVII perches; V acres, vaut l'acre XIIII s.—Guillaume et Hue Goncelin pristrent l'acre por XVIII s.

Eu Hamel au Prestre, tant en terres quant en jardin, XVI acres, l'acre XV s.

Item, est ileques le dit jardin, contient I acre, et est comtée es dites XVI acres, et sont ballie a icels Guillaume et Hue, l'acre por XVIII s., sanz les quesnes et les arbres qui sont sus terre.—La somme outre les chamz, XIX lb. IIII s. X d.

fol. 61v

Item ileques X setiers de forment, le pris du setier X s. a la petite mesure.

Item, II moeuz et VIII setiers d'orge et I mine, le pris du setier VI s.

Rentes

Item, ileques III moeuz III setiers et plene mine d'avoine, le pris du setier IIII s.

Item, XXII capons, et XVI d. Item, X gelines, X d.

Les preeres ileques aianz carues. Item, II.C oeus, et XVI d.

Le cens ileques, XVI s.

Ices rentes devant dites valent XXIIII lb. VIII s. VI d.

Rentes[3]

Anvers Hanguemare,[1] XIII acres, l'acre IX s.—Robert le Flamenc prist icestes XIII acres; c'est assavoir III acres et demie, por tout XXIIII s. VI d.; et les autres IX acres et demie, l'acre pour XIIII s.

La somme VII lb. XVI s. VII d., quer XX perches defaillent de la meillor.[2]

---

[1] *cf.* note, fol. 57v.

---

[1] Honguemare-Guénoville, Eure, a. Pont-Audemer, c. Routot.

[2] These figures show that here again the acre contains 160 *perches*.

[3] This marginal note should have been written lower.

L'avoine, II moez et demi, le setier IIII s. Item, setier d'orge, le pris du
setier VI s. Item, III setiers V boiss. de forment, le pris du setier X s.
Le cens, XXIII s. Item, XIIII capons, XIIII d. Item, XIX gelines,
et XVI d. Item, II.C.LXIII oeuz, XX d. ob.; preeres de II car[ues]
et autant d'erches II foiz en l'an, valent VI s.
La somme d'iceles rentes XII lb. XVII s. IIII d.

fol. 62

Anvers Vateville,[1] VIII acres, le pris de l'acre V s.
Sus le castelain IIII acres, l'acre II s.
Anvers le maret, XX acres, le pris de l'acre VI s.
La somme par la mesure XVIII acres et demie et
XXVIII perches, sanz le maret euquel leu sont XX
acres.
Le cens, XLIIII s., VIII d. Item XVIII capons, IIII d. Item XXI
gelines. Item XI.XX oeus, et IIII d. A Noel, VIII s. por bres, XII
formages, II s. Les preeres de III carues.
Ices choses lesqueles sont en la devant dite ferme sont ballies a Mahieu
Boutin por XIIII lb. XIII s. por la cresence et por tout.

N'estoit
pas en
ferme le
bosc des
haies

Anvers Berneville,[2] XVI acres; la mesure anvers Berneville, XVIII
acres.
Item, VI acres de gastines. Es haies, III acres, dont le bosc est vendu,
ne sont pas plusors forz les terres par la mesure.
Es haies est le bosc sus terre, vendu est por LXV lb.
Item, en la faleise, VIII acres, l'acre V s.
Anvers Mondestuit, VI acres, l'acre II s.

fol. 62v

Item, IIII setiers et plene mine d'avoine, le pris du setier V s.
Item, le cens, LXXIII s. VIII d.
Item, XXXVII capons, et XXXVII d., et VIII gelines.
Item, V.C oeus et XV mansois.
Les preeres de III carues II foiz en l'an, vaut la iornée XVI d.
Item, les hommes du fieu doivent clorre LX perches de closage, valent
XX s.
Item, VIII herces II foiz en l'an, valent VIII s.
La somme XVI lb. VI s. VIII d.

Les choses lesqueles sont anvers Berneville—Ballies sont a Thommas
de Cailloel et a Lucas de Brotonne por la crescence et por tout, XXII
lb.

---

[1] Vatteville (?), Seine-Inférieure, a. Yvetot, c. Caudebec.
[2] Barneville, Eure, a. Pont-Audemer, c. Routot.

La bosc sus la terre qui n'estoit pas a ferme est ballie au devant dit Thommas et a Gefrey Tornetout pour LXV lb.

Anvers la Boissiere,[1] X acres, comté le iardin, le pris de l'acre XII s.

Item, vers le bosc IX acres, le pris de l'acre III s. Par mesure XVII acres et demie por tout.

Le cens ileques, XXIIII s. III d. Item IIII capons, III d. Item XII gelines, XII d. Item, XVII.XX.X oeus, XIIII s. Chascune vache doit por le pasturage par an VII d., valent XIIII d. Por chascune ouaille VIII d., valt XVI d.

fol. 63

Les choses lesqueles sont en la ferme de la Boissiere baillies sont a— Mons. Nichole de la Londe[1] por XI lb., o les rel. et la justice, et por l'encreissement des terres XXV s. VI d.

        La somme de totes ices fermes devant dite XII.XX lb. XXIII s.

Iceste somme devant dite creist de VII.XX.XVIII lb. III s. VI d. mes enaprez n'en descomte LV lb. XVI s. por la crescence de Tierreville la quele crescence n'est pas comtée—au Baillif.

Anvers la haie du Parc, demie acre de terre, VI s. Ballie a Guillaume du Parc qui la tenoit por VIII s.

fol. 63v

La ferme de la terre de la Bataille,[1] XXXIII lb.

    Eu camp de la Bataille ioste le maneir, XVI acres, l'acre XII s.

    En I piece au chemin de Roem, X acres, le pris de l'acre XIII s.

Jurée

    Eu camp de l'Essart, II acres et demie, le pris de l'acre XIII s.

    Anvers Borneville,[2] III acres, a cel pris.

    Entre Saint Estiene et la meson Robert Baut, VI acres, l'acre XV s.

    Item, au chemin de Roem, I acre, XV s.

        La some XXXVIII acres.

Mesure

    Par mesure XLIIII acres.

    Les cens IIII lb. XI s. Item, XLII capons, et II s. VI d.

---

[1] *cf.* fol. 57v.

---

[1] *Cart. Nor.*, no. 511. Nicolas de la Londe, knight, had a usage in the forest of Londe in 1253.

Delisle, *Ech.*, no. 813. "Nicholaus de Londe," a knight, attended the Exchequer in 1258. *H.F.*, XXIII, 728, 745. Nicolas de la Londe was summoned to the army in 1242 and 1272, the second time, however, as a knight of Caux.

---

[1] La Bataille, Eure, a. Pont-Audemer, c. Quillebeuf, cne. Bourneville.

[2] Bourneville, *ibid.*

Item XXIII gelines, et XVIII d. Les preeres de IIII carues II foiz en l'an, vaut la iornée XVI d. Item bres por tout X s. Le campart XL s. Item, IIII herces II foiz en l'an, vaut la iornée VI d. Rel[iez].

La somme XXXIIII lb. XV d.

Icele ferme est baillie a Morice de la Noe et a Robert Baut por LIII lb. XVIII s., et creist de XX lb. XVIII s. et sont les terres mesurées.

La ferme de la terre Nichole Lecomte, que l'en dit Goolonc, XXIIII lb. En la garene de Groolonc, XII acres, l'acre XV s.

Item VI acres de terre a meteerie perpetue, vaut l'acre XV s., quite au—Roy.

Les cens ileques IIII lb. XIX d. Item XLII capons et XL d. Item VIII gelines, VIII d. Por oeus VII s. IX d. Item, XXX setiers d'avene, vaut le setier IIII s. Les preeres des carues, V, II foiz en l'an, vaut la iornée XVI d.

La somme XXV lb. XVI s. III d.

La ferme devant dite est baillie—a l'abbé de Corneville por XXX lb. Iceste creist de VI lb.

La ferme de la terre Guillaume Harenc,[1] que l'en dit de Lidetot,[2] XVII lb.

Au Plesseiz delez Lidetot, XI acres III verg. et XX perches, l'acre XV s.

Les cens en deniers, LXXV s. Item XX capons, XVIII d. Por oeus et por deniers, XIX d. ob. Por une coignie, IIII d. Une livre de poivre II s. Une oue, X d. Un setier de forment, XX s. Item, VIII boiss. d'avoine, IIII s. Item, IIII boiss. de forment, VI s. VIII d.[3] Les relevees et esples. Les preieres des carues, les esples et rel.

La somme XIIII lb. IIII s. VII d.

La devante dite ferme est baillie a Robert de Sollie Mare por XVIII lb. XII s. Ele creist de XXXII s.

La ferme de la terre Raoul le filz Guy, X lb.

Prez de la haie de Rootot,[4] X acres, XV s. l'acre.

---

[1] *M.A.N.*, 2ᵉs., V, 157. Land of Guillaume Harenc at St. Christophe was confiscated by Philip Augustus at the time of the conquest.

[2] Lilletot (?), Eure, a. and c. Pont-Audemer, cne. Fourmetot.

[3] These prices show that in this district there were 12 *boisseaux* to the *setier*.

[4] La Haye de Routot, Eure, a. Pont-Audemer, c. Routot.

Item, es haies ileques, IIII acres, l'acre VI s.

Les cens en deniers, XII s. Item IIII capons, et IIII d. Item XX oeus, I d.

La somme IX lb. VIII s. III d.

Robert le Barbe prist icele ferme por XVI lb. X s., et creist la somme de VI lb. X s., et sont les terres mesurées.

fol. 65

La ferme de la terre Rogier du Mor, VII lb.

En I clos a herbage, une verge, VIII s.

Les cens en deniers, IIII lb. V s. V d.

Item XXXVIII capons, et III s.

Item, mil oeus, et o X oeus I d.

Les releveies ileques, XII s.

La somme VII lb. XII d.

Icele ferme prist Renaut du Mor[1] por VII lb. X s., et creist de X s.

La ferme de la terre Aalis de Gauge, XI lb.

Eu camp du jardin, III acres, l'acre XIII s.

Ileques desus, III acres, por tout XV s.

Jurée

En la costure prez terre, IIII acres, l'acre XI s.

Joste la terre Ricart de la Voie, I acre et demie, le pris de l'acre XI s.

Au puiz Symon du Puiz, II acres, le pris de l'acre XI s.

fol. 65v

Sus le chemin de Roem, I acre, au pris devant dit.

A la fosse Belleum, III acres, le pris de l'acre X s.

A la meson Gefrey du Jardin, I acre, XI s.

Item, I acre en III pieces, vaut IX s.

Item, en la riviere, II acres en II pieces, por tout XX s.

A la meson Roncelin, demie acre, vaut IIII s.

Item, prez de Magneville, I acre et demie, por tout XVI s.

Sus le chemin de Roem, demie acre, por tout por tout [sic] X s.

Sus la meson Marcel, III verges, por tout IX s.

Mesure

Par mesure XXVI acres, I verg. de terre et la verg. et demie de pré.

Les cens en deniers, XIIII s. Item III capons, III gelines, et IIII.XX oeus.

---

[1] *Quer. Nor.*, no. 80. A Renaut "del Mor" of the viscounty of Pont-Audemer complained that the king seized half his inheritance (worth 15 l.) because two of his uncles fled to Poitou. The farms of Rogier and Renaut du Mor (*cf.* fol. 85) listed in this manuscript are farmed at 17 l. and may well be the lost half of Renaut's inheritance.

La somme XIII lb. IX s. V d.

La ferme devant dite est ballie a Ingouf Marivint por XV lb. XV s., et creist de IIII lb. XV s.

fol. 66

Lesclusage de la rue au Pareors anvers le Pont Audemer, valent XXIIII s., tout a la Seint Michiel et est en la ferme devant dite.

Jurée

La ferme de la terre Nichole de la Londe[1] IX lb.—Laquele autres fiees est apelée la ferme Ermeneust, et est baillie par le viscomte por VIII lb.

> Au chemin de Roem a Clo luis, I acre, XII s.
> Au Feugueray,[2] I acre, XIII s.
> A la fosse Coudreuse V acres, le pris de l'acre XIII s.

Mes.[3]

> Les cens en deniers, III s. X d. Item, IIII capons, et XXX oeus. Item XX boiss. d'avoine, valent X s.
> La somme CVI s. VIII d.

fol. 66v
N'estoient
pas en
ferme

Une forfaicture anvers Toberville,[1] laquele contient II acres, ou la entor, laquels n'estoit pas a ferme—Ballie a Gefrey le Court por XVI s. l'acre.

Item I acre de terre, qui est ioste la terre Gefrey le Court anvers le bosc Goet, qui n'estoit pas en ferme—Ballie a iceli Gefrey por XVI s.

La ferme du Busc de Hatingues,[2] XXXVI lb.

> Eu terreor du Buc de Hatingues, XXXVI acres I verg., l'acre XVII s.

Jurée

> Item, eu tallieiz du Buc, l'erbage de V acres, le pris de l'acre XX s.
> Le bosc n'est pas en ferme.

Mes.[3]

> Item XLVI capons, I geline, et o les chapons III s. I d.
> Item III.C oeus, XX oeus meinz, et II tor[tiaulz], a Pasques, LXXI s. IIII d.

---

[1] Stapleton, I, 146; II, 488. "Nicolas de Londa" accounted for the *bailliage* of Londe in 1195 and 1198.

[2] Le Feugré, Eure, a. Pont-Audemer, c. Routot, cne. Bourg-Achard.

[3] Partially erased.

[1] La Trinité de Touberville, Eure, a. Pont-Audemer, c. Routot or St. Ouen de Touberville, *ibid.*

[2] Le Busc de Hastingues, Eure, a. Pont-Audemer, c. Routot, cne. Hanville.

[3] Partially erased.

Item III aigneles ou III s. Item XVI boiss. de forment, vaut le boiss. XII d. Les preeres de IIII carues II foiz en l'an, vaut la iornée XVI d.,/ et tout autant d'erches. Les reliez et les justices.

La somme XXXVII lb. XII d.

La ferme Juliane de Neuville anvers Coletot et Corneville,[1] LI lb.[2]
Le remanant d'iceste ferme est ballie par le viscomte por XXIX lb. VIII s. I d.

Anvers Corneville I molin, vaut XII lb.

La moute seiche ileques, VIII lb.—empre—l'abbé de Corneville ia XL s.—Gefrey de Camz et Pierres des Camz pristrent por XXII lb. o la moute seiche.

Les cens XI lb. XXII d., capons XXVIII et XXVI d.

Item VII gelines, III.C oeus, et XXX d.

Anvers Saint Maarc,[1] le pasturage sus le Pont Audemer, por tout XLVIII s.

La sexte partie por le—Roy du molin, XLI s., quite au—Rey.

Item V seetes ferrées, por tout X d.

Les cens ileques, XI lb. XV s. IX d.

Item, XXVIII capons, et XX d. Item, VI.XX oeus, VI d.

II acres de bruere, ne sont pas comtées.

Item, sus le castel du Pont Audemer, IX acres et demie de bois de la Soulleite lesqueles deivent remaneir en boscage. Et ballies a Dyonis Canterel[2] por IIII lb. V s. VI d.

Anvers le Maret d'icele ferme, I acre, par mesure V verges, le pris de l'acre XVI s.

Item, ileques III jardins continans III acres, par mesure IIII acres et demie, por tout LX s.

---

[1] Corneville-sur-Risle, Eure, a. and c. Pont-Audemer; Colletot, *ibid.*

[2] *Cart. Nor.*, no. 952. The abbot and convent of Sainte-Marie-de-Corneville announce that "ad firmam perpetuam recepimus in firma que fuit Juliane de Nuevilla apud Cornevillam, unum molendinum cum molta sicca et pertinentiis; 11 l. tur. 22 d. annui redditus; 28 capones con 26 d.; 7 gallinas; 300 ova et 30 d.; item apud Sanctum Medardum pasturagium, et costas super Pontem Audomari; item, sextam partem cujusdam molendini; 5 sagittas ferratas; 11 l. 15 s. et 9 d. annui redditus; 28 capones et 20 d.; 120 ova et 6 d.; relevia rusticorum et simplicem justiciam eorumdem, pro 45 l. tur." . . . 1280.

H.F., XXIII, 709. "Juliana de Novilla" held one-fourth knight's fee in the *bailliage* of Pont-Audemer shortly after the conquest.

---

[1] Saint-Mards-sur-Risle, Eure, a. and c. Pont-Audemer.

[2] *Cart. Nor.*, no. 476. "Dyonisius Canterel" was mayor of Pont-Audemer, *c.* 1248.

Jurez

Item, ileques IIII acres de pré, le pris de l'acre XII s. VI d., paié la rente.

Item, le viez cortil par mes.   vaut por tout XVI s.

Item, eu camp Juliane, II acres de pré, par mesure III acres, por tot XLII s.

N'estoient en ferme

Item, ileques IIII acres et XXVIII perches—de novel nos est dit.

fol. 68

Item, XXV capons, XXII d., et VI gelines.

Rentes

Les cens en deniers, LXXII s., por oeus II s.

Les preeres, se les chevaus soient ileques.

La somme LX lb. XIII s. X d.

Les choses lesqueles en la ferme du Maret.—Ballies sont a Henri de Columbieres. Item, a iceli IIII acres XXVIII perches de bois por XXXIII s. sanz le defiement.

La somme Henri de Columbieres, tam por la crescence des terres quam por le bosc, XXIIII lb. XV s.

Iceste ferme desus dite creist de XXIII lb. XI s. I d., sanz le bosc de la Soillete, et IIII acres et XXVIII perches d'autre bois.

fol. 68v

La ferme de la terre de la Valée, VIII lb. X s. Iceste ferme doit estre en la serganterie de Montfort.

Envers la Valée, V acres d'erbage, n'est pas plus par la mesure trové, le pris de l'acre VIII s.

L'avoine, XIIII setiers, le pris du setier IIII s.

Les cens, XXXIII s. II d. Item XXVII capons et XXVII d., II gelines. Item XIII.XX oeus, et o X oeus I d.

La somme VIII lb. VII s. VI d.

Iceste ferme devant dite est ballie a Berthelemeu de Briorne por XII lb., et creist de LXX s.

Item, por une partie de la ferme de la Valée apud Willeville[1] a nos de noviau dite, XVII s.

La ferme d'une acre de terre X s. de Laquese.

fol. 69

La ferme de la terre du Plesseiz[1] XXX lb.—Ballie est par le viscomte por XXV lb.

Anvers Faudeis, II acres, le pris de l'acre IIII s.

A la meson Robert Larchier, II acres, a celi pris.

Sus le Plesseiz, III acres, a celi pris.

---

[1] Illeville, Eure, a. Pont-Audemer, c. Montfort-sur-Risle.

---

[1] Le Plessis (?), Eure, a. Pont-Audemer, c. Quillebeuf, cne. Bouquelon.

Jurée

Sus la fosse Gefrey, II acres, a celi pris.
Au jardin Harenc, I acre, vaut V s.
Au Plesseiz, III acres, le pris de l'acre IIII s.
Eu camp de la vigne, II acres, por tout X s.
Anvers les mares, XXXII acres, le pris de l'acre VIII s.

Mes.[2]

Le campart de V acres, por tout VII s.—Robert Larchier tient
IIII acres. Iceli Robert prist le campart de IIII acres, por
tout VIII s.

Rentes

Robert Buost, III acres; Symon Auquier, I acre.
Le cens en deniers, XXXVII s. V d. III services a chevauz,
IIII lb. V s. Item XLIX capons, et o les capons III s. X d.;
II gelines; IIII.C.LXX oeus. Les preeres de III carues II
foiz en l'an, et V d'erche; les rel. et les justices.
La somme XXII lb. II s. IIII d.

fol. 69v

La ferme de la terre de Columbieres,[1] XVII lb.
Anvers le Maret, XXV acres, le pris de l'acre VII s.

Juré

En la terre sablose, XXX acres, le pris de l'acre IIII s., sanz
les brueres.

Mesure

Trouvé est tout autant par la mesure.
Item, sont ileques entor II.C acres de bruiere non pas mesurées,
ne ne nos estoient pas dites—Icestes XII acres sont ballies en
la some desus dite.

n'estoient
pas en
ferme

Les cens en deniers, XXXII s. Capons XX, et VIII d. Gelines
IIII. Item IX.XX.X oeus, et VII d. Le service d'un cheviau
X s. Les preeres de III carues une fiee en l'an, herches, reliez
et justice.
La somme XVII lb. XIIII s.

Guillaume de We et Jehan de la Nois pristrent icele ferme por XXIII
lb. XVI s.—et creist de VI lb. XVI s.—sanz les II.C acres par ledit
dudit Guillaume de We.

fol. 70

Andreu Estoupecto que l'en dit la terre Guiart de Trapaville por III
acres XVIII s. por tout—Ballie par le viscomte por XII s.

Comtez
par
sey

Les ples anuels XXX lb., perpetuel, comtez par elz.
Les menues rentes de Wateville, XXX s., perpetuel, comtées par eles—
Comté est des ples et des rentes a la Saint Michiel.

---

[2] Partially erased.

---

[1] Columbeaux (?), Eure, a. Pont-Audemer, c. Quillebeuf, near Bouquelon.

Le jardin de Vateville, XX s. comté par li.

De la meson Jehan d'Appeville, LIII s. IIII d. L'en comte du jardin et de la meson a la Saint Michiel.

Comtez
par sey

Item, II saumons, por tout X s.—comtez par elz.

L'ennor

Du mestier de Soriaumare,[1] C lb.

Le mestier de la Haie du Mor,[1] LIII lb.

de
Brotone

Le mestier de Hauville,[2] LXI lb. X s.

L'estallerie de la Vigoie de Boute avant, XXVIII lb.

ou plus
ou mainz

La somme XII.XX lb. L s.—Baillies par le viscomte por XI.XX.XIX lb. IX s. et est comté[s] par sey.

fol. 70v
comtez
par
eulz
comtée
par sey

Les mares de Vateville, XXIIII lb.—comtez sont par eulz a la Saint Michiel.

La pesquerie du Pont Audemer—Ballie a Guillaume Canterel por XII lb.[1]—comté est par sey.

La terre de Freschiesnes, VI lb.

La ferme de la terre de Buesemoncel, XIIII lb.

Les cens en deniers, XXIX s.

Item, II capons et demie, et II d. et ob.

Item, III gelines, et III d. Item L oeus, et V d.

Le molin o le preel X lb., et por moute XXX s.

Por les moutes de Cauerville[2] et d'Appeville,[3] X s.

La somme XIIII lb. II s.

fol. 71

La ferme de la terre Boutevilain, VI s.

La ferme de la terre Baboin, VI d.

La serganterie de Romois desus dite creist par tout XI.XX lb. VIII s. XIII d.

---

[1] Delisle, *Etude sur la condition de la classe agricole*, p. 337. The *Grael de Vatteville* (early thirteenth century) indicates "ministeria Haye Mauri . . . Hauville, Sorelle mare. . . ." Haye du Mor, Eure, a. Pont-Audemer, c. Routot.

[2] Hauville, Eure, a. Pont-Audemer, c. Routot.

[1] *Cart. Nor.*, nos. 957, 958. In 1281 Gringoire and Robert du Bois-Gencelin, knights, gave the king 15 l. in rents owed them at Esquetot and Epreville in order to free "Guillaume Canterel, bourgeois du Pont-Audemer" from paying 12 l. for the "iaue du Pontiaudemer, la quele le devant dit Guillaume tient a ferme perpetuel" and 3 l. for half the fief of Bonesbouz. *ibid.*, no. 963. Shortly thereafter, Guillaume Canterel and Raoul d'Elbeuf, squire, took all of the fief of "Bornebez." *ibid.*, no. 476. One of the Canterel family was mayor of Pont-Audemer in 1248.

[2] Cauverville-en-Roumois, Eure, a. Pont-Audemer, c. Routot.

[3] Appeville-Annebaut, Eure, a. Pont-Audemer, c. Montfort.

La serganterie de Killebue[1]

La ferme de la terre Goolon, vaut XL s.

> Eu camp de Saint Uriout,[2] III verges et XVIII perches, le pris de l'acre XV s., paié la rente.
>
> Eu camp que l'en dit la fosse a l'aieue, VII verg. et X perches, l'acre XV s., paié la rente.
>
> En iceli camp, VII verges et V perches, a celi pris.
>
> En celi camp meismes, demie acre et XXVIII perches, a celi pris.
>
> Joste le jardin Ricart du Mont Quevrel, I acre VIII perches par mesure, a celi pris.
>
> Eu camp ioste la terre Gautier le Large III verg. a celi pris.
>
> La somme VI lb. VI s. VI d.

> Joste Saint Uriout[2] III verg. XVIII perches.
>
> As Genestoiz III verges.

Mesurées
sont

> Joste la meson Ricart du Mont Quevrel I acre VIII perches.
>
> Eu camp de Goolon IIII acres et demie et IIII perches.
>
> La somme VII acres et I verg.[3] Icele ferme devant dite n'est pas ballie.

fol. 72

La ferme de la terre de La Mare XL lb.[1]

> Est ileques le masnage continant IIII acres, le pris de l'acre VI s.
>
> En une cousture environ le maneir devant dit, XXVI acres, le pris de l'acre VI s.

Jurée

> A la granche de la campaigne en un camp, XXIII acres et demie, l'acre XV s.
>
> Item, en celi meismes camp sus le jardin, II acres et demie, l'acre XV s.
>
> Les prez sus Seinne, VI acres, le pris de l'acre XIIII s.

---

[1] Quillebeuf, Eure, a. Pont-Audemer. It is strange to find Quillebeuf the seat of a sergeanty since it was part of the land which William Longsword gave Jumièges with "quicquid ex his ad fiscum suum pertinebat. . . ." (Delisle-Berger, II, 92).

[2] Saint-Thurien, Eure, a. Pont-Audemer, c. Quillebeuf.

[3] This would make 30 *perches* to the *vergée*. This proportion appears nowhere else in the document. The scribe has probably omitted an X in writing down the number of *perches*.

---

[1] There was a fief of La Mare at Sainte-Opportune-près-Vieux-Port, Eure, a. Pont-Audemer, c. Quillebeuf. *Cart. Nor.*, no. 614. This may be the land of Guillaume de la Mare, which was included in a farm to Jumièges in 1259. *cf.* fol. 73v.

Mesure

La moute seiche LX s. La moute des garbes XXX s.
Item, VI.XX.XVII capons, et o les capons VI.XX d., et I geline.
Item, XI oees, vaut l'oie X d.

Rentes

En la Pasque en oeus et en deniers XX s., et en la Mi-caresme XVI s. A la feste de Saint Michiel VIII lb. XV s. En la feste Saint Jehan XXVIII s. En la feste Saint Andreu XII d.

fol. 72v

Item, I setier et IIII boiss. de forment a la mesure de Bone-ville, le pris du setier XX s.
Item, demi moe d'avoine et I quartier, le pris du setier VI s.
Item I setier et V boiss. d'orge, le pris du setier X s.
Les preeres de V carues II foiz en l'an, vaut la iornée XVI d.
Item IIII herces II foiz en l'an, vaut la iornée VI d.
Item, sont les autres redevances, lesqueles sont deues au maneir, c'est assavoir le feniage, saclage, tassage et pilage.
Les herbages des bois, XX s. par an.
Item, II bateals en la mer, por tout XX s.
Les rel., les ples, et les justices.

La somme LVIII lb. XIIII s. V d.

Item, un bolengier anvers Killebue, vaut VIII s.
Item, un bouchier ileques, se il fust ileques, fust quite de la costume, qui vaudroit VIII s.
Item, se le fermier mainsist eu fieu il peust avoir chascun—ior une carete eu bosc—a l'abbé de Jumeges.

fol. 73

Iceles choses lesqueles sont en la ferme devant dite sont ballies—a l'abbé de Jumeges pour LXX lb.—et creist iceste ferme devant dite—c'est assavoir por terres, por prez, por usage de bois, por un bouchier et por un bolengier issi que tout vaut IIII.XX.VII lb.—et en tel maniere creist iceste. La somme XLVII lb.

fol. 73v

La terre du vivier Henri le Cambellenc, XIIII s.
Baillie est a Ricart Canos por XXX s., et creist de XVI s.

La ferme de la terre Goobout XX s.	La somme X lb., de laquele les parties sont cestes ensuivant.[1]
La ferme de la terre Godelon XL s.	
La ferme de la terre Galeran Duve XX s.	
La ferme de la terre Deudonné VI lb.	

---

[1] *Cart. Nor.*, no. 614. In 1259 Louis IX farmed to Jumièges the tenement of Guillaume de la Mare and "quicquid habebamus in tenemento Deudonne, in tenemento Goubert, in tenemento Godelent, et in tenememento Waleranni fillii Duve. . . ."

Por XVII acres de terre, le pris de l'acre IX s.

Por demie acre de pré, IX s.

Por le site du molin a vent, XX s.

Por une place que Guillaume Aubin tient, II s. VI d.

Les estiaulz as poissons, L s.

Item, I place en la Rue Laictiere, le pris n'est pas mis.

Nichole Heron, XXXII s. II d. de rente, II capons, XX oeus, II d.

Les rel. et les esples.

La somme XII lb. XVII s. X d.

N'estoient
pas en
ferme
fol. 74
Item, IIII masures d'une voeve, ne sont pas en ferme.

Les fermes desus dites sont baillies a Lucas Lenevou et a Gefrey du Fay o les IIII masures por XVI lb. X s. Por l'encressement de la terre XXVII s.

En tel maniere creist de VII lb. XVII s.

La terre Andreu Legrant et Kenivet XX s.

La ferme Guillaume Crassi,[1] XV lb.[2]

Anvers Blaqueville,[3] II acres et demie d'erbage, por tout XXVIII s.

Les cens en deniers, XIII lb. XIIII s. VIII d.

Item, LVIII capons et LVIII d. Por oeus et deniers V s. III ob.

Les preeres de IIII carues II foiz en l'an et V d'erche II foiz en l'an.

La somme XVII lb. XI s. I d.

Rogier du Fay[2] prist tote la ferme por XVIII lb.

fol. 74v
La ferme Rogier de Torville[1] XII d.

Du molin as malades de Killebue XX s.

Iceste serganterie de Killebue devant dite creist de LXIII lb.

---

[1] *Cart. Nor.*, no. 136. Guillaume's lands were confiscated about 1206. *cf. Quer. Nor.*, nos. 382, 399, 406, 407, 412, etc., for descriptions of Guillaume's rather arbitrary methods in building up his estates.

[2] *Cart. Nor.*, no. 642. "En 1259 S. Louis concéda le fief de Blacarville à Roger du Fay, avec quelques rentes, 58 chapons, prières de charrue et droit de justice sur les vassaux. Dans la donation il est appelé 'la terre qui fut a Guillaume Crassi'"; (quoted by Delisle from M. Canel, *Essai sur l'arrondissement de Pont-Audemer*, t. I, p. 359). *ibid.*, no. 1046. In 1285 master Richard du Fay held this farm.

[3] St. Mards de Blacarville (?), Eure, a. and c. Pont-Audemer.

---

[1] *cf.* fol. 85.

La serganterie d'Espayngne[1]

La ferme de la terre Guillame de Condé, XIII lb., comtée est par sey.[2]

> Eu camp au Quesney, VIII acres, desqueles IIII acres vaut l'acre III s. Les autres IIII acres, c'est assavoir eu camp Germein, vaut l'acre V s. VI d.
>
> Devant la porte, VI acres, desqueles IIII vers le iardin, valent por tout XXII s.

Jurée

> Eu camp Hermeri, II acres, vaut l'acre VI s.
>
> Au Corbez en IIII pieces XIII verg., vaut l'acre V s. VI d.
>
> Eu camp Viel, I acre a celi pris.
>
> En mie le mont, II acres a celi pris.
>
> Es lons seillons, II acres a celi pris.
>
> Es cortes pieces, II acres, le pris de l'acre III s.
>
> Eu camp Renier, III acres a celi pris.
>
> Es marleiz et es lonz seillons, III acres a celi pris.
>
> En glisois ioste le doict, III acres a cel pris—Eu camp Lovier, I verg.
>
> La somme XXXIII acres et demie.

fol. 75v

> Item, I gardin continant II acres, por tout XL s. et creist de demie acre par la mesure.
>
> Item, est ileques I vergee de pré, vaut IIII s. et creist de X perches par mesure.
>
> Item, I cortil, contient XII perches, nos l'estimames a XII d.

> En la cousture du Quesney, VIII acres L perches.
>
> Eu camp du Monte Lenmie, IIII acres XX perches.
>
> Eu Mont Viel, es camz Renier, et es cortes pieces, VIII acres et XX perches. Eu Val Viel, II acres.
>
> Eu camp de l'Angle et de Roont Buisson, III acres et demie.

mesure

> Eu camp du Gort, I acre et demie.
>
> Eu camp des Arbres, demie acre et XXIIII perches.
>
> Eu camp de Romperol et le camp Robert, II acres I verg. XVI perches.
>
> Eu camp de Glises, III acres et demie, XX perches.
>
> Eu camp de Marleiz, Viel, et les lons seillons, VII acres.
>
> Eu clos Lohier, LX perches.

---

[1] Epaignes, Eure, a. Pont-Audemer, c. Cormeilles.
[2] This farm was probably near Condé-sur-Risle, Eure, a. Pont-Audemer, c. Montfort, *cf.* fol. 77.

En la couste [*sic*] devant la porte, XI acres XXX perches.
Item, eu camp Colet, I acre et demie, XVI perches.

> La somme des mesures des terres devant dites, LIIII acres et XXVI perches.[1]

Les cens LV s. IIII d. Item, XXVI capons et XXV d.
Item, II.C.LX oeus et II d.
Les preeres d'une carue II foiz en l'an, vaut la iornée XVI d.
Les homes residens doivent clorre les jardins, coidre les pommes, et tribler, le fienz coidre et espartir, vaut X s.
Les rel. et les justices.

> La somme XIII lb. VI s. VI d.

Ices choses devant dites lesqueles sont en la ferme de Condé sont ballies a Robert le Fol por XVIII lb.
Les terres creissent de XXIII lb. IX s.—et le jardin vaut CIX s.—et creist de X lb. IX s.

La ferme de la terre Torpin de la Chambre XV lb.

En la Saucie, III acres, le pris de l'acre IX s.
A la Croiz, VII verges, por tout XX s.

A Haute Planque,[1] II acres, le pris de l'acre X s.
A la Planque Laictiere, III acres a celi pris.
Eu pré Aubec, I acre et I verg., por tout XII s.
Item, sus les prez III acres, le pris de l'acre IX s.
Au moulin du pré, II acres a celi pris.
Au molin du Crochet, II acres, por tout VIII s.

> La somme XXXVIII acres et demie.

Le pré sus Rille, III acres, le pris de l'acre XX s.
Le—baillis a le fein.
Joste Saint Goufram,[1] VII verg., le pris de l'acre IX s.
Anvers Montenay,[2] III acres, le pris de l'acre XI s.
Joste la terre Mahieu de Launey, I acre, VII s.
Sus la rue Maagnel, demie acre, III s.

Devant Saint Gofren,[1] V acres et demie, le pris de l'acre VIII s.
Au molin de la mare, V acres a cel pris.

---

[1] According to these figures, there would be 46 perches to the virgate in this region, unless we are to assume an error of 30 perches in the scribe's record.

[1] Les Hautes Planches, Eure, a. and c. Pont-Audemer, cne. Saint-Paul-sur-Risle.

[1] Saint-Wufran, Eure, a. and c. Pont-Audemer, cne. St. Paul-sur-Risle.
[2] Montenay, Eure, a. and c. Pont-Audemer, cne. St. Paul-sur-Risle.

Joste la terre Mahieu de Launey, II acres, por tout XIIII s.
Eu camp du Quesne, V verges, por tout XII s.
A la croiz Robert le Grant, I acre en III pieces, por tout VI s.
La mesure creist de XXVII s.

Mesure[3]
fol. 77v

Les cens en deniers, LXIX s. IIII d.
Item, IX capons, IX d., II oees, XX d.
Item, IIII.XX.X oeus et III d.

Rentes

Les preeres de II carues et II d'erche, V s. IIII d.
La moute seiche, XX s.
Les rel. et les justices.
Item, le—roy a ileques VI aides a coedre les feinz et le patron-
nage d'une chapele.
La somme XXII lb. III s. VII d.
Robert li Vilains prist la ferme devant dite et le pré sanz le patronnage
de la capele por XXXI lb.
Icele ferme est ballie par le viscomte—a l'abbé de Cormelles por XXXII
lb.—et por la crescence des terres XXVII s.—n'estoit pas en ferme.
En tel maniere creist iceste de toute la somme, comté le
pré, XVIII lb. VII s.

fol. 78

La ferme de la terre Ernaut de Torville[1] VII lb.
Eu camp devant la porte, VII verg., le pris de l'acre XII s.
Aus II turz, II acres, le pris de l'acre VIII s.

Jurée

Es monz Guernier, V acres, por tout XXV s.
Eu pre Auboc, III verg., por tout IX s.
Envers Campignie,[2] XI acres, X s., par mesure XII acres III
verg. et XXXV perches.
Le pré tout autant par mesure, vaut l'acre XX s.

le bosc
n'est pas
en ferme

Item, l'erbage de l'acre et demie de bois et du jardin san le bosc,
por tout—XL s.—par mesure II acres LX perches.

fol. 78v

Robert Leber, I boiss. de forment, XII d., et II capons.
Gillebert Poubele, VI s., IIII capons.
Le fieu Michiel Harenc, VI s. et I oeie.

---

[3] Very faint.

[1] *H.F.*, XXIII, 710. "Ernaudus de Torvilla" held one-fourth knight's fee under Philip
Augustus in the *bailliage* of Pont-Audemer.
Delisle, *Ech.*, nos. 433, 468. The land of "Ernaudi de Torvilla" was in the king's
hands, in 1229 and 1231, by reason of wardship.
[2] Campigny, Eure, a. and c. Pont-Audemer.

Le fieu Roncelin, II s., II capons.

Le fieu Henri des Mares, II s., II capons, et VI poucins.

Ricart Loinctier—II s.

Le seige d'un molin anvers Campigni, XX oeus et XVI d.

La preere d'une carue II foiz en l'an, por tout II s.

Por la herce XII d.

Item, les hommes du fieu doivent fener, tasser, auner, amener et le lin coedre.

Item, en la paroisse de Saint Germain,[1] IIII acres de terre, le pris de l'acre V s.

Item II setiers d'avoine, ne sont pas balliez.

La somme VIII lb. XII s.

En la ferme devant dite est l'acre et demie de bois.

Ballie est a Guiart Legrant por XV lb. XII s.

Le bosc sus terre, III acres et demie a este estimé, et nous rendra ledit Guiart l'estimacion.

Et creist de VI lb., XII s. et le bosc XL s.

Est ileques en la ferme desus dite un douaire, lequel est ballie por VII lb. XV s.—et est comté par sey.

La ferme de la terre au Poignoor[1] XV lb.

Joste le bosc, XIX acres et demie de terre, le pris de l'acre IIII s.

Item ileques XVIII acres de bois.

Les cens en deniers, VIII lb. Item, LXV capons et LXIII d.

Item IIII gelines. Por oeus et deniers, XII s.

Les preeres de V carues II foiz en l'an, et tout autant d'erches.

Item, I setier d'avoine, vaut VI s. et I esprevier.

La somme XIIII lb. XIIII s. IIII d.

Ices choses devant dites lesqueles sont en la ferme au Pognoor ballies sont a Adan de la Blaerie por XVIII lb.—L'abbé de Preaulz li encheri de XX s. Item il prist XXI acres et demie de bois sanz le superficie por IX s. l'acre.

L'abbé de Preaulz doit tam por la ferme que por le bosc XXVIII lb.

---

[1] Saint-Germain, Eure, a. and c. Pont-Audemer.

---

[1] *Quer. Nor.*, no. 79. The fief "Poingnatoris" in the parish of Epaignes was forfeited when the tenant went to England at the time of the conquest.

XIII s. VI d.—Ele creist de IIII lb. VI s. et por le bois IX lb. XIII s. VI d.[2]

fol. 80

La ferme de la terre de Litebec[1] et Jehan de Launey[2] XXV lb. Ballie est par le viscomte por XXVIII lb.

Eu camp des II Londeiles, I acre, XX s.

Es jardins de Litebec, II acres, por tout XXII s.

Eu camp de la Marete, I acre et demie, por tout XV s.

Jurée

A la fosse Quideber, I acre et demie, por tout XII s.

Eu camp sus la porte, IIII acres, por tout L s.

Sus les prez qui sont diz les parrelles, IIII acres, por tout XXX s.

A la Planque Laictiere, I acre, X s.

Outre la Planque Laictiere es Burez,[3] IX acres, desqueles VII acres por tout XXXIIII s. et les II autres por tout XVI s.

Eu camp des Bequeiz, I acre, X s.

Eu camp joste les Faudeiz, III acres, por tout XVI s.

Item, ileques I acre, por tout V s.

Item, demie acre sus les haies, et demie aillors, por tout V s.

Item, demie acre sus les prez, VIII s.

Les prez, III acres et demie, le pris de l'acre XX s.

fol. 80v

Les cens ileques, IX lb. XIIII s. IIII d.

Item, XXXI capons et XXVIII d.

Item I geline, XII.XX.XV oeus.

Rentes

Item, les hommes du fieu doivent coedre les feinz et espartir.

Robert Brehale, IIII s. de rente.

Les esples, les rel. et les justices.

---

[2] *Cart. Nor.*, no. 610. In 1259 Louis IX gave "Poigueor" to Préaulx as a perpetual farm for 28 l. 19 s. 6 d. The farm included "19 acras et dimidiam terre, 21 acras et dimidiam bosci sine tercio et dangerio, 8 l. tur. censuales, 50 capones et 63 d., 4 gallinas, ova et denarios redditus cum eisdem, precarias carrucarum et herciarum, 7 sextaria avene, relevias rusticorum et simplicem justiciam eorumdem. . . ." *ibid.*, no. 620. In 1259, June, Préaulx, in acknowledging the grant, enumerated "19 acras et dimidiam bosci sine superficie, que debent remanere in boscum sine tercio et dangerio, 7 l., 18 s., et 10 d. censuales, 63 capones et 4 gallinas, et cum caponibus et gallinis 5 s. et 8 d., 1 sextarium avene, 80 et 50 ova, et cum ovis 5 s. et 6 d., item, 1 speverium, 1 par calcariorum deauratorum . . . [the rest as above]."

[1] Lillebec (?), Eure, a. and c. Pont-Audemer, near St. Paul-sur-Risle.

[2] *Quer. Nor.*, no. 81. Jean de l'Auney, knight, lost his land because he adhered to the king of England. He may be the Jean de l'Auney who held one-third knight's fee of the honor of Pont-Audemer, *H.F.*, XXIII, 710.

[3] Les Burets, a place-name in the valley of the Risle, just above Pont-Audemer.

Anvers la Haie Daniel, V verg., por tout XII s.

Item, eu maneir Milcas, V acres, valent por tout XXX s.

Eu camp des Faudeiz, II acres, le pris de l'acre VIII s.

Jurée

Item, III vergies, por tout VIII s.

Eu camp de la Peliconniere,[1] II acres, por tout XVI s.

Item, es pré de Rille, demie acre, vaut XV s.

fol. 81

Item, sus launey, V verges, por tout XX s.

Item, por II residences, VIII s. VI capons, VI d.

Item, XLV oeus et VI d.

Robert Brehale, IIII s. de rente.

La somme XXXII lb. XVII s. VII d.

Iceste serganterie d'Espaigne devant dite creist de XXX lb.

comtée
par sey

La tierce partie du marcié de Preaulz, XXIII lb. VI s. VIII d. por le consentement du—Rey qui consenti—a l'abbé de Preaulz que il feist marcié.—Ballie par le viscomte por XXV lb.—comté est par lui.[1]

comté
par sey

Por les poissons qu'il ont a costume a presenter au—Roy C s. anvers Killebue—Et XL s. por chen meismes les quelz le viscomte a costuma a prendre—et est par sey comté.

La serganterie du Mesnil[1]

(fol. 81v
is blank)
fol. 82

La ferme de la terre Bloiout[2] XXVIII lb.

N'est pas
en ferme

Es auneiz, I verg. et demie, vaut por tout XV s.

Les cens en deniers, IIII lb. IIII s. VI d.

---

[1] *Quer. Nor.*, no. 81. A three-acre field, called "Pelicon," was forfeited to Jean de l'Auney by one of his tenants for failure to pay manorial dues, and was seized with Jean's land by the king. The petition by a descendant of the first holder for the return of this land was apparently denied, since the land was still held by the king when our document was written.

[1] *Cart. Nor.*, no. 585. ". . . Nos, per inquestam de mandato nostro factam, abbati et conventui Beati Petri de Pratellis mercatum ejusdem ville reddiderimus . . . salvo nobis tercio dicti mercati in omnibus et placito ensis . . .," 1257.
Quer. Nor., no. 76. Louis VIII granted Préaux a market in return for their tithe of the mills of Pont-Audemer, lost at the time of the conquest. Between 1238 and 1240 (approximately), Louis IX revoked this grant of a market, although the monks were paying him about 22 l. a year for the privilege (*H.F.*, XXI, 256). The act cited above restored the market. *cf.* fol. 90.

[1] Le Mesnil-Ferrey, Eure, a. Pont-Audemer, c. Beuzeville, cne. Saint-Pierre-du-Val.
[2] Blohioust (?), an old fief of Pont-Audemer, near Bois-Hellain, a. Pont-Audemer, c. Cormeilles.

Item, XLVIII capons et XLIIII d.
Item, IIII.C.XXX oeus et II s. II d.
Item, une oie, X d., VII boiss. d'avoine, III s. VI d.
Le molin et la moute seiche XXXII lb.
　　　　La somme XXXVIII lb. XIII s. I d.
Guillaume le Torneor prist icele ferme por XLIIII lb. X s. Les super-
ficies est nostre de launey.
Et creist de CXV s. et por launey XV s.

fol. 82v　La ferme de la terre Mahieu de Foulebec[1] IX lb.
　　　　En une costure souz le mostier, VI acres, l'acre XV s.
　　　　Item, II acres de pré, le pris de l'acre XIII s. Item II aloeuz por
　　　　　　tot VI s.
Ichi est la mesure.
　　　　Eu camp du Castenier, V acres, XX perches meinz.
　　　　Eu jardin de Folebec, I acres.
　　　　Eu camp de la vigne, LXIII perches de roncereiz.
　　　　En II aloeuz, I acre XIII perches meinz.

　　　　Les prez II acres, et en I noe demie acre.
　　　　Item, V oies. Item, XXIX capons et XXV d.
　　　　II maslarz, por tout X d., por oeus V s.
　　　　Por balanc[er?] et cens, LVI s. VI d.
　　　　Item I buisson, contient entor I vergie.
　　　　Les preeres se les chevaulz fussent ileques.
　　　　Les rel. et les justices
　　　　　　La somme X lb. III s.

fol. 83　　Les choses qui sont en la ferme devant dite sont ballies por XII
　　　　lb. XVIII s. a Thommas de Baalie.
　　　　　　Et creist de LXXVIII s.

N'est pas
en ferme
　　La ferme de la terre de Bouleville[1] XIX lb. X s. perpetuel.
Item, sont ileques IX setiers de bernage. Le—Ballif le receit et n'est
　　pas comté.
Item, anvers Marteinville[2] VIII setiers d'avoine de bernage.

---

[1] Foulbec, Eure, a. Pont-Audemer, c. Beuzeville. *Quer. Nor.*, nos. 68, 84. Mathew forfeited his land because he went to England and died there. According to his heirs he
had license to go, and the *bailli* Cadoc wrongfully seized the land. The heirs rated the
value of the land as 12 l.

---

[1] Boulleville, Eure, a. Pont-Audemer, c. Beuzeville.
[2] Martainville, *ibid.*

Item, anvers Abelon[3] XIII setiers d'avoine de bernage et est comté icest bernage a la Saint Michiel.

fol. 83v La ferme de la terre Pevrel[1] L lb.

En la cousture des Joubles,[2] XVI acres et demie, l'acre XII s.

Anvers le Mesnil, III acres et demie, por tout IIII setiers d'avoine et III mines d'orge.

Jurée En la paroisse de Cramonville,[3] XXV acres, le pris de l'acre X s.

Eu camp de la mare et de Maupestiz le meillor.

Au Bequeiz le peior.

Le campart XIX s. Item, I morsel de reue.

Eu camp de Bequeiz, II acres.

Eu camp de l'Espine, III acres et demie.

Eu clos Pevrel, VI acres.

Eu camp de Maupestiz, V acres.

Mesure Item, ileques acre et demie.

Eu camp au prestre, III acres.

Eu camp de la mare, III acres.

Anvers Jobles es II masures de Fiqueflue,[4] XXXVII perches.

En la grant cousture, XVIII acres.

fol. 84 Eu fieu de Gaillon, IIII acres et demie.

Les prez, por tout IIII acres.

Les bois en III pieces, X acres.

Eu grant jardin, demie acre, XVII perches.

Eu jardin et eu maneir de Jobles, I acre et demie, XIIII perches.

Les cens en deniers, VI lb. X d.

Item XLII capons, IIII gelines.

Item III.C.XXX oeus. Item oies IX.

Rentes Item L chiez d'ail, mil et L oignons, valent VI s. III d.

La moute seiche XXX s.

Item, II setiers et XIII boiss. de forment, le pris du setier XVI s.

---

[3] Ablon, Calvados, a. Pont l'Evêque, c. Honfleur.

---

[1] Stapleton, I, cxxxv and 105. Guillaume Pevrel forfeited his land in 1155. It was farmed to Guillaume du Hommet in 1180.

[2] Joble, Eure, a. Pont-Audemer, c. Beuzeville, cne. Fiquefleur-Equainville.

[3] Cremanville (?), Calvados, a. Pont l'Evêque, c. Honfleur, cne. Ablon.

[4] Fiquefleur-Equainville, Eure, a. Pont-Audemer, c. Beuzeville.

Avoine X setiers X boiss. et demie, le pris du setier IIII s.

Item I setier et II boiss. d'orge, vaut le setier VIII s.

Item II reons de chous.

fol. 84v Item, l'erbage dune acre et demie de jardin, XI s.

Le jardin vaudroit en heritage XL s.

Item, III acres et demie de pré, vaut l'acre XII s.

Item XX raseaulz de forment, III setiers III boiss. meinz, vaut le setier XIIII s.

Avoine, X setiers III boiss., vaut le setier IIII s.

Item, XXXIIII capons et XXXIIII d.

Item III.C et X oeus et o X oeus I d.

Item VIII oies. Item un molin, VII lb.

Les preeres de III carues II foiz en l'an, et tout autant d'erches.

Les cens en deniers, VI lb. IX s. IIII d.

La somme LXII lb. IX s. II d.

La ferme devant dite est ballie a monseignor Enioiran de Villequier por LXX lb. et por le bois VII lb. X s. Les superficies du bois est nostre.

Et creist de XX lb. et por le bois VII lb. X s.

fol. 85 La ferme Renaut du Mor VII lb.

Anvers Luerai, V acres, le pris de l'acre X s.

A la Mare Cauchese, eu camp de la Marliere, es viez jardins, et eu camp devant, XIII acres, le pris de l'acre X s.

La somme IX lb.

Icele ferme est ballie a iceli Renaut por X lb. et creist de LX s.

La ferme de la terre Rogier de Torville[1] XV lb., comtée est en recete et est demenée en despenz quar ele fu rendue.

fol. 85v La ferme de la terre Aaline des Loges XXX lb. Rendue est et d'iceste nen nen comte pas quar ele est rendue a Olivier des Mares.[1]

Le molin de Bueseville, lequel est entitulé de Lacye,[2] L lb. et n'est pas ballie—Ballie est par le viscomte encore por LX lb. comtée la moute.

---

[1] cf. fol. 74v.

[1] cf. Olim, I, 52. "Oliverus de Maris" proves by inquest that land in the king's hand belongs to him (not later than 1258).

[2] Beuzeville, Eure, a. Pont-Audemer. Delisle-Berger, II, 334. "Buesevilla" was part of the honor of Le Pin, held by Hugh de Lacy under Henry II.

Et est ileques un petit pré euquel sont prises les motes a rapareillier la caucie dudit molin et sont iches choses comtées es deniers desus diz.

La ferme du marcie de Bueseville XIII.XX.X lb.—n'est pas ballie en l'an LX fors por XII.XX.X lb.[3]

fol. 86

La ferme de la terre Robert de Sainte Marie XXIII lb.

Anvers le Monthoquier, XXXVI acres, vaut l'acre V s.

Jurée

L'erbage de XII acres et I vergie de bois, vaut l'acre III s.

Item I clos XXX s.

Item, VII setiers d'avoine, le pris du setier IIII s.

Item, XII boiss. d'orge, valent VI s.

Item, II boiss. d'avene a la petite mesure, valent XII d.

Item, I boiss, de farine de forment, vaut XII d.

Item, le campart de XVIII acres de terre, valent por tout XXIIII s.

Rentes

Item, XXIX capons et V gelines et XXVII d.

Les preeres de IIII carues et tout autant d'erches II foiz en l'an.

Item, I oie, X d., I aignel, XII d., les rentes en deniers L s. VI d. Item II.C.LX oeus et XXVII d.[1]

fol. 86v

Item, l'autre ferme o la devant dite, anvers Berville,[1] CXI s. VI d. de rente. Item XXXIIII capons, I geline, III.C. IIII.XX et X oeus, une oue, vaut X d.

Un setier d'orge, vaut VI s.

Les rel. et les justices.

La somme XXIII lb. VI s. II d.

Icele ferme devant dite est ballie a Ferri du Mesnil por XXXVI lb. X s.—et creist de VII lb. X s., et por le clos et le bois VI lb.

---

[3] *H.F.*, XXI, 256. This market brought in only 150 l. in the year 1238.

---

[1] This line is written in a very crowded hand and was probably inserted later.

---

[1] Berville-sur-Mer, Eure, a. Pont-Audemer, c. Beuzeville. *Quer. Nor.*, no. 62. Two knights claimed that the land of Robert de Sainte Marie at Berville and other places was wrongfully seized by Cadoc, on pretext of a voyage by Robert to England. They asked for the land in the name of their wives, daughters of Robert. Cadoc was accused of seizing the land because Robert would not marry these daughters to Cadoc's sergeants.

Delisle, *Catalogue des Actes de Philippe-Auguste*, no. 1590. Robert's land was in the king's hand by 1215.

La ferme de la terre du Booley[1]—XX lb.

> Les terres ileques XL acres, par mesure L acres et demie et XIX
> perches et vaut l'acre VIII s.—Guillaume Malesovres prist
> les terres sanz le bois por X s. l'acre.
>> La somme selonc la mesure XXV lb. VI s.
>
> Item, livre de poivre, II s., les cens, LIX s. X d. Item, XXVI
> capons et VIII gelines, II.C.XL oeus, XIIII oies, vaut l'oie
> · X d.

> Les feires de S. Oen et de S. Laurenz, IIII s. Item, II setiers
> d'avoine, vaut le setier IIII s.—La somme XXI lb. II s.
> VI d.
>> La somme d'ices rentes qui sont ballies CIII s. II d.

Et creist selonc ballie et a ballier X lb. IX s. II d.

Anvers Tigerville, I acre de terre, vaut VI s.

La ferme de la terre Guiart de Forinval[1] XLV s.

> Sont ileques III acres de pré et un closel, por tout LX s.
> Ballie a Ferri du Mesnil por LX s. et creist de XV s.
>> Icele somme est en la somme Robert de Sainte Marie.

La ferme de la terre Raoul Morel, II acres et demie de terre, por tout
XX s.—Ballie a Jocelin Brichart pour XXIIII s., et creist de IIII s.

La terre Crespin Malesoevres, III acres, por tout XXXVI s.

Ballie a Ricart et a Hue Waquelin et a Guillaume le Fevre por XLV s.
et creist de IX s.

La terre Jocelin de Moiaz, X s. perpetuel.

La commune du Pont Audemer por les hales, XV lb.[1]

En aprez sont deuz—a l'abbé de Preaulz XXX s. por la diesme.[2]

La meson Guillaume Despeville, LIII s. IIII d., perpetuel, comté est
par sey a la Saint Michiel.

Les avoines de Goditonne, XXX setiers a la petite mesure. Un offri
de ceste ferme au—Ballif, XX lb. Est ileques la terre—le viscomte

---

[1] La Boulaie (?), Eure, a. Pont-Audemer, c. Beuzeville, cne. Equainville.

[1] *Cart. Nor.*, no. 106. The land of the son of Gérard de Fournival was in the hands
of Philip Augustus in 1205.

[1] *Cart. Nor.*, no. 317. Louis VIII granted the burgesses of Pont-Audemer the right to
build "halla" in 1224, in return for an annual payment of 15 l.

[2] *ibid.*, no. 495. A list of the rights of Préaux in Pont-Audemer, includes "30 solidos per
manum vicecomitis pro decima novarum aularum." c. 1250.

receit et en comte au—Roy et est comtée par sey a la Saint Michiel.
Le fieu au Boite, III setiers d'avoine et XX boiss. d'orge comté a la
Saint Michiel.

fol. 88v
La ferme Paien de Sainte Marie IIII lb. X s.
    Le pasturage de XXV acres de terre, por tout L s.
    Les cens en deniers, LXXVII s.
    Item, XXVII capons. Por oeus, II s. VI d.
    Item, X oies, vaut l'oie X d.
    Le siege d'un molin—La moute seiche, X s.
    Le pré du vivier, X s., C chiez d'aulz, valent X d.
    *   La somme CXVI s. XI d.

fol. 89
La ferme de la terre Malet XXV lb.
    Le molin Malet, XV lb.
    La coillete de la semainne, L s.
    La viez ville, XX boi[ss]. d'orge, valent VI s.
    Jehan Maillart por I mole a coutiaulz, X s.
    De la plante Robert Watel, IIII s.
    Les cens Malet, XL s.
    Les fourages valent X s.
    *

La ferme Henri le Cambellenc XXV lb.[1]
    Les hales au pain et au bouchiers, XVI lb.
    Rad. du Four, XXV s.
    Es prez VI lb. Un petit isle ileques, XX s.
    Item, l'autre petit isle, X s. Item les prez, VI lb.
    Un jardin, XXX s. Guillaume Hoel, V s.

fol. 89v
    La vielle geole, IIII s.
    Robert Debin, IX s.
    Berville en deniers et en orge, IIII lb.
    En capons, IIII s. VI d.
    Ricart Joce et Thommas Julian, XX s.
    Guillaume le Quarqueor, VI s.
    Saint Laurenz de Quarteville,[1] LVII s. I d.

---

[1] *Quer. Nor.*, no. 75. Henry "Camerarius," knight, forfeited his land by going to England at the time of the conquest.

---

[1] Quetteville, Calvados, a. Pont-l'Evêque, c. Honfleur. The parish was Saint Laurence's.

Por II setiers d'avoine et III capons, XI s.
Guillaume le Warsaut, XXX s.
La Geole, IIII s.
Henri le Despensiers, XX s.[2]
Le pressorage, XXX s.
Le vivier, XVI s.
Le four Osmont, XX s.

Iceles II devant dites fermes joignantes sont comtées o les fieuz et les eschaietes por IIII.XX lb.

La prevosté du Pont Audemer.[1]
    La costume du denier et de la maaille, les cens et les estalages valent VII lb. X. s. chascune semainne.
En aprez est deue la disme—a l'abbé de Preaulz.[2]
Et ices choses paiés remaignent au—Roy XVII.XX lb. C.XII s.
Les molins du Pont Audemer, c'est assavoir IIII fors le molin Malet—valent VII.XX lb.[3]
En aprez le—Roy rendi LX sommes de forment, valent IIII.XX lb., ne fu pas dit a cui.

A la porte de Corneville la terre que Ricart le filz Jude tient est de froc—le Roy, et touz icelz qui en tienent entre la Blaerie et la porte des Molins de la partie de Saint Oen ont sorpris sus le fro le—Roy.

La ferme de la terre Rogier du Bosc X lb., les parties sont cestes—
    Avoine, XIII setiers, III quartiers meinz, a la petite mesure.
    Item, XXXII capons et II s. a Noel, VIII gelines et VIII d., C oeus et X d. a la Saint Michiel, IX oies.
    Item, une acre et demie de pré, vaut l'acre XII s.
    Eu clos Wicart, I acre de terre, vaut III mines d'avene.

---

[2] *Quer. Nor.*, no. 75. Henry "Dispensator" complains that he is being made to pay 40 s. a year to the king for his house, which had been pledged to Henry "Camerarius" for a debt. The debt was to have been paid in four 40 s. instalments, but the conquest intervened, the king took all the lands of Henry "Camerarius" and forced Henry "Dispensator" to pay the 40 s. every year.

[1] Stapleton, II, cci. Pont-Audemer was part of the Meulan lands, confiscated by both John and Philip. *cf.* fol. 43.

[2] *Cart. Nor.*, no. 495. Préaux has the tenth week of all the income of Pont-Audemer, *c.* 1250.

Delisle-Berger, I, 390. This tithe was granted by Waleran, count of Meulan, and confirmed by Henry II, *c.* 1165.

[2] *cf.* fol. 81.

La moute seiche, XXX s., et enpres ches choses il nos fu dit que ele valoit C s.

fol. 91 Item, le siege d'un molin, lequel vaudroit X lb. se il fust fet. Icele ferme devant dite est ballie a Estiene Alain por XXI lb. X s.—et creist de XI lb. X s.

La ferme de la terre de Conteville IIII.XX lb., perpetuel.[1]
La terre Tostain Fromont XX s.—et est enquis d'icele anvers Cramiaville.

La somme de la serganterie du Mesnil LXX lb. III s. VI d.

fol. 91v La sergenterie de la Londe[1]

La ferme de la terre Guy de Briorne, Guillaume de Caumont et Angnes de Gisorz, et Guerart le Forestier VIII.XX.XVII lb.

Jurée Anvers le Teillol, CVI acres, vaut l'acre XXII s.
Item, ileques XXV acres d'erbage, une o le jardin le—Roy, vaut l'acre XVI s.

Mesure Par mesure VII.XX.IX acres et demie, XXXV perches et demie.

fol. 92 Les cens ileques, X lb. Item, IIII.XX capons, valent XL s.
Por oeus et deniers, X s. Por le fenage, II s.
Item, III setiers de forment, valent XL s.
I setier d'avoine, IIII s.
Item, III oies, vaut l'oie X d.
Les preeres de VII carues II foiz en l'an, vaut la iornée XVI d.
Rentes Item, VI herces, valent VI s.
Item, le service d'un homme, XII d.
Item, XII fers a cheval, valent II s.
Item por le carriage que IIII hommes doivent en aoust, por tout XVI s. Item III hommes doivent tasser, vaut III s. Item, ileques II hommes qui doivent chascun I iornée de carriage en aoust, vaut por tout II s.

---

[1] Conteville, Eure, a. Pont-Audemer, c. Beuzeville. *Cart. Nor.*, nos. 179 (p. 297), 255. Richard gave Conteville to the monks of Jumièges in exchange for Pont de l'Arche. Under Richard they paid 20 l. a year for Conteville (Stapleton, II, 450). Philip Augustus, in return for confirming the exchange, which had been cancelled by John, raised the rent to 80 l. a year.

[1] La Londe, Seine-Inférieure, a. Rouen, c. Elbeuf, or the forest of La Londe, *ibid.*

Thommas du Clos por icen, II s.
Les rel. et la justice, LX s.

fol. 92v Icele ferme devant dite est ballie a monseignor Robert/ du Bosc; c'est
assavoir, l'acre de la terre por XXIIII s., le setier de forment por
XIIII s., le setier d'avoine por V s., et les autres rentes a la value.

La somme II.C lb. XXXVIII s. VI d.

L'aide du Sap vaut de III anz en III anz C s.

Anvers le Borc Toroude,[1] IIII acres et demie de terre, valent por
tout XLIIII s.—Item XVI galons de vin, valent XVI s.
Item, ileques II capons, XIIII pains, valent XIIII d.,
I oie X d.

Ices choses sont ballies a Guillaume de Longue Ville por IIII lb.
IIII s.—et creist de XXI s.

fol. 93   La ferme Guillaume de Caumont que il tenoit por
XX lb.

Anvers Briorne II acres de terre, l'acre XII s.

Item, ileques II acres, vaut l'acre X s.

En somne d'iceli camp a la croiz, V acres, l'acre XII s.

Jurée Sus le vivier, V acres, l'acre XII s.

En somne de la cousture du dit Guillaume, II acres, l'acre
XIII s.

Item ileques I acre de ronce, vaut XV s.

Trouvé est par mesure XVI acres et XXIIII perches par tout.

Rentes Les cens ileques, LXX s.

Item XXXI capons, IIII oies.

fol. 93v Item, V.C oeus et a les oeus L d.

Item, est ileques le pasturage en la riviere, vaut LX s.

Item, X setiers et pleinne mine d'avoine, vaut le setier IIII s.

La moute seiche XII s.

Les preeres d'une carue, les preeres d'erche, XXXIIII d.

Les rel. et les ples.

Icele ferme devant dite est baillie a Guillaume de Chaumont por XXIIII
lb.—Descreist la terre d'une acre et XXIIII perches meinz, vaut X s.
VI d.—et issi remaignent XXIII lb. IX s. VI d.

fol. 94   La ferme de la terre Guy de Briorne.

---

[1] Bourgthéroulde, Eure, a. Pont-Audemer.

Eu pré de la Vacquerie,[1] I acre et demie de pré, por tout XVIII
s.—Richart Pivot prist por XXXII s.

Eu pré de Pestiz, I acre et demie, par mesure II acres XII
perches, por tout XV s.—Estiene Coyct prist l'acre por
XVII s.

Eu pré a l'Omme, I acre et demie, por tout XVIII s.—Estiene
Coyt prist, par mesure, II acres XXVI perches, por tout
XX s.

Eu pré du Molin de Rille, I acre de pré, vaut XVI s. Ricart
le Sainneor la prist, par mesure por l'acre et XXVIII perches,
por XXX s.

fol. 94v

Eu camp Watinel I acre de terre, vaut VI s.—Estiene Coyt la
prist por VII s.

Eu camp des Cortilz, V verges XV perches, par mesure I acre
et demie, XXXV s.—Guerout le Prince prist tout por XLV s.
Item, iceli Guerout prist por II iornées de carue II s. La
somme por tout LI s.

Eu pasturage souz Saint Michiel, I acre et demie, por tout XV s.
Rogier Vesin prist por XX s.

Eu Val Hais, II acres de terre, por tout XXXV s.—Rogier
Vesin, par mesure I acre et demie, I vergie et XIIII perches,
por tout XLV s.

Eu val Aubert, IIII acres de terre, por tout XXX s.—Guillaume
le Charon,[1] par mesure VI acres, et I vergie, et I perche.
Item, ileques I acre et demie de parrei, por tout XX s.—et
iceli Guillaume tout emsemble prist por LXXIX s.

Item, une place joste la porte qui mainne a Biaumont, XII d.
Hue de Cailloel la prist por V s.

fol. 95

Item, une piece de terre joste la meson au Torneor, vaut X s.
Raoul de la Fosse la prist por XX s.

Es furces des aioues, IX acres de pré, et de pasturage, por tout
LXXV s.

L'isle Oede, I piece de terre, vaut XII s.

Item, I piece de terre eu Buquet Fouqueron, por tot XVIII s.

Item, I piece de pré joste Karentine, vaut VII s.

---

[1] La Vacherée, Eure, a. Bernay, c. and cne. Brionne.

---

[1] *Quer. Nor.*, no. 347. A Guillaume le Charon was a burgess of Le Sap (not far from
here) in 1247.

Le pré du gué, VI s.

Le camp as anglez, VI s.

Gefrey Pelerin prist tout por VIII lb.

Item, ileques en la ferme devant dite, VI.XX.XII capons, et o les chapons IIII s. VIII d.

Les cens en deniers et por fenage, XXXVIII s. II d.

Por le service de Launey XL s. A rendre Caresme Prenant VII lb., en la feste Saint Martin d'yvel XIII s.

Le molin de Briorne, XIIII lb. X s. por la metie le—Roy. Ballie est a Pierres de Caumont, chevalier, por XVII lb.

Anvers Valleville,[1] I jardin, XV s.—A rendre en la feste Saint Martin d'esté, X s. En la feste Saint Michiel, V s.

Les chars d'un mouton, VI s.

Les chars de II angniaulz, II s.

Item, IIII galons de vin, valent IIII s.; XI.C.L oeus.

Le jardin le—Roy, continant I acre, XXX s.

Une place joste la porte, II s. Une livre de poivre.

Item, VII setiers de forment, vaut le setier XIIII s.

Avoine ileques, XXI setiers et une mine, vaut le setier IIII s.

Item, I setier d'orge, vaut VIII s.

Item, XIIII oies, vaut l'oie X d.

Item, es haies III verges, por tout XV s.

Item, II places voides—Ballie est a Robert Ogier por XXXII lb. eu jor de samedi en landemaine de la nativité nostre seignor, en l'an M.CC.LX et V, par encherissement de XL s., et mist en contreplege son man[eir] continant I acre et demie de terre.

La ferme Angnes de Gisorz[1] anvers Telloil, VII acres de terre, vaut l'acre XVIII s.

La ferme de la terre Guerart le Forestier anvers Telliol, VII acres, vaut l'acre XVIII s.

La somme XII.XX lb. LXVII s.

Iceste ferme des ballies et a ballier, III.C lb. XXII s. et creist de VI.XX.IIII lb. II s. IX d.

Gefrey de Cantelou prist I petit isle deriere la meson por V s.

---

[1] Valleville (?), a. Bernay, c. and cne. Brionne.

---

[1] Stapleton, II, 491. The land of Agnes of Gisors in the *bailliage* of La Londe was in the king's hands in 1198. It brought in only 8 s. that year.

Robert de Periers I autre isle prez du jardin Morel por IIII s.

Icestes
n'estoient
pas en
ferme

Guillaume le Fevre prist II acres eu camp Goucelin por XII s., l'en dit que ileques sont V acres.

Raoul Wallart prist le maṣurage Guerost tout por X s., l'en dit que ileques sont III acres de terre es queles est une acre de bois.—Baille est sanz le bosc sus terre.

Le cotil Laurenz Rousee, demie acre, III s.—Ballie a Guillaume le Fevre por III s.

Robert le Periers, une place joste la porte de Roem por IIII s. Iceli Robert la rencheri sus li jusques a VI s.

Iceles valent XL s.

fol. 97

La ferme de la terre de Columbieres,[1] por tout XL s., perpetuel.

Les ples au viscomte de la Londe, XXX lb.—comtez par eulz.

Le porcage en la viscomté, XIX lb.—et est assavoir que se le pasnage ait est es foreis demene sont deuz V s. por chascun porc, le porc autre foiz ne paia fors II s. VI d.

Le bigrage, XIIII s. VI d. perpetuel—C'est assavoir icelz qui prennent les mes des musques.

Le fieu du Pont Cardon[2] XV s.,—par ces parties.

Sont ileques IIII galons de vin.

Item, XII capons et XII d., item, VII.XX.X oeus. Ballie a Nichole le Moinne por XXI s.—et creist de VI s.

fol. 97v

Le jardin de Boissey,[1] VI s.

La terre Mau rous, VI s.

La terre Guillaume Lempereor, XX s.

Une acre de terre anvers Berville,[2] V s.

Une acre de terre de Phelippe Tale, V s.

La terre Guillaume Pelous, II s. VIII d.

La terre Ricart Burnel, VIII s.

La terre Guillaume de la Faleise, IIII lb.

Une mote prez Boissoy.[1]

La haie de Saint Michiel est en doute et dit l'en que ele vaut XV lb. ou XL lb.—et est apelée par autre nom la terre Girart du Marc.[3]

---

[1] Colombier (?), Eure, a. Pont-Audemer, c. Bourgthéroulde, cne. Berville.

[2] *cf.* note, fol. 136v.

---

[1] Boisset-le-Châtel, Eure, a. Pont-Audemer, c. Bourgthéroulde.

[2] Berville-en-Roumois, Eure, a. Pont-Audemer, c. Bourgthéroulde.

[3] *cf.* fol. 36.

Estoient deuz a monseignor Ricart de Buiebec[1] du Roy XIIII lb.
De cen achata le—Roy XII lb.—comté par sev.

> La somme de icele serganterie de la Londe IIII.XX.IIII lb. X s. XI d.
> La somme de tote la—viscomté du Pont Audemer VII.C.LXI. lb. V s. VIII d.

La ferme de Cyerre, XIIII lb. IIII s.
La ferme de Hotonne, XVI lb. X s.
La ferme de Fraxines XVIII lb. VI s. VI d.
La ferme de la Bussiere, VI lb. II s. IX d.
La ferme Ernaut du Bosc,[1] XLIX lb. XVIII s. I d.
En enprez sont fieufées, XXXI lb.
La ferme Rogier Tactoris, XLIIII s.
Demie acre de terre, IIII s.
La ferme Guy de Garbarville, XII s.
La ferme Baboin, III d.
II saumons, V s.
Le bosc de la Soillete, XLII s. X d.
La ferme Rogier de Torville, VI d.

Le campil du Noefborc, L s.
Item, VI setiers d'avoine de rente par an, lesquelz doit le praier.
La ferme Leyciarum por la metie, XII s. IIII d.
La ferme de Lacye, XXII s. VI d.
Guillaume Moisson, XII d.
Estiene Vincent, XII d.
Le molin ad Esmoloors, VI s. VI d.
La ferme de Bigarz, XII d.
La ferme Rogier Harenc, XXX s.
Une acre de terre, IIII s.
La ferme Robert de Montfort, VI s.

La ferme Thomas dit Lepetit, VIII s. VI d.
La ferme Herbert le Lou, X s.
Le forestage de Montfort, XXV lb.

---

[1] This is probably the Richard, lord of Bébec (Seine-Inférieure, a. Yvetot, c. Caudebec, cne. Villequier) mentioned in *H.F.*, XXIII, 251 (after 1237).

[1] Stapleton, I, 101. The king obtained 49 l. 19 s. 4 d. from the land of "Ernaldi de Bosco" in the Roumois in 1180. *cf.* fol. 57v.

(fols. 100, 100v, are blank)

La terre de la rente de Waurey, XXX s.
La terre Morel de Lortiey, III s.

fol. 101

ICI COMMENCHE LA VISCOMTÉ DE BERNAY[1]

La ferme Rogier de Mortemer anvers Droecourt[2] vaut VIII.XX.X lb.
En la couture aus Bordarz, IIII acres et demie de pré, le pris de l'acre XXV s.
Item, en iceli camp, IX acres, le pris de l'acre XVIII s.
Eu camp des arbres de Droecourt sont par mesure IX acres, le pris de l'acre XXV s.—Baillies sont a Andreu de Droecourt sicomme la premiere.

Jurée

Eu camp du chemin de Droecourt, IIII acres, vaut l'acre XXIIII s.—Andreu de Droecourt prist l'acre por XXVI s.—et sont ileques par mesure LIII acres et demie.
Item, ileques demie acre, VII s. Ballie a iceli Andreu sicomme la premiere.

fol. 101v

Eu camp souz le chemin deriere la meson Mauree,[1] VIII acres et I vergie, l'acre vaut XVI s.—Andreu de Droecourt prist l'acre por XVIII s.
Item, prez iceli camp IIII[2] acres, par mesure XIII acres et XX perches, vaut l'acre XXV s.

Jurée

En la cousture du mostier, XII acres, le pris de l'acre XXX s., par mesure XII acres et VI perches. Guillaume de Montfort prist l'acre por XXXV s.
Item, souz la dite cousture, I acre, vaut XXIIII s.
Eu camp au Fevre, IIII acres, par mesure III acres et III vergies, le pris de l'acre VIII s.—Guillaume de Montfort prist l'acre por XII s.
Entre la meson Gaudin et le chemin—le Roy, VI acres, le pris de l'acre XXIII s.
Item, I acre, laquele Herveu le Fevre tient, vaut XXVI s.
Le Blaier Macelin, demie acre, vaut XIII s.

---

[1] Bernay, Eure. While no sergeanty is named, the farms given from fol. 101 to fol. 118 cover an area no larger than many sergeanties, with Bernay as its center. It is possible that the scribe neglected to write "sergenterie de Bernay" because of the repetition of the name of the viscounty.

[2] Drucourt, Eure, a. Bernay, c. Thiberville. Quer. Nor., no. 95. Roger Mortimer is said to have forfeited this land by going to England. cf. fol. 26 and note.

---

[1] There is still a farm named "le Maurey" to the north of Drucourt.

[2] An "X" has probably been omitted here.

Guillaume le Court, I acre, vaut XXVI s.—Le devant dit Andreu les prist sicomme la premiere.

   . . et queir dedenz la mesure

fol. 102

En la cousture Guillaume Mauree et eu camp abotissant, XII
acres XX perches,

En la couture aus Bordarz, XIII acres et demie.

Eu camp au Fevre, III acres III verges, en la couture du mostier
XII acres VI perches; Guillaume de Montfort prist selonc la
somme de la mesure por XVI lb. X s. III d.

Mesure

En la cousture des arbres, XX acres.

Eu camp au Court et eu Traveisein, III acres et demie, I verg.
et IIII acres et XX perches.

Eu clos Hardoin, II acres et demie et XX perches.

Joste le Pestiz, demie acre de terre.

Les prez

Es prez des Ferieres, II acres, por tout L s.

Est ileques I acre et demie par mesure—Jehan le Masuier et
Andreu de Droecourt pristrent l'acre por XXX s.

Le maneir de Droecourt, I acre, XXX s., tout autant a l'en
trouvé par mesure.

fol. 102v
l'erbage

Item, sont en la ferme devant dite IIII.XX acres d'erbage, le
pris de l'acre, une par autre, VI s.

Sont trouvées ileques LIII acres et demie par mesure. Jehan le
Masuiers et Andreu de Droecourt ont pris une o II acres de
bois barbe, l'acre por VIII s.

Avoine ileques de rente, XXV setiers et I mine, le pris du setier
VI s.

Por LIX capons, I geline, oeus et L s.

Les cenz por tout IIII lb.

Anvers Droecourt, XV carues.

Anvers Bornanville,[1] VIII carues.

preeres
de carue

Saint Vincent de Boolay,[2] VI carues.

Saint Martin le Viel,[3] V carues.

fol. 103

Anvers Faveroles,[1] VI carues.

[1] Bournainville, Eure, a. Bernay, c. Thiberville.
[2] Saint-Vincent-du-Boulay, Eure, a. Bernay, c. Thiberville.
[3] Saint-Martin-du-Tilleul, Eure, a. and c. Bernay.

[1] Faverolles-les-Mare, Eure, a. Bernay, c. Thiberville.

Anvers Duranville,[2] X carues.

Chascune jornée vaut XVI d. et doit chascune carue III iornées.

Anvers Droecourt une iornée d'erce, vaut VIII d.

Le molin d'Oillie,[3] vaut LXXV lb.

La moute seiche vaut ileques XXX lb.—Ballie por XX lb. et C s.

Item, sont ileques les rel.

fol. 103v

Item, ileques les ples de Brotonne, sont estimez par le fermier a
XII lb.

Ne sont
en ferme

Anvers Droecort, II acres de bois, ne sont pas en ferme. Ballies a
Andreu de Droecort por XVI s.

Andreu de Droecort prist le remanant d'icele ferme, exceptez les choses
baillies desus dites, lesqueles anciez estoient fetes, et exceptez II acres
de bois barbe qui n'estoient pas en ferme lesqueles il retenoit por le
pris il vaudront.

La somme XI.XX.XVIII lb. V s. VIII d.

La somme du bail ou des bauls II.C.IIII.XX lb. LXI s.
IIII d.

Et en tel maniere creist la somme de CXIII lb. XXI d.

fol. 104

La ferme de la terre Hue Datin[1] a Duranville LII lb.

Eu camp Malloe, IIII acres, vaut l'acre XVI s.

Aus Haus Sellions, V acres, I verg. mainz, l'acre XVIII s.

Anvers Mombaton,[2] I acre, vaut XV s.

Jurée

Souz Mombaton, I acre et demie, vaut l'acre XII s.

Item, ileques I verg., vaut III s.

Deriere la meson Raoul le Bochier,[3] II acres, vaut l'acre XX s.

Deriere la meson Raoul Mallart,[4] I acre et demie, vaut l'acre
XX s.

Au Fresnot, VII verges, vaut l'acre XX s.

---

[2] Duranville, Eure, a. Bernay, c. Thiberville.

[3] Saint-Léger-du-Houley, Calvados, a. and c. Lisieux, cne. Ouilly-du-Houley.

Quer. Nor., no. 95, a complaint by representatives of the men of the Mortimer farm,
from Drucourt, Bournainville and Duranville, that the charge for milling at this mill has
been more than doubled since it came to the king's hand.

---

[1] *Quer. Nor.*, no. 318. Hugh d'Astin adhered to John and forfeited his Norman lands
at the time of the conquest.

[2] Mont-Bâton, Eure, a. Bernay, c. Thiberville, cne. Le Theil-Nolent.

[3] *Quer. Nor.*, no. 299. "Radulfus dictus Carnifex" of Duranville complains that his
dues have been increased.

[4] *Quer. Nor.*, no. 294. "Radulfus Maslart" of Duranville asks for 7 acres seized by Hugh
d'Astin for non-payment of rent, and later taken with Hugh's lands by the king.

Eu camp de la Croiz, VII acres, le pris de l'acre XXIIII s.
Eu camp du Lievre, III verg., vaut l'acre XX s.

fol. 104v

Au Courtieres, III acres, vaut l'acre XXIII s.
A la Huanniere, demie acre et V verg., l'acre XX s.
En la cousture entor le maneir, X acres, vaut l'acre XXIIII s.
Eu camp ioste Malloe, demie acre, vaut l'acre IX s.
Vers la gastine, I acre et demie, vaut l'acre XVIII s.
Sus la meson Gefroy Tiecelin, III verg., vaut l'acre XX s.
Au Teil Noolent, demie acre X s.
          La somme XLII acres et demie.

Eu camp du Lievre, III verges.
Eu camp Feron, I acre et XX perches.
Eu camp Fendre, II acres, X perches meinz.

Mesure

Eu camp deriere le maneir, IX acres et demie, I verg., et IIII
    perches. Raoul de Laquese prist l'acre por XXVII s.
Eu camp de Cortieres, III acres I verg. et XX perches. Iceli
    Rad. prist l'acre por XXVII s.

fol. 105

Eu petit camp des gastines, demie acre et IIII perches.
Eu vergie du Lievre, I verg. XXV perches.
En la couture Hapel, V acres et LX perches.
Eu camp Warin, I acre XXXVII perches.
Eu camp de la Vallée Biaugendre,[1] III acres XLIIII perches.

Mesure

Eu camp de Monbaton, I acre XII perches.
Eu camp du Muterel, II acres XXXV perches.
Eu camp de Chiefville, II acres XII perches meinz.
Eu camp Quevrel, demie acre XXXI perches.
Sus le clos Henri Malliart,[2] I acre et demie—Ballie a Laurenz
    Hapet por XXVIIII s.
Eu camp du Fresnot, II acres.—Guillaume Freuz prist l'acre por
    XXVII s. quite au—Roy et est quite le—Roy de I setier de
    avoine que de cen devoit.
Eu camp deriere la meson Raoul le Bouchier, II acres XXXVI
    perches—Raoul le Bouchier[3] prist l'acre por XXVII s.
En la couture entre la croiz et le Petit Mesnil,[4] VIII acres.

---

[1] *Quer. Nor.*, no. 277. A Gautier Beaugendre held land at Duranville before the conquest.
[2] *Quer. Nor.*, no. 298. Henri Mallart complains that two acres of his father's land were wrongfully seized by the king with the Astin forfeiture.
[3] *cf.* note, fol. 104.
[4] Le Petit Mesnil, Eure, a. Bernay, c. Thiberville, cne. Duranville.

fol. 105v

Eu camp de la Huenniere, I acre et demie, IX perches meinz.

Item, I iardin est ileques, le bosc contenant III verg. XXVI perches. Ballie a Raoul Quese por XLVIII s., et vaut la verg. X s.

Item, est ileques le superficie du jardin por LX s.—et icele superficie fu ballie a iceli en nostre voie quant nous aliom a Caem a l'eschiquier de Pasques en l'an LX.

La somme de la mesure XLVIII acres.

Sunt ileques V preeres de carue III foiz en l'an, chascune iornée vaut XVI d.

Item, V herces chascune foiz en l'an, estimée la iornée a VI d.

Rentes

Item, sont ileques II services, por tout XXXVII s.

La meson Robert de Sarnieres, XVIII s.

Item, LIX capons, le capon V d., oeus V.C.IIII.XX.X, por le cent X d.

Le cens en deniers, IIII lb. VII s. IX d.

Le rel.

La somme LIIII lb. VIII s. VIII d.

La some des choses ballies et a ballier LXVIII lb. X s. IIII d. et creist de XVI lb. X s. IIII d.

fol. 106

La ferme de la terre Rogier Alis a Maneval[1] vaut VIII.XX lb.

Eu camp des Moleins, XI acres, l'acre XV s.

Es vaulz souz la court, IIII acres, l'acre XX s.

Anvers la Mare au Borc, IIII acres a celi pris.

Anvers la Marverie au Seignor, IIII acres, l'acre XX s.

Anvers la Mare Wacie, III acres a celi pris.

Jurée

Anvers Tellium, III acres a celi pris.

Eu camp Heliot du Mesnill V verges, vaut l'acre XX s.

Eu camp Vallellies, I acre et demie, l'acre XX s.

Devant la meson Orellion, IIII acres, l'acre XII s.

Anvers les Erabliaus, I acre et demie, l'acre XVIII s.

Eu val Ricart, VII verg., l'acre XVIII s.

Anvers les Ardilliez, demie acre X s.

Anvers les mares I acre XVI s.

fol. 106v

Sus la Mare Gacon, V verges, l'acre XX s.

---

[1] Menneval, Eure, a. and c. Bernay. *Quer. Nor.*, no. 324. The lord of Menneval forfeited his land to Philip by going to England.

Es closages, V verg., l'acre XVI s.

A la couture Roole, I acre et demie, l'acre XII s.

A la Rouge Couture, II acres et demie, l'acre VI s.

Jurée Eu camp Floris, I verg., VIII s.

A la Mare Durant, a la fosse Gautier, a la Haie Baniart et sus le petit chemin, II acres, XX s.

Le clos Laurenz, por tout V s.

Le clos du petit molin, XX d.

Anvers la court I iardin, contient III verg., por tout XX s.

Item, ileques le petit iardin continant I verg., VIII s.

Item, le clos Rafart, demie acre, XVI s.

Item, III petiz isle, por tout XIII s.

Anvers Campflor[1] la metie d'un pré, demie vergie, IIII s.

Item, ileques entor II acres d'erbage, por tout L s.

Item, ileques II masures lesqueles le prestre tient, por tot XVIII s.

Mesure
fol. 107 Item, ileques I conrey en l'abbeie de Bernay III foiz en l'an. Et ileques devient estre le seignor o III chevalz, le prevost, son forestier, por tout X s.

Icelz de Maneval quicunques a cheval doit le cariage des iarbes en aoust et le tassage.

Les cenz de Saint Remi, XII lb. XIII s.—a la feste de Saint Jehan, VIII lb. X s.; a la Saint Hylaire, ~~IIII lb.~~ [sic] V s.

Rentes Les capons ileques LVIII. Gelines XXXIII et demie et oeus dedenz VI.C et X, sanz le diesme, et o les capons et les gelines, IIII s.

Anvers la Chavigniere,[1] I setier de forment, vaut IX boiss.

Anvers Bernay, vaut le setier XII s.

Anvers Toussue,[2] II setiers et I mine d'orge, vaut le setier VI s.

Au molin Sain, I mieu d'avoine, vaut le setier IIII s. a la mesure de Bitone.

Item le molin au ble o la seiche moute de Maneval, XXXIIII lb.

La pesquerie de l'aieue, L s.

fol. 107v Demie oie, VI d.

Une livre de poivre, II s.

II iornées en aoust, II s.

---

[1] Campfleur, Eure, a. and c. Bernay.

---

[1] La Chauvinière, Eure, a. and c. Bernay, cne. Saint-Clair-d'Arcey.

[2] Toussue, Eure, a. and c. Bernay, cne. Menneval.

Item, ileques le pilage, VII s.

Por I aignel, XVIII d.

Le moulin au ble de Fomucon,[1] por la tierce partie—le Roy, L s.

II molins foulerez, por tout XXX lb.

La terre Alalim, XL s.

Le pasnage des porz, X s.

Les esples et les rel., VI lb.

Item, sont ileques IIII preeres de carue, desqueles chascune doit
    III iornées, et vaut la iornée XVI d.

Por III herces II foiz en l'an, por la iornée VI d.
              La somme VII.XX.XVIII lb. XIX s. VIII d.

fol. 108   La ferme de la terre de la seignorie le—Roy de Faveril,[1] XL s.
    Sont ileques IIII acres de terre, vaut l'acre X s.—Rogier Marmion prist
        la seignorie—le Roi de Faveril por LIII s. VI d.

    La ferme Raoul de Repentigni[2] XIII lb.
        A la Bouleie,[3] III acres et demie et I vergie, l'acre XX s.
Jurée   A Marguerin, III acres et demie, le pris de l'acre XX s.
        Eu camp vers le moustier, VI acres, l'acre XX s.

Mesure   Sunt ileques par mesure XIII acres III verg. VIII perches.
fol. 108v

        Les cens en la devant dite ferme, XVI s.
        Item, II setiers d'avoine, vaut le setier VI s.
Rentes   Item, XI capons et XI d. Item V gelines et IIII d.
        Item, VI.XX oeus, II d.
        Por une carue, XXXII d.
              La somme XV lb. III d.
    La seignorie de ceste ferme est ballie por XVI lb. Guillaume du Roset
        encheri l'acre de II s. et prist le remanant de la ferme, c'est assavoir
        les rentes, por LII s.
              La somme toute XVIII lb. IX s. III d.
              Et creit de CIX s. et III d.

---

[1] This might be either Fumechon, cne. Thibouville, or Fumechon, cne. Ecardenville,
both in the canton of Beaumont-le-Roger.

---

[1] Le Favril, Eure, a. Bernay, c. Thiberville. Stapleton, I, 85. In 1180 the king obtained
13 s. from the land of Favril.

[2] *cf.* note, fol. 112v.

[3] La Boulaie (?), Eure, a. and c. Bernay, cne. Plasnes.

La ferme a la dame de la Mare anvers Fresnose[1] VI.XX.XV lb.

En la cousture d'outre le doict, XV acres, vaut l'acre X s.

En la couture entor le mostier, X acres, l'acre XI s.

Souz les Bucallies, XV acres, desqueles II vers le jardin valent XII s. l'acre.

Les autres XIII acres, vaut l'acre VIII s.

Les prez anvers Frenose, XIII acres, le pris de l'acre XL s.

L'erbage ileques d'un jardin, XVI s.

Les fruiz ileques, VIII s.

Item, l'erbage plessen, XV s.

L'erbage en I auney deriere le ballium, XXIIII s.

En la couture deriere le iardin, XIIII acres LX perches.

En la couture ioste le mostier, XII acres.

En la couture Berruier, XVII acres.

En la grant piece, XI acres LXVII perches.

Joste la meson Robert le Comte, I verg. XV perches.

Au vivier, VII.XX.VIII perches.

Au petit pré, I acre XXIX perches.

En la place du molin, XX perches.

L'erbage de l'auney, II acres XXXVI perches.

L'erbage du Plesseiz, qui autres fiees est apelé le lieu du maneir, et de la mote, III acres et demie, LX perches.

Le jardin, II acres XVII perches.

La pesquerie de l'aieu, VI lb.

Le campart ileques, X lb.

Les pesqueries feaulz, por tout XIIII s.

Le molin o la moute seiche, XX lb.

Item, V setiers et I quartier de forment, vaut le setier, XV s.

L'avoine ileques, XXIII setiers et I boiss., le pris du setier VI s.

Un setier d'orge, VI s.

Item, CXIIII capons, sanz ceuls de Roncenoi.

En deniers, VIII s. IX d.

Anvers Roncenoi, XXXIIII capons.

Por les oeus de Fresneuse, XVIII s. II d.

Item, ileques I oues, le pris de l'oie VIII d., et II s. de rente.

Les cens de Fresneuse et de Hotot et de Roncenoi, XXIII lb. III s.

---

[1] Freneuse-sur-Risle, Eure, a. Pont-Audemer, c. Montfort-sur-Risle.

Le pasturage de Fresnouse, LXIIII s.
Por le pasturage forain, X s.

Anvers Roncenoi en la cousture de Quiquenpoit, VIII acres, por
    tout LX s.
Joste icele couture, III acres, por tout XXX s.

Jurée   Sus le Vidoit, II acres arables et IIII acres de pastur[age], por
    tout XL s.
Eu pré Gambon, III acres, en la ferme Rogier l'Angleiz, III
    acres, en la couture de la capele, III acres; por ices III pieces,
    por tout, C s.

fol. 110v   Anvers Roncenoi estoient seronc la jurée XXXIIII acres de
    terre, valent XVII lb.
Ileques est trové par mesure LXVIII acres.
        Donc la somme creist de XVII lb.

Jurée   Eu camp du clos et es noers, IIII acres, por tout XL s.
Le pré novel et le camp au prestre, IIII acres, por tout L s.
Le camp Valen, III acres; II acres d'erbage, et II acres de pré,
    et sont les terres arables por tout IIII lb.

Mesure   Par la mesure de Vincent sont ileques IIII.XX.XVI acres et
    demie, desqueles sont XXVIII acres en auneys.

Le Mort Doict XX s. por tout, et por l'aieu de Roncenoi.
Anvers Roncenoi et a Auto[1] III.C.X oeus et o les oeus IIII d.
    Les rel. et les justices.
Les sieges du maneir et la mote.
        La somme VII.XX.XI lb. III d.

fol. 111   Icele ferme devant dite est baillie a Monseignor Jehen de Harecort[1] et a
    Mons. R. son frere por IX.XX.X lb., sanz l'erbage du Plesseiz.
Item, il doit XX lb. IX s. VI d. por l'encressment des terres et des prez.
        et en tel maniere creist iceste ferme de LXXV lb. IX s.
        VI d.
Les prez creissent anvers Fresnouse de III verg. XXIX perches de terre
    et creissent de III acres LX perches.

---

[1] Authou, Eure, a. Pont-Audemer, c. Montfort-sur-Risle.

---

[1] The Harcourts, one of the great families of Normandy, had important holdings in this region. *cf.* fol. 47v.

La crescence des terres vaut XXXII s. VI d.
La crescence des prez XXXVII s.

fol. 111v

La ferme Jehan de Jerpouville anvers Francheville[1] vaut LX lb.
Devant la porte de Francheville, IIII acres, l'acre XX s.
Des demises du maneir, IIII acres, a celi pris.
Eu camp de Blanchart, V acres, a celi pris.
En la mare Hersent, VII acres, l'acre XX s., exceptez en II
lesqueles sont estimées por tout a XX s.

Jurée

Es Fauqueis, XIIII acres, vaut l'acre XX s.
L'erbage eu maneir de la ferme, I acre, XVIII s.
Anvers la Haie du Chemin, I acre, XVIII s.
En la Haie Fosse, demie acre, VII s.
En Longue Haie et eu frique, I acre, V s.
Eu pré Parreus, I verg. III s.
La Bruiere l'Anglez, I acre, VII s.
La somme XXXVIII acres III verg.

fol. 112

En la grant piece joste le maneir, XXXVII acres.

Mesure

Eu maneir, I acre et LX perches.
En bruieres, III acres et demie et IIII perches.
Des demises du maneir, IIII acres, LX perches.
Eu prael de la ville demie acre, et VIII perches.
La somme XLVI acres, III verg. et XII perches.[1]

Le cens en deniers, VII lb., V s.
Item, IIII.XX.IIII capons, XIIII gelines, et XL d.
Une oie, VIII d. Item, IX.C oeus.

Rentes

Item, X setiers et plene mine d'orge, vaut le setier VII s. et IIII
boiss. d'avoine.
Les preeres de XII hommes qui doivent coedre le fienz et porter
as camz, une iornée en aoust, tasser, piler, fouir les cortilz,
coedre le lin, por ices services XII s.
La moute seiche C s. Item sont ileques VIII redevances, XXIIII
s. por tout. Les esples ileques XL s.
La somme LIX lb. I d.

fol. 112v

Icele ferme devant dite est ballie a Colin dit Quarrel por LXXV lb.

---

[1] Franqueville, Eure, a. Bernay, c. Brionne. Stapleton, II, cclix, Jean had held one knight's fee of the honor of Montfort before the conquest.

---

[1] According to these figures there were 40 *perches* to the virgate in this region.

La crescence des terres por VIII acres de terre, VII lb. IIII s.

Et en tel maniere creist icele ferme XXII lb. IIII s.

La ferme de la terre qui fu Hue de L'Auney et Raoul de Repentignie[1] XXVI lb.

Au Buisson en I couture, VI acres de pré, le pris de l'acre XXIIII s.

Item, en iceli camp, II acres a celi pris.

Jurée

En l'autre camp du Buisson, V verg., por tout XXV s.

Item, ileques II acres, l'acre XXIIII s.

Au Lou Pendu, II acres, le pris de l'acre XX s.

fol. 113

A la Herodiere, XII acres d'erbage, l'acre XII s.

En la couture du bosc du Buisson, XIIII acres et demie, VIII perches.

Eu camp Harel ioste la couture, III acres XVI perches.

Eu camp devant dit, II acres.

Mesure

Eu clos du hamel Juin, XXXIII perches.

Eu camp du Lou Pendu, II acres et demie et I verg.

Eu camp Rich[er]i, II acres.

Eu camp Poiree, II acres XXV perches.

Eu camp de la mare du chemin, II acres et demie, LX perches.

Eu camp des Herodieres, XIIII acres.

Le cens ileques, LXXI s. VIII d.

Rentes

Les preeres de carue, II, II foiz en l'an, XXXII d.

Item, V verg. de bosc, ne sont pas ne ferme.

fol. 113v

La ferme de la terre Henri du Pont Audemer[1] XL s.

Ileques estoient devant le bail par le dit Michiel de la Boolaie XXXIX acres.

Par mesure sont trovées XLI acres, L perches.

Icele ferme est ballie a Mons. Michiel de la Boolaie[2] por

---

[1] *Cart. Nor.*, no. 1091. In 1207 Philip Augustus granted to Jean d'Asnières, with other holdings "quicquid Radulfus de Repentigni et Hugo de Alneto similiter habebant in Algia. . . ."

---

[1] *Quer. Nor.*, no. 326. Henri de Pont-Audemer forfeited his land by going to England at the time of the conquest. He had been *bailli* of Caux before the conquest; *cf.* Stapleton, II, cxxvi.

[2] *Cart. Nor.*, no. 647. Accounts of the commune of Rouen, *c.* 1260: "Domino Michaeli de Bouleia pro suo sallario, 15 l., et pro expensis 7 l., 10 s." Delisle, *Ech.*, nos. 789, 813. "Michael de la Boelaie," knight, attended the Exchequer in 1248 and 1258.

XVIII lb.—et creist issi de XVI lb.

La ferme de la terre Robert de Cantelou anvers Neuville[3] XLII lb.

Entor le maneir, XXVI acres, desqueles X acres valent l'acre XXII s.; les autres X, vaut l'acre XVIII s.; et les autres VI, l'acre VIII s.

A Maleare—II acres et demie, vaut l'acre XXII s.

Anvers Berceucort, qui est apelée Longue Raie, I acre et demie, l'acre XX s.

En la Corte Acre, II acres, vaut l'acre XVIII s.

Au puiz Garnier et a la fosse Rouele, III acres, l'acre XXII s.

A la fosse Jumelle, III verg., l'acre XXII s.

A la Mare Celee, I verg. et demie, l'acre XVI s.

La somme XXXVI acres XX perches.

En la grant piece de la mare du Bosc, XXI acres et demie et LX perches.

En la couture ioste le iardin, X acres XLIIII perches.

Au puiz Garnier, III acres XXVI perches.

Eu camp de la Courte Acre, II acres XL perches.

Eu camp de Longue Raie, I acre et demie et XL perches.

Eu camp Malare, III acres XII perches.

En la piece iost Robert Maurree, demie acre XXV perches.

En la Mare Celee, demie acre, IIII perches meinz.

En la mote et eu jardin, I acre, XV perches.

La somme XLIII acres et demie et III perches sanz le jardin et sanz la mote.

De cen deivent estre ostées IIII acres et LVI perches por la mesure et demorent XXXIX acres XXVII perches.[1]

Le cens de la devant dite ferme en deniers, LXXV s.

Une mine d'orge, III s.

III mines d'avoine, IX s.

XI oues, vaut l'oie X d.

---

[3] *H. F.*, XXIII, 617. Robert de Canteleu had held one-fourth of a knight's fee at Neuville-sur-Authou (Eure, a. Bernay, c. Brionne) from the abbot of Cormeilles; he forfeited it by going to England at the time of the conquest.

---

[1] All these sums work out at the rate of 40 *perches* to the virgate.

Rentes

Capons XIX, et XXXIII d.

VI gelines, XII.XX.X oeus, XXXIII d.

Les preeres de V carues II foiz en l'an, vaut la iornée XVI d.

Une quarete en aoust, II s.

Esplez et reliez, XL s.

  La somme XLI lb. V s.

Le jardin et la mote, XXV s.

Les terres valent XLV lb. VI d.

Les rentes valent VIII lb. X s. X d.

  La somme LIIII lb. XVI s. IIII d.

  En tel maniere creist la somme de XII lb. XVI s. IIII d.

fol. 115

Ligier de Bretigni prist toutes les terres lesqueles sont en la ferme devant dite por XXIII s. l'acre. Et les autres rentes selonc cen que il sont estimées. Et donna en contreplege l'oictieve partie de son fieu de hauberc anvers Noville.

  Le jardin et la mote XXV s.

  Les terres XLV lb. VI d., et sont demenées a iceli IIII acres LVI perches par mesure.

  Les rentes valent VIII lb. X s. X d.

    La somme de tout LIIII lb. XVI s. IIII d.

    et creist issi la somme de XII lb. XVI s. IIII d.

fol. 115v

La fermes Angnes de Tillie[1] vaut VI lb.

  Sont ileques VII verges de terre desqueles vaut l'acre XX s., et

Jurée

  III verges X s.

En I camp une acre et X perches.

Mesure

Eu camp de la Rue Morel I acre, XV perches.

Les preeres de III carues feoaulz, por tout II s.

Item, III vavassories, por tout L s.

Item, II oues, valent XVI d.

Item, XIIII capons, et II s. IIII d.

Rentes

Item, VII.XX oeus, XIIII d.

Avoine III setiers I mine, vaut le setier VI s.

Gillebert du Hamel doit III s. de rente.

Jehan du Val, II s.

  La somme VI lb. XII d.

---

[1] *cf.* above, fol. 96.

Icele ferme est ballie a Guillaume du Buisson et a Guillaume Goin por VII lb., et creist de XX s.

fol. 116
Comté
par sey
par sey

La terre Romain de Caorses, XX s., perpetue.
La terre Michiel du Bosc, VIII s.
La terre Crespin du̇ Val, X s.

La terre Guillaume de la Lequeroie, LX s.
    Les terres arables IX acres, vaut l'acre V s.
    Une vavassorie, vaut XXXV s.
        Icele ferme est ballie a Mons. Jehan de Morcent por VI lb., et creist iceste some de LX s.
Sont ileques par mesure X acres et demie de terre par Rogier Harenc.
    La somme VI lb. XIIII s. II d.

fol. 116v

Le fieu Harpin,[1] C s. par parties
Le cens vaut C s. IIII d.
Le vivier de Bernay, X s., perpetuel.
Le molin du Gort, XX s., perpetuel.

Comtée
par sey

La seignorie le—Roy anvers Fresnouse, VII lb.
    Eu camp ioste Thommas Hunost, V verg., l'acre V s.
    Eu camp ioste Nichole de Salecraus, I acre, V s.
    Joste le brueray, III acres, vaut l'acre V s.

Jurée

Item, XXI acres de brueray, vaut l'acre IIII s.
Item, I acre de pré, vaut XXIIII s.
Item, I verg. de pré, vaut VI s.
Item, I iardin continant I vergee, III s.
Item, I acre de terre en la riviere, vaut V s.
    La somme XXVI acres et I verg. sanz le pré et le iardin.

fol. 117

Mesure

Prez de l'aumosne, I acre LV perches.
En sardeaus, I acre XXV perches.
En la grant piece, XXVI acres.
Eu maneir I acre, LXVI perches.
    La somme XXIX acres III verg. XXVI perches.[1]

Les preeres des carues se il sont ileques.
Item, sont ileques II residences desqueles—Robert Lague doit

---

[1] There was a fief Herpin at Saint-Pierre-de-Salerne, c. Brionne, and a fief Harpin at La Herpinière, Beaumontel, c. Beaumont-le-Roger. This is probably the latter.

---

[1] This gives 40 *perches* to the virgate.

une, c'est assavoir, VII s. a la Saint Jehan, VII capons a Noel
et XXX oeus a Pasques.

Rentes

Guillaume Lorence, a la Saint Michiel V s., II capons, II d., XX
oeus, I d.

Estiene d'Autoil, V s, IIII capons, IIII d., XL oeus, IIII d.

Angnes Labodine, XIII mansez, I d., X oeus, I capon, I d.

Raoul Hunost, a la Saint Jehan, XV d.; a la Saint Michiel, IIII
s. III d., I capon, I d., une geline, X oeus, I d.

fol. 117v

Raoul du Buc, VI s. I capon et demie, III obol., XV oeus, I d.

Item, Robert Boi vin, III s. a la Saint Michiel.

Robert Estiene, V d., X oeus, I d., et de l'autre partie XII d.

La somme IX lb. II s. III d.

Jehan Delivet prist icele ferme por XII lb.

La somme prisie et de la crescence de la terre XIII lb. IIII s. VI d., et
en tel maniere creist iceste somme de VI lb. IIII s. VI d., et encore
doit d'une acre de terre.

La ferme de la terre de Pelee Ville[1] XL s., perpetuel.

fol. 118

Veci la Sergenterie de Gaci[1]

La ferme de la terre du Sap[2] IIII.C.L lb.—comtée par sey

Anvers Noville[3] eu camp de Biau Fou, XI acres, l'acre VI s.

A la meson Jehan de la Ferté, I verg., II s.

En la couture sus le iardin, X acres, l'acre X s.

Eu camp Efforcie, IIII acres, l'acre V s.

Jurée

Eu camp Goiot, V acres, vaut l'acre IIII s.

Es terres Hue Lamie, III acres, l'acre II s. VIII d.

Au Partuit Lecarc, VII verg., por tout VIII s.

En la couture du doit de Torgion, XI acres, l'acre VII s.

A la fosse de Baugi, V acres, l'acre V s.

En pestiz, V acres, l'acre X s., au gué Hanon, IIII acres, l'acre
VI s. Ballies a Mons. Helloin de Aurival, l'acre por XI s.—et
n'a pas letres a fin.

Eu pré Destouallies, I acre, XXVI s.

Es lons prez, VII verges, l'acre VIII s.

---

[1] Plainville (?), Eure, a. and c. Bernay.

[1] Gacé, Orne, a. Argentan.

[2] Le Sap, Orne, a. Argentan, c. Vimoutiers. *H. F.*, XXIII, 710; *Quer. Nor.*, no. 328.
The lady of Le Sap is said to have given her barony to the king.

[3] Neuville-sur-Touques (?), Orne, a. Argentan, c. Gacé.

fol. 118v

Item, au Gui Amere, IIII acres, l'acre VI s.

Une acre et demie de brueray, por tout IIII s. VI d.

Jurée

Es Pomerey l'Ermite, II acres, l'acre X s.

La terre au Telliers, II acres I verg., l'acre X s.

Sus le ver eger, VII verg., l'acre VI s.

Item ileques, III acres, vaut l'acre VII s.

les prez
Mesure

Eu pré au vavassor, III verg. por tout XX s.

Entre les II aioues, VI verg. et I quarter[on], l'acre XX s.

Eu viverel, VII vergies, por tout L s.

fol. 119

Les cens, IIII lb. IX s.

Ricart Ernaut, I service de chevalz, I mine I boiss. et demie de
forment, et tout autant d'avoine.

Le molin et la moute seiche, IIII.XX lb.

Le bucage, VII s.; por oeus, XLIIII d.; II capons, II d., et
XX gelines.

Rentes

La mote o le maneir contient II acres, por tout XX s.

Lesclusage, V s.

Les preeres de XXVI carues III foiz en l'an, vaut la iornée
XVIII d.

Item, une piece de bois, V acres—n'est pas en ferme.

Anvers le Sap au terriers, IIII acres, vaut l'acre VIII s.

En la longe piece, III acres, vaut l'acre VIII s.

Jurée

Sus le chemin d'Orville,[1] III verg., l'acre VIII s.

Sus la sente de Valosot,[2] V verg., vaut l'acre V s. Ballie a Jehan
de Gargesale, l'acre por XII s.—Il a en ices pieces VIII acres
et demie et XXXII perches par mesure.

fol. 119v

Item, un iardin continant demie acre, vaut X s.

L'autre jardin continant II acres, L s. sanz la cohue—Ballie a

Jurée

devant dit Jehan por LXV s.

Une mote, le bail et les fossez, I acre, por tout XXX s.

Ballie a iceli Jehan por L s.

Mesure

Le cens ileques, L s.

Le menu cens, XV lb.

Rentes

Les rentes des terres, XX s.

XXII setiers de vin, vaut le setier XXXII d.

---

[1] Orville, Orne, a. Argentan, c. Vimoutiers.
[2] Le Val au Sou, ibid., cne. Orville.

Avoine, XIX setiers, vaut le setier VI s.

La costume du denier et de la maille, et d'une foire, VII.XX lb.

fol. 120

Le loage des estaulz des hales, X lb.

IIII capons, IIII d., XL oeus, II d.

Les corvées des carues, XII, II foiz en l'an, por tout L s.

Les ples de la baronnie, VIII lb.

Rentes

Item, demie acre de pré et XLIII perches, vaut l'acre X s. Ballie a Jehan de Gargesale por XII s. Item I broce continant II acres, par mesure III acres, vaut l'acre X s.—Ballie a iceli Jehan, l'acre por XVI s. VIII d. et en tel maniere creist la somme d'icecles qui sont ballies a celi Jehan de CVII s. VI d.

Les enclumages au ferons, XXV s.

Por la rente des forges, VI espardites, vaut chascune VI d.

Por les estalages as borgeiz et au ferons, por tout IIII lb.

fol. 120v

Anvers Meules[1] eu feu de Pilarderie, XII acres, l'acre III s.

Eu fieu au Chien, VIII acres, vaut l'acre III s.

Jurée

Eu fieu Estiene Pepin, VII acres, a celi pris.

Le campart ileques IIII s. por tout.

Les prez ileques anvers l'aieue Reide, II acres, III vergies, por tout XL s.

Les rentes ileques, XIII setiers VII boiss. et demi de forment, vaut le setier XVI s.

Rentes

Avoine XLV setiers III boiss., vaut le setier VI s.

Le cens en deniers, XLV s. VI d.

Item, de la Boucardiere, XV s. de rente.

Demie livre de cire, vaut XII d.

Item, I livre de commin, V s.

Item, XLII capons, XXI d., IIII gelines, IIII poucins, et IIII d.

fol. 121

Item, IIII.C et L oeus, et o XX oeus II d.

Item, les preeres feaulz d'erces II foiz en l'an, XXV s.

Les preeres des carues, XL s.

Rentes

Reliez et esples.

Le moulin de Meules anvers Canapeville,[1] LVI lb.

Les esples ileques, XL s.

---

[1] Meulles, Calvados, a. Lisieux, c. Orbec.

[1] Canapville, Orne, a. Argentan, c. Vimoutiers.

La somme IIII.C.XXIII lb. XVIII s.

fol. 121v

La ferme de la Mare Augier XVIII lb.

Au chemin Hue, III acres, vaut l'acre XVI s.

Ileques prez—VI acres a celi pris.

Item, ileques III acres a celi pris.

Jurée

En descendant de la rue de la Mare Augier, VII verges a celi pris.

Joste le genestal, I verg. et demie a celi pris.

Eu genestey, en pestiz, en jardins, et en broces V acres et demie, par mesure IIII acres et demie de bosc et n'est pas en ferme.

Mesure

Par mesure XVIII acres et demie de terre et I acre et XX perches de jardin.

fol. 122

La moute seiche, XL s.

Les preeres de V chevaulz III foiz en l'an, XII s.

Rentes

Une mine d'avoine, III s.

Le cens, XLVIII s., XI d., capons XXIII.

Item, IIII gelines, III.C et X oeus.

Uns esperons d'argent, II s.

Item, II paniaulz, II chevestres, et II cengles, por tout VIII d.

Les rel., dangiers, et les justices.

La somme XVII lb. VIII s.

Le priour de Saint Nicholas du Pas por—l'abbé de Lira Verne o V acres et demie de bois prist por XXVI lb., sanz le bosc sus la terre—vaut le bosc X s. l'acre—et issi creist iceste ferme de CV s. et LV s. por le bosc.

Por la cressence de IIII acres et demie de terre, LXII s.

Por I acre XX perches du jardin, XI s.

La somme, par mesure, XXIX lb. XIII s.

fol. 122v

La ferme Guillaume Crassi[1] anvers Bauquency et a Lonvigni IIII lb.

Eu camp de Lovigni, VII acres, vaut l'acre IIII s.

Jurée

Eu grant camp, III acres a celi pris.

Au mostier de Bauquency I acre a celi pris.

Mesure

Le cens ileques, XLVI s.

Rentes

Item, II capons, II gelines.

Les preeres de III carues II foiz en l'an, vaut la iornée II s.

La somme CVIII s.

Baudri le Menant prist tout por VI lb. X s., et creist de L s.

---

[1] *cf.* fols. 74, 163v.

fol. 123

La ferme de la terre des Portes VII lb.

Eu camp de Long Raie, sont ileques les espinais, VI acres, vaut l'acre IIII s.

En la couture ileques, III acres, vaut l'acre IIII s.

Es Haulz Pestiz, V acres, vaut l'acre III s.

En la Ruelle, II acres, I vergee, vaut l'acre III s.

Eu camp du Buat et eu camp du Clos, II acres, l'acre III s.

A la mare, III acres et demie, vaut l'acre III s.

Eu camp de Marches, IIII acres, vaut l'acre III s.

En forieres, I vergee, vaut II s.

Entre la Fosse Barne et Longue Raie, III acres de pré, vaut l'acre XXII s.

Item, une noete sus moire, vaut II s.

Item,

Item, II gelines, II d., II s., et XL oeus.

fol. 123v

La ferme qui fu au conte de Lencestre a Crosillie[1] XXXV lb.

Eu camp ioste le mostier et eu traveis du Quesne,[2] V acres, l'acre VI s.

Au Houletes, II acres, vaut l'acre II s.

Au hoi Hellenc, III acres et demie, por tout IIII s.

Le pris d'une acre et demie, por tout XII d.

Jurée

Eu camp d'entre les II cheminz, I acre, XII d.

Sus le chemin du Booloi,[3] I acre, II s.

Es corteries vers le bosc, I acre, XII d.

Eu camp vers le bosc, II acres, l'acre II s.

Eu travers du camp du bosc, III acres, l'acre XII d.

Au partuis de Mauremme, III acres, l'acre XX d.

Es monz IIII acres, l'acre XII d.

Eu camp Gaudin, II acres, l'acre II s.

A Cisi,[4] I iardin, contient demie acre, XX s.

Eu camp Perce Haie, XX acres, l'acre II s. IIII d.

Eu camp Robert le Testu, I acre, II s.

Eu fieu a la Tropele, I acre et demie, por tout X s.

Eu camp Crestian, II acres, l'acre XII d.

---

[1] Croisilles, Orne, a. Argentan, c. Gacé. *Cart. Nor.*, no. 113. The land of the earl of Leicester was confiscated by Philip Augustus after the conquest.

[2] Le Chêne, *ibid.*, cne. Coulmer.

[3] Boulaie, *ibid.*, cne. Croisilles.

[4] Cisai-Saint-Aubin (?), *ibid.*

En a la Bochete, XX acres, l'acre VI s.

En mie la forest, III acres, por tout XX s.

les

Item, ileques, I acre et demie, por tout XX s.

prez

L'erbage de V verges et I vergie de broutillie, por tout X s.

mesure

Rentes

Du fieu Gontier por le cens, IX lb. XI s.

Du fieu le comte, XXXIIII s.

A la Saint Remi, XII boiss. de forment, XXIIII boiss. d'avoine.

Item, I quartier d'avoine et VI s. tor.

Du fieu Gonnon L gelines, por pains XXV d.

Du fieu au comte, XVII gelines, por pains XII d. et III.C oeus.

Item, anvers Crosillies VI carues III foiz en l'an, vaut la iornée
XVIII d.

Le fieu Chanu d'une residence, III s.

La masure Berenger Fouquet, II s.

La masure Robert Testu, por la residence, II s.

Rentes

Adan de Chanai por icen, II s.

Avoine ileques XIX setiers, vaut le setier VIII s.

Le cens en deniers, VIII lb.

Et ileques est comtée la vavassorie de Bouci.

Les preeres de carues et d'erces, por tout LXVI s.

Item, IIII capons, XI gelines, et XIII d.

Item, IIII.XX.X oeus, XIII d.

Reliez et esples et justices, XX s.

Les amendes de la forest, XL s.

La somme LIII lb. VIII s. VIII d.

La terre Jehan du Val,[1] VI s., en doute est.

La terre Auberi de la Capele, L s., perpetuel.

Veci la Serganterie d'Orbec[2]

Comtée
par sey

La ferme de la terre d'Orbec qui est apelée la terre au Mareschal[3]
VI.C.XL lb.

La costume du ble XL lb.

---

[1] *Quer. Nor.* no. 308. A Jean du Val claimed five-eights of an acre of land near Bernay. At prevailing prices this might very well be worth the 6 s. annual income mentioned above. The fact that title is in doubt also indicates that this is the land referred to in the *Querimoniae.*

[2] Orbec, Calvados, a. Lisieux.

[3] Richard Marshal, *cf.* fol. 5. *H. F.*, XXIII, 708. This fief was rated at two and one-half knights.

fol. 125v

Item, la costume du ble et du fruict, XXXIII s. IIII d.

La costume du file et de la leinne, LXIIII lb.

La costume des IIII piez, LXIII lb.

La costume des seans, IIII.XX.X lb., quant a la maaille et au denier.

La costume de souz semainne des quaraites, VI lb.

La costume des toniaulz lier,   XIII s. IIII d.

Le hasvage de la ville, XX s.

Ices choses desus dites du commenchement de la ferme remainnent au—Roy et valent II.C.LXXI lb. VI s. VIII d.

Item, XX lb. IX s., tant en rentes quant en seignories.

Le cens en deniers, XXXIII lb.

Troiz molins o la moute seiche, VIII.XX lb.—et d'ices molins rendoit le—Roy CIX s. au malades d'Orbec que le fermier des ore en avant rendra.

fol. 126

Le gort d'Espreville, XXX s.

Ices choses devant dites, c'est assavoir le cens, les molins et le gort sont ballies a Mons. Jehan de Tordoict oveques les II viviers qui n'estoit pas de ferme et les ples sicomme le fermier ices choses avoit por XII.XX lb.

Les capons ileques XXVIII, le pris du capon V d.

Item, II gelines, le pris de la geline III d.

Et o les capons IIII d.

Les preeres des carues, L s.—Ices preeres sont ballies a Estiene de Bienfete.

II viviers anvers Orbec sont baillies sicomme est dit par devant— et n'estoient pas en ferme.

fol. 126v

Les terres arables eu camp Traharderie,[1] XI acres, vaut l'acre VII s.

Eu camp de la Vionose, VII acres, vaut l'acre V s.

Jurée

Eu camp d'entre les II bois, qui est dit les Vaulz Basson, VII acres, vaut l'acre V s.

Item, por II pieces de terre sus le bosc, contient VI acres, XIIII s. por tout.

Ballies sont a Estiene de Bienfete[2] por VI lb.

---

[1] La Trehardière, Calvados, a. Lisieux, c. and cne. Orbec.

[2] This is probably the father of the Etienne de Bienfaite, Master of Forests under Philip the Fair, whose farms in Orbec were made a free fief in 1301. See A.N., JJ 38, no. 74, and JJ 49, no. 116.

Item, eu camp as Dueaulz por l'erbage, II setiers d'avoine, vaut le setier VI s.

En la cousture de la Trahardiere, XI acres et demie, XLV perches. Richart Renaut prist l'acre por XV s.

Mesure

En la cousture d'Orbequet,[2] V acres LX perches.

En la cousture Vionose, IX acres et demie, XXIX perches.

Eu Val Basson, X acres, LVI perches—Ballies sont a Estiene de Bienfete.

Les esples de la ville, C s.—Ne sont pas balliez fors sicomme le fermier ices choses tenoit sicomme est dit en la devant dite page.

fol. 127
Iceste
est
des
jurée

Entre Orbec et la Planque de Launey,[1] les prez le comte, VIII acres, les pris de l'acre XII s. Sont ileques par mesure IX acres et demie.

Eu pré Robert de Auqueinville, qui est apelé le Pré Noef, I acre XXII perches—Ballies a Estiene de Bienfete l'acre por XIII s. La somme VII lb. II s., selonc la mesure.

Le pasturage vers les forques d'Orbec, I setier d'avoine de VI s.— et sont ileques entor XX acres.

Anvers Bien Feite,[2] XXXI acre, des queles XXIII acres sont ballies por VII lb. X s.

jurée

Au Sellions, VIII acres, VIII s.

En la couture Judoc et desouz, IX acres, l'acre V s.

Sus le vivier en la couture, XIIII acres, l'acre V s. VI d.

fol. 127v
mesure

Eu camp des Sellions et au camp aus Asniers, IX acres III vergees X perches.

En la couture Judoc, VIII acres LX perches.

En la couture du vivier, XV acres et demie, LX perches.

L'erbage ileques de VI.XX acres de bois, ou la entor. Por chascune vache, I boiss. d'avoine—et les reiz d'ongnons sont estimées a IIII lb.

Le cens et les borgages, XIIII lb.

Item XXX capons, vaut le capon V d.

---

[2] Orbiquet, Calvados, a. Lisieux, c. Orbec.

[1] Launai, Calvados, a. Lisieux, c. Orbec, cne. Saint-Martin-de-Bienfaite.

[2] Bienfaite, Calvados, a. Lisieux, c. Orbec, cne. Saint-Martin-de-Bienfaite.

Jardins
et
Rentes

Item, II molins ileques, LXX lb.

La moute seiche ileques, VI lb.

II pesqueries ileques, c'est assavoir le gort de la Rosiere et d'aillours, LX s.

Item, ileques I cortil, contient entor II acres, por tout LX s.

Item, le regort du vivier, XXV s.

Item, l'autre partie du regort lau ou icreist herbe, V s.

Les preeres des carues, por tout L s.

fol. 128

Le jardin de Larballetiere,[1] XX s.

Item, I cortil as Planques de Launey, por tout X s.

La costume de la maaille, XX s.

Les esplez ileques, XL s.

Item, le maneir ileques.

Iceles choses devant dites qui sont anvers Bien Fete, o le maneir et le vivier, balliez sont a Estiene de Bienfete qui tient la meson por VIII.XX.VIII lb. XXII d.

La creissement de la terre vaut XXIII s. VI d., encore demore a mesurer.

fol. 128v

Anvers Aubernon[1] en la couture de Saint Berthelemeu, XXI acre, desqueles VI acres sont eu camp de Amaucis et a la grosse Testiere, le pris de l'acre VII s.

Item les autres XV acres d'icele masure, estimée l'acre a X s.

En la couture de la Forestiere, XVI acres, vaut l'acre IX s.

En la petite couture, V verges, et I prael d'une vergee, vaut l'acre IX s.

Eu camp du molin,[2] V verges, le pris de l'acre IX s.

Eu camp Beneet, V verges, l'acre IX s.

Eu camp de Biaumont, II acres, l'acre VIII s.

Jurée

Eu camp de Lalbeie, I acre et demie, l'acre X s.

Eu camp Berte, II acres, l'acre V s.

Eu camp Avesne, II acres, l'acre IX s.

Eu val Codre, XVII acres, l'acre IIII s.

Eu camp de Bone Vaulz, III acres, l'acre III s.

La somme LXVIII acres et demie.

fol. 129

Eu Grant Pré, XIII acres et demie, vaut l'acre XI s.

---

[1] La Balletière, Calvados, a. Lisieux, c. Orbec, cne. St. Martin-de-Bienfaite.

---

[1] Abenon, Calvados, a. Lisieux, c. Orbec, cne. La Folletière-Abenon.
[2] There is still a mill of Abenon.

Eu Petit Pré et en la Cruere, II acres, l'acre X s.

II acres de auney, l'acre VII s.

Les auneiz et le jardin du Viel Molin, IIII acres, l'acre VII s.

L'erbage de III acres, l'acre V s.

La brueire de Biaumont, I acre, IIII s.

En la grant couture de la Foletiere,[1] et en la petite souz le chemin, et en la couture de Saint Berthelemeu, XX acres et demie et X perches.

Eu camp de Avesne, II acres, XXVIII perches.

Eu camp Berte, I acre, XXIIII perches.

Eu camp d'Aubernon, I acre, XL perches.

Eu camp de Biaumont, I acre et demie et XL perches.

Eu camp du molin et eu camp Beneet, XVIII acres, XX perches.
tout n'est pas mesuré.

Ices choses qui sont anvers Aubernon ballies sont a . . . mons. Jehan de Tordoict por C.VIII lb.

Les preeres de XIIII herces feaulz II foiz en l'an, vaut la iornée VIII d.

Les preeres de III carues II foiz en l'an, vaut la iornée XVI d.

Les vavassories feoaulz, XI, valent XI lb.

Un fieu anvers Bone Val, VI lb.

Item, ileques IIII setiers d'avoine, vaut le setier VI s.

Les cenz et les bordages, IIII lb. II s., o chapons LXXVII et chascun chapon I d.

Item, VII.C.XX oeus et o XX oeus, II d.

Le fieu Coquerel, VI sos de carue, valent X s.

Les esples et les rel, XL s.

La somme VI.C.IIII.XX.XIIII lb. V s. IX d.

Iceste ferme creist de VIII.XX.VIII lb. XXII d. Nos creon que encore crestra.

De cest encreissement desconte por ices choses esqueles le fermier a son terme de LXIX lb. XIII s., et XX lb. les queles il achata.

La ferme Nichole de Meules anvers Meules et Sarqueus[1] C lb. LX s.

[1] La Folletière-Abenon, Calvados, a. Lisieux, c. Orbec.

[1] Meulles, Calvados, a. Lisieux, c. Orbec. Cerqueux, Calvados, a. Lisieux, c. Orbec.

Jurée

A Meules au Pomeret, XXII acres, l'acre VII s.
II acres d'erbage, l'acre XXV s.

Rentes

Les formenz de rente, VI setiers, XI boiss., vaut le setier XVI s.
Avoine, XIX sext., VI boiss., vaut le setier VI s.
Le cens, IIII lb. X s. VI d.

fol. 130v

Item, XL capons et XXX d.
Por oeus et por deniers, VII s.
Item, XIIII gelines, II galons de vin, II s.

Rentes

Uns esperons de fer, VIII d.
Item, ileques la diesme, XLV lb.
Les preeres de IIII carues II foiz en l'an, vaut la iornée XVI d.,
II herces II foiz en l'an, vaut la iornée V d.
Les rel. et les esples.

N'est pas
en ferme

Item, II acres de bois, ne sont pas en ferme, vaut l'acre XI s.
Anvers Sarqueus, eu camp de Briorne, XIIII acres, vaut l'acre
XII s.

Jurée

Deriere la meson Henri de Sarqueus,[1] III acres et demie, l'acre
XII s. Ballies a iceli Henri, l'acre por XX s.
Entre le mostier de Sarqueus et le chemin eu camp Ermenosc,
XXII acres, l'acre VI s.
Joste la Haie du Mont, II acres et demie, l'acre XII s.

fol. 131

Le molin de la Baretiere[1] por la siste partie—le—Roy, LXXV s.
Les services de VI vavassories, VIII lb. II s. VI d.

Rentes

Le cens, XXII s.
Item XXXVI chapons et o le capon I d.
Item, XVIII.XX oeus, et o X oeus, I d.
Item, IIII preeres d'erce feoaulz, vaut la iornée VI d.
Les preeres de II carues II foiz en l'an, vaut la iornée XVI d.
Le cens ileques, XLVIII s.

Jardin

Le jardin ioste le mostier, I acre, sanz le maneir se il soit ileques,
vaut XIII s.—Ballie a Henri de Sarqueus sanz le maneir por
XX s.
Au Boolet, entor V acres de bois, l'acre sanz le superficie VI s.
Item II acres de pasturage, por tout X s.
        La somme CIX lb. XVI s. IIII d.

---

[1] *Quer. Nor.*, no. 333. A Henri de Sarqueus is mentioned.

[1] La Balletière (?), Calvados, a. Lisieux, c. Orbec, cne. St. Martin-de-Bienfaite.

fol. 131v
Comtée
par sey

La ferme Guillaume de Villiers anvers Meules[1] et Hamau Viel[2] X lb.

    Les terres arables, VIII acres, desqueles II acres et demie valent, c'est assavoir l'acre, XVII s.

Jurée

    Les autres II acres, vaut l'acre XII s.

    Eu camp as croiz, I acre, XIIII s.

    Eu camp de Minere,[3] V verg., l'acre XV s.

    Eu camp de la Noete demie acre, eu camp de Vibrey, III verges, vaut l'acre X s.

Mesure

    Une residence, XIIII s., VI d.

Rentes

    Guillaume le—Roy, II d. por oblations.

    Item, ileques I jardin qui contient I acre et demie, vaut l'acre sanz le bois XIIII s.

fol. 132

    Item, IX capons et IX d.

    Item, IIII.XX oeus, et o X oeus I d.

    En la paroisse de Saint Pierre de Meules[1] V setiers et IX boiss. d'avoine, desquelz—le Roy doit a Richart de Monpoignant XXII boiss., a Jehan Delivet I quartier, a Robert du Val III boiss.

Rentes

    Item, ileques XXIII boiss. de forment, desquelz le—Roy doit a Ricart de Monpoignant X boiss., a Jehan Delivet I quartier et a Robert du Val I boissel. En apres le—Roy en doit avoir VI boiss., et de la fille Guillaume de Villiers II boiss. por le tiers.[2]

    Item, I acre de terre qui est commune au—Roy et a une autre partie du—Roi, vaut IIII s., et ont ileques les filles le tiers.

        La somme IX lb. VII s. VI d.

fol. 132v

La ferme du Mostier Hubert[1] XVII.XX.XVI lb.

    En la couture souz la forest, XXXVIII acres, l'acre XIIII s.

   * Vers le val est meillor, vers le bosc

---

[1] Meulles, Calvados, a. Lisieux, c. Orbec. *Quer. Nor.*, no. 330. The six sisters of Guillaume de "Villeriis" of Meulles ask for a third of his land, forfeited because he was living in England when their father died *c.* 1240. They estimate the extent of the holding at 8½ acres. Judging by the entries on fol. 132, their request was granted.

[2] Viel (?), Calvados, a. and c. Orbec, west of Meulles.

[3] There is a hamlet called "Le Minerai" north east of Meulles.

[1] Meulles. The parish church was St. Peter's.

[2] These figures would indicate a quarter composed of 4 bushels.

[1] *Cart. Nor.*, no. 113. The barony of Les Moutiers-Hubert (Calvados, a. Lisieux, c. Livarot) was seized by Philip-Augustus at the time of the conquest. *Quer. Nor.*, nos. 346, 348. Hugh Painel lost his lands in Les Moutiers-Hubert when he adhered to John.

Eu jardin du Mostier Hubert, VI acres, vaut l'acre XX s. Hubert Corcon prist l'acre por XXVIII s.

Eu val Corcon,[2] XVI acres, vaut l'acre XII s.

En marneis XX acres, vaut l'acre II s.

Entre le mostier Corcon[2] et Moutier Hubert, XXX acres, vaut l'acre X s.

Entre le bosc Hubert et la Cocardiere,[2] XX acres, l'acre V s.

Entor la Mare Boulliant,[2] XX acres, vaut l'acre III s.

Au Belloet,[3] XXIIII acres, vaut l'acre X s.

Souz les Magnieus,[2] I acre, XXIIII s.

Entre le mostier et les Magnieus, VIII acres, l'acre VIII s.

Eu camp Homfroy, III acres, por tout X s.

L'erbage des acrez, por tout XXX s.

Le pré de l'Aube Espine, VI acres, l'acre XV s.

Souz la Trihenniere, IIII acres, l'acre XX s.

Souz les Magniens, III acres, l'acre XX s.

Es Roserez, VII acres, l'acre XV s.

Estiene, prestre des Mostiers Hubert, tient VIII acres de terre que il a porpris et a jostée a son aumosne, et siet cele terre anvers la Mare Boulliant, et vers le Pomier Hardoin, et cen seit Guillaume de Friardel,[1] Guillaume le Neveu, Hubert des Haies, Ricart Elies, Ricart Basire, Damien Semion, Martin le Fornier, Ernol de la Montée, Gervaise le Prevost, Symon de la Ville, Guillaume Pihoet, Thomas le Monnier, Jehan Torel, Ricart Griet, Huesel.

A la Herodele, I chevalage, vaut XL s.

A la Belliere,[1] XL s. Au Magniens XIIII s.

A la Blandivoie, XVI s.

Au Belloet, Robin Bernart, XX s.

Anvers Bele Aioue,[2] XX s. Au Belloet, XVI s. VIII d.

De la Bataille, IIII lb. De l'aide.

---

[2] The valley leading to Notre-Dame-de-Courson, la Cocardiére, la Mare Bouillante, les Magnans, are all places in the commune of Moutiers-Hubert.

[3] There are several places named Bellouet in this region. This may be Bellouet in the cne. of Bellou, c. Livarot.

---

[1] cf. note, fol. 146v.

---

[1] La Bellière, Calvados, a. Lisieux, c. Livarot, cne. Notre-Dame-de-Courson.

[2] Probably near the Bois de Belleau, ibid.

Le fieu l'Angleiz,[3] VII lb., IIII s.

Le clos au Cibot, XX s.

Rentes

Item, XXVII capons et XVII d., LXVI gelines.

Por pain LXVI d. Por pains et gelines du fieu a l'Angleiz XVIII s. Item, d'iceli fieu XIIII gelines.

Item, XVIII.C oeus et XXXVIII d.

Le forment, VII setiers, XII boissels, vaut le setier XVI s.

Avoine X moez, II setiers et demie, vaut le setier VI s.

L'erbage des viviers et des jardins, LXVIII s.

L'erbage qui est de noviau coupé, IIII lb.

Por carues et herces de la Bataille, por tout XL s.

Por les carues et les herces du Mostier Hubert et de Belloet, XL s.

Les preeres du fieu a l'Angleiz, XII s.

Les preeres de Belle Aioue, XII d.

fol. 134
**Ne sont
en ferme**

Item, les sieges de III viviers, ne sont pas en ferme.

Item, le gerbage de la forest, III mines de forment, I mine d'orge, et une mine d'avoine, valent LX lb.[1]

Anvers le Mostier Hubert II molins et le gerbage.

Rentes

La prevosté XXIX lb., c'est assavoir II fours, VI lb.; I oue de X d. Le cens et le fenage C s. Le gerbage XX s. Les foires LX s. Le marcié LX s. Les esples LX s.

Item, les esples de la baronnie, XXX s.

Livairon[2] por les esples, CX s.

Les fruis des jardins du Mostier Hubert, XL s.

Guillaume Friardel, II s. de rente.

Le fieu a l'Angleiz, es prez Liegart et a Lisoures,[3] IIII acres, vaut l'acre XVI s.

Vers la Maladerie, II acres, l'acre III s.

En la couture du mostier de Lisores, I acre et demie, vaut l'acre X s.

fol. 134v

Anvers Saint Ouein[1] en la couture des Martiaus, VI acres, l'acre VII s.

---

[3] *cf.* note 2, fol. 134.

[1] This is obviously a mistake; the scribe should have written "s."
[2] Livarot, Calvados, a. Lisieux.
[3] Lisores, Calvados, a. Lisieux, c. Livarot. *H. F.*, XXIII, 645. One-fourth of a knight's fee at Lisores was seized by the king at the time of the conquest.

[1] Saint-Ouen-le-Houx, Calvados, a. Lisieux, c. Livarot.

A la Bordiniere,[2] III acres, l'acre VII s.

Eu jardin Paienel, I acre et les arbres, por tout XX s.

Eu camp Raoul Gefroy, I acre et demie, l'acre II s.

Jurée Eu camp de la Quese, III acres, vaut l'acre II s.

A la Garence, I acre, vaut II s.

A la fosse Belot, V acres, vaut l'acre II s.

En la lande Suart, demie acre d'erbage, vaut XX d.

Item, ileques II acres de pré, vaut l'acre XV s.

Le jardin Raoul Gefroy, demie vergée, III s.

Rentes Le cens en deniers, XIII lb. Item L gelines, XII capons, VI d.

Item, II.C oeus et o X oeus I d. Les preeres de VII carues II foiz en l'an, XXX s. Le molin a Choisel, VII lb. X s. quite au—Roi.

Item, I petit isle, III s.

fol. 135 Anvers Equamville,[1] le fieu de Caorses eu camp Martin, III acres et demie, vaut l'acre III s.

Eu camp des Raies, III acres, vaut l'acre III s.

Eu camp Hermon le Vilain, I acre, XVI s.

Eu camp de la mare, V verges, por tout XX s.

Jurée En la couture de Launey, II acres et demie, vaut l'acre III s.

Eu camp Guerart, IIII acres et demie, l'acre IIII s. VI d.

Rogier le Lievin, V acres, l'acre III s.

Jehan du Val, II acres, l'acre IIII s.

Johost, I vergee II s.

Les bruerez, IIII acres, l'acre III s.

fol. 135v Le pré de la Caucie, I acre, XX s.

Es prez de Launey, VII verges, l'acre XXXII s.

Item, III verges ileques, XXII s.

Le jardin et le clos II acres, l'acre XVI s.

Eu bosc de Launey, II acres d'erbage, por tout XVI s. Sont appresagies en heritage XXX s., sanz le bosc sus terre qui vaut XL s.

Les prez et l'erbage L'erbage des autres III verges, por tout VIII s. Sont estimées par autre XII s. par an.

---

[2] *Quer. Nor.*, no. 346. A vavassory of this parish was called "la Blondignère."

---

[1] Auquainville (?), Calvados, a. Lisieux, c. Livarot.

L'erbage de l'autre auney, por tout VIII s. En heritage valent XV s.

Item, l'erbage de demie acre de lande, IIII s., vaut VIII s. sanz le bosc sus terre.

II vavassories, por tout XX s.

Le cens, VII lb. VIII s. VI d.

Capons, LXII, et o le capon I d.

Item XV gelines, VI.C oeus, et o X oeus I d.

Les preeres, por tout XVIII s.

Avoine X setiers, I boissel meinz, vaut le setier VI s.

La somme XVI.XX.XIX lb. XI s.

La graverie de Tigerville,[1] IIII lb.

Le froc de Prestreville,[2] III s.

Les terres de la Capele Yve,[3] XV s.

La terre Robert Harenc, X s.

La terre Martin de Tornetot, II s.

La terre Robert le Sut, VI d.

La terre Jehan du Val,[4] VI s.

Le fieu a l'Anglez de Meules, XX s.

En doute, est assavoir mon se c'est ferme ou fieu.

La ferme de la terre du Pont Cardon, du Bosc Renout et de Avesnes,[1] por tout XIIII.XX.XVII lb.

Anvers le Bosc Renout et anvers Avesnes, VI.XX acres, l'acre III s.

Guillaume Goulafre prist l'acre por V s.

Sont ileques par mesure VI.XX et II acres

Les chevalages des vavassories et le cens en deniers, XI lb. et V s. du Bosc Renout.

Item, anvers le Bosc Renout, anvers Avesnes, et anvers le Pont Cardon, IX moez d'avoine, vaut le setier VI s.

Item, anvers Avesnes, II oues, valent por tout XVI d.

---

[1] Ticheville, Orne, a. Argentan, c. Vimoutiers.

[2] Pretreville, Calvados, a. and c. Lisieux.

[3] La Chapelle-Yvon, Calvados, a. Lisieux, c. Orbec.

[4] *cf.* note 1, fol. 125.

---

[1] Pontchardon, Le Bosc-Renoult, and Avernes-Saint-Gourgon, Orne, a. Argentan, c. Vimoutiers. *M. A. N.*, 2ᵉs., V, 156. Guillaume de Pontchardon had held much land in this region. His holdings were granted to Ancouf, castellan of Exmes, by Philip Augustus in 1216. *cf. Quer. Nor.*, no. 332.

fol. 137
Rentes

Item, I cent de poires, vaut XII d.

Item, ileques XXII setiers de forment, vaut le setier XVI s.

Item, X boiss. d'orge, valent VI s.

Item, les chevalages de Avesnes, XII lb. V s.

Anvers le Pont Cardon, sus le jardin, VII acres, l'acre XII s.

Item, anvers la Ruppe,[1] IIII acres, vaut l'acre XII s.

Eu Val Borde, I acre et demie, l'acre XII s.

Sus le bosc de la Heunodoie, IIII acres, l'acre III s. VI d.

En la couture du chemin d'Orbec, II acres, l'acre XX s.

Jurée

Eu camp Haro, I acre et demie, vaut l'acre IIII s.

Eu camp sus la couture, I acre et demie, vaut l'acre VIII s.

Item, entre le camp Haro et la dite couture, I acre, III s.

Eu camp de Lardillier, demie acre, vaut l'acre XIIII s.

Eu camp Bouchart, I acre et demie, vaut l'acre VI s.

fol. 137v
Eu camp sus Touque, I vergie, IIII s.

Eu val Nichole du Molin, I acre, XII s.

Jurée

Item ileques, I vergie, V s.

Eu camp du cemetiere, I caneviere, vaut XII d.

Eu camp Brune, demie acre, II s.

Anvers la Heronnoie, VII acres, vaut l'acre III s. —Ballies a
Jehan Heraut, l'acre por V s.

Eu pré Doquet, I acre et demie, por tout L s.

Eu Petit Pré, I acre, XXV s.

Eu Lonc Pré, II acres, vaut l'acre XX s.—de cen est deue la
diesme.

Herbages
et
jardinz

Eu pré du Molin, III acres, vaut l'acre XX s.

Eu vivier, I acre et demie, vaut l'acre XL s.

En Bonete, III verg. de pré, vaut l'acre X s.

Eu pré du Gué Reide, I acre et demie, vaut l'acre XXV s.

Item, l'auney ileques o le bosc, II acres, vaut l'acre XXX s.

Item II jardins qui contienent III acres et demie, le pris du
mellor LX s., de l'autre XX s.

fol. 138
Item, anvers le Pont Cardon, la masure Dyonis le Priour, I
vergie, vaut II s. VI d.

Item, l'autre masure ioste la masure Aubert de la Hellebodiere,
VI d.

Mesure

Le cens anvers le Pont Cardon, XII lb.

---

[1] La Roche, cne. Pontchardon.

Anvers Nueville,[1] XXV s.

Anvers Saint Germain des Camz,[2] XL s.

Sus le molin Gillebert du Hamel, L s.

II poires d'esperons, XVI d.

Item, uns esperons dorez, valent III s.

Les capons de tout la ferme du Pont Cardon et des autres villes, et por oeus et por gelines, IX lb.

Les preeres des carues et d'erces, VIII lb.

Le molin du Pré, XXXVII lb.

Le molin de Bonete, XXII lb.

Le molin du Fric, XXIIII lb.

Le molin Denmie, XXX lb.

Les esplez et les reliez, LX s.

La somme XIII.XX.XVII lb.

La somme de la serganterie d'Orbec VIII.XX.IX lb. IIII s. II d.

Veci la Serganterie de Cormeilles[1]

La ferme de la terre Guillaume de Homez anvers Gloz[2] IIII.XX.X lb.

---

[1] Neuville-sur-Touques (?), Orne, a. Argentan, c. Gacé.
[2] Probably Saint-Germain d'Aunai, Orne, a. Argentan, c. Vimoutiers.

---

[1] Cormeilles-en-Lieuvin, Eure, a. Pont-Audemer.
[2] Glos, Calvados, a. and c. Lisieux.

Cart. Nor., no. 1018. "Universis, etc., Guido, . . . Lexoviensis episcopus, salutem. . . . Notum facimus quod nos ab excellentissimo domino Philippo . . . rege Francorum . . . recepimus ad firmam perpetuam, pro nobis et successoribus nostris, in terra que fuit Guillermi de Hommez, in parrochiis de Glocio, de Cornu Bubali, de Cortonnel, de Fontenellis, de Maierolis et de Sancto Johanne de Liveto 85 acras et 46 perticas in terris arabilibus, in brueriis, in pratis et alnetis; item, in masagio et gardinis 13 acras, 1 virgatam et dimidiam; 16 l., 9 d. annui census; 5 ansseres; 25 sextaria et 12 boissellos avene redditus; 8 boissellos frumenti; 119 capones, 29 gallinas, et cum caponibus et gallinis 11 s. et 7 d., 1 libram et dimidiam piperis; 1162 ova, et cum ovis 3 s., 6 d. et obolum; 66 acras et 20 perticas bosci sine tercio et dangerio; quoddam molendinum situm in dicta parrochia de Glotio cum moltis siccis et madidatis . . . item medietatem cujusdam molendini siti in parrochia Sancti Martini Veteris . . . pro 126 l., 10 s., 7 d. tur." 1283.

Quer. Nor., no. 1. This land was taken into the king's hand at Guillaume's death in 1243, though Robert de Montfort, who claimed to be nephew and legal heir, objected. Robert estimated the value of the estate at 80 l.

ibid., no. 349. Guillaume's brother died in England. He may have technically inherited and then automatically forfeited the land, thus barring Robert.

Olim, I, 123. In 1260 "domina Lucia de Grae" asked for this land once held by her uncle. The claim was denied.

Entre l'aioue d'Orbec et Cortonne,[3] VII acres, vaut l'acre XVII s.

Jurée

Item, ileques III acres, vaut l'acre XVI s.

Vers la couture Lopin, V acres a celi pris.

fol. 139v

Souz le mostier de Gloz, III verges, por tout XII s.

Anvers la Pierre Marie, IIII acres desqueles II valent l'acre XVIII s., les autres II vaut l'acre XVII s.

Anvers le Quesne Hervei, II acres et I verg., vaut l'acre XX s.

Eu camp du Pommeret, IX verg., vaut l'acre XX s.

Jurée

Eu camp Roussel, VII acres, por tout VIII s.

La couture Porquet, vaut por tout VII s.

En parreiz, XVII acres, vaut l'acre XVIII d.

Anvers Gloz VI acres a celi pris.

Anvers la croiz de Viliers,[1] III verg. et demie, por tout XV s.

La parsone du Cor du Bugle,[2] VI acres, de cen il l'en rent por tout III s., enquis est de qui il la tient.

La somme LXI acres XX perches.

En prez et en auneiz V acres, desqueles III verg. valent XVI s.

Les prez
et
auneiz

A la cengle V verg., por tout XX s., et III autres, por tout XLV s., sanz le superficie de l'auney—

Ileques sont trovées par mesure V acres et demie et XXVIII perches.

Le jardin ileques III acres et demie, por tout VII lb.

fol. 140

Anvers le Cor du Bugle, XIIII acres et demie et XXIIII perches.

Por la terre au prestre du Cor du Bugle, VI acres.

Anvers Maeroles,[1] I acre.

Anvers le Castele en bruieres, VII acres et demie.

A la croiz de Viliers, III verg. et XX perches.

Eu camp du Quesne Hervei, II acres, I verg., XII perches.

Eu camp de la Pierre Marie, IIII acres, V perches.

En la couture de la Maladerie,[2] IX acres et demie, I verg.

Mesure

En la longue raie Saffrei, I acre et demie, XVI perches.

[3] Courtonne-la-Meurdrac, Calvados, a. and c. Lisieux.

[1] Villers-sur-Glos, cne. Glos.
[2] Cordebugle, Calvados, a. Lisieux, c. Orbec.

[1] Marolles, Calvados, a. and c. Lisieux.
[2] La Maladrerie, Calvados, a. and c. Lisieux, cne. Glos.

Eu clos Anquetin, III acres, XVI perches.

Les gennes parrez, VI acres XXXII perches.

Le genne jardin, II acres et demie, LX perches.

Le jardin de la mote, II acres et demie.

Le camp souz le mostier, III verges, VIII perches.

Eu camp du Pomeret, II acres, XXV perches.

En la couture Lopin, IIII acres, LX perches.

  La somme de la mesure LXIIII acres I verg. XVIII perches.[3]

fol. 140v

La commune. Les pasturages forainnes por la partie le—Roy XIIII s.

Et est comté ileques I quartier de mouton que le—Roy prent ileques.

La moute seiche anvers le Cor du Bugle et a Puillete, XXX s.

Le grant molin de Gloz por la partie le—Roy, XII lb.

  De cen prendront les moines de l'Auney C s. de l'aumosne.

Le petit molin por la partie le—Roy, XII lb. XIII s. IIII d.

Rentes

  De cen prendront les moines du Mont Argis, XIIII s. de l'aumosne.

Le cens en deniers, XII lb. X s.

Capons, LXXV, et XXVII gelines.

Item, ileques III oues, vaut l'oie XII d.

Item IX.C.IIII.XX.X oeus ileques.

Les preeres de IX carues II foiz en l'an, valent XIIII s.

Por XIIII herces, VII s.

Avoine, XVIII setiers et X boiss., vaut le setier VI s.

Une mine de forment, VIII s.

Demie livre de poivre XII d.

Une mote sanz priez.

Jehan du Mesnil-Guillaume, por I coutel VI d.

Item, sont ileques XIII hommes qui doivent coedre les pommes et tribler. Item, I autre doit faire le marc.

fol. 141

Item, sont ileques V hommes qui doivent clorre les iardins, carier, et tasser les garbes en aoust.

Les esples ileques C s.

Item, sont ileques—les reliez de hauberc, I douaire qui vendra au—Roy, et LXXVII acres de bois. Icestes ne sont pas en ferme ne ballies.

---

[3] This total is wrong. It should be 69 acres 3v. 5p.

La somme IIII.XX.IIII lb. XVII s. VI d.
Icele ferme desus dite n'est pas ballie—.[1]

fol. 141v
Comté est
par sey

Por la partie le—Roy eu molin de Moiaz,[1] XXXII lb., perpetuel.
Es vaulz d'Asnieres, I mare, VI d.
Les monz d'Asnieres,[2] XII d., perpetuel.

Jurée

La ferme Jehan de Homez anvers le Mesnil Godement[3] LVI lb.
 En la couture du Pomier, X acres, vaut l'acre XIIII s.
 En la couture Traverseinne, VI acres a celi pris.
 En la couture Filliastre, V acres, vaut l'acre XIII s.
 En la couture du Quesnel, V acres, l'acre XIIII s.
 Eu camp Avenel, III acres et demie, l'acre XV s.
 Eu camp du fosse, V verges, l'acre XV s.
 Eu camp de Lame Lebelle, VII verg., l'acre VII s.

fol. 142
Ne sont
pas en
ferme

 L'erbage en quatre acres et demie de terre, l'acre XV s.
 Item, sont ileques II acres et demie de bois de XII anz, sanz
  le bosc X s.
 Item, sont ileques III acres et demie de pré, por tout IIII lb. X s.
 Item, I place qui fu jardin, o le siege du maneir qui contient II
  acres et demie, por tout LX s.
  La somme XXXVII acres.

  La mesure par Odart[1]
 En la couture du Pomier, XI acres I vergee.
 En la couture Traverseine, VII acres I verg. III perches.
 En la couture Filliastre, VI acres I verg. et X perches.
 En la couture de Quesnel, V acres XXVI perches.
 Eu camp Avenel, III acres I verg. XXX perches.

Mesure

 Eu camp du fosse I acre et demie, XIIII perches.

---

[1] *cf.* note on fol. 139.

---

[1] Moyaux, Calvados, a. and c. Lisieux.
H. F., XXI, 255. This farm had been made at least as early as 1238, since in that year the mill brought in 16 l. a term.
[2] Asnières, Eure, a. Pont-Audemer, c. Cormeilles. Stapleton, I, 85. The king drew a revenue of 62 s. from "terris de montibus de Asneriis" in 1180.
[3] Le Mesnil-Godemont, Eure, a. Bernay, c. Thiberville, cne. Fontaine-la-Louvet.
Delisle, *Ech.*, no. 145. Jean de Hommet had not made his peace with the king by 1214.
Olim, I, 123. In 1260 "domina Lucia de Grae" asked the king to restore Mesnil Godemont, which had belonged to her father. Her claim was denied, and the court stated that her father had forfeited the land before 1210 by adhering to the king of England.

---

[1] *cf.* fol. 231.

Eu camp de Lame Belle, II acres.

L'erbage en nois, V acres et I vergie.

Eu jardin, en la place, et eu siege du maneir, XI acres.

Et en bosc et en pré, IIII acres.

En I clos joste le mostier, XXXVI perches.

Eu camp de La Vergie, I verg. et XXXVI perches.

La somme LIIII acres.[2]

L'aide feal, CXII s. III vavassories ileques LX s.

Le cens ileques, XL s.

Item, I setier de forment, vaut XVI s.

Item, III setiers d'avoine, por tout XVIII s.

La moute seiche ileques, X lb.

Item, XXXII capons et XXXII d.

Item, XXVII gelines, XXVII d.

Item, VI.C.VIII oeus et XXX d.

Un conrei euquel deivent estre VIII hommes a chevalz, XVI s.

Les preeres de VIII carues II foiz en l'an, XVI s.

Item, XVI herces II foiz en l'an, XVI s.

Les esples LX s.

Item, sont ileques redevances de VIII hommes qui doivent clorre les jardinz, les pommes coillier et tribler, les estoubles coedre et sarcler quant mestier en sera, tasser, porter a la meson, fener et quarier et les taupes prendre.

La moute moiste, IIII lb.

Item, lessiau du vivier et le siege du molin.

La some LXIII lb., IX s., V d.

Iceles choses qui sont en la ferme desus dite sont ballies a Guillaume Louvel por IIII.XX.VI. lb. XIII s., o II acres et demie de bois sanz le superficie, qui n'estoient pas en ferme, boen bosc est.

Iceli Guillaume delessa iceste ferme—a mons. Ricart de Bosc-Gencelin[1] por le pris que il l'avoit prise.

La ferme de la terre Jehan de Morchans, Jehan Basset, Gautier de Laci,

---

[2] Another case of faulty addition. It should be 58 acres 3 v. 5p.

---

[1] *Cart. Nor.*, no. 499. A Richard de Bois-Gencelin was with St. Louis on his first crusade, and was given 30 l. a year from the *prévôté* of Evreux, *c.* 1252.

ibid., no. 915. Before 1278 Richard had given St. Taurin of Evreux two acres in his fief of Bois Gencelin.

Delisle, *Ech.*, no. 830. "Ricardus de Bois Gencelin" is listed among the knights present at the Easter Exchequer, 1266.

Guillaume de Escuredoict, Guillaume de Boutemont et la tierce partie du molin de Moiaz, LXV lb. III s.

> Anvers le Pin[2] entre les camz Jehan du Mostier et la Fosse as Louz, IX acres, vaut l'acre VIII s.

Jurée

> Eu camp entre Ricart du Perier et la Fosse as Louz, XVIII acres, l'acre VIII s.

fol. 143v

> En une torniere eu camp de Lieblai, VIII acres, l'acre VIII s.
> Eu camp Quevillion, II acres, l'acre IX s.
> Entre les cans Robin du Mont et la terre Basset, IX acres, l'acre VIII s.

Jurée

> Entre le Plesseiz et la terre Jehan Malliart, IX acres, l'acre VIII s.
> Sus la forest du Pin, I acre, V s.
> Joste la terre Anquetin de la Bataille, demie acre, V s.
> Es devant dites pieces demie acre de la crescence VI acres et demie, l'acre VIII s.

> > Ballies ices choses devant dites sicomme dedenz est dit.

Jardinz

> Le jardin continant II acres d'erbage, valent por tout XVI s.
> L'erbage des autres VI acres, vaut l'acre IIII s.
> Anvers la Haie du Fauc, VII verg. de terre, vaut l'acre VII s.

fol. 144

> Eu fieu du Bequeto, l'erbage de IIII acres et demie.
> Item, ileques les terres arables, V acres, anvers le Pin.
> En la couture vers la meson Robert du Jardin, VII acres et demie et XX perches.
> En la couture souz le bosc, XIII acres et demie.
> Eu camp Kevillion, I vergie.

Mesure

> En la couture du camp Souvre, XIX acres et demie, VIII perches.
> Es bruieres de la Noeve Forest, V acres et demie, I verg.
> Item, ileques en herbages, IIII acres.
> Eu jardin Fessart, I acre XXIIII perches.
> Anvers le Quesnot Pendant, I acre XX perches.
> Eu camp a l'Angleiz, II acres, XX perches meins.
> Joste le jardin Fessart, demie acre.
> En la couture du Pin, XXI acres I vergie.
> En la couture sus le Plesseiz, XVIII acres et demie et VIII perches.

---

[2] Le Pin-en-Lieuvin, Calvados, a. and c. Lisieux.

Eu camp Ose, VII verges.

Eu pré du Broil, demie acre.

fol. 144v

Le cens ileques, L. s. VI d. en la feste Saint Michiel, a Noel XIX capons, XIII gelines, et o les capons et les gelines XXIII d., a Pasques IIII.C oeus XI d.

Por III vavassories, XXVIII s.

Rentes

Les preeres des carues et l'erces, por tout XXX s.

L'aide le comte, XVI s. par an.

Item, sont ileques II summages, valent IX s.

Avoine ileques III setiers et I mine, le pris du setier VI s., quant l'en coeut le foage; eu molin de Bievredoit V s. quant l'en mue le monnier; le seignor a II s. por vin.

Les rel.

Anvers le Bequet au Bosc Costentin, VIII acres, l'acre VI s.

Anvers Botemont,[1] VII acres de pré, valent por tout XXXV s.

Item, demie acre, por tout VIII s.

Anvers Canseure, XVIII acres et demie de terre, le pris de l'acre VI s.

Jurée

Anvers Moiaz eu clos Mahieu, III acres, l'acre XII s.

Item, ileques VIII acres de bois qui sont ballies par le fermier, l'acre por VI s.

I capon, I d.; XX oeus et I d.

Anvers Castelion,[2] VIII acres et demie, le pris de l'acre X s.

Le maneir o la moute.

fol. 145

Anvers Castellion eu camp Blandin, II acres XVII perches.

Eu camp Girart, III verg. XX perches.

Eu camp de Leblai, II acres XV perches.

Mesure

En I clos demie acre XX perches.

Eu campil Pompein, V verg. VI perches.

Eu camp Guerost, I acre et demie, I verg.

En jardinz, I acre.

Eu camp du clos Mahieu, II acres.

Avoine XVIII setiers a la mesure Robert Bertran, vaut le setier IIII s.—forment III setiers, I mine a cele mesure, vaut le setier XII s.

---

[1] Bouttemont (?), Calvados, a. and c. Lisieux, cne. Ouilley-le-Vicomte.
[2] Castellain (?), Eure, a. Bernay, c. Thiberville, cne. Saint-Aubin-de-Sallon.

Le cens a la Saint Michiel, XLI s.

Rentes   Por capons et gelines, XXVIII s.

Por oeus, IX s. III d.

Les preeres du carue, V, II foiz en l'an, vaut la iornée XII s. [sic].

Anvers Escuredoit, XLVIII s. de rente. Item, I setier de avene, VI s.

Les preeres de VIII carues II foiz en l'an, vaut la iornée XII d.

fol. 145v   Item, IIII herces II foiz en l'an, valent IIII s.

Le molin ileques, XIX lb., V s.—Le molin de Moiaz ballie est au seignior de Biaufou por XXV lb.—c'est assavoir la partie le —Roy.

Rentes   Avoine de rent, X setiers, II boiss. meinz, les pris du setier VI s.

Por moute, VII setiers d'avene.

Por un service et demie, XXI s. A Pasques II s., XL oeus, III d.

Item VII d. et maalle, VIII capons et o les capons X d. et ob.

Une geline et demie—a Penthecoste XVIII d.

Les rel., XX s; a la feste Saint Hylare XVIII d. de rente.

Non estoient pas en ferme   En la forest du Pin,[1] XIIII acres de bois.

Eu Plesseiz, VII acres et demie.

Au Bosc Costentin, VII acres et demie.

En la Noeve Forest, I acre.

fol. 146   Eu Plesseiz du Pin, IX acres I verg.

En la Grant Forest de bosc, XIX acres et demie.

Mesure   En la Noeve Forest, I acre et demie.

En baille, demie acre.

La somme IIII.XX.XV lb. IIII s. X d.

Iceles choses qui sont en la ferme devant dite, sanz le siege du molin, sanz la moute seiche et mollie, sanz le siege du maneir, et sanz les arbres, et sanz les acres du bois devant nommées, qui n'estoient pas en ferme sicomme est devisé par la mesure desus dite, sont ballies— a mons. Guillaume de Bouquetot, ne ne poet estre enchirie sus iceli Guillaume por meinz que VIII lb.—et prist le maneir audit mons.— Julian de Peronne et Oede le Rous[1]—Mons. Guillaume de Biaufou[2]

---

[1] Le Pin-en-Lieuvin, Calvados, a. and c. Lisieux.

---

[1] Delisle, *Etude sur la condition de la classe agricole*, p. 409. Julien de Peronne (later *bailli* of Rouen) and Eudes le Roux, *pannetier* of the king, had been making arrange-

et Jehan de Morchans pristrent l'enchirissement por IIII.XX.XIIII lb.

La crescence des terres vaut VI lb. V s.

Por le maneir, IIII lb.—Iceste ferme creist de LXIIII lb. II s., que por le molin dedenz, que por autres choses.

fol. 146v

La ferme de la terre de Sirefonteinne,[1] laquele Guillaume de Friardel[2] tient, XIX lb. X s. VIII d.

    En jaireit sus la meson Rad. de Boneval, IIII acres et demie, le pris de l'acre XII d.

    Es parreiz sus la Hamel, VII acres, vaut l'acre III s.

    Eu camp Hausart, III verg., por tout III s.

Jurée

    Le gardin ileques, X s.

    En bosc, acre et demie, por tout X s.

    Eu camp de Launey, sus le sentier de Lixioes, V acres, l'acre X s.

    Eu camp de la fosse, VII verges, l'acre X s.

    Es parreiz de Sirefonteinne sus le mont, III acres, l'acre III s.

    En la haie de Mangneville, I acre et demie, por tout X s.

    Eu val Osmont, V verg., por tout VI s.

fol. 147

    Le pré V verges, le pris de l'acre XXIIII s.

    Eu camp Bovet, I acre, X s.

La seignorie de la petite ferme

    Le pré des Ouailles, III verg., por tout XX s.

    En genestei, III verg., por tout II s.

    A la meson Guillaume des Parreiz, V verg., por tout III s.

    Eu Val des Ouailles, IIII acres, l'acre VI s.

    Eu pré des Ouailles, III verg.

    Eu pré—a l'Abbé—I verg. XXIIII perches.

    Eu pré de Sirefonteinne, LXXII perches.

---

ments for clearing part of the forest of Evreux shortly before 1260. Part of this farm may have consisted of such clearings.

[2] Delisle, *Ech.*, no. 813. Guillaume de "Bello Foco," knight, attended the Exchequer in 1258.

---

[1] Cirfontaines, Calvados, a. and c. Lisieux, cne. Marolles.

[2] This is perhaps the "Guillelmus de Friardel, miles," mentioned in *Olim*, I, 303 who unsuccessfully claimed the sergeanty of "Loutelerie," formerly held by "Reginaldu: de Sirefontaine," 1269.

B. N., *Ms. Lat.* 9018, p. 10. Pledges for "Guillelmus de Friardello" owe 37 l. 10 s. ir 1275.

Mesure
de l'une
et de
l'autre
ferme

vol. 147v

Eu camp de Cantelou,[1] I acre et demie, XXVIII perches.
Eu camp de Launey, IIII acres III verg.
Eu camp de La Fonteinne, I acre et demie.
En la haie ileques, demie acre, XVI perches.
Es gardins au saunier, demie acre, XX perches.
Eu val Avion, VII acres VIII perches.
Es haies et en auneis, I acre.
En I jardin, LX perches.
Es parreiz Lovet, I acre XVIII perches.
Eu camp Pastinel, II acres I verg.
Item, ioste iceli camp, I acre.
En bruieres anvers le Hamel, VI acres I verg.
Item, ileques VIII acres.
En pardins, I vergee de parprestures.
Anvers Cantelou du bosc, VII verg. XXVIII perches.
Des jardins ileques, III verg. XX perches.
Item, ileques en parreiz, X acres LX perches.
Eu camp Hansac, I acre et demie.

Rentes
de la
grant
ferme
fol. 148

Les preeres feaulz II foiz en l'an, III s.
Item, les preeres de VI carues II foiz en l'an, XVIII s.
Le cens ileques, VII lb. XIX s.
Forment III setiers, III quartiers, le pris du setier XVI s.
Avoine VII setiers, IIII boiss., le pris du setier V s.
Capons LVI. Item, XVII gelines.
Item, VII.C oeus. Eu fieu Poz, III iornées de I homme de fener,
     de tasser, de clorre les haies, et des autres services, por tout,
     XVIII d.
Le fieu au maistre de Cortomel,[1] I service de cheval, XX s.
Touz les hommes du fieu doivent le fenage, triblage, tassage,
     closage de jardin, esceptez le maistre de Cortomel et le fieu
     au Poz, qui est fieufé por XVIII d.
Eu fieu de Sirefonteinne sont XXXIIII residences.
Le cens en la Pasque Florie, X s. VI d.

---

[1] Saint-Hippolyte-de-Cantelou (?), Calvados, a. and c. Lisieux.

---

[1] Courtonnel, Calvados, a. and c. Lisieux.

Item IIII.XX oeus, VIII d.—Les rel. et les esples, XX s.
La somme XXX lb. XVI d. sanz les residences.

fol. 148v　Icele ferme devant dite—ballies sont les terre et les autres choses selonc
la mesure a Guillaume de Friardel[1] por XXXIII lb.

La somme de toute la seignorie d'icele ferme, sanz les
prez et sanz le jardin, selonc la jurée XXXII acres
et demie, par mesure XLVIII acres III verg. XXXVI
perches.[2]

La somme des prez selonc la jurée III acres, par mesure
I acre et demie, XVI perches.[2]

Les jardins selonc la mesure II acres XX perches.[2]

Les terres creissent de XVI acres XXXVI perches.

La serganterie de Cormeilles creist de VI.XX.XI lb. XI s. IX d.

fol. 149　La seignorie le—Roy anvers le Pin, XLV s., perpetuel.
La terre de Brevedan,[1] VII s.
La terre Rogier Belot, X d., perpetuel.
La terre Gautier Gernago, V s., perpetuel.

Veci la Serganterie Hoschie

fol. 149v　La ferme de la terre Batorz de Saint Lambert[1] VII lb.

En la couture, VI acres, I verg. meinz, le pris de l'acre VI s.

En la couture deriere le bosc, VI acres, le pris de l'acre VII s.

En la couture devant le bosc, III acres et demie, l'acre VI s.

En gastine XXV acres, desqueles XVIII acres entre la meson
Hue du Bosc et le Lonc Essart[2] vaut l'acre V s.—et les autres
IIII s.

Entre ladite couture et la Bardoliere,[3] XV acres, vaut l'acre
III s.

Rogier Bardol, Hue de Bosc-Jehan, Nichole Herfroi et Gautier

---

[1] *cf.* fol. 146v.
[2] Comparison of these figures with the measurements given on preceding folios show
that in this district there were 40 *perches* to the virgate.

---

[1] Le Brèvedent, Calvados, a. Pont-l'Evêque, c. Blangy.

---

[1] Saint-Lambert, Eure, a. Bernay, c. Beaumesnil.
[2] Long Essard, *ibid.*
[3] La Bardouillière, *ibid.*

de Footel XV acres et demie pristrent, l'acre por VII s.; anvers le Lonc Essart XVIII acres, l'acre VI s.; a la Bardoliere XV acres, l'acre IIII s.

Enolf du Bosc-Jehan prist les rentes por IIII lb. X s.

Item, VII acre de bois, XIIII d'auneiz, l'acre sanz le superficie VII s.

La somme des terres, comté le bosc, LV acres I verg.

Pa [*sic*] mesure sont ileques LVI acres et demi.

Le cens ileques, XLV s.

Item XXXV capons, XXV d. et II.C oeus.

La some XV lb. X s.

Rogier Bardol et son compaignon pristrent l'acre de bois por XVIII s., sauf le tiers et le dangier, a lui por LVI acres et demie de terre, laquele du bois XVI lb. XI s.

Item, iceli Rogier prist le bosc sus terre por VII lb. par encherissement de X s. en l'acre—la premiere paie a la Saint Michiel.

La ferme de la terre de la Harengerie[1] VI lb.

Eu camp Oson, IX acres marlées, l'acre VI s.

Item, ileques, XL acres, vaut l'acre IIII s.

Sont ileques par mesure LVIII acres et demie de terre.

Le cens ileques, XIII s.

Item X capons. Item, XL oeus et o X oeus I d.

La somme XI lb. XIII s. II d.

Robert de Montevrai, chevalier, prist XLIX acres de terre a la Harengiere, l'acre por V s. VI d.

Et Gillebert Herfroi prist por XX s. quite au—Roi, et la superficie du jardin qui est comtée o les terres por XL s.

Les terres creissent de IX acres et demie, vaut sanz la superficie du jardin LI s. IX d.

Iceste ferme creist de XI lb. XXI d., quite au—Roi.

La ferme Dyonis de Corneville XXIIII lb.

En la couture de l'Espine Beneete, X acres, l'acre X s.

Eu Fons du Val, III acres, l'acre V s.

Es Friez III acres, l'acre III s.

---

[1] La Harangère, Eure, a. Bernay, c. Beaumesnil, cne. Thevray.

Jurée
Es Gaudieres, III acres, anvers le mont Frielouz VI acres, vaut l'acre IIII s.

Eu camp au Peletier, II acres a celi pris.

A la marniere, I acre a celi pris.

A la mote, III verges a celi pris.

La somme XXVIII acres III verg.

En la couture de Corneville[1] des haies, X acres, esqueles est acre et demie de bois.

En la petite couture, IX acres.

Mesure
En la couture ioste le maneir, VI acres.

Item, en II pieces petites qui sont sus les vaulz, IIII acres et demie.

Anvers le mont Frielous, VII acres XX perches.

fol. 151v
Le cens en deniers, IX lb. XII d.

Item, XXXVIII capons, XIIII gelines et XLV d.

Rentes
Item, V.C oeus—la moute seiche III s. par an.

Les preeres de IIII carues II foiz en l'an, vaut la iornée II s.

Et por XXVIII iornées de hommes, XIIII s.[1]

Por les herbages, VIII s.

Les rel., les dangiers par la reson de la justice.

Item, en la ferme de Fontanis sont II s. de rente.

Une masure por le deffaut du resident, IIII s.

La some XXII lb. II s.

Icele ferme desus dite est ballie a Jehan le Masuier por XXVIII lb.

Les terres creiscent de VI acres I verg. et XX perches, valent XXXVIII s., et creist iceste ferme en deniers de CXVIII s.

fol. 152
La ferme qui est apelée le fieu Harpin[1] XXV lb.

Eu camp Guillaume Aaline, II acres, l'acre II s.

En l'autre camp sus Rille, II acres, l'acre II s.

---

[1] Corneville-la-Fouquetière, Eure, a. and c. Bernay.

---

[1] *Quer. Nor.*, no. 275. The men of Corneville complain that Guillaume de Friardel, who held the farm of Corneville twenty years ago, compelled them to do a day's harvest work each year, or pay 8 or 10 d., though they had never done this before.

---

[1] There was a fief Harpin at La Herpinière, Eure, a. Bernay, c. Beaumont, cne. Beaumontel.

Jurée

Eu camp sus les prez, II acres.
Ab oppositis prator., II acres.
Joste la terre Anquetin du Buisson, V verg.
Devant la terre d'iceli Anquetin, VIII acres.
Au bosc desus, II acres et demie.
Sus le bosc Berengier, II acres et demie.
Sus le dit camp, II camp, II acres.
En somme de celi camp, V verges.
A la voie de Bernay, I acre I verg.
A la voie de Sarquigni,² III verges.
En la couture du Perier, VII verges.
Eu Val Jehan, II acres.

I acre par autre vaut X s.

fol. 152v

Mesure

En la couture de la Fontenelle, III acres, XVIII perches meinz.
Eu Canelete, I acre et demie, I verg.
En la parrelle, III verg. VI perches.
En l'erables, IIII acres X perches.
Ileques en I autre piece, III acres VIII perches.
A l'Espine, I acre VIII perches.
Au Pin, X acres III verg. I perche.
A la Herodiere, I acre et demie.
Eu camp as Boes, I acre XXIII perches.
Item, II camz ioste les prez, IIII acres et demie, XXII perches.
Eu camp sus Rille, II acres, XX perches meinz.

Rentes

Le cens et les rentes, VI lb. XI s. VI d.
Item, IIII.XX.XI capons, VI gelines, IX poucins, IIII oues.
Item, VIII.C et XL oeus, II setiers d'avoine, vaut le setier VI s.
Les preeres en marz de XXXIII hommes de lor cors, valent VII s. VI d. Les preeres de carue, se ileques soient hommes du fieu de Harpiniere,¹ doivent les feinz coedre, curer le doict.
Item, ileques le campart de XXX acres, vaut L s.
Iceli qui a le fieu a touz les anz I fou de V s. en la forest.

fol. 153

Item, le iardin et l'erbage du jardin, por tout XLV s., et contient II acres et demie et XXX perches.

---

² Serquigny, Eure, a. and c. Bernay.

---

¹ La Herpinière, Eure, a. Bernay, c. Beaumont. cne. Beaumontel.

Les prez, III acres, l'acre XXVII s.; par mesure III acres et demie.

La some XXXVIII lb. II s. VI d.

La ferme Ernaut de Torville,[1] qui est apelée Monpincon,[2] VIII lb.

En la Noete, II acres, l'acre V s.

Eu jardin Lacon, V acres, l'acre V s.

A la Huleniere, XVIII acres, l'acre III s.

Par douaire et par tout sont ileques XXXVII acres XXIIII perches par mesure.

Le cens, LI s. VIII d.

Capons, XXV, et III d.

A Pasques VII.XX oeus, III s. IIII d. de rente.

Une piece de terre ileques doit II roes de carue, qui valent XII d.

Item, sont ileques II setiers d'avoine, vaut le setier VI s., por moute.

Item, V jornées de seage, la iornée VI d.

Les preeres de carue III foiz en l'an, vaut la iornée XVIII d.

VII herces II foiz en l'an, vaut la iornée VI d.

Les rel. et les esples—le presentement de la capele.

Une dame tient la tierce partie de la terre Ernaut en doaire.

Icele chose qui est en ferme ensemble o le doaire baillie est aprez le deces a la dame a Henri Boudrot por XXII lb., sanz le patronnage, en tel maniere que de cen ne paera fors que les II parties et donra le doaire qui descendra, et met en contreplege sa terre qui vaut C s.

Et creist iceste ferme de VI lb. XIII s. IIII d.

Le molin au Hure VI lb.—Ballie a mons. Gefroi de Moiaz por VIII lb., quite au—Roy. Et rendra desore en avant II setiers d'avoine qui li sont deuz.

La terre Robert de Tevrai, XXVI s.

Sont ileques X capons, C oeus, XIX s. III d.

Les corvées se il soient ileques.

Item, ileques II residences.

Iceles choses sont ballies a Guillaume Torode por XXXV s., et creist iceste ferme de IX s.

---

[1] cf. note, fol. 78.

[2] Montpinchon, Eure, a. Bernay, c. Beaumesnil, cne. Epinay.

Les porprestures de la forest de Biau Mont.

> Entor le bosc de Biau Mont, III acres et demie.
>
> Ad Maram Putridam, IX acres et demie.

mesure

> Entre le Chemin as Porz et le maneir Henri du Pont Audemer,[1] II acres et demie et XII perches.
>
> Entre les fossez Henri et la Soudiere,[2] XI acres VIII perches.

fol. 154v

> A la Hermeroie,[1] X acres.
>
> Au Gros Quesne, I acre.
>
> En la piece devant la Soudiere, XXVII acres et demie et XX perches.
>
> > La somme LXV acres I verg.[2]

Robert le Galois prist d'ices terres devant dites I acre ioste la Soue por VI s.

Pierres de Bosc Rogier demie acre ioste la Soue por III s.

Mons. Guillaume du Bosc les fossez dehors le maneir Henri du Pont Audemer, c'est assavoir XVI acres, l'acre por VI s., sanz le bosc sus terre.

Raoul le Blanc de la Sodiere, V acres.

Robert Jehan, V acres et demie.

Estiene Soude, V acres et demie.

Alexandre Soude, IIII acres.

Jehan Hochart, III acres.

Henri Hochart, III acres.

Jehan de Hermer[oie] X acres—chascune acre por VI s.

fol. 155

Ices choses qui sont baillies des gastines de Biaumont por XVII lb. X s.

Le bosc est en la terra que mons. Guillaume du Bosc prist.

> La serganterie de Hochie, XXXVI lb. XVIII s. VII d.

> Veci la sergenterie de Leurre[1]

La ferme Ricart de Rouvres[2] anvers Cramiauville, LXX s.

La ferme Guillaume de Bosc, V s., perpetuel.

---

[1] cf. note fol. 113v.
[2] La Soudière, Eure, a. Bernay, c. and cne. Beaumont.

---

[1] La Hermeraie, Eure, a. Bernay, c. Beaumesnil, cne. le-Noyer-en-Ouche.
[2] This is another case of a virgate containing 40 perches.

---

[1] Lieurey, Eure, a. Pont-Audemer, c. Saint-Georges-du-Vièvre.
[2] Delisle, Ech., no. 589. The land of Richard de Rouvres was in the king's hand in 1236.

La ferme Rogier des Haies, II s. VI d., perpetuel.

La ferme Fortin de Leurre XVIII s., perpetuel.

La ferme Robert du Mesnil Gacon[1] XXX s.—et est en tel choses, c'est assavoir, III m[ines] d'orge, XX s. de rente, IIII capons, IIII d., XL oeus, IIII d.

Tout est en certainnes rentes, vaut la dite ferme XXXV s.

> Symon Pootel et Robert Gregoire pristrent tout por L s.
> Iceste ferme creist de XX s.

La ferme de la terre Baldoin et Nichole du Coudrai[2] XVI lb.

> En la couture du Ramier, XVI acres, l'acre XII s.
> Le pasturage de VIII acres, l'acre IIII s.

> En la couture du Ramier, XV acres.
> En fritages ioste la mote, VII acres.
> Eu camp des Gripiaus en herbage, XII acres et demie.

> Eu bosc du Ramier, V acres.

> Le cens en la feste Saint Michiel, LX s.
> Item, XL capons et XL d., XV gelines, XV d.
> Item, en oeus et en deniers, IX s.
> Avoine IIII setiers I mine, vaut le setier VI s.
> Item, III oues, vaut l'oie VIII d.

> Les preeres de III carues II foiz en l'an, por tout IX s.
> Item, IIII herces II foiz en l'an, valent IIII s.
> Le service d'une jument, III s.
> Item, les services de III vavassor[s] qui doivent tasser le fienz. porter as camz et espartir, et coedre l'estouble.
> Item, sont ileques bordiaux qui doivent tasser, et sarcler par I iornée.
> Les rel. et les justices.
> > La somme XVIII lb. VII s. VII d.

Mons. Jehan de Morchans prist iceste ferme por XXV lb.

Item, iceli prist V acres de bois, l'acre por X s., sauf le tiers et le dangier.

Item, il prist la Leiqueroie[1] por VI lb.

Icestes II fermes sont ballies a Jehan por XXXI lb., por le bosc L s.,

---

[1] Le Mesnil-Gacé, Eure, a. Bernay, c. Thiberville, cne. Heudreville-en-Lieuvin.

[2] Le Coudray, Eure, a. Pont-Audemer, c. Saint-Georges-du-Vièvre, cne. Lieurey.

[3] St.-Jean-de-la-Lequeraye (?). Eure, a. Pont-Audemer, c. Saint-Georges,du-Vièvre.

por l'encreissement des terres LXXVIII s. Some de tout XXXVII
lb. VIII s.

fol. 156v
Nos terres creiscent de LXXVIII s.

fols. 157
and 157v
are blank
Icele ferme creist de XII lb. XVIII s. sanz les bois.

La viscomté de Bernay creist de VI.C.XII lb. XIX s.
VIII d. en pures fermes.

La terre Coulliart qui forfist terre X s.—par Jehan Guiart.

fol. 158

ICHI COMMENCHE LA VISCOMTÉ D'AUGE

Veci la serganterie sus la mer

La ferme de la terre Raoul de Tilli[1] anvers Darnestal[2] IX.XX.X lb.
A la Fosse Espie Quevre, II acres et demie.
La terre souz l'Espine, I acre et demie, LXVI perches.
Le Marqueis au Fevre, I vergie.
Les monz Biauventre, XXV acres et demie, XXX perches.
En icestes XXV acres sont demie acre et VI perches de bois.
Eu camp de Chevremont, XII acres et demie, XX perches.
En la couture de Branville,[3] XVIII acres LXX perches, des-
queles III acres sont de la prevosté.
Es monz des Pommiers et en apartenences, LII acres demie.
Eu camp Fevrier XII acres III verg.
Icestes terres valent, I acre par autre X s.
La somme VI.XX.IX acres XXXI perches.[4]
Valent LXIIII lb. XII s.—de cen doivent oster XXX s.
por III acres qui sont de la prevosté de Branville.

fol. 158v
Sus le vivier, XI acres et demie, LXVI perches.
Le jardin au Fevre, XIIII perches.
Le jardin sus le molin, IIII acres III verg. V perches.

---

[1] Delisle, *Catalogue des Actes de Philippe Auguste*, no. 817A, indicates a grant of
the land which Raoul de Tilli had held at Darnétal-en-Auge, to Guillaume d'Argences.
However, the grant, dated 1204, was later cancelled.

H. F., XXIII, 635. The fiefs of Raoul de Tilli at Darnétal and Drubec were still in
the king's hands, *c.* 1220; *ibid.*, 709, they owed one knight to the king and two to the
lord.

cf. fol. 181v.

[2] Darnétal, Calvados, a. Pont-l'Evêque, c. Dozulé.

[3] Branville, *ibid.*

[4] The only way in which this total can be obtained is by assuming that the half-acre and
6 *perches* of wood and the 3 acres of the *prévôté* must be added to the area of the fields
of which they are apparently a part. When this is done, the virgate of 40 *perches* appears.

Le jardin du Hamel aus Harderiaus, II acres et demie, IIII
  perches.
Le jardin Aubret, I acre et I verg.
Eu jardin souz le vivier, XXX perches.
Eu camp aus Anceulles, III verg. XXX perches.
Eu jardin de Branville, I acre III verg. XXX perches.
Le jardin de la vielle court dedenz le bosc, L perches.
b[1] L'eschaete des Lormiers, I acre LI perches.
a[1] Le jardin au Faucons, demie acre XXVI perches.
c[1] Eu fieu Gefroy le Petit, LX perches.
Souz le mostier, demie acre, XV perches.
    Touz ices jardins valent XXX s. l'acre.
    La somme XXIII acres I verg. XXVI perches, valent
    XXXV lb. II s. VI d.[2]

fol. 159
N'estoit
pas en
ferme
N'estoit
en ferme

*Le bosc   au maneir de Darnestal, IIII.XX.XVIII
  acres XXX perches, vaut l'acre IX s. III d.
    La somme XLV lb. VIII s. V d.
Le bosc d'Angerville[1] XX acres LX perches.
En la mote demie acre, vaut l'acre X s.
    La somme X lb., VIII s., IIII d.
    Mons. Guillaume d'Angerville[2] prist le bosc et les poissons
      du vivier sus terre por LXV lb., la tierce partie a
      Pasques.
En la couture de Quevremont, I acre de pré, que l'en apele le
  Pré de l'Essart, vaut XXXII s.

fol. 159v

Le molin au ble, la moute seiche, et le vivier, CXIX lb.
La meson et le patronage, X lb.
Le molin foulerez et les foires, XVIII lb.
Le four, XL s. La prevosté, XII lb.
Les services de XV vavassories, XXII lb. X s.

---

[1] These letters perhaps mean that the entries should be rearranged.
[2] There is something very strange about this addition. Some of the land obviously has not
been included, but the return in money shows that we are still dealing with the virgate
of 40 *perches*.

---

[1] Angerville, Calvados, a. Pont-l'Evêque, c. Dozulé.
[2] Delisle, *Ech.*, nos. 793, 831. A Guillaume d'Angerville, knight, attended the Exchequer
in 1252 and 1267.
H. F., XXIII, 635, 709. An elder Guillaume d'Angerville held fiefs in the *pays d'Auge*
and was marshall of Normandy under Philip Augustus.

Les dangiers des mariages, la justice de la ville, les rel., que le fermier devant avoit, tout por X lb.

L'avoine de rente, XXXIII setiers, vaut le setier V s.

Le cens en deniers, XV lb.

Les regarz de Noel, por les pains, por les capons et por les gelines, IIII lb., II s. A la feste Saint Michiel, XVIII oues, vaut l'oie VIII d. Por oblations, IIII s.

A la feste Saint Nicholas, IIII s.

A Noel, IIII pardris, vaut la pardris III d.

Les regarz a Pasques, por les pains et por les oeus, XL s.

Les redevances et les pilages des jardins, XXII s. VI d.

La somme III.C.IIII.XX lb. XLIII s. X d.

Icele ferme est baillie a Mons. Guillaume d'Angerville por III.C.IIII. XX lb. XLIII s. X d., la terce partie a Pasques, et creist de VI.XX.VI lb. VII s.

fol. 160

La ferme de la terre qui fu Robert d'Angerville[1] VII.XX lb.

Es chans de la Tellioe et de Formieres, X acres, par mesure, XXIX acres et XX perches, vaut l'acre V s.

Sus le bosc d'Angerville, VIII acres, par mesure IX acres I verg. et demie, vaut l'acre IIII s.

Jurée

A la Burgaudiere, II acres I verg., par mesure I acre et demie et demie verg., por tout IX s.

Sus le clos Robert Flamingi, III verg., par mesure demie acre et demie verg., vaut por tout III s.

A Caudemuche,[2] XX acres, par mesure XXII acres III verg., l'acre IIII s.

Item, le bosc I acre XXXIIII perches.

fol. 160v

Les prez V acres; par mesure IIII acres LIIII perches; vaut l'acre XX s.

Les
prez
et les
iardins

*I iardin a la Burgaudiere, I verg., X s.

I autre jardin, qui est apelé le iardin a l'Archid[iacre], VII s.

---

[1] Angerville, Calvados, a. Pont-l'Evêque, c. Dozulé.

H. F., XXIII, 635. A certain Robert Teillart held two knight's fees of Robert Bertran, at St. Etienne-la-Thillaye, Beaumont, Branville, Bloville, and Angerville, which escheated to the king at the time of the conquest. He is probably the Robert d'Angerville of our text, since the holdings of Robert d'Angerville mentioned here and on fols. 168v. *ff.* coincide with Robert Teillart's lands, and the place-name "Teilliart" occurs repeatedly in the description of these holdings (fols. 160v, 168v, 169, 170, 171, 175).

[2] Caudemuche, Calvados, a. Pont l'Evêque, c. Dozulé, cne. Cresseveuille.

*

Le jardin de la Plante, XXV perches, III s.
Le jardin Telliart,[1] II acres; par mesure VII verg., XXII perches; por tot XL s.

*

Eu Clos Viel, demie acre, X s.

N'estoit pas en ferme

En bosc II acres, par mesure III acres XXXIII perches meinz, l'acre XX s.

Item XXXII oues, capons CV et CV d., gelines CV et CV d.
II.M oeus et o chascun X oeus I d.
Item, L anguilles, valent XX s.

*

ʻ Item XVIII askes de sel, chascun IX d.
Le cens en deniers, XXIIII lb.
Les rel. et la justice, les preeres de carues, XL s.

fol. 161

Les II parties du molin de Villequier, XX lb. por—le Roy.
Le molin de Caudemuche, XX lb., de cen est deue la diesme.

Rentes

Le molin de la porte et du vivier o la moute seiche, XX lb.
Le molin foulerez o le prael, VII lb.

*

Avoine V moez, VII setiers, vaut le setier V s.
Item, VI cartiers de forment, XXXV s.
Robert le Fevre, I mine de feves, VI s.
       Toutes ices desus dites valent VII.XX.XI lb. IX s. VI d.

Mons. Robert le Bouteillier prist iceste ferme toute, chascune acre por XII d. outre l'estimatiom. Item chascune [*sic*] por X d. Item chascun setier d'avoine por VI s. Item, chascun hasket de sel por IX d.

fol. 161v

Anvers Waseville devant la meson au Fricher, I acre et demie de terre, por tout L s.
Les prez, por tout LX s.
Le cens, XVI s.
Item, II capons, XVIII gelines, et XIX d.
Item, VI.XX.X oeus et o X oeus I d.
Item, IIII setiers d'avoine, vaut le setier VI s.
Item, XIIII asques de sel, l'asquet vaut IX d.

Waseville

Les preeres des herces, por tout XXV s.

---

[1] *cf.* note 1, fol. 160.

Les foires du Val d'Antre[1] por la partie—le Roy, LX s.
Le molin ileques, XI lb.
La some VI.XX.IX lb. XVII s. VI d.[2]
Ices choses qui sont en ceste ferme sont ballies a Ricart de Sillye, prestre, por XXXIII lb.[2]
Et creist de XLIIII lb. IX s., VI d.[2] et nequedent ele est mesurée.

fol. 162

La terre qui fu a la dame de Darnestal a Criqueville[1] XL lb.
    Anvers Bruetot, III verg., valent por tout XII s.

Jurée

    Anvers Criqueville, I acre et demie, por tout XXX s.
    Les fruiz des arbres d'icele terre, X s.
    Une vergie en jardin, por tout II s.

Les prez

    Eu pré de Losier, I acre, XXIIII s.—Ballie est a Pierres de Balliet, prestre, por XXVIII s.
    En Lonc Pré, demie acre, XII s.
    Au seillion Sommier, demie acre, XII s.
    Eu pré de Vaudos, III verges, por tout XXIIII s.
    Eu pré de la Ruelle, demie acre XX s.—Ballie a Jehan Boitin por XX s., et a letres et mist en contreplege I acre de terre eu Coupier.
    Eu pré Escarbot, III verges, por tout XXIIII s.
    Devant Herouville, demie acre, XVI s.
    Devant la meson Ansel le Prevost,[2] demie acre, XVI s.
    Es courtes pierces, XXX perches, por tout VI s.
    Anvers Briecort, I acre de pré, XXIIII s.

fol. 162v

    Es prez des Carrieres, I acre, XX s.
    Eu pré Aloe, III verges, por tout XVIII s.

les prez

    Eu pré Estiene le Gay, I acre, XXIIII s.
    Es prez des Hermeriaus, I verge, VI s.
    Eu pré du molin, XXX perches, por tout V s.
    En la rosiere de Bruetot, V verges de ros, por tout XX s.

---

[1] Valley of the river Ancre, a tributary of the Dive which flows past Angerville.

[2] The meaning of these figures is far from clear, but the first sum seems to be the value of the farm if the value of Waseville be subtracted from the total given on fol. 161. Then, if the value at which Waseville is farmed be added to this total, you get the increase in value given in the last figure.

---

[1] Cricqueville-en-Auge, Calvados, a. Pont l'Evêque, c. Dozulé.

[2] This house is mentioned in *Cart. Nor.*, no. 529 (A.D. 1255).

Mesure

Le molin de Criqueville et la moute seiche ou le—Roy a la
metie, por sa partie VIII lb. quite au—Roi.

*II services   et un demie, por tout LX s.

Por demie service XV s.

Rentes
fol. 163

Por le cens et por I esprevier, CXII s., VI d.

Ricart de Aseville, VI d. de cens.

Item VIII capons, XXXIIII gelines et XXXIX d.

Item II.C.XL oeus, et o X oeus I d.

Item X oues, vaut l'oie VIII d.

Les preeres de II carues et d'erces, por tout VI s.

Rentes

Por III quartiers de feves, VI s.—I setier d'avoine, V s.

Item II quaretées de ros et II de fein, por tout XX s.

Item, sont ileques V bordiers qui queurent l'aioue au molin et
doivent curer le bief.

Item, sont ileques VII bordages qui doivent seer le ros et auner,
lier, fener, coedre les pommes, tribler, por tout XIIII s. IX d.

Item, sont ileques III bordiers qui doivent aler a Caen.

Item, sont ileques les vavassors qui doivent porter le merrien du
molin jusques a l'aioue et servir le rapareilloor du molin et
doivent amener la moele au molin.

Les Rel. et les justices.

La some XXXVII lb., XVIII d.

fol. 163v

La ferme de la terre Guillaume Crassi, Guy de Dive,[1] et la quarte
part du molin de Bueseval[2] VIII.XX.X lb.

Sus les monz de Houlegate,[3] XIII acres et demie, l'acre VI s.

Les coutures ileques contiennent VI acres, l'acre VIII s.

Eu terreor de Rougemont, III acres et demie, l'acre VI s.

La Tuilliere, V acres, l'acre VI s.

En la couture de Roncemont, III acres, l'acre VI s.

Aus Hoquetes sus la mer, III acres a celi pris.

Eu grant pré, I acre et demie a celi pris.

Es Dehez, II acres et demie, l'acre IIII s.

---

[1] *Quer. Nor.*, no. 18, mentions the confiscation of this part of the lands of Guillaume
le Gras. *cf.* fol. 74.

Quer. Nor., no. 7. Guy de Dive was castellan of Chinon, and forfeited his lands for
adhering to John.

Cart. Nor., no. 996. Portions of this farm were leased to the monastery of St. Etienne
de Caen for 170 l. in 1282.

[2] Beuzeval, Calvados, a. Pont L'Evêque, c. Dozulé.

[3] Butte de Houlgate, *ibid.*

Joste Saint Aubin, demie acre, V s.

Joste la Holegate,[4] IIII acres, l'acre VIII s.

Eu camp de la Cortereuse, demie acre II s.

Sus le molin, V verges, l'acre VI s.

Item, ileques I vergee, XVIII d.

En la Rouge Terre, I vergie et demie, XVIII d.

Jurée

Es Faudeiz, demie acre, IIII s.

En la Cortereuse, III verg., IIII s.

fol. 164

Es Faudeis eu camp Sommier, VII verg., l'acre V s.

Eu camp de Lalierai, demie acre, II s. VI d.

Eu Valet, I vergie et demie, XXII d.

En la Vinge des Asnes, I acre et demie, VI s. por tout.

A la Hasidiere, demie acre, II s.

A Monchaulitel, V verges, por tout VII s. VI d.

Item, ileques demie acre a celi pris.

A la Mare de la Fonteinne, demie acre, III s.

Es cours seillons, I verg. et demie, II s.

A la Hoguete, I verg., XII d.

Es Cossetes, I acre, XII s.

b[1] Eu val, I verg. et demie, por tout XVIII d.

Ileques demie acre, II s.

Eu camp Raoul Davy,[2] I acre, VI s.

Ricart Symon, demie acre, III s.

Eu val, XXX perches, XII d.

Jurée

Eu camp Noel, III verg., IIII s. VI d.

Item ileques I vergee, XVIII d.

c[1] Es noires terres, I acre, XII s.

a[1] Es Quevesches, I acre, XIII s.

fol. 164v

Item, es Noires Terres, demie acre, III s.

Ileques I acre, XII s.

Aus Quevesches, demie acre, IIII s.

Eu camp Rad. Davy, I acre, XIIII s.

Eu camp que l'en apele les Prez, VII acres et demie, l'acre XII
s.—des queles III verg. sont du fieu de Dives.

---

[4] Houlgate, ibid.

[1] cf. fol. 158v.

[2] Quer. Nor., no. 18. Osana, daughter of Raoul Davy of Beuzeval, complains that
Guillaume le Gras took six acres of land at Beuzeval from her father for failure to pay
dues, and that this land was seized with the rest of Guillaume's holdings by Philip Augustus.
cf. fol. 164v.

Item, en iceli camp V verges, por tout XV s.

En la crote, I acre et demie, X perches, l'acre XII s.—ballie a Garin d'Auge por XXIIII s. La terre creist, vaut VIII d.

A la voie de Wateville, III verg., por tout VI s.

Jurée Eu camp Agu, XXX perches, por tout XII d.

En la Terre Roge, III verg., por tout IIII s. VI d.

Eu camp qui est apelé Cortirat, III verg., por tot IIII s. VI d.

Souz Touracle, I acre et demie, por tout VII s. VI d.

En Maret, III verg., por tout III s. IX d.

En la couture au Gras, VII verg., por tout XIIII s.

En I jardin, I acre et demie, IIII perches, por tout XXV s.—Ballie a Andreu de Robraque por XL s. La terre creist et vaut VIII d.

Eu chief du jardin, IX perches, XVIII d.

A la meson Davy, demie acre, IIII s.

fol. 165 A Meseres, demie acre, II s.

A Bapaumes, demie acre, II s.

A Caufosse, III verg., III s.

La terre souz Caufosse, demie acre, III s.

Eu camp au XXX perches I verg. et demie, XXVII d.

A la meson Hue Lebouteillier, I verg. et demie, XXVII d.

Eu camp Daguichon, III verg., III s.

Ileques, V verg., V s.

Es mortes terres, III verg., IIII s. VI d.

Eu camp Eurot, III verg., XII s.

Ileques vergie et demie, IIII s. VI d.

Eu camp de la Miteinne, demie acre, VIII s.

Es mortes terres, XXX perches, XVIII d.

Jurée Eu camp de la Fortillie, verge et demie, XXVII d.

Anvers la haie, demie acre, II s.

Ileques verge et demie, XVIII d.

Anvers Mortefonteinne, demie acre, II s. VI d.

Es haies, vergie et demie, XXII d.

Eu camp Motiau, III verg., IIII s. VI d.

fol. 165v Les Droerus, V verges, l'acre V s.

Ileques le petit iardin et les fruiz, V s.

En la rosiere, demie vergie, III s.

Anvers Caumondel, demie acre, III s.

A la Fossete, demie acre, XII d.

En l'autre piece, demie acre, II s.

Robert Mutel, II acres, por tout VIII s.

Au Quesneu, V vergîes, V s.

Au Caumont,[1] V verg., V s.

Ileques verge et demie, XXII d.

Item, ileques verge et demie, XVIII d.

Jurée Anvers Mie Voie, demie acre, II s.

Ileques III verg., III s.

A la Voie de la Croiz, III verg., III s.

A la Maeinne Voie, III verg., III s.

Sus le fes de Chaumont,[1] III verg., III s. VI d.

Ileques demie acre, II s.

A la Hoguete, III verg., IIII s. VI d.

Aus Buaus de Houlegate, III verg., III s.

fol. 166 La somme de toutes les terres qui sont en la ferme devant dite semonte C.V acres III verg. IX perches, selonc cen que il ont esté jurées—et selonc la mesure CX acres et LX perches.

> Et sont toutes ices terres desus dites ballies ensemble o les preeres deues as dites terres et o une graverie qui vaut III s. a Ricart le Prevost, a Ricart Mouton, Osber Bacheler, a Guillaume Osber, a Gascon Lasne, a Symon de la Pierre, a Ricart Canquere,[1] a Guillaume Beicu, a Robert Malclerc, a Robert de la Pierre,[2] a Ricart Anquetil. Por XLVIII lb., chascon por tout, c'est assavoir par mesure de CVII acres.
>
> Et creiscent les terres et vaut XXXVIII s. X d.

fol. 166v Le Pré au Cheval, I verge, V s.

Le molin de Beuseval[1] et la moute seiche, XVII lb.—Ballie a Richart le Prevost et a Guillaume Osber por XIX lb.

Item, l'autre molin euquel le—Roy a la quarte partie, LX s. Ballie a Mons. Guillaume de la Pierre[2] por IIII lb.

---

[1] Caumont, Calvados, a. Pont-l'Evêque, c. Dozulé, cne. Beuzeval.

[1] Or "Tanquere"; the letter is not clear.

[2] *Quer. Nor.*, no. 8. A Robert "de Petra" held at Beuzeval, which is in this district.

[1] Beuzeval, Calvados, a. Pont-l'Evêque, c. Dozulé.

[2] *Quer. Nor.*, no. 2. "Willelmus de Petra, presbyter" of Beuzeval, complains that he was forced by the Exchequer in 1242 to repair this mill, though the king did not pay his share of the expenses.

Item, XLVIII sommes de sel et II haquez, vaut la somme III s.

Item, anvers Dive,[3] VIII setiers d'avoine.

Le cens en deniers, XXXIII s.

Et de l'autre partie, XV lb. IIII s. VI d.

Rentes

Capons, VI.XX, et XIX gelines; item, II.C.I geline.

II.M oeus, IIII.C.XXXIII.

Item, III oues, I aignel.

Item, VI vavassories, vaut la vavassorie V s.

Item, XV setiers et I mine de forment, vaut le setier XV s.

Item, IIII.C.LXIII pains.

Le pré Gervaise, V verges, ne sont pas estimées.

fol. 167

       Anvers Dives eu terroor de Chaumont, XXX acres es lieus par dedenz.

Eu Petit Pré, IX verges, vaut l'acre XXVIII s.

Eu camp de la Bercherie, V verg., l'acre XVI s.

Eu camp du Moncel, V acres, vaut l'acre XII s.

Eu camp des Petites Vignes, II acres et demie, vaut l'acre VI s.

Es Planes, demie acre, vaut l'acre II s.

En la Crote, demie vergie, XII d.

Eu pré Bonel, I verge, II s.

Raoul le Monnier, I verg., XIIII s.

Jurée

Eu camp Dri, I acre, XVI s.

Eu camp des Vaulz, I verg., XVIII d.

Eu mont du Pommier, I verg., II s.

Au Bracet, demie vergie, XII d.

Sus le Clos as Malades, IIII acres, l'acre XII s.

Item, ileques XXVI acres, vaut l'acre VI s.—Richart le Prevost prist en la longue couture V acres, l'acre por VII s.

Une verge de caneviere, II s.

fol. 167v
N'est pas
en ferme

Rogier le Fevre, I verg. de cortillage, IX s.

Es preaulz, X perches de pré, por tout XVIII d.

Les rentes en deniers, XV lb. XVII s. XI d.

Item, XXXIIII oues, II setiers de forment.

Avoine II muiz V setiers I quartier.

Anvers Garengues[1] la metie de I molin, ballie por I mui de ble, duquel le setier vaut VIII s.

---

[3] Dive, Calvados, a. Pont-l-Evêque, c. Dozulé.

[1] Grangues, Calvados, a. Pont-l'Evêque, c. Dozulé.

Le four, por tout XXV s.

Les preeres de XV carues et d'erces, por tout XXXV s.

Anvers Saint Martin de Viliers,[2] XXXV s. VII d.

Item, XXI capons, et X gelines.

Item, XII.X oeus; item, V quartiers d'avoine, III mines de

ble de/ mouture, LI pain.

Le services par aoue, XV s.

La somme VIII.XX lb. C.X s.

Iceste ferme creist selonc baillie et a ballier de XXII lb.
XVII s. III d.

La ferme Robert d'Angerville a la Teillaie, VII.XX lb.

Es closages, VIII acres, por tout C s.; par m[esure] X acres
L perches.

La cousture Remi, VI acres, I verg. meinz, vaut l'acre V s.

Eu camp Anquetin, VI acres a celi pris; par m[esure] V acres
et demie.

La terre Ricart Gervaise, I acre, V s.; tout autant par m[esure]
—Ballie a Ricart Bruhart por VIII s.[1]

Es marleis, V verg., tout autant, por tout VII s.

Eu jardin au seignor, I acre, VIII s.

Le fruict vaut XX s.

Es parreaulz Telliart, IIII acres et demie, vaut l'acre IIII s.;
par mesure IIII acres III verges.

Eu camp Heudig[er], IIII acres; par m[esure] III acres III
verg. X perches; por tot. XLIX s.—Ballies a Henri le
Bouvier por L s. Iceli acompaigna Jehan du Lugan.

Eu camp Telliart anvers Saint Estiene,[2] III acres, por tout
XVIII s.—Ballies a Henri et a Ricart du Lugan por XXX s.

L'erbage de IIII acres de bois de la Teillaie, por tot. L s.

Les fruiz III s.—et est apelé l'autre bosc de Saint Vincent.

La su[mme] sanz le bosc et sanz I acre de jardin par
m[esure] XXXV acres et demie, XXVI perches.

Les prez des seignories, por tout IX lb.[1]

---

[2] Villers-sur-Mer, Calvados, a. Pont-l'Evêque, c. Dozulé. The parish church was St.
Martin's.

---

[1] Apparently inserted after the page had been written.

[2] St. Etienne-la-Thillaye, Calvados, a. and c. Pont l'Evêque. cf. notes on fols. 160 and
172.

---

[1] cf. notes on fols. 160 and 172.

Par mesure X acres III verg.

A la Jonchere, V verg., por tout XII s.

prez Eu Lonc Boel, I acre, XVI s.

Eu Roont Pré, V verg., l'acre XVI s.

A la Pescherie, III acres a celi pris, par m[esure] III acres et XX perches.

Es Auneiz, II acres a celi pris.

En la Rosiere, XI acres I verg., vaut l'acre X s.

Mesure Par mesure XXIX acres I verg. et XX perches de pré.

Les preeres de fener et d'auner.

Le danger de fauquier—c'est assavoir que nul ne poet fauquier de ci la que les prez le—Roy soient fauquiez.

Rentes Le molin Telliart[1] o la moute seiche et I verg. de pré, por tout XVI lb.—Item, LXIII oues, vaut l'oie VIII d.

fol. 169v Item, VI pardriz, vaut la pardriz II d.

Item, XVI fers a cheval o les clouz.

Item, II vavassories, chascune doit I mieu d'avoine.

Item, l'autre qui doit demie mui d'avoine, et vaut le mui LX s.

La livrée des pasturages des prez, por tout VII lb.

Le pracage, c'est assavoir iceli qui garde les prez, C.V s.

Le fieu de Biaumont.[1]

Anvers Ardanne,[2] VII acres et demie, por tot XLV s.; par mesure VIII acres.

Jurée En la couture de la Fontainne, IX acres, vaut l'acre VIII s.; par mesure XI acres et demie, XVI perches.

Eu camp d'entre les II bois, II acres, por tot XXX s.; par mesure V acres I vergie.

Eu camp souz l'auney et eu clos desus, III acres, por tout XXX s.; par m[esure] V acres, I verg.

fol. 170 Eu camp au Pleidoor, I acre et demie, l'acre VIII s.; eu Mont au Pleidoor I acre, VII s. VI d.; par mesure III acres I vergie VI perches.

En la couture Telliart souz Biaumont, X acres, por tot L s.;

---

[1] Beaumont-en-Auge, Calvados, a. and c. Pont-l'Evêque. *cf.* note, fol. 172.

[2] *Quer. Nor.*, no. 26. Complaint that the land of "Ardena" was seized by the lord of Angerville six years before the conquest, because the plaintiff's father failed to pay the rent. The king now holds it as a result of the confiscation of the lands of the lord of Angerville. *cf.* note on fol. 160.

Jurée

par mesure XI acres I verg.—Ballies a Henri de Biaumont por LXVII s. X d.—et creist la terre.

L'erbage d'un jardin continant I acre et demie,[1] XX s. por tot, tout autant par mesure.

Le fruict ileques XX s.

N'est en ferme

Item, XXXIII acres de bois—ne sont pas en ferme ne ballies.

Le fruict d'iceli bois, vaut XXX s.

Le molin et la moute seiche, o I setier d'orge, XXX lb.[1]

fol. 170v

Es plesseiz, en la saucee, et en l'auney, XVI acres de bois sanz le superficie, eu bosc Brunel, II acres par mesure; eu bosc de la Garende, III acres et demie—Ballies au priour de Biaumont, l'acre por IX s.[1]

Rentes

Avoine ileques, II moez VII setiers.[2]

Le cens de la Teillee et de Biaumont, IIII lb. XI s. VIII d.[2]

Por capons, por gelines, et por oblations a Pasques.

Por gelines, por oeus et por deniers, LXIX s.[2]

A la feste Saint Jehan en deniers, C s.[2]

Por une vavassorie a la feste Saint Michiel, VII lb. XIII s. IIII d.

fol. 171

Le fieu au Pele, sus le molin Teilliart I acre et demie, por tout VI s.

Item, ileques V verg., por tout IX s., et por l'acre demie VIII s.

Item, ileques II acres et demie, XXV s.; par mesure VIII acres III verg.

Anvers le Buisson, I acre, tout autant par mesure. Lau est le bosc, n'estoit en ferme—le superficies sus terre valent XXXV s.

Es prez de la Loge, V verg., tout autant par mesure, por tout XX s.

Ballie a Robert le Bouteillier, chevalier, por VII lb., et crut la terre et l'avoit pris por VI lb.

Le fieu de Blanville,[1] es clos Telliart II acres, por tout XII s.

L'erbage de II acres de bosc, nequedent le bosc est comté o les

---

[1] cf. note on fol. 172.

---

[1] Cart. Nor., no. 641. Twenty-four and one-half acres of woodland ". . . in plesseis et in bosco Burell', in bosco de la Garende et in bosco Londe . . ." were farmed to the priory of Beaumont in 1260.

[2] cf. note on fol. 172.

---

[1] Branville, Calvados, a. Pont-l'Evêque, c. Dozulé. cf. notes on fols. 160 and 172.

Jurée

terres, por tout XXX s. Le superficie du bois est en la main du forestier, par mesure VIII acres, X perches.

Eu camp Merdeuz, I acre et demie, por tout VIII s.

Hue Aubert, demie acre II s. Rad. Goncelin, I verg., XII d.

Une [*sic*] et demie de pré, par mesure III acres, por tout XXXV s.

La somme jurées LX acres III verg., sanz H. de Biaumont et Robert le Bouteillier, et sanz le jardin.

fol. 171v

III vavassories, por tout XXIIII s.[1]

Le cens en deniers, C s.

Item, VII sommes de sel, et le quart d'une somme, vaut la somme III s.

Rentes

Item, XL capons et XL d. Item, XL gelines et XL d.

Item, III.C oeus, et o X oeus I d.

Avoine, III setiers VI boiss., vaut le setier V s.

Les preeres de carue, por tout X s.

Item, le patronage d'une chapele vaillant XXV lb.

N'estoient pas en ferme

Item, III acres de bois, tout autant par mesure, qui est apelé la Lande[1] souz Biaumont, sanz le superficie. L'en dit que deriere le maneir est une piece de terre que nos n'avons pas en escris.

La somme VIII.XX.XV lb. VIII s., II d.

Ballies sont sanz le superficie—au priour de Biaumont, l'acre por XII s.[2]

Iceste somme creist de LV lb. XVI s.—Memoire de la capelle.

fol. 172

Item, les choses qui sont en la ferme desus dite tant ballies que a ballier sont ballies—au priour de Biaumont en Auge, ensemble o le patronage, sanz XXXIII acres de bosc qui n'estoient pas de ferme, por IX.XX.X lb. par an; en tel maniere que ces choses qui estoient anciez ballies remaindront ballies aussi comme devant—et seront tenues du—prior, mes sont ostées de sa somme IX lb. por Robert le Boutellier et por Henri de Biaumont. Item, iceli priour prist le fonz de IIII acres de bois lau ou il avoit l'erbage por IIII lb., sanz le superficie qui est ballie par ledit Guiart de Selves.[1]

---

[1] *cf. Cart. Nor.*, no. 641, and notes 1, fols. 170v, 172.
[2] This probably refers to the wood mentioned four lines above.

---

[1] This is obviously the farm given in *Cart. Nor.*, no. 641. If certain items from fol. 168v are included as part of the prior's holding, the correspondence is almost perfect.

La somme selonc la mesure, comte le bosc, II.C lb. LIIII
s., VI d., sanz Robert de Biaumont et Henri le But.—

fol. 172v

La ferme Guillaume Espec anvers le Quesnoy,[1] Guillaume Boutemont[2]
anvers Wanville,[3] Guillaume Triten et Robert de Saint Estiene que
l'en apele la terre au Nouricon—LVIII lb.

En la grant couture de Saint Estiene, III acres, vaut l'acre X s.

Eu camp au Heulebec, I verg., V s.

Devant la meson au prestre, demie acre, VIII s.

Jurée

Eu camp du jardin le—Roy, I acre, XII s.

Devant la meson Ricart Jehan, III verg., por tout XII s.

Joste les haies, III verg., por tout X s.

Joste la mare Fouquet, I acre, VI s.

Joste le molin foulerez, demie acre, III s.

Mesure

Par mesure VII acres et demie de terre.

Icestes choses lesqueles sont en la partie d'iceste ferme,
laquele partie est apelée le fieu le Norrecon o le jardin

". . . nos priori et conventui de Bellomonte in Algia ad firmam perpetuam concessimus,
pro 200 l. et 54 s. et 6 d. tur. . . . in firma Roberti de Angervilla a la Telloie 35 acras
et dimidiam et 26 perticas terre arabilis; quoddam jardinum continens unam acram; 10
acras et 3 virgatas bosci qui vocatur Boscus Sancti Vincentii; 29 acras, unam virgam et
20 perticas pratorum, cum redeventiis eorumdem; molendinum Telliart cum molta sicca,
et una virgata prati contigua molendino; item 63 anseres de redditu, 16 ferra ad equum
cum clavis, duos vavassores, quorum quilibet debet unum modium avene de redditu; item
unum vavassorem qui debet dimidium modium avene; livreiam pasturagii pratorum et
pratagium. Item, in feodi Bellimontis, 28 acras terre arabilis; quoddam jardinum continens
unam acram et dimidium; quoddam molendinum, cum molta sicca; unum sextarium ordei
de redditu; duos modios et 7 sextaria avene de redditu; censum apud la Teilloie, et apud
Bellum montem 4 l. 11s. 8 d.; pro caponibus, gallinis, oblacionibus, ovis et denariis ad
Pascha, 69 s.; ad festum Sancti Johannis in denariis, 100 s., quos debet quidam vavassor;
ad festum Sancti Michaelis 7 l. 13 s. 4 d. censuales. Item, in feodo de Blanvilla 8 acras
et 10 perticas terre arabilis, 3 acras pratorum; 3 vavassores et 100 s. censuales; 7 summas
et quartem partem unius summe salis; 40 capones, 40 d.; 40 gallinas et 40 d.; 300 ova, cum
singulis decem ovis unum denarium; 3 sexteria et 6 boissellos avene redditus; precarias
carrucarum; patronatum capelle de Tylleia. . . ." 1260, February.

¹ Le Quesnay, Calvados, a. Pont-l'Evêque, c. Dozulé, cne. Glanville.

H. F., XXIII, 635, 709. Guillaume Espec had held one knight's fee of R. Bertran at
"Kesnoi Espec" which was confiscated by Philip Augustus.

² *Cart. Nor.*, no. 998. "Universis presentes litteras inspecturis et audituris Guillermus
Harenc et Hugo Heudeer, salutem. Notum facimus quod nos a domino rege ad firmam
perpetuam recepimus in firma Guillelmi et Johannis Espec et Guillelmi de Botemont 117
acras et 65 perticas terre, 4 acras bosci cum fundo sine tercio et dangerio, 5 acras prati,
quoddam molendinum ibidem cum molta sicca, 8 l. 6 s. 10 d. annui census, 70 capones,
30 gallinas et cum caponibus et gallinis 8 s. 2 d.; 905 ova et cum ovis 7 s. 5 d., 12
anseres, 11 sestaria et unam minam avene, 5 s. annui redditus pro decima feodi de
Quesneio . . . pro 70 l. tur." 1282.

³ Is this an error for "Glanville"? *cf.* fol. 173.

—le Roy et la Haie au Norricon—ballies sont a
　　Robert de Biaumont, chevalier,[4] por XV lb., XII d.
　Item a iceli la superficie de la haie por L s.

Anvers la Haie au Norricon, I acre et demie de bois.
Eu clos au Fevre, V verges, por tout XXV s.
Souz Saint Cloout, I acre, XVI s.

Avoine de rente, II setiers, I mine, et I mine de forment qui
　　vaut VIII s. Une livre de poivre II s.
Les rentes en deniers, LVIII s. et IX d.
Capons XXIIII. Gelines VII.
Item, XIII.XX.X oeus, pains XXVII, et VIII fers a cheval.
　Ballies a iceli Robert sicomme devant est dit.

Anvers le Quesney Espec, IIII.XX acres de terre, desqueles
　　XL acres de la meillor entre Saint Pierre Angis[1] et Glan-
　　ville,[2] vaut l'acre X s.
Vers le chemin de Biaumont, XL acres, vaut l'acre VI s.

En la praerie de Ronceville,[3] es prez Roons, V acres, por tout
　　IIII lb. XV s.
L'erbage de VIII acres, por tout L s.
L'eschaete de la terre a la fille Robert le Clerc du Mont Ainsi,
　　c'est assavoir por XIII acres, por tout LXVI s.

Le jardin—le Roy, I verg. et demie, por l'erbage VI s.
Le fruict II s.
Le jardin Hue, por l'erbage XX s.
Le jardin Roset, por tout XII s.
Por l'erbage de l'autre masure, laquele Rogier Toquet tient,
　　VI s.
L'erbage de la court au seignor, XII s.
Jehan Brunel, I piece de terre a Grantville, XIIII s.
　　Colin Espec prist les devant dites IIII.XX acres et XIII
　　acres de la fille Rogier le Clerc, l'acre por IX s. VI d.

---

[4] *Quer. Nor.*, no. 8. A Robert de Beaumont, knight, held the farm of Beuzeval, in this region, *c.* 1239. He may possibly be the same as the Robert mentioned above, since he was made a knight only after 1228 (*Quer. Nor.*, no. 19). In view of his business interests it is worth noting that he was accused of being of bourgeois origin, and that he paid a heavy fine for being knighted without the king's permission.

[1] St. Pierre-Azif, Calvados, a. Pont-l'Evêque, c. Dozulé.
[2] Glanville, Calvados, a. Pont-l'Evêque, c. Dozulê.
[3] Roncheville, Calvados, a. and c. Pont-l-Evêque, cne. Saint-Martin.

Item, l'erbage de VIII acres de terre, le jardin—le Roy, le jardin Hue, et le jardin Rosez a ce pris, et touz l'erbages a celi pris. Les prez et le molin por XXII lb.

Item, III pieces de bois qui n'estoient pas en ferme et les autres seignories du Quesney, d'Auriville, et de la Herodoie a ce pris.

Item, les services de la ferme por X s., et les autres rentes la value a la value les rentes delessa, et apres ces choses il les prist et vaut por tout IIII.XX.XV lb. XIX s.

Et issi creist de LI lb. XIII s.

fol. 174

Nous feismes a Colin Espec une somme de IIII.XX.XIII lb. XIIII s. VI d. d'iceste ferme, et nous donna a entendre que en icele ferme estoient tant solement VI.XX acres par toutes choses, tant en bosc que en autres choses, et cen fu eu castel du Pont Audemer, au jor de mercredi aprez les octaves de Pasques en l'an M.II.C.LX.—Item, sera mesurée.—

Avoine de rente, XI setiers et I mine, vaut le setier VI s.

Le molin de la Planque, XIIII lb.

Rentes

Le cens en deniers, VI lb. II s. IIII d.

Les preeres des carues et d'erces, VII s. VI d.

Capons LXVI, et LXII d. Gelines XXVI et XXI d.

Por oeus et por deniers, XIII s. IIII d.

Item XVI oues, vaut l'oie IX d.

Pains, IIII.XX.VII, le pain I d.

Ballies sicomme desus est dite a Colin Espec.

fol. 174v

La terre du Mesnil, VIII acres et demie, XI perches.

En la paroisse de Vaqueville, III acres et V perches de terre qui fu Pierres Hoel, por tout XVI s.—Ballie a Guiart du Pont l'Evesque por XVIII s.

Eu fieu de Boutemont por pains, por capons, et por deniers, XII s.

N'est pas en ferme

Au Quesney[1] sus la Longue Alne, III acres de bois.

Joste le chemin en II hayes, demie acre.

Eu bosc a la Pastee, I acre—Ballie a Colin Espec sicomme desus est dit.

Item, au Quesnoy, I jardin continant III acres, por tout XXX s.

[1] Le Quesnay, near Glanville.

Anvers Auriville, I vergee de terre, vaut VII s.

Anvers la Herodoie, I acre et demie, vaut IX s.

Item, sont ileques XII bordiers qui doivent por lor masures I
jornée de fener et l'autre de faire seer, et ne son pas feoaulz.

La somme IIII.XX.IIII lb. X s. IX d.

Ballie a Colin Espec toutes ices devant dites choses
sicomme desus est dit.

fol. 175

La ferme du molin Telliart et de Bloville,[1] LIIII lb.

La ferme Hue de Aub[er]teinville, XV lb.

Robert le Fornier, II acres, por tout VIII s.

Item, iceli II autres acres a celi pris.

Item,   I acre, tout autant par m[esure], a celi pris—
Ricart Lieve Haste la prist por IX s.

Robin le Fornier, demie acre, IIII s.

Guillaume Coispel demie acre par mesure, IIII s.—Ballie a

Jurée

     iceli por VI s.—Hebert Vassart IIII perches de maresc, II s.

Iceli Hebert prist et I acre et demie ileques prez de li por
XXVI s.

Rogier Flori, I acre, IIII s.

Hebert Wassart, I acre et demie, par mesure VII verg., XVI s.
    —Iceli la prist sicomme desus est dit.

Anvers Bloville,[1] IIII acres de pré, por tout IIII lb. X s.

fol. 175v

Le molin, et les services de curer le doict, o la moute seiche,
XXI lb.

Item, III vavassories, por chascun XV s., et por demie VII s.
VI d.

II bordiers, qui doivent le fiens porter et espartir, IIII s.

Item, les autres XI doivent fener et coedre.

Avoine ileques VII setiers, et I mine, vaut le setier VI s.

Item, VII sommes de sel, XXI s.

Les preeres des carues et des herces, por tout XII s.

Le cens ileques, VII lb.

Rentes

Item, XVIII capons et XVIII d.

Gelines XXXVII, et XXXVII d.

Item, IIII.C oeus et XL d.

---

[1] Blonville-sur-Mer, Calvados, a. Pont-l'Evêque, c. Dozulé. This mill is probably part
of the fief of Robert Telliart, who held land at Blonville, which escheated to the king at
the time of the conquest, *H. F.,* XXIII, 635. *cf.* fol. 160.

Ne sont
pas en
ferme

Item, III acres de terre qui furent au—comte qui fu pendu, por
tout XX s.

Raoul Tolemer prist ensemble o V acres de terres
lesqueles il tenoit dedenz, tout por XXX lb.

fol. 176

Anvers Bernoville,[1] I acre de terre, vaut VII s. VI d.

Item, ileques demie acre de pré, vaut XV s.

Item, III sommes de sel, et III asquez, por tout XI s., III d.[2]

Item, VIII capons et VIII d. VIII gelines, VIII d.

Item, VIII.XX et XVI d.

Le cens en deniers, XLVII s.

Odart des Ponz anvers Bloville, XVII acres, vaut l'acre VIII s.

Houe le filz Gilon, II acres, por tot. XVI s.

tout[3] par mesure
XXIII acres

Colin Beuse, III acres, por tout XVIII s.

Guillaume le Bovier, I acre et demie, por tout IX s.

Odart des Pons prist une acre par l'autre pour XVIII s.,
VI d.

fol. 176v

Durant Bovier, I acre, VI s.

Le clos de Dyve, II acres, tout autant par m[esure], por tout
XXVI s. Gefrey Govion prist por XXX s.

Gefrey Gougion, I acre et demie, por tout VI s.

Thomas Gougion, III acres, por tout XVI s.

Maquerel, I acre, V s.

Hue Aubert, I acre et demie, por tout VI s.

Raoul Tolomer, III acres, por tout XVIII s.⎤ tout autant par
Item, iceli II acres, por tout VIII s.   ⎦ m[esure]

—Baillies a iceli Rad. o le molin sicomme desus est dit.

Souz la Londe, I acre et demie, por tout VI s.

Anvers Auberville,[1] demie acre de pré, IIII s., et les services
des hommes qui font le fein.

*Por I   V s.

Le cens en deniers, XLI s. IIII d.

---

[1] Bénerville, Calvados, a. Pont-l'Evêque, c. Dozulé.

[2] In this case 4 *asquez* make a *somme*, assuming that the *asquez* is 9 d., as it is on fols.
160v and 161.

[3] This sum must include the land of Odart above.

---

[1] Auberville, Calvados, a. Pont-l'Evêque, c. Dozulé.

Avoine, XXV setiers et III quartiers.

Capons, XLIII, et III gelines.

Item, II.C.IIII.XX oeus, II oues, et LX painz.

La some LXXIII lb. XIX s. IIII d.

fol. 177

Icele somme devant dite creist selonc baillie et a baillier de XXX lb. XV s. I d.

Ici metras la mesure

La ferme de la terre d'Angoville,[1] LXXIIII lb. XV s. VI d., de cen sont rendues por les aumosnes XVII lb. et remaint—au Roy LVII lb.

Eu camp de l'Arbre, III acres, vaut l'acre XVI s.

Eu camp de la Fonteinne, V verg., vaut l'acre XII s.

Jurée
fol. 177v

Eu camp du Mont Avignie,[2] I acre et demie a celi pris.

Eu camp de Vateville, I acre a celi pris.

Joste la meson Guillaume le—Roy, VII acres a celi pris.

Eu camp Sale, I acre a celi pris.

Eu camp Vimarc, II acres a celi pris.

En la Plate Couture, IIII acres a celi pris.

La some XX acres III verg., selonc la jurée, mes par la mesure XXIII acres I verg. et XIIII perches, desqueles una acre et demie et X perches sont tenues en douaire.

Les preeres d'Angoville eu camp de la Tresceinne, IIII acres, IIII lb.

Eu camp de la Delle, II acres a celi pris.

Item, en l'autre camp qui est apelé la Delle, II acres a celi pris.

Item, ileques III verg. a celi pris.

Jurée

Anvers la Sausedelle II acres a celi pris.

A la Grant Delle, V acres a celi pris.

La Courte Raie, I acre et demie a celi pris.

Eu chef de deille eu Doquet, II verg. a celi pris.

La some XVII acres III verg.

fol. 178

Les prez selonc la mesure, XIX acres III verg. V perches.

Le molin d'Angoville et la moute seiche, XIIII lb.

Item, XIII asquez de sel, valent IX s. IX d.

Capons LXVI et LXVI d.

Item, XLV gelines et XLV d.

---

[1] Angoville, Calvados, a. Pont-l'Evêque, c. Dozulé, cne. Cricqueville.

H. F., XXIII, 709. The fief of Angoville in the *pays d'Auge* owed the service of one knight at the time of Philip Augustus. It had been held by Hugh Painel.

[2] Lieu Mont à Vigny, south of Cricqueville.

Item, XL oues. Item, IX.C.LX oeus, et o X oeus I d.

Le cens en deniers, VI lb.

Forment, XXXII setiers et I mine, vaut le setier XV s.

Avoine, VIII setiers et I mine, vaut le setier V s.

Item, uns esperons dorez, valent II s.

Les preeres de XV carues, XXX s.

Item, por V vavassors, X lb.

Guillaume du Val doit I crenune de let, vaut IIII d.

Item, sont ileques II bordiers qui doivent mener les bestes au seignor d'un maneir en autre.

Item, V vavassors qui doivent porter le bernage d'Angville anvers Bonneville, fener, auner, tasser, et amener en la ville de Angoville, et le merrien du molin amener de Ronceville anvers Angoville—Les rel. et justices X s.

La somme IIII.XX.VII lb.

Icele ferme desus dite est ballie au—priour et au couvent de Realpré,[1] et paieront l'anmosne, por C.IIII lb. XIX s. VII d., quite—au Roy. Se plusors terres ou prez soient trouvées iceli paiera selonc plus et meinz—et son parchonniers Robert de Saint Cler[2] et Guillaume le—Roy.

Iceste ferme creist de XLVII lb. XIX s. VII d.

La somme du bail selonc lor letres CIX lb. VI d. et creist de LII lb., VI d.—La so[mm]e Ric. le Clerc.

La terre Wilequier des granches XV s., perpetuel.

Les foires de Biaumont en Auge, XV s. perpetuel.

La viscomté Bertran, XX lb.,[1] perpetuel.

La terre Jehen Espec, XL s.

L'avoine ileques, III muiz, II setiers.

La somme de la crescence de toute la serganterie XIIII.XX.IIII lb. III s. IIII d.

---

[1] *Cart. Nor.*, no. 586. Louis IX had already given this community eight and a half acres of meadow at "Angovilla" in 1257. The lands of the abbey were very close to this fief.
[2] *ibid.* Robert held a meadow at "Angovilla" in 1257. *cf.* fol. 177v.

---

[1] Delisle, *Ech.*, no. 658. "Inquistio utrum pater Robini Bertran saisitus erat die et anno quando obiit de vicecomitatu inter aquam de Touqua vel non. . . . Dicunt omnes quod nunquam habuit saisinam de dicto vicecomitatu. Judicatum est quod dominus rex habeat saisinam suam in pace. . . ." 1230.

La Serganterie de Bevron[1]

La ferme du Pont l'Evesque[2] C lb.

En la riviere, II acres et demie, vaut l'acre IX s.

Eu camp Crasset, I acre, vaut V s.

Eu camp Torgot, I acre, VIII s.

En marleiz, I acre et demie, vaut por tout XIII s.

Juree

Es parrez, II acres, vaut l'acre VI s.

Eu camp qui est apelé le Jardin, II acres, vaut l'acre X s.

En mie le val, I vergie, vaut II s.

Sanz pris

Le fosse as larrons, I acre, sanz pris.

Le jardin et la masure, I verg., por tout XII s.

Au Noiers, I verg., de bordage, II s.

Item, demie acre de pré, vaut VIII s.—Ballie a Mons. Richart de Bois por X s.

Ices terres devant dites sont ballies a Guiart de Silvanet por

*

La some por la descrecence des terres IIII lb. XII s.

fol. 180

Par mesure X acres IX perches, sanz la fosse au larrons qui n'est pas comtée.

Le molin XL lb., de cen est deue la deesme.

Une foire ileques, XX lb.

La coustume de la hale au ble, XX lb.

Rentes

Item, IIII lb. de poivre, vaut la livre IIII s.

Item, I mieu d'avoine, vaut le setier IIII s.

Item, IIII sommes de sel, vaut la somme III s.

Le cens en deniers, XVIII lb. IIII s.

Les preeres de II carues.

La prevosté du Pont l'Evesque, XII lb.

Item, II oues, valent XVI d.

Item, XXVIII capons, et o les capons II s.

Item, VIII.C oeus et VIII d. Por II lampraies XVI s.

Item, III troites III s.

La somme CXVII lb. II s. VIII d.

Et creist iceste ferme de XXII lb. II s. VIII d.

La valor de la ferme de Nival doit enquise estre.

---

[1] Beuvron-en-Auge, Calvados, a. Pont-l'Evêque, c. Cambremer.

[2] Pont-l'Evêque, Calvados.

La ferme de la terre Thomas Basset[1] XLII lb.

Eu Hamel aus Amelines, V acres, l'acre XII s.

En une piece devant la porte, VII acres a celi pris.

Entor le maneir Basset, XIIII acres a celi pris.

Item, ileques II acres et demie de pré, L s.—par m[esure] III acres X perches.

Par mesure XXX acres XX perches.

Avoine, II moez, vaut le setier VI s.

Le cens en deniers, X lb. XI s. VI d.

Le fieu de Guerres,[2] XIIII s. en deniers.

Item, VI oeus, vaut l'oie VIII d.

Item, XVI gelines et XVI d.

Item, XI.XX.X oeus et V s. V d.

Les preeres des carues, por tout XXVIII s.

La somme XXXIX lb., II s.

La ferme Basset, la ferme au seignor de Darnestal, la ferme Hue Boute Vilain, et la ferme de Duremare[1] ballies sont a la parsonne de Clebec[2] por VII.XX lb.

Item, le bosc des dites fermes ballies ensement, l'acre por X s., sanz la superficie.

La valor de la terre que l'en dit qui fu donnée a une damoisele est ostée de la somme desus dite.

Les terres creiscent de V acres, valent LX s.

Le bosc I acre, vaut X s.

Et creist de XXII lb. XIIII s.

---

[1] Delisle-Berger, II, 12, 116, 119, 140, etc. Thomas Basset was in constant attendance at the court of Henry II in the latter part of his reign, and frequently witnessed royal acts. *H. F.*, XXIII, 635. Thomas "Basseit" had held a knight's fee at "Drubec" and "Fauguergnon" in the *bailliage* of Bonneville, which was seized by Philip after the conquest.

[2] *H. F.*, XXIII, 635. A fief of "Guirros" is listed in the *bailliage* of Bonneville.

---

[1] Drumare, Calvados, a. and c. Pont-l'Evêque, cne. Beaumont-en-Auge.

cf. note on fol. 182v.

[2] Clarbec, Calvados, a. and c. Pont l'Evêque. These four fiefs were all held of the Bertran baronny, and were listed fairly close together in the registrar of fiefs (*H. F.*, XXIII, 635) as well as here.

La ferme de la terre de Darnestal anvers Drubec,[1] LXI lb.

En la couture Aoul, VIII acres et demie, vaut l'acre XII s.

Au maneir de Drubec, XXVI acres a celi pris.

Les prez, I acre et demie, por tout XXX s.

Item, ileques I piece de bosc, V acres, vaut l'acre XII s., par mesure VI acres.

Par mesure XXXV acres L perches.

Item, ileques XIII boiss. de forment, valent XXX s., et XVI boiss. feront le setier.

Le cens en deniers, XI lb. V s. VI d.

Item, LX gelines et LVIII d.

Item, II capons et II d.

Item, VI.C oeus et o X oeus I d.

Le molin ileques, XXX lb.

Les preeres de XIIII carues, valent XXVIII s. VI d.

Le fieu Osmont doit une residence, vaut XII d.

Por la terre du molin, I setier d'avoine.

Raoul Onfrey por I residence, XII d.

Item, Ricart de Seiqueval por I residence, II oues qui valent XVI d.

Item, por I autre residence, XII d.

Item, I vivier, I mote.

Les esplez et les rel.

Le patronage d'une iglise—n'est pas en ferme.

La somme LXVIII lb. X s. II d.

Iceste ferme est ballie sicomme desus est dit.

La ferme Hue Boutevillein[1] L s.

Les rentes en deniers, XLII s. Item, XXIII capons, IIII gelines.

Item, IX.XX oeus; XXVI pains, vaut le pain I d.

La somme LVII s. VIII d.

---

[1] Drubec, Calvados, a. and c. Pont-l'Evêque. This is the other part of the land of Raoul de Tilli, lord of Darnetal, cf. fol. 158.

[1] Quer. Nor., no. 4. The property of Hugh Boutevilain in Auge was seized after his death because it was claimed that the nearest heir was living in England. Another heir denied this in 1247, apparently to no effect.

H. F., XXIII, 620. Hugh had held two and one-half knight's fees in the bailliage of Caen under Philip Augustus.

fol. 182v La ferme Henri de Gurneville que l'en apele Grumare[1] vaut XIIII lb. X s.

> La quarte partie du molin de Grumare,[1] VII lb.
>
> Item—le Roy a la seignorie de meitre ileques le monnier.
>
> Anquetin de Grumare por l'acre et demie de terre, III setiers d'avoine, vaut l'acre XII s.
>
> Les rentes en deniers, XLVIII s. IX d.
>
> Item, XXVII capons et demie.
>
> Item, VIII gelines. Item, XVI.XX.V oeus.
>
> L'avoine, V setiers, et X boiss. de forment, et XXXVI pains, vaut le pain I d. Les preeres des carues X s.
>
> Les rel, les esples, les justices, les services des hommes qui doivent amener le merrien du molin, coedre le fein et tasser.
>
> Item, le bosc de Druremare, entor II acres, l'acre VIII s.,—par mesure III acres et I verg.
>
> > La somme sanz le bosc XIII lb. XVII s. V d.
> >
> > Ices IIII fermes devant dites creiscent de XXII lb. XIIII s.

fol. 183 La ferme de la terre Robert de la Mare a la Fonteinne XIX lb.

> En la valée Robert de la Mare, VI acres, l'acre VII s. VI d.
>
> Au Buisson Guerosc, VII acres XXX perches, XLV s.—Henri Cousin prist l'acre por VIII s.
>
> **Jurée**
>
> Eu fieu Crupes, IIII acres, par m[esure] III acres et demie et demie vergie, por tout XXIIII s.—Rad. de la Mare prist l'acre por IX s.
>
> A la mare du don Ricart, V verg., par m[esure] VII verg., por tout IIII s. VI d.—Rad. de la Mare prist l'acre por V s.
>
> Joste le bosc I acre, IIII s.
>
> Item, II acres et demie d'erbage de bosc, vaut l'erbage X s.
>
> L'erbage d'un jardin IIII s.
>
> Le fruict X s.

fol. 183v

> Item, demie molin vaut VIII lb.—meit ileques—le Roy le monnier por la metie—Ballie a Symon de la Fonteinne por IX lb. X s.

---

[1] The scribe has probably made an error hre. He should have written "Drumare" (Calvados, a. and c. Pont-l'Evêque, cne. Beaumont-en-Auge).

H. F., XXIII, 635. A fourth part of the knight's fee of Drumare was in the king's hands c. 1220, "ex parte magistri Henrici de Guinevilla."

Quer. Nor., no. 41. A request for this fief, which is said to be in the king's hand because the priest who last held it died in England.

Le cens ileques, XVII s.

Item, IIII capons et demie et IIII d.

Le fieu au Fouliart, IIII capons, IIII d.

Raoul Morpain por I regart, IIII d.

Item, L oeus, IIII d.

Les preeres d'une carue et demie vaut III s.

La somme XVI lb. XI s. X d.

La ferme Hue de Roies,[1] XI lb.

Eu camp Pesson, III acres et demie, par mesure V acres et X perches, tant de terre quant de pré, por tout IIII lb. X s.

Le molin et la moute seiche IX lb.

Le cens en deniers, XXIIII s.

Item, XXII capons et XIX d.

Item, II gelines. Item IX.XX oeus et XVI d.

Les preeres d'une carue, II s.

Les esplez et les rel.

La somme XV lb. IX s. IIII d.

Renout Bigart prist icele ferme por XVIII lb. II s.

Et creist de VII lb. II s.

Anvers Brootes I setier d'avoine, item, demie acre de terre, et demie acre d'auney, un jardin, por tout XV s. Icen est ballie a Rad. Beuron, clerc, por XX s., sanz la superficie, et creist de V s.

La ferme de la terre de Cauqueinvillier[1] XLV lb.

La terre qui fu a l'oncle Hervei Lartuier, demie verg., III s.

Eu camp Richeber, I acre, XX s.

Eu camp de la Vigne, III verg., X s.

Eu camp Morant, I acre, VIII s.

Eu camp des Gotieres, demie acre, VI s.

Es parrez Ermeneut, I acre et demie, por tout X s.

Es fosses Alberee, demie acre, V s.

Eu camp as Gans, I acre, XII s.

---

[1] Delisle, *Ech.*, no. 98. "Hugo de Rotis" was outlawed in 1212 for failing to appear at the assizes of Bonneville to answer "de morte W. de Torvilla et de morte Ricardi de Navare. . . ."

H. F., XXIII, 711. He had held one-eighth of a knight's fee from Hugh de Montfort.

---

[1] Coquainvilliers, Calvados, a. Pont-l'Evêque, c. Blangy. *cf.* note, fol. 185v.

H. F., XXIII, 634. The barony of Coquainvilliers escheated to the king from Hugh de Montfort. Much of it lay in the *bailliage* of Caen.

Eu camp Hoteri, III verg. et demie, valent XII oues par an.

Eu camp au Houlez, III acres, por tout XXIIII s.

Une piece de pré, vaut VIII s.

La some X acres et I vergie.

Mesure   Par mesure, XXIII acres et I verg.

fol. 185   Avoine V moez et demie, le setier VI s.—desquelz II moez a la
mesure sont du bosc foulée.

Item, IX quarters de forment, vaut le setier XVI s.

Item, XXXIX capons et XXXIX d.

Item, IIII.XX.II gelines et V d.

Item, XIIII aingniaulz, valent XIIII s.

Rentes   *Item, XIIII moutons. Item XIIII.XX.V oeus.

Le cens LXV s.   Une verge de[1]

Un esprevier, III s. Por pos,[2] XXX d.

Une livre de poivre, vaut II s. VI d.

Un past, ou XL s.

Les preeres des carues, VII lb. X s.

Les preeres des herces, XXX s. IIII d., por la iornée.

Et sont deues en ces villes, c'est assavoir—Anvers Cauqueinvillier,
carues et herces; anvers Saint Ymer,[3] carues sanz herces;
anvers Le Tort Quesne,[4] carues sanz herces.

fol. 185v   Item, sont ileques XII bordiers qui doivent les pommes coedre et
tribler, faire le sidre, fener et auner, et soleit prendre por
chascun service XXX d.

Rentes   Item, en la ville de Cauqueinvillier sont aucuns bordiers qui
*   doivent en aoust tasser les blez et   [1] et fener, vaut
XX s., c'est assavoir la iornee de tasser VI d., de fener IIII d.

*La prevosté   [1] IIII lb. X s.

Les amendes XL s.

N'est pas   Item, est ileques la garenne.
en ferme   La somme LVII lb. XV s. IIII d.

---

[1] The detail of this farm is given in *Cart. Nor.*, no. 116. The phrase in Latin was
"unam virgam stallate," corrected by Delisle at no. 810 to "scallate," scarlet cloth.

[2] *ibid.*, "pro potis 30 denarios."

[3] Saint-Hymer, Calvados, a. and c. Pont-l'Evêque.

[4] Le Torquêne, Calvados, a. Pont-l'Evêque, c. Blangy.

---

[1] These omissions may be supplied from the document quoted in the note below, as
"legumina," and "et messeria."

Toutes ices choses qui sont en la ferme desus dite sont ballies a—Mons. Phelippe d'Autoil[2]—por—LXXII lb. et creist de XXVII lb.

Le molin de Herouessart[3] por la partie—le Roy, VIII lb., et I setier de forment de XVI s.

fol. 186 La ferme de la terre Robert de Bloville a Lehan,[1] XXXV s., perpetuel.
La ferme Rogier le Prevost—le viscomte la bailla por L s.
La ferme de la terre Le Han,[1] XL s., perpetuel.
La ferme de la terre Robert de Beteville, XX s.

Comtée
par sey La ferme de la terre Guillaume Bardol,[2] XVIII lb.

*

[2] *Cart. Nor.*, no. 611. ". . . nos dedimus et concessimus ad firmam perpetuam Philippo de Autolio, militi, . . . pro 72 l. tur. annui redditus . . . in firma de Cauqueinviller 23 acras et unam virgatam terre, dimidiam acram prati vel circiter; 5 modios et dimimium avene, 9 quarteria frumenti; 39 capones et 39 d.; 82 gallinas cum 5 d.; 14 agniculos et 14 arietes; 285 ova; 65 s. censuales; 1 virgatam stallate [should be 'scallate']; 1 espreverum; 30 d. pro potis; 1 libram piperis; 1 pastum vel 40 s.; . . . precarias carrucarum et herciarum, . . . servitia 11 bordariorum, qui debent poma colligere et triblare, facere sidrum, fenare et adunare; item servititia quorumdam bordariorum in valle de Cauqueinviller qui debent in Augusto tassare blada et legumina et fenare; preposituram et messeriam; relevia rusticorum et simplicem justitiam eorumdem. . . . Premissa autem eidem concessimus una cum garenna que ibi esse dicitur. . . ." 1259.

ibid., nos. 160, 403. Two Gui's d'Auteuil had held at Coquainvilliers since the time of Philip Augustus, who confiscated the land from Hugh de Montfort.

M. A. N., 2[e]s., 5, p. 155. In the original grant of land at Coquainvilliers to Gui d'Auteuil in 1207, Philip especially reserved some of the land for himself. This is probably the land which was later granted as a farm to Philip d'Auteuil.

Cart. Nor., no. 810. St. Louis later conceded this farm to Robert Loremier, priest, for 65 l. a year. Robert, in 1271, surrendered the farm to Nicholas, archdeacon of Pont-Audemer. The description of the domain in this last lease is almost identical with the one given above.

ibid., no. 707. Financial difficulties probably caused Philip to lose the farm, for in 1265 he surrendered a rent of 9 l. *par.* on the exchequer in return for 95 l. *tur.* According to Delisle's note, he was with the king on the Crusade of 1270, which probably increased his financial troubles.

[3] Héroussards (?), Calvados, a. Pont-l'Evêque, c. Dozulé, cne. Branville.

H. F., XXIII, 709. The fief of "Herovexard" in Auge was in the king's hand after the conquest.

[1] Le Ham, Calvados, a. Pont-l'Evêque, c. Cambremer.

[2] *Cart. Nor.*, no. 410. In 1235 Louis IX gave "Hamelino de Blagone" the rents in kind from the land of Guillaume Bardol at Putot (Calvados, a. Pont-l'Evêque, c. Dozulé), reserving for himself "bosco, prata, et roserias." *H. F.*, XXI, 256. The king obtained 8 l. from the land of G. Bardol in 1238.

H. F., XXIII, 634. A Guillaume "Bardof" held a knight's fee at Putot under Philip Augustus.

Sont ileques XII acres de prez es lieuz dedenz nommez—

En la delle outre le Viel Fosse, II acres I verg., l'acre XVIII s.

La delle entor le Viel Fosse, II acres I verg., a celi pris.

Eu pré Pierres, I acre et I verg., l'acre XXIIII s.

parties

Eu pré de Roies, II acres I verg., l'acre XVI s.

Eu pré des Rues, demie acre, XII s.

Eu pré de Haudem[er], demie acre a celi pris.

Es prez de Bruecort,[3] I acre, XIIII s.

fol. 186v

Eu pré a la Fauresce, demie acre, XII s.

Au Buisson du Pré, I verg., VI s.

Es prez de l'Osier, III verg., l'acre XXIIII s.

Eu pré du Maret, III verg., por tout XII s.

Eu pré Moret, III acres I verg., por tout XX s.

Item, X acres de ros a Briecort, l'acre XII s.

Souz le mostier de Saint Cler,[1] V verg., por tout XX s.

La somme XXI lb. XVIII s.

*

La somme de la serganterie de Bevron LXVII lb. VII s. VIII d.

fol. 187

Veci la Serganterie de Bonneville[1]

La ferme de la terre de la Faleise,[2] CXV lb.

En la couture de la campagne vers Helot, XV acres, l'acre XII s.

En iceli camp vers la Gouannie, XXII acres, l'acre X s.

Joste le molin des Autielz,[3] II acres XX perches, l'acre XV s.

Ballies a Mons. R[i]cart de Buesemoncel por XXXVI s. et creist de II s. VI d. por XX perches.

Prez le hamel de Crotes, III verg., por tout IX s.

Jurée

Sus les prez de la Faleise, III acres, l'acre V s.

En la couture du Parreus, III acres, l'acre XIII s.

En iceli camp I acre et demie, l'acre X s.

---

[3] Brucourt, Calvados, a. Pont-l'Evêque, c. Dozulé.

[1] Saint-Clair-en-Auge, Calvados, a. Pont-l'Evêque, c. Dozulé, cne. Goustranville-Saint-Clair.

[1] Bonneville-sur-Touques, Calvados, a. and c. Pont-l'Evêque. The dukes of Normandy had had holdings in Bonneville at least as early as the reign of Richard III, and Henry II assigned a 10 l. rent on the town to the nuns of Lisieux. (Delisle-Berger, I, 320; II, 143.)

[2] Falaise, Calvados, a. Pont-l'Evêque, c. Blangy, cne. Saint-André-d'Hebertot.

[3] Les Authieux-sur-Calonne, Calvados, a. Pont-l'Evêque, c. Blangy.

Eu camp ioste le jardin du frique, II acres a celi pris.

Es auneiz Roncelin, V acres a celi pris.

fol. 187v

Eu camp du Re, demie acre, VI s.

Eu camp Hebert, I acre et demie, por tout XV s.

Eu camp Basin et eu camp de Launey, III acres, l'acre VIII s.

En iceli camp demie acre V s.

les
prez

Le jardin du frique, I acre et demie.

Por le fruict et por l'erbage, XXIIII s.

Eu jardin de la Vigne, I acre, por tout X s.

N'est pas
en ferme

Item, XXV acres de bois. L'erbage, XV s.

Eu pré Morcean, V verg., por tout XXX s.

Eu pré de la Faleise vers les Autielz, III acres et demie, por tout
LX s.

Mesure

Le molin de la Faleise et la moute seiche XXXV lb.

fol. 188

Vers les Autielz demie molin, XX lb.—Ballie a Mons. Ricart de
Biaumoncel por XXIIII lb. et creist de IIII lb.

Eu molin de Tillie, II setiers de forment, vaut le setier XVI s.

L'avoine ileques, VIII setiers V. boiss., vaut le setier V s.

Item, I mui de sidre, vaut X s.

Rentes

Item, CIII capons et o les capons VIII s. V d.

Item, XXXIII gelines et o les gelines II s. V d.

Item XL oues, vaut l'oie VIII d.

Item, VI pocins, valent XII d.

Item, VI.C.XX oeus, et a X oeus I d.

Le cens en deniers, VI lb. X s.

Item, VII vavassors qui valent CXIIII s.

Les preeres de XIIII carues II foiz en l'an.

Les preeres de XX herces II foiz en l'an.

Touz les bordiers doivent coedre, amener et auner les feinz.

Anvers Faleise auner et coedre les pommes.

      La some CXVI lb. VIII s. II d.—et creist iceste somme
de CXIIII s. II d. selon l'estimation et le bail.

fol. 188v La ferme Guillaume Escuredoict, C s.

Eu camp Jehan du Bosc, I acre, XII s.

Eu clos Widecoc, I verg., IIII s.

L'erbage d'un jardin lequel tient V acres, por tout XXV s.

Le pré III acres, I verg. meinz, por tout LX s.

Le cens, L s.

Item, XXIX capons et XX d.

Item, III gelines et II d.

Item, XIX.XX et X oeus, et o X oeus I d.

Les preeres d'une carue et d'une herce.

Item, les bordiers doivent fener les feinz des prez.

La somme IX lb. VIII d.

Ballies sont ices choses a Guillaume de Tornay, au seignor de la Cort Herbert por XII lb.—et creist de VII lb.

Le molin de Kalunde, por tout IIII.XX lb.

fol. 189

La praerie de Bone Ville por carues et por herces II foiz en l'an.

Canapeville,[1] XIX carues II foiz en l'an, et IX d'erche III foiz en l'an.

Englesqueville,[2] XVIII carues II foiz en l'an, V d'erches III foiz en l'an.

Ronceville,[3] IX carues et VI d'erche II foiz en l'an.

Daube,[4] IIII carues et IIII d'erche II foiz l'an.

Heudequeinville,[5] XI carues, XI herces.

Toroville,[6] X carues, X herces.

(Rouceville IX carues et VI d'erche II foiz en l'an.)[7]

Les pestiz sus les Mares, por tout IIII lb.—Les parties sont cestes.

parties

Le pestiz sus les Mares, XL s.

Le pestiz devant les Mares, XX s.

La foullerie sus les Granz Prez, XII s.

Ballies a Robert Anquetil, a Herbert Orellion et a Pierres Hebert por C s. et creist de XX s.

fol. 189v

Le fieu Jorfarin[1] X lb.

Eu Lonc Boel, demie acre, VIII s.—Guillaume Herosc prist por XIII s.

---

[1] Canapville, Calvados, a. and c. Pont-l'Evêque.

Stapleton, I, 68, 69. The king had an income from the meadows of Canapville at least as early as 1180.

[2] Englesqueville-sur-Touques, Calvados, a. and c. Pont-l'Evêque.

[3] Roncheville, Calvados, a. and c. Pont-l'Evêque, cne. Saint-Martin-aux-Chartrains.

Delisle-Berger, II, 143. One of the early dukes (Richard II) had granted rights at Englesqueville and Roncheville to Chartres. Henry II confirmed this grant c. 1180. Apparently this district is one of the oldest parts of the domain.

[4] Dauboeuf, Calvados, a. and c. Pont-l'Evêque, cne. Touque.

[5] Hennequeville, Calvados, a. and c. Pont-l'Evêque, cne. Trouville.

[6] Tourville, Calvados, a. and c. Pont-l'Evêque.

[7] This entry, in a small and almost effaced hand, merely repeats the entry for Roncheville above, and is probably a correction, later seen to be unnecessary.

---

[1] Stapleton, I, 68. Roll of 1180, "et de IIII li. et X so. pro terra Japharin."

Eu camp qui est apelé le iardin Iorfarin, III verg., XX s.—Jehan
Bardol por XXII s.

Eu pendan de Male Terre, VII verg., l'acre XVI s.—Crestian
le Cambellenc[2] por XVI s.

Sus la fosse Sevestre Gaudon, demie acre, VIII s.—Nichole du
Molin por IX s.

Item, ileques demie acre, VII s.—Crestian le Cambellenc por
VII s.

A la fosse Hurel, I acre, XX s.

Souz la meson Robert le Boulengier, I acre et demie, l'acre XIIII
s.

Jurée

Ricart le Meteer, l'acre por XVI s., tout autant par mesure.[3]

Item, ileques VII verg., par me[sure] II acres et XIX perches,
l'acre XVI s. Thommas Sevestre, por tout XXXII s. et por
la crescence de la terre II s. III d.

Sus la Male Terre, I verg., IIII s.—Ansel Orellion[4] por IIII s.

Souz la voie d'Englesqueville, I acre et demie, l'acre XIII s.

Sus le mont de Bone Ville, II acres, l'acre IIII s.—Jehan l'Escot
et Rad. Bardol, l'acre por VIII s.

Eu pendant de la Male Terre, demie acre, VIII s.

fol. 190

Es Essarz Viel, II acres, por tout XVI s.—Jehan l'Escot et
Raoul Bardol, por tout XXII s.

A la Retaillie, I acre, XIIII s.—Crestian le Cambellenc por
XIIII s.[1]

Souz le clos Seri, demie acre, VIII s.

Item, ileques I acre, XII s.—Thommas Sevestre por XIIII s.

Au Marleiz, I verg., IIII s.

A l'Essartel, III verg., por tout IX s.—Ansel Orellion por X s.

Au Doitel, demie acre X s.—Climent le Cambellenc por XIIII s.

Eu camp Jorfarin, I verg., et demie, por tout VII s. VI d. Henri
Mode por XI s.

Item, ileques ioste le Doitel, demie acre, VI s.; II capons, II d.;
et XX oeus, II d.

---

[2] See note on fol. 190v.

[3] This probably refers to the entry above.

[4] "Ansellus Orelon" of Bonneville appears in *Quer. Nor.*, no. 16. He asks that the
past income from four librates of land, long held by the king, but recently adjudged his,
be given him.

---

[1] See note on fol. 190v.

Sus la granche Coquet, I verg., II s.

Eu camp Jorfarin joste la meson Robert le Bolengier, I acre, par mesure demie acre LX perches.—Ballie a iceli Robert l'acre por XVIII s.

Item, demie acre d'erbage ioste les mares, V s.

Item, I verg. en garez, V s.—Thomas Sevestre por V s.

La somme XIIII lb. XIII s.—et creist iceste ferme selonc ballie et a ballier de VI lb. XV s.

fol. 190v

Les prez de Bonne Ville, VIII lb.

Sont ileques XXI acres de pré en ces lieus—c'est assavoir

Eu pré de la Voillie, IIII acres et demie, X perches.

Eu pré du Fenil, IIII acres III verg.

Eu pré de Sequillion, III acres et demie.

Es II prez des Viez Mesieres, I acre I verg.

Eu pré de la Noe, IX acres L perches. Vaut chascune acre des terres desus dites XV s.—quite au—Roy.

La somme XXIII acres LX perches, et sont ballies a Crestian le Cambellenc[1] por XV s. l'acre.

Ne sont pas en ferme

Es granz prez VIII acres et I verg., valent por tout VII lb. X s.

Ballies a Clement le Cambellenc et a Guillaume, l'acre por XXIIII s. o les services de fener, et de carrier sicomme—le Roy les avoit.

La somme d'ices choses X lb. XII s., selonc la mesure.

fol. 191

Item, sont ileques III villes, c'est assavoir Bone Ville, Escanapeville, et Escamiauville[1] qui doivent fener, coedre, et auner les feinz et mener a la ville.

Item, est ileques I praier qui garde les prez et a une quaretée de fein a IIII beus et a II chevauz de rente et de cen rent—au Roy I setier d'orge.

La somme XXIII lb. V s., de cen doit caer VII lb. X s. por le grant pré.

Le campart de Boneville, por tout LXX s.

Les foires de Saint Andreu, VI lb.

---

[1] This is perhaps the Chrétien le Chambellan who was a burgess of Caen, viscount of Caen in 1269, and *bailli* of the Cotentin in 1274. *cf.* my *Administration of Normandy*, p. 96.

[1] Equemauville, Calvados, a. Pont-l'Evêque, c. Honfleur.

La grande crote, VI lb.—Ballie a Guillaume Prentout, a Thomas Hure, a Gillebert Hubert, sanz les redevances des carues, l'acre por VIII s.

Sont ileques XII acres de terre, L perches, l'acre X s.

Item, les redevances des carues en ces villes.[1]

> A Bonneville, XIIII carues et tout autant d'erches I fiee en l'an.
> A Canapeville, XIX carues, IX herces, I fiee en l'an.
> Anvers Englesqueville, XVIII carues, VI herces, I fiee en l'an.
> A Ronceville, IX carues, V herces, I fiee en l'an.
> A Daubou, IIII carues, IIII herces, I fie en l'an.
> Anvers Heudequeinville, XI carues et autant d'erches, I fiee en l'an.
> Anvers Toroville, X carues et autant d'erches I fiee en l'an.

Ne sont pas en ferme
fol. 192
Comté par sey

Les herbages de marz, por tout X s.

Item, LXII s. IIII d. por XXXIIII sommes de sel.

Le molin de Gibellenc, XL lb.

Le molin de Wacul, XXVIII lb.—Henri le Moiteer prist por XXXII lb.

La pesquerie de Bonne Ville, XX lb.

*Le pré des Autielz, por tout VIII s.—Giles de Gerpouville le prist por demie acre et por XII s.

La terre Ricart du Vergier, XXX s., perpetuel.

Les cens et les rentes de Boneville et de Canapeville, LII lb. XVI s. II d. —perpetuel.

Les regarz ilequez, C s. XII d.—perpetuel.

La terre Henri le Prevost, X s.—perpetuel.

La jonciere de Wacul, XVI s.—Renaut Orellion[1] et Henri le Meteer prist por XVIII s.—sont ileques entor III verg.

Les herbages d'avril, X s.—perpetuel.

La terre Thomas le Mercier, II s. ou I lb. de poivre—perpetuel.

La terre Robert de Roies a Bone Ville, XXXV s.—perpetuel.

La terre Pelicon de Hebertot, VIII s.—perpetuel—Sont ileques III setiers d'avene dites a nos par le viscomte, et II acres de terre non comtées de cen fors VIII s.—

La vacquerie de Bone Ville, XXVII s.—perpetuel.

La gravarie ileques, XXVII s.—perpetuel.

---

[1] For these place-names, *cf.* fol. 189.

[1] Quer. Nor., no. 37. Renaut "Oreilon" must have been a man of some prominence in the town, since he was chosen to present a petition, in behalf of the community of Bonneville, to the *enqueteurs*.

Les aides aus costumiers du fieu Paienel,[1] IIII lb.—perpetuel.

Les herbages de Bone Ville, XXIIII lb. IIII s.

L'avoine ileques, III moez XI setiers X boiss.

Le bernage[2] de la ballie de la prevosté, XV setiers.

Item, du bernage par Escot et Bardol[3] XVII setiers I mine d' avene.

Forment, III moez IX setiers III quartiers.

Le fieu Hue Seri, jardin continant III verg.—Ballie a Renaut Orellion
por I setier de forment et I quartier, et II sommes de sel.

*La ferme de l'aioue   VI setiers d'avoine.

fol. 193
N'estoient
pas en ferme

Eu camp du mostier, III acres I verg., l'acre XVIII s.

Eu jardin le—Roy, I verg. a celi pris.

Joste la meson Gautier Ostart, I verg. a celi pris.

Item, XII d. du cens, I pain, I capon.

De cen rent le Roy I mine de forment, I oue.

La somme LVII s. XI d. quite—au Roy.

Ballies sont a Guillaume Morel por LXX s., quite—au
Roy.

Icest serganterie sanz la ferme de l'aioue creist de
XXVIII lb. XVII s. VIII d.

fol. 193v

Veci la Serganterie[1]

La ferme de la terre Robert de Viez-Pont,[2] Henri du Noef-Marcie et
Olivier de Quesne VII.XX.XV lb.

Eu camp de Livieres, V acres, l'acre V s.

Eu camp du Longuel es Lot[er]aulz, IX acres, vaut l'acre VIII
s.

Eu Val de la Court, eu Camp Pendant, et es Ruaulz, XI acres,
vaut l'acre VIII s.

Eu camp des Faudeiz, II acres, l'acre IIII s.

---

[1] This is probably the fief of "Angovilla," once held by Hugh Painel, mentioned on fol.
177.

[2] Stapleton, I, 234. Bernage of the viscounty of Bonneville, for the three years ending
1195, was 129 mines and 1½ quartiers, or 21 setiers 1 mine a year.

[3] cf. fol. 190.

[1] Royal holdings in this sergeanty are not concentrated enough at any one point to
suggest a name for the district. Perhaps the clerk who drew up this document found it
difficult to select a name for the sergeanty for the same reason.

[2] Stapleton, II, ccliv, cclxi, cclxv, cclxvi. "Robertus de Veteri Ponte" was a trusted
agent of John in the years just before the conquest and followed John to England, thus
losing his Norman lands. cf. M. A. M., 2es., V. 116-122.

Devant luis Durant du Juin, I acre et demie, l'acre VI s.

Eu jardin de la Court du Plesseiz, V acres, l'acre XII s., desqueles II acres sont en bosc, duquel la superficie n'est pas comtée est ileques le bosc. Des autres III acres vaut le fruict par an XX s.

Eu camp du Val Restout, XII acres, desqueles III acres sont del bosc de III anz, des autres IX acres, vaut l'acre VI s.

Es parrez des essarz, XVII acres, l'acre IIII s.

Item, I verg. et demie de pré, por tout XII s.

Item, XXX acres de bois—n'est pas en ferme.

Anvers la Belotiere, IIII acres et I verg., l'acre VIII s.

Avoine, X setiers XIIII boiss., vaut le setier VI s.

Le cens ileques, IIII lb.

Item, XLII capons, XLII gelines, I d.

Item, IIII.C oeus, et o X oeus I d.

En la bruere de l'essart, XIIII s., une mote.

Les rel. et les justices.

Le patronage d'une capele.

Item, V acres de bois de la deffense ioste Brotonne, vaut l'acre IIII s.

La terre Robert du Viers Port.

Eu camp de l'Angle au Loet, III verg., por tout XV s.

En la Longue Haie et Corbe Londe, IIII acres et demie, l'acre XX s.—Guillaume le Comte et Guillaume Huret pristrent l'acre por XXII s.

Eu camp Rolant, III acres et demie, l'acre XII s.—Guillame Wiret prist l'acre por XIIII s.

Eu camp Sevestre, V verg., por tout XII s.—Guillaume Goves et Guillaume Wiret, por XIIII s.

Eu camp Guerin et en la petite piece, III acres et demie, l'acre vaut VI s.—Guillaume Wiret prist l'acre por VII s.

Eu camp Lohoret, verge et demie, por tout IIII s.—Jehan Rachine por V s.

En la couture souz le mostier et desus, II acres et demie, vaut l'acre VIII s.—Robert le Hesne prist por IX s.

Eu camp Ourriet, III acres, l'acre XIIII s.

Eu camp de la Guisiere, VII verg., por tout X s.

Sus le Lonc Pré, VII verg., por tout VII s.

Entre le bois et le chemin, I acre, IIII s.

fol. 195

Eu camp Feitout, III acres, l'acre VII s.
Sus le camp Farou, demie acre, IX s.
Eu camp a la Felenesse, I acre, VIII s.
Eu camp de la Quesnoie, II acres et demie, l'acre X s.
Eu camp de Huterel, I acre et demie, l'acre X s.
Eu camp Osmo, II acres, l'acre X s.
En la couture sus la meson Robert Hardel, III acres, l'acre VI s.
Eu jardin du Quesne,[1] IIII acres, l'acre et l'erbage XX s.
Le fruict, IIII lb.
Item, demie acre, X s.
La court devant le mostier, III verg., vaut l'erbage XII s.

Jurée

Le fruict, IIII s.—Item, est la mote haute.
En la couture au Cat, II acres, l'acre IIII s.—Raoul le Fevre
    prist l'acre por V s.
Eu fieu des Vauz, I acre, VI s.
Joste la meson Jehan Blanchart, I verg., XVIII d.
Eu camp des Vaatres, III verg., por tot VIII s.
Eu Cauvei Berte, IIII acres, l'acre VI s.—Robert Renaut l'acre
    prist por VII s.
Eu camp Hellot, III acres, l'acre IIII s.
Eu pré du Quesne,[1] VI acres, l'acre XXXII s.—Guillaume
    Goves et Guillaume Hure l'acre prist por XXXIII s.

fol. 195v
N'est pas
en ferme
Mesure

Item, eu pré Davy, I vergie, V s.—Rad. le Fevre por VI s.
Eu fieu du Quesne, C.V acres de bosc.

Le molin du Quesne, XLV lb. Le prestre prist ileques la disme.
    Et sont ileques XXI baniers.
Un four vaut X s.

Rentes

La moute seiche vaut V boiss. de forment de rente.
L'avoine, I quartier, vaut XVIII d. de rente.
Le cens en deniers, X lb. II s. VIII d.
Item, LXXVII capons, et o les capons VI s. IIII d.
Gelines II, oeus VI.C.IIII.XX et X, et o X oeus I d.

fol. 196

Item, les services des fauqueors en XV verg. de pré, vaut le
    fauquage de chascune verg. VIII d.
Guillaume Wiret doit querre les fers d'une carue, valent IIII s.
Item, il doit querre III cotiaulz a trenchier le pain.

---

[1] Le Chêne-aux-Dames (?), Calvados, a. Pont-l'Evêque, c. Dozulé, cne. Glanville.

Item, un videre ou V s., I chien ou II s.

Item, LX fers a cheval, ou X s.

Durant le Fevre, III coutiaulz ou XVIII d.

Item, sont ileques III residences, valent XII s.

Les preeres de XXX carues II foiz en l'an, valent LXXV s. VI d.

Item, XXIII hommes qui doivent fener et amener les feinz;
    item, les pommes coedre, amener et tribler.

Touz les hommes du fieu doivent amener le mesrien a faire la sale.

Les rel. et les justices X lb.

Et le patronage d'une iglise.

<table>
<tr><td>

fol. 196v
Comtée par
sey

</td><td>

La ferme de la terre de Glanville[1] IX lb.

</td></tr>
</table>

La terre Olivier du Quesne.

Eu camp de l'Erablet, III acres, vaut l'acre VI s.

Eu camp Franque, I acre, V s.

Eu camp du molin, II acres et demie, l'acre VII s.

Eu camp Martinet et eu camp Hueline, III acres, l'acre VIII s.

Jurée

Eu jardin de haut, I acre et demie, l'acre X s.

Le fruict XX s.

Eu camp de Pinardieres, III acres, l'acre VI s.

Au fou de Foucheres, XVI acres, l'acre VI s.

Eu camp Roberge, IX verg., por tout XII s.

A la Billiotiere, I verg., por tout II s.

Eu jardin du doict, I acre, XX s.

Le fruict IIII lb.

Le pré, III verg., por tout XV s.

*N'est pas
en ferme*

Le bosc XVII acres.

Item, une haie joste les prez continanz entor III acres, vaut l'acre
    XXV s.

fol. 197
Mesure

Le cens IIII lb. XI s. VI d.

VII vavass[ors], XX s. Item, XLI capons et III s. V d.

Item, IIII.C.XXX oeus, et o X oeus I d.

Item, sont ileques les hommes qui doivent le fienz espartir, les
    feinz amener, les pommes coedre, tribler et amener.

Rentes

Les rel, et les justices.

---

[1] Glanville (?), Calvados, a Pont-l'Evêque, c. Dozulé. *cf. Quer. Nor.*, no. 50. A fief at
Glanville was forfeited when the holder went to England, but there is no proof that it is
this fief which is referred to here.

Un siege de molin—Sont ileques XI baniers.

La moute seiche vaut III s.

Le patronnage de l'iglise du Quesne.

Et III quartiers d'avoine.

La terre Ricart le filz Hue anvers Quartel—N'est pas comtée par le—ballif de Caan.

Au Buquet, V verg., por tout V quartiers d'orge.

Es Mortes Terres, V verg. a celi pris.

Item, en icele delle, V verg. a cel pris.

Eu camp de la Saete, V verg. a cel pris.

Joste le chemin de la Falese, demie acre, demie vergie, por tot
b[1] III quartiers d'orge.

Es Hautes Mortes Terres, III verg., valent III quartiers d'orge.

a[1] Sus l'erable de Mourteres, demie acre, demie verg., por tout III quartiers d'orge.

Eu maneir au seignor, I acre, vaut VII quartiers d'orge.

En la Campaigne, VII verg. en frique, valent por tout I quartier d'orge.

Le pré ileques, III verg., valent IIII s. tor.

Le molin ileques, por la tierce partie le—Roy, XI setiers pleinne mine d'orge a la mesure de Saint Pierre.[2]

Le cens en deniers XXIIII s. V d.

Une livre de poivre, vaut III s.

Item, IX capons, IIII gelines XIII d.

Item, C.X oeus et VI d.

Item, en la paroisse du Quartel en la rue de la Faleise, Jehan de Morens, VII s.

Les heirs Gaubert de Breteville, V s., II pains, II capons, I geline, I d., XXX oeus, II d.

De ces
rentes
doit estre
enquis
en la
ballie
de
Roem

Robert de Breteville, V s. II d., II capons, XXX oeus, II d.

Robert Lebel, XII d.; I geline, I d.; X oeus.

Robert Richier, XVIII d.; I capon, I d.; I geline, I d.; XXX oeus, I d.

Andreu Herbrichon, I lb. de poivre. Item, eu molin de Chairon VII setiers XI boiss. et demie d'orge a la m[esure] de Saint Pierre de Dive, valent LXII s.

Item, VI acres et demie de terre, valent VI setiers d'orge.

[1] cf. fol. 158v.

[2] Saint-Pierre-sur-Dive.

Item, II perches de pré, valent II s.

Item, eu molin de Grant Camp, VIII lb.

Item, ileques I acre et demie de pré, vaut XXX s.

Eu fieu Lovel, XVI d.

Les preeres des carues du Quesne, por tout IIII lb.

Item, les residences, por tout XX s.

Le fruict sauvage de haes XX s.

La somme IX.XX.XI lb. XIIII s. I d.

Iceste ferme creist selonc ballie et a ballier XXXIX lb. XII s. I d.

<table>
<tr><td>N'estoit pas es roules</td><td></td></tr>
</table>

N'estoit pas es roules
Anvers le Hamel Ricost, XX s.

Le cens, IIII capons, XL oeus, IIII d. et II pains.

fol. 199

La ferme de la terre Robert Fromentin au Grant Doict[1] LVI lb.

En la couture sus le mostier, VIII acres, l'acre VII s. VI d.

Eu clos sus le mostier, XLIX perches, por tout XX s.

Eu camp de Lorfarderie, VII verg., por tout VIII s.

Sus la meson au Chevrre, demie acre, V s.

En la couture devant la meson Jehan l'Angleiz, IIII acres et demie, vaut l'acre X s.

Jurée
Item, ileques desus, IIII acres, l'acre VI s.

Item, ileques III acres de brueray, l'acre IIII s.

Les terres es Sellions, VII verg., por tout X s.

N'est pas en ferme
Anvers la croiz Boissier, X acres, vaut l'acre V s.

A l'aunay Mallevrier, I verg. et demie de bosc, por tout V s., la superficie vaut IIII lb.

Eu clos Aubert, III verg. et demie de jardin, por tout XV s. Le fruict vaut VII s.

fol. 199v
Mesure
Le jardin Sevin, IX verg., por tout XLV s. Le fruict XL s.

La metie d'un molin, XIII lb.

Le cens ileques, CXII s. IX d.

Les preeres por toute la ferme, XX s.

Rentes
L'avoine ileques XXIIII setiers II boiss., vaut le setier VI s.

Item, VI.XX et I pains, III capons, LXXII gelines.

Item, VI.C et XLV oeus et IIII poucins.

---

[1] Grandouet, Calvados, a. Pont-l'Evêque, c. Cambremer, *Quer. Nor.*, no. 53. The nephews of Robert "Formentin" ask a portion of his land, on the grounds that Robert never gave their father his rightful share of the estate. Robert forfeited the land by remaining in England after the conquest. The nephews estimate the value of the land at only 25 l.

Item, touz ceulz du fieu doivent le fein coedre et auner; item, les pommes coedre et tribler.

fol. 200

La ferme Erneys de la Roque.

Est ileques I acre de pré, vaut XX s.

Le cens, XXIX s. II d.

Item, IX capons et I geline, I cent de poires.

Item, X fers a cheval o les clouz, I coutel ou III d.

N'est pas
en ferme

Item, VII acres de bosc, ne sont pas en ferme.

La ferme Robert de la Mare.

Eu camp Flour, I acre demie, por tot VII s. VI d.

Sus la Tremblaie, I acre, V s.

Eu camp que le apele la Vigne Galeran, demie acre, II s. VI d.

Eu camp du Home, VII verg., vaut l'acre X s.

Jurée

Eu camp souz la Buignie, II acres et demie, l'acre VIII s.

Eu val de l'Espinay et sus le doict, V verg., l'acre VI s.

Eu camp de Crevecour,[1] demie acre, X s.

Le fruict, III s.

Item, demie acre de pré, X s.

fol. 200v
Rentes

Le cens en deniers, XXII s. III ob.

Item, XV capons, III gelines.

Item, II oues, VIII.XX.XV oeus.

La terre Robert Formentin anvers Manerbe.[1]

Sont ileques IIII acres de bruerie, vaut l'acre V s.

Le cens en deniers, XIIII s. II d.

L'avoine, IIII setiers, vaut le setier VI s.

Item, VII gelines, VII d.

Item, LXX oeus et VII d.

La ferme Guillaume Brichart anvers Quevrel, a la Planque[2] et a Hotot.[3]

Es broces—le Roy III acres, vaut l'acre V s.

Eu jardin le—Roy de Platel, II acres et demie, l'acre XII s.

Jurée
fol. 201

Le fruict vaut XII s.

Eu camp de Noviau Clos I acre, XII s.

Le fruict, XVI s.

L'auney du Noviau Clos, I acre, XII s.

---

[1] Crèvecoeur-en-Auge (?), Calvados, a. Lisieux, c. Mézidon.

---

[1] Manerbe, Calvados, a. Pont-l-Evêque, c. Blangy. cf. note, fol. 199.

[2] La Planche (?), Calvados, a. Lisieux, c. Mézidon, cne. Crèvecoeur.

[3] Hotot-en-Auge, Calvados, a. Pont-l'Evêque, c. Cambremer.

Le fruict, III s.
Anvers Naire Val, II acres, l'acre VI s.
Sus la meson Osbert le Potier, I verg. et demie, por tout V s.
Le pré Quevrel, demie acre, XI s.

Le cens en deniers, CX s. II d.
Item I setier et IIII boiss. de forment, vaut le setier XVI s.
Avoine ileques, VIII setiers, vaut le setier VI s.

Item, XL capons, XL gelines, III.C.LXX oeus.
Robert le Potier I boiss. de noiz, vaut XII d.
Les preeres de III carues II foiz en l'an.
Item, icelz du fieu doivent clorre les iardins, coedre les pommes,
    et le fruict tribler et auner.

A la Planche.
Eu camp de la Planche, I acre, XXIIII s.
Le cens en deniers, XXXIII s. VIII d.
Item, III quartiers d'avoine, I quartier de forment, X capons,
    IIII.XX oeus.
Les preeres de II carues II foiz en l'an.
La somme LXXVIII lb.

La ferme de la terre Robert Lefevre, XVI d., ou VIII fers a cheval.
La terre Guillaume Aubert, II s., perpetuel.
La terre Morel du Livet, XII d., perpetuel.
La terre Paein de Sainte Marie, XVII s.
L'avoine ileques, XVI setiers, vaut le setier VI s.

La Serganterie de Honnefleu[1]

La ferme Guillaume Boutemont du gardin de Penne de Pie[2] et de la
    garde de Waseic, XVI lb.

Deriere la meson Guillaume Hoccan, demie acre, vaut XII s.
Item, a Renele, III vergies, XVIII s.
Item, ileques I acre et demie, vaut l'acre XX s.
Es Corteriz, demie acre, XIIII s.
Item, ileques I acre, vaut XXIIII s.
Es Graveles, III verg., XVIII s.

---

[1] Honfleur, Calvados, a. Pont-l'Evêque. Most of Honfleur was held by the Bertrans, cf.
Cartulaire de Bricquebec (ed. C. Bréard), pp. 224, 227.
[2] Pennedepie, Calvados, a. Pont-l'Evêque, c. Honfleur.

Item, ileques et a la Fonteinne au Tur, I acre, XXVIII s.

Item, I vergee, VII s.

Item, I autre verg., VII s.

Sus le clos Renaut, demie acre, XIIII s.

Jurée

Item, I verg., VII s.

Au Choucay, I acre, IX s.

Joste le Lonc Bouel, I acre, XVI s.

A la voie porquier demie acre, VIII s.

Sus le vivier, III verg., IX s.

Au molin foulerez, I verg., VIII s.

A Clebec, I verg., IIII s.

Robert Marcade, I acre, XVI s.

Es Graviers, I verg., IIII s.[1] Somme, par mesure, XIII acres et demie perche meinz.[1]

Les prez, III acres et III verg., por tout L s.

fol. 203

Le jardin continant I acre et I verg., por tout XL s.

Rentes

Un gort, XVI s.—Thomas le Moine III d. ou I ganz.

Gefroy Alori, V s., III capons, III d.

Les preeres, se il sont ileques.

Les rel. de vilains.

La some XVIII lb. VI s.

Item, est le siege du molin.

Le relief et la justice n'est pas ballie.

Rogier Boutel prist la ferme devant dite en renchierissant por XXX lb. XIII s.

Et est ileques le siege du molin, n'est pas en ferme.

Item, il n'a pas la iauue de Waseic ne de Penne de Pie.

Les terres creiscent de V verg., valent XIII s., et en tel maniere creist icele ferme de XIIII lb. XIIII s.

fol. 203v
Mesure

Comtée
par sey

La ferme Agace Troussebout[1] VI.XX lb.—comtée par sey.

Eu camp du Puiz, XIIII acres, par mesure XVIII acres LX

---

[1] Very crowded, apparently inserted after the page was written.

---

[1] *Quer. Nor.*, no. 57. Agatha Trousebout was given land at "Formevilla" by the king "in maritagium." It later reverted to him, on her death without heirs. *cf.* Stapleton, II, lxxvii, lxxviii.

perches, vaut l'acre XII s.—Ricart de Tyville d'Escamiauville prist l'acre por XV s.

Eu clos de la couture de Frommeville,[2] VII acres, par mesure VIII acres et demie, XXVI perches, l'acre XII s.—Mahieu de la Croiz prist tout por C s. et creist por la seignorie des terres de XXII s.

Anvers Landebroc, VII acres a celi pris, par mesure VI acres— Ricart prist por XII s. l'acre.

Anvers Bonneville, II acres, III verg., por tout L s.—Anssel Orellion[3] por XXV s. l'acre.

I jardin que le chastelain tient, vaut IIII lb.—Icest jardin est ballie a Ricart de Tyville por C s.—et est ileques le colombier qui n'est pas en ferme, vaut C s.—Ricart prist por C s.

fol. 204

Le molin de Frommville et la moute seiche, XL lb.—Guillaume Gromet por L lb.

Le molin de Berneville[1] o la moute seiche, XXXV lb.—Rogier Boutel por XLVI lb.

Item, ileques XLIII setiers d'avoine, vaut le setier V s.—Ricart por XVI lb. XII d.

Rentes

Item, XX boiss. de forment, valent XX s., XVI boiss. font le setier, Ricart por XV s.

Item, III lb. de poivre, VI s.—Ricart por VI s.

Le cens, IX lb. IX s. Item, XXXVI capons.

Item, XI s. V d. ob. Item, VI.C.XV oeus. Gelines, LXIII et III oues. A Pasques, XLVIII s. Les preeres de VI carues II foiz en l'an, et tout autant d'erces, rel. et justices por tout XXX s. Ricart prist por XXX s.

fol. 204v
N'est pas
en ferme

Le campart ileques de IIII acres et demie et XXVIII perches, XX s., n'est pas en ferme—Ricart prist por XX s.—Iceli Richart prist le remanant a la value et vaut sa somme LVI lb. II s. I d.

La somme VI.XX lb. CXVII s. VIII d. ob.

Iceste ferme creist de XXXVI lb. V s.

Ceste serganterie creist de XLIIII lb. VII s. IIII d.

---

[2] Fourneville, Calvados, a. Pont-l'Evêque, c. Honfleur.
[3] *cf.* fol. 190.

---

[1] Barneville, Calvados, a. Pont-l'Evêque, c. Honfleur.

Comté par
sey
Le molin a l'abbé de Saint Euvoult,[1] VI lb., perpetuel, comté par sey.

Le cens d'Escamiauville,[2] XV lb. XV s., perpetuel. Les regarz a Noel
et a Pasques, VI s. II d., perpetuel. Raoul le Miere prist o les rel. et la
simple justice por XX lb. es octaves de Noel en l'an LXI.

L'abbé de Saint Richier encheri tout de XL s.—Item, encheri sus lui de
XL s.—Renaut Dablon l'enchiera de XL s. sus l'abbé et mist en contreplege VI s. d'anuel rente.

La somme de toute la viscomté IIII.C.LXIII lb. VIII s.
I d.

fol. 205

La some de toute la baillie de Roem, II.M.IIII.C.XXI[1]
lb.

Les parprestures de la haie du Teil,[2] XII d. perpetuel.
Les regarz au Pigre, XII d.—perpetuel.
La terre de Moliniaus,[3] IIII s.
Les regarz au forestier, IIII lb.—perpetuel.
Le fieu Juguel, XX s.—perpetuel.
La terre Chairon, IIII s.—perpetuel.
La porcherie de Bone Ville, XXX s.
La prevosté de Penne de Pie,[4] C s.
Robert Erart, X s.
L'erbage de Roval, VII s.
La prevosté de Honneflue, IX lb.
Anvers Formeville,[5] VI setiers, III quartiers d'avoine.
Anvers Escamiauville, IX setiers—l'abbé de Saint Riquier prist par le
pricor VII setiers, le setier por VIII s. en l'eschiquier de Pasques en
l'an LXII.[6]

---

[1] *Cart. Nor.*, no. 657. Louis IX ratifies the grant by Queen Blanche of a "platea . . .
sita inter Molinellos et Honefiendam . . . ad faciendum quoddam molendinum" to St.
Evroul for six pounds a year. *c.* 1260.

[2] Equemauville, Calvados, a. Pont-l'Evêque, c. Honfleur.

[1] This figure can be obtained only by adding the total increase of the viscounty of
Pont-de-l'Arche (fol. 231) to the total of the increases of the other viscounties (fols.
39v, 98, 156v, 204v). This indicates that the items on this page were entered after the
record was finished.

[2] Le Theil, Calvados, a. Pont-l'Evêque, c. Honfleur.

[3] Moulineaux, Calvados, a. Pont-l'Evêque, c. Honfleur, cne. Equemauville.

[4] Pennedepie, Calvados, a. Pont-l'Evêque, c. Honfleur.

[5] Fourneville, Calvados, a. Pont-l'Evêque, c. Honfleur.

[6] The entries on this page, added after the scribe had made his totals, seem to refer
to the sergeanty of Honfleur.

Item, par le forestier, VIII setiers, I quartier.

Du mestier de Formeville, par le forestier, VIII setiers, I quartier.

Sus le mes Guerart, I acre de terre anvers Vierval, VII s., le seignor prist tout.

Les gastines de Bonneville.

> Por devers Escamiauville, IIII.C.XXV acres et demie.
> Item, II.C.XIII acres.
> Item, C acres et demie.
> Le joncheiz a mesurer et une noeue vente entor IIII.XX acres.
> La somme VII.C.XXXIX acres.

Anvers Saint Aysnier d'une terre, X s. par Thomas le Clerc—l'en enquist et des arrerages.

Item, la meson plaideresse joste le chastel de Bonneville—Ballie a Ricart de la Fonteinne por V s.—en l'eschiquier de Pasques en l'an LX.

Veci la viscomté du Pont de l'Arche[1]

La Serganterie de Wauvrai

Nous devons descomter et descomteron par le viscomte du Pont de l'Arche XXXIII s. por les aumosnes et les fieuz trop comtez, c'est asavoir por la metie XVI s. VIII d.

En toutes les fermes de la viscomté du Pont de l'Arche le tiers est paié a Pasques et les II pars a la Saint Michiel.

Veci la Serganterie du Pont de l'Arche.

La ferme de la prevosté du Pont de l'Arche XVI.XX lb.[2]

> Le cens, LXX s.   Les hales, XX lb.
> Le campart, IX lb.
> II molins, IIII.XX lb.
> Le travers, LX lb.
> La costume du vin et des borgeiz, XL lb.
> La costume du pain forain, XII lb.
> La costume de la guesde, L lb.
> Les estaulz au suours, XX s.
> Les estaulz au ciriers, XII s.
> La costume de l'arche et la pesquerie des gorz, XLV lb.

---

[1] Pont-de-l'Arche, Eure, a. Louviers.

[2] *Cart. Nor.*, no. 179 (p. 297), 255. Richard gained Pont de l'Arche by an exchange with Jumièges in 1195; Philip Augustus later confirmed this. *cf.* above, note, fol. 91.

Le musel et l'arrinage des tronz, XX s.

Les hales as merciers, XXV s.

Les misericordes, XX s.

La costume du ble forain, XXX s.

Une acre de terre en la paroisse de Igoville,[1] VIII s.

La somme III.C.XXI lb. V s.

fol. 208

La ferme de la terre Mons. Pierres de Preaulz,[1] que l'en dit de Caudebec,[2] C lb. C s.

Item, XIIII acres et demie de terre, chascune XXI s.

L'avoine, IIII muiz et VII setiers.

Por XIII masures et demie, por chascune VII s. IIII d., II capons, VIII oeus.

Item, por les dites XIII masures, III setiers I quartier de ble.

Por la couture Aguillon, X capons, XIII s. IIII d.

Por I fieu est apelé le Bordage, IX s.

Por les campars, XVIII lb.

*Por le jardin au seignor de Harecourt XL [sic][3]—perpetuel.

Eu molin d'Eullebue,[4] XXVIII lb.—perpetuel.

Au Bosc Asceline,[5] I acre et III verg. de terre, valent I setier de forment de XVIII s.

Por le fieu Raoul d'Eullebue, LX s., perpetuel.

I jardin anvers Eullebue[4] en la Poterie, XX s.

Ileques prez I cortil, V s.

Au Tuit Anger,[6] IX acres, VIII lb. III s.

fol. 208v

Anvers Marretot,[1] XXX acres, desqueles V sont en masure.

La masure Rose, XIII s.; II gelines, II d.; XX oeus et II d.

Enmeline de l'Escalier, V s.; III capons, II d.; et XII d.

Por le service—Guillaume Ogier, V s., II capons, II d.

Por III services, XII d.—La fame Robert du Val, VI s.

---

[1] Igoville, Eure, a. Louviers, c. Pont-de-l'Arche.

[1] Stapleton, II, cxlv. Pierre was a prominent noble of Normandy under Richard and John. He adhered to John after the conquest and died in England.

[2] Caudebec-les-Elbeuf, Seine-Inférieure, a. Rouen, c. Elbeuf.

[3] *Cart. Nor.*, no. 371. In 1230 Louis IX granted Richard de Harecourt "jardinum nóstrum de Eullebue super secanam" at an annual rent of 40 s.

[4] Elbeuf, Seine-Inférieure, a. Rouen.

[5] Saint-Nicolas-du-Bosc-Asselin, Eure, a. Louviers, c. Amfreville-la-Campagne.

[6] Le Thuit-Anger, Eure, a. Louviers, c. Amfreville-la-Campagne.

[1] Martot, Eure, a. Louviers, c. Pont-de-l'Arche.

Guillaume Tovel,[2] V s., II capons, XX oeus, II d.

Anvers la Mare Tassel,[3] demie acre, vaut XVIII s.

La somme CVII lb. XVII s. X d.

La masure de la terre de Caudebec.

Sont ileques en II coutures XIIII acres et XIII perches.

Item, anvers Maretot,[1] XVII acres et demie verg. et doit la meson Robert de Feugueroles ileques parfaire XXX acres, sicomme l'en dit, et doit estre enquis.

Item, ileques I acre et demie d'autre fieu.

Item, anvers le Tuit Anger, X acres.

Item, anvers le Bosc Ascelin, I acre et demie.

Item, anvers la Mare Tassel, demie acre.

fol. 209

Icele ferme devant dite est ballie a Mons. Jehan de Harecourt por VI.XX lb. VIII s. VI d.

La some des baulz dechiet la somme du—Ballif en XVII lb. VI s. VIII d.

N'estoient pas en ferme

En la paroisse de Saint Amant[1] et du Tuit Signol[2] sont XIIII mines d'avoine de bernage qui doivent estre renduz au Pont de l'Arche a la Saint Michiel, et XIIII gelines a cele feste, cen est ballie o la ferme.

N'estoit pas en ferme

Anvers Evraville,[3] VI setiers d'avoine de bernage, et est enquis.

N'estoit pas en ferme

Anvers Dameneville,[4] est ileques prez XI setiers et I mine d'avoine de bernage ensement—est enquis.

fol. 209v

Veci la Serganterie del Val de Rooil[1]

La ferme des masures du Val de Rooil IIII.XX.XV lb.

Anvers Wauvrai,[2] XVI masures et demie, chascune doit IIII setiers d'avoine, vaut le setier VI s. Item, III s. Item, chascun IIII d., III gelines. Item, XII oeus. Item, I quartier de forment, vaut le setier XII s.

Por bordages VI s.—Henri de la Cort prist ices bordages por

---

[2] Or Covel.

[3] La Mare-Tassel, Eure, a. Louviers, c. Amfreville, cne. Le Thuit-Signol.

---

[1] Saint-Amand-des-Hautes-Terres, Eure, a. Louviers, c. Amfreville.

[2] Le Thuit-Signol, Eure, a. Louviers, c. Amfreville.

[3] Vraiville, Eure, a. Louviers, c. Amfreville.

[4] Damneville (?), Eure, a. and c. Louviers, cne. Quatremare.

---

[1] Le Vaudreuil, Eure, a. Louviers, c. Pont-de-l'Arche.

[2] Saint-Pierre-du-Vauvray, Eure, a. and c. Louviers, or Saint-Etienne-du-Vauvray, *ibid.*

XIIII s. Item, il prist la terre Jehan le Senescal por XXX s., escripte est dedenz.

Por le cens des autres masures, VI lb.

Anvers Portigoie,[3] XII masures, desqueles X rendent chascune
* IIII setiers d'avoine, III—III gelines, XII oeus, I quartier de forment, VI d.

Des autres II, une est en la main le—Roy, vaut XL s.

L'autre doit XX s.

Por II bordages, XII d., XII oeus.

Anvers Tornedos,[4] XII masures, chascune por tout XX s.

fol. 210

Anvers le Val de Rooil, V masures, desqueles chascune doit IIII setiers d'avoine, III s., III gelines, XII oeus, I quartier de forme.nt.

Les rentes des autres masures, IX lb.

Le cens des coutures, IIII lb.

Chascune des masures devant dites qui doit avoine doit campart de terres qui apartienent as masures et vaut III moez, tant d'orge que d'avoine, par an, qui valent X lb. XVI s.

Guillaume Letort, II capons.

Anvers Wavrai et Portigoie, por les cens des masures XIIII lb.
La somme CVIII lb. IIII s. III d.
Iceste somme dechiet la somme des fermes XIII lb. IIII s. III d.

Dehors le castel, VI acres de terre, IIII lb., par mesure VI acres et demie, XXIIII perches—Ballie a Mons. Raoul le castelain de Val de Rooil por C s. Mons. Robert de Warrcline[1] l'encheri de XX s.—Jehan le Tarvernier le rencheri de XX s. et remainst a Mons. Raoul por VII lb. XIIII s. VIII d., selonc la mesure.

fol. 210v

Robert du Parrey, III s., perpetuel.

La prevosté de Tornedos, LX s.

Sont ileques XII masures—Phelippe Lebret et icelz qui les tienent ont pris iceles por IIII lb.

Comtée par sey

La terre que len dit d'Esquetot,[1] qui fu Tiebaut de Chartres, L lb.[2]

---

[3] Portejoie, Eure, a. Louviers, c. Pont-de-l'Arche.
[4] Tournedos-sur-Seine, *ibid.*

---

[1] *Cart. Nor.*, no. 632. In 1259 "Robertus de Warclive, miles," sold the king a house which he had held at Vaudreuil.

---

[1] Ecquetot, Eure, a. Louviers, c. Le Neubourg.

Ricart de la Haie, por II acres de terre, demie mui d'avoine, perpetuel.

La terre de Poses,[3] XII d., perpetuel.

Le pré Guillaume Havart, VI d., perpetuel.

Le molin de Lery,[4] C s., perpetuel.

Comtée
par sey

La terre Pierres le Suor, XVIII d., perpetuel.

La terre de Pintarville,[5] C s., perpetuel.

La terre au comte de Meullent, C s., perpetuel.

I montier en l'aioue Destuire, VII d.

La terre Mabile du Bosc Normant, C s., perpetuel.

La malliere de la prée, X d., perpetuel.

La terre Robert Malliart, II s., perpetuel.

La terre Rogier Crespin, V s., perpetuel.

La terre Jehan le Senescal, XIII s. IIII d.—Ballie sicomme desus—[6]

fol. 211

La masure Ernaut de Torville,[1] II s., perpetuel.

La terre a la Toupete, XII d.—perpetuel.

La somme VIII.XX.XV lb. XIII s. X d.[2]

La ferme de la prevosté du Val de Rooil, XVI.XX lb.

Troiz fours, C s.

II forges, X s.

II molins, IIII.XX.X lb.[3]

La costume ileques, XX lb.

Unes foires en la feste Saint Dyonis, X lb.

I pestiz, CX s.

Les censuiers de l'aiue por la licence de pesquier, XVIII lb.

L'avalage de l'aioue, C s.[4]

Les II pars del montage de l'aiue, XXV s.[4]

---

[2] *Cart. Nor.*, nos. 313, 342 (p. 309). Philip Augustus and Louis VIII had given Thibaut land at Ecquetot, Criquetot and Villettes, for which he paid 50 l. a year.

Delisle, *Ech.*, nos. 675n, 675r. Thibaut was dead by 1239 and his estate was then being divided among his children. Ecquetot had already reverted to the king, since in 1238 the *bailli* of Rouen accounted for 25 l. from Ecquetot for one term. *H. F.*, XXI, 255.

[3] Poses, Eure, a. Louviers, c. Pont-de-l'Arche.

[4] Léri, Eure, a. Louviers, c. Pont-de-l'Arche.

[5] Pinterville, Eure, a. and c. Louviers.

[6] *cf.* fol. 209v.

---

[1] *cf.* note, fol. 78.

[2] This seems to be the sum of the whole sergeanty to this point.

[3] *Cart. Nor.*, nos. 1094, 1103, 250 (p. 302), are acts of Philip Augustus concerning the mills of Vaudreuil. Granted to minor officials, they returned to the king as a result of a series of exchanges.

[4] This probably refers to tolls for the use of the Eure. Beaurepaire, *op. cit.*, p. 239, states that as late as 1755 *péage* was still taken at the port of Vaudreuil.

Item, les hales du Val de Rooil, IIII lb.
                La some VII.XX.XIX lb. V s.

Le fieu au Boutellier[1] anvers Portigoie, XII masures.
        Chascune XII d., II capons a Noel.
        Item, XII oeus et XII manseis a Pasques.
        A la feste Saint Jehan XVIII d. por le foage.
        A la feste Saint Michiel X d. de cenz.
        III setiers d'avoine, III boiss. de forment par chascune masure.
        Item, III desdites masures doivent III.C pipeniaulz, chascun
            vaut I d. Item, II anguilles a Caresme Prenant, chascune
            vaut XII d.
        La costume des dites masures, X s.
        Item, doivent fener, le fain coedre en II acres de pré, vaut VI d.
        Le campart des dites masures, XVIII setiers, tant d'orge que
            d'avoine, chascun mui LXXII s.
        II acres de pré, XL s.
        Por une masure anvers Gavray,[2] V s.

Une masure anvers Poses,[1] II capons a Noel, XX oeus a Pasques,
            III setiers d'avoine a la feste Saint Michiel, III boiss. de
            forment et une almoniere valante XII d.
        Le campart d'icele masure, I setier d'avoine, vaut VI s.
        Anvers Lery[2] le cens vaut LVIII s.
                La somme XXX lb. XII s. VIII d.

Le fieu au mareschal, VIII acres de terre, valent X lb., sont ileques par
    mesure IX acres et demie, XXXIII perches.
Anvers le Val de Rooil, IIII acres de terre sablouses, l'acre IIII s.
La metie de la coillete por les bestes, VI lb.
                Icele terre est ballie a Henri de Portigoie, prestre de
                Sainte Marie du Val de Rooil,[3] chascune acre por
                XXX s.

---

[1] Is this fief, or the marshal's fief on the next folio, a remnant of lands assigned to ducal
officers in their official capacity? This is a very old part of the domain, and these official
fiefs may go back to Richard II.

[2] Probably Saint-Pierre or Saint-Etienne-du-Vauvray, Eure, a. and c. Louviers.

[1] Poses, Eure, a. Louviers, c. Pont-de-l'Arche.

[2] Léry, *ibid.*

[3] Notre-Dame-du-Vaudreuil, *ibid.*

> Item, ballie est a iceli la meson qui fu Frambert[4] por XL s. et fist assignement a cent soudées de terre de son fieu par an.

Les moinnes de Bon Port por la premiere falce, XX s.—Ballie a Henri le prestre du Val de Rooil por XXII s.

Demie acre de pré anvers Hom,[1] Xs.

*La metie   [2] des prez le—Roy du Val de Rooil, de Lery   [2] et
*   de Hom[1]—Ballie as moinnes de Bon Port

Item, les rentes que l'en apele les manseiz.

Item, la metie de jogie[2]

Item, XIX charree de fein por XXV lb., et X s. par an.[2]

*   et les mareschiaulz anvers le Val de Rooil en cenz a la feste Saint Michiel, C s. et XXXIII capons a Noel.

Anvers Gavray le campart d'une masure, I setier d'avoine, vaut VI s.

Item XX borgages, valent VI s. VIII d.

> La so[mme] XXVIII lb. XIIII s. VIII d., sanz la meson Franbert.

De la terre Pierres du Crues, por tout XV s.

La forest du Val de Rooil anvers Lery, XXII masures et demie, chascune doit VIII boiss. d'avoine; I pain, vaut II d.; I geline, IIII oeus; XII gerbes, c'est assavoir IIII de mesteil, IIII d'orge, IIII d'avoine, et vaut chascune garbe IIII d.

Et se la masure est devisée chascun tenant feu en eulz il doit iceles costumes.

Item, sont ileques III fours, valent LX s.

---

[4] J. Andrieux, *Cartulaire de Bonport* (Evreux, 1862), p. 66. There was a Frambert who was clerk to the viscount of Vaudreuil in 1227. This entry suggests that the government may have provided lodgings for even minor officials.

---

[1] Isle l'Homme, Eure, a. Louviers, c. Pont-de-l'Arche, in the Eure at Vaudreuil.

[2] The scribe was obviously copying here a document which he could not read, or could not understand. Omissions may be supplied from *Cart. Nor.*, no. 607. In 1259 Louis IX gave Bonport "19 scharreias feni prout eas percipiebamus in pratis Vallis Rodolii, medietatem subtrabum praerie Vallis Rodolii, Hummi, Leriaci et de Loviers, cum medietate logie ibidem, si fuerit, sicut fieri consuevit, et quemdam redditum ibidem percipiendum qui vulgariter dicitur les Manseis" for 25 l. 10 s. tur. As Delisle points out, later readers have also found it difficult to interpret this charter.

Stapleton, I, 92. These 19 loads of hay were part of the farm of Vaudreuil as early as 1180. *ibid.*, cxxxvii. The dukes of Normandy had had important holdings in these meadows as early as the reign of Richard II.

Item, II bordiaulz, chascun IIII boiss. d'avoine, I pain, I geline, et V garbas.

La so[mme] XIII lb. XII d.

Anvers le Val de Rooil, XV masures et demie, chascune I boiss. d'avoine; VI garbes, II d'orge, II de mesteil, II d'avoine; II gelines; II pains, vaut chascun II d.; et VI oeus.

Item, sont ileques XIIII bordages et demi, chascun IIII boiss. d'avene; III garbes, I de mesteil, I d'orge, I d'avoine; I pain; I geline; III oeus. Item, IX borgages, chascun doit V d.

La so[mme] VIII lb. XXII s.

fol. 213v

Anvers Poses por le cens, L s.

Anvers Montoire[1] et Escroville[2] sont entor VI.XX feuz, desquelz IIII anvers Escroville doit chascun I capon a Noel et VI oeus a Pasques.

Item, ileques VI autres feuz, desquelz chascun doit IIII d. a Noel et IIII d. a la feste Saint Jehan Bapt.

Item, sont ileques X autres feuz, desquelz chascun II d. a Noel et II d. a Pasques et a la feste Saint Jehan II d.

La commune d'icele ville[3] doit por l'erbage de la forest X s. a la feste Saint Jehan, et a la feste Saint Remi VI.XX garbes, c'est assavoir la metie de mesteil et l'autre metie d'avoine, c'est assavoir la garbe de mesteil VI d., d'avoine III d.

Item, doit icele commune X setiers de seigle.

Nichole Darrable, II poucins a la Saint Remi.

Chascun feu de Montoire doit I pain ou II d. a Noel et VI oeus a Pasques.

Le priour ileques doit I setier de mesteil a la Saint Remi et IIII poignies de candeles a chascune feste de Sainte Marie et X d. ensement.

fol. 214

Anvers Escroville et anvers Montoire sont III fours boulengieres, / valent por tout XL s.

Robert d'Escroville tient le fieu par la reson duquel i paie au—Roy eu tens de pesson XXV s., ou V pors a la volenté le—Roy et quant il n'est pas pesson il paie XII s. et VI d.

Ices de Montoire et d'Escroville donnent por le porc qui est envoié en la forest eu tens de pesson IIII d., a l'autre tens rien ne doivent.

La somme, XII lb. X s.

---

[1] Montaure, Eure, a. Louviers, c. Pont-de-l'Arche.
[2] Ecrosville, Eure, a. Louviers, c. Pont-de-l'Arche, cne. Montaure.
[3] Ecrosville.

Anvers la Haie Malherbe[1] por IIII.XX.XVII feuz et XIIII quaretes C.XII s.

Por II fors, de chascun XXX s.

La somme VII lb. VI s.

Anvers Evraville[2] sont C feuz, desquelz chascun doit III garbes de bernage et III garbes de marc[age].

Item, por   et le cheval, XIII.XX boiss. d'avoine.

Item, por chascun feu, I pain ou II d. et VI oeus.

Item, sont ileques VIII.XX et X gelines.

fol. 214v

Item, por l'erbage, XX s., c'est assavoir por une vache I d.

Item, V fours, valent L s.

Item, chascune meson quant ele est vendue doit IIII d. de vente et IIII de revestement.

Item, est en la costume des estaulz, des arches, et des closages, c'est assavoir par an V s.

La some XXV lb. XVIII s.

Anvers Surtoville[1] sont IX setiers et VIII boiss. d'avoine.

Item, chascun feu doit XII d.

La somme IIII lb.

Anvers les Dans[2] sont masures, chascune doit VIII boiss. d'avoine, I pain, I geline, et IIII oeus.

La some XLIX s. XI d.

Anvers Portigoie sont XXIII masures, chascune masure doit IIII bois. d'avoine, I pain, II oeus, II garbes d'orge.

La somme LXII s. III d.

fol. 215

Anvers le Bequet sont VI.XX masures, chascune doit XV d.

Item, sont ileques IX autres masures, chascune doit V garbas, V oeus a Pasques, I pain a Noel.

Item, chascune masure aiant cheval doit corvée.

Item, sont ileques VIII autres masures, chascune doit IIII garbes, IIII oeus a Pasques, I pain a Noel.

Item, sont ileques III fours, valent XL s.

---

[1] La Haye-Malherbe, Eure, a. and c. Louviers.
[2] Vraiville, Eure, a. Louviers, c. Amfreville.

[1] Surtauville, Eure, a. and c. Louviers.
[2] Les Damps, Eure, a. Louviers, c. Pont-de-l'Arche.

Item, chascune quarete doit II s.

La somme XI lb. III s. VII d.

Anvers Criquebeu[1] sont divers feuz, c'est assavoir LXIII feuz et demie;
chascun feu doit IIII garbes, II de seigle et II de tramoiz ou XII d.
por garbes; IIII oeus; I pain, ou II d.

Item, IIII d., chascun feu.

Item, sont ileques IIII feuz, valent IIII lb.

Item, XXVIII autres feuz desquelz chascun doit IIII oeus, I pain, et
IIII d.

La some IX lb. XII s. IX d.

fol. 215v

*

Anvers Frenose[1] sont LXXVI feuz, desquelz chascun doit XII d.
I pain, et V oeuz.

Item, IIII mines d'orge, les queles doivent IIII autres feuz par la
raison de

Somme IIII lb. XI s.

Anvers Maretot,[2] XLV feuz, chascun doit III d.

Item, sont ileques VI autres feuz; chascun doit III garbes, c'est assavoir
I d'ybernage et II de marc[age]; I quartier d'avoine; III oeus a
Pasques; I geline a Noel; I pain ou II d.

Chascune vache d'icelz hostieux,[3] III d. por l'erbage.

Item, sont ileques X autres feuz d'iceli feu, chascun doit XII d.

Item, autres II feuz qui paient III gerbes, I geline a Noel.

Somme XLI s. III d.

Anvers Wicarville[4] sont II fours, valent XXIIII s.

Anvers le Pont de l'Arche sont VIII.XX feuz, chascun feu doit II d.

Item, VIII fours, chascun XX s. Item, I potier doit XX s.

Item, chascune vache, I d., valent VIII s. Item, chascun porc maalle,
vaut II s.

Somme X lb. XVIII s. IIII d.

Somme des parties devant dites XVII.XX lb. LXVI s.
X d.

---

[1] Criquebeuf-sur-Seine, Eure, a. and c. Pont-de-l'Arche.

---

[1] Freneuse (?), Seine-Inférieure, a. Rouen, c. Elbeuf.

[2] Martot, Eure, a. Louviers, c. Pont-de-l'Arche.

[3] Note the use of the word "hostieux." Apparently much of the land of this viscounty had
been recently cleared and was settled by *hôtes.*

[4] Incarville (?), Eure, a. and c. Louviers.

fol. 216   La porcherie du Val de Rooil,[1] XXV s.—Ballie a Jehan du Bosc et as
heirs Laurenz Rossel por XL s.

Comtée   Les misericordes de la forest du Bort.
par sey   La pesquerie de l'aioue a Rez, VIII lb.—comtée par sey.

La ferme Ricart de Ry XVI lb.

Les terres arables, VII acres, l'acre XXIIII s. ⎱ par mesure
Item, II acres, chascune acre V s.   ⎰ XI acres, III
Item, I acre et demie, valent II s.   ⎱ verg., et XV
La tierce partie du molin, C s.   ⎰ perches
Item, XXXI capon, valent XV s. VI d.
Item, XVI.XX.X oeus, valent XXXIII d.
Le cens en deniers, LXVI s., II oues valent II s.
Un aignel, vaut XII d.
Les reliez, justices, et les services.
      Somme XVIII lb. VII s. III d.
      Iceste ferme est ballie a Mons. Baldoin,[2] chastelain du

fol. 216v   Val de/de [*sic*] Rooil por XXVIII lb.
      Et creist de XII lb. et fu delessie a iceli por XII lb. de la
      crescence.

Comtée   La ferme de la terre que l'en apele le fieu de Marly LXX lb.
par sey   Un molin, XXV lb.
      Les prez de VIII acres de terre et demie, VIII lb.
      Les cenz, XV lb. Item, les cenz, IX lb.
      Item, XVI setiers et demie de forment marchaant, valent X lb.
      Item, XLIII capons, III gelines et I oue.
      Un aignel ou XII mansoiz.
      Item, XII.XX oeuz, qui valent II s.
      Por le jardin, XXX s.—Ballie a Nichol Basin por XL s.
      Somme LXIX lb. XVII s. VI d.

fol. 217   Veci la Serganterie de Craville[1]

La ferme de la terre de Magneville[2] vaut IIII.XX.VII lb.

---

[1] Stapleton, I, 99. There were two *porcariae* in the forest of Bort in 1180, each yielding
10 pigs. This may represent one of them.
[2] *Cart. Nor.*, no. 808 (p. 338). Philip III gave Baldwin a rent of 50 l. on the prefec-
ture of Vaudreuil in 1271.

---

[1] Crasville, Eure, a. and c. Louviers.
[2] Mandeville, Eure, a. Louviers, c. Amfreville.

Les terres arables, XXII acres, valent XXII lb.

Sont ileques par mesure XXXIII acres et demie.

Un molin, XX lb.

Avoine VI setiers, valent XXXVI s.

N'est pas
ballie
fol. 217v

Item, VI setiers d'avoine por l'erbage, XXXVI s. N'est pas ballie.

Item, forment, XVII setiers et I mine, vaut le setier XII s.

Le cens en deniers, IX lb.

La prevosté et l'erbage de la Haie Aaline, XXX s.

En herbage sont XXXVIII acres et XX perches, par mesure—
Ballies sont a Michiel de la Haie, a Martin et a Jehan du Bosc, freres, a Guillaume de Can et a Ricart Gontier, chascune acre por VIII s.

Por III services de III vavassors, IX lb.

est ead.
fir [ma]

Le campart LX s.

Un jardin, XXX s.

Capons, VII.XX. Galines, VIII. VI.C oeuz et V s.

En deniers, VI s.

Les corvées, XX s.

Por les dangiers d'icelz qui doivent la residence, c'est assavoir Guillaume XX s.; Laurenz, XV s.; Herbert, XV s. et Renout du Val, V s.; Andreu Duremont, V s.; Hemart, V s.

Les ventes et les reliez et les justices, XL s.

fol. 218

Item, monseignor le—Roy a en la granche de Trossebout[1] tout l'estraim qui vient a la granche et est estimé a XXX s., et est assavoir que—l'abbé du Bec qui tient la granche doit ileques amener la diesme toute d'iceli terroor.

Item, a ileques le—Roy quarete bastarde o le herneiz, vaut VI d.
Icele ferme desus dite est ballie a Mons. Guillaume de Tornebuc, chevalier, sanz VI setiers d'avoine qui sont deuz por l'erbage du bosc Trossebot et sanz le bosc, por CX lb., en tel maniere que la baille faite as homes de la Haie remaindra sicomme devant, et icelz respondront a iceli et sont comtées en sa somme.

Item, en cele ferme XL acres de bois qui ne sont pas de ferme, ne ne sont pas ballies.

La somme IIII.XX.XIII lb. XIIII s. VIII d.

Renaut Trossebout,[2] chevalier, prist IIII acres d'iceli bosc, eu lieu que

---

[1] Troussebout, Eure, a. Louviers, c. Amfreville, cne. la Harengère.

[2] *Cart. Nor.*, no. 600. Renaut Trossebout, knight, held land at St. Cyr and made many donations to religious houses between 1258 and 1274.

l'en dit Lescoallie vers Magneville, de l'aage de VI anz, l'acre por XX s., sanz la superficie. La chose Avebert eu boscage sanz le tiers et le dangier et obiliga son maneir de la Trosseboutiere[3]

La ferme de la terre de Dameneville[1] vaut LXVII lb.

> Le cens en mesons, VII lb. IX s. II capons, lesquelz Thomas Pinchon doit desus sa meson a Noel.
>
> XX capons, VI gelines, II.C oeus.
>
> Item, III pastz qui valent XV s.—lesquelz Thomas du Jardin doit, et de cen tient eu fieu environ VI acres de terre a Orne de Craville. Ileques doivent venir les menganz, le seignor et la dame, la damoisele, le prevost, l'escuier, les chienz veneors et les serganz a pie—Ballie a iceli Thomas por XX s.
>
> Item, III oues, valent III s.
>
> Item, sont ileques les corvées qui valent X s.
>
> Item, II perches de terre que Thomas le Vaquier tient por XXX d. Iceli Thomas prist iceles por II s. VI d.
>
> > Item, les terres arables, XLVIII acres, valent L lb.—Les parties sont cestes:
>
> Anvers Dameneville eu camp de [*sic*], III verges et IIII perches.
>
> Eu camp du Quesne, III verg., XXXIIII perches et demie.
>
> Eu camp du Tronquet, IIII acres III verg. et XXIIII perches.
>
> Item, a l'Aispine Berte, V acres et demie, XXIII perches.—Icestes sont ballies a Guillaume de Dameneville, chevalier,[2] ensemble o le jardin et o l'erbage dedenz escrites, tout por XXVI lb. V s.

> A l'Espine, Rogier Fouchier demie acre I vergie et XIII perches.
>
> Eu camp des Roies, II acres XXXIIII perches et demie—Icestes sont ballies a Thomas de Quatremares por IIII lb. XI s.
>
> Eu camp de Lamie Costure, II acres et I verg.—Ballies a Ricart Hamelin et a Thomas le Vaquier, l'acre por XXIIII s., la tierce partie a Pasques et out letres.
>
> Item, en celi camp, lequel camp est apelé les autres le camp de V verges, sont V verg. XX s. l'acre.

---

[3] La Trousseboutière, Eure, a. Louviers, c. Amfreville, cne. St.-Cyr-la-Campagne.

[1] Damneville, Eure, a. and c. Louviers, cne. Le Mesnil-Jourdain. *H. F.,* xxiii, 636. The lord of "Danevenvilla" held five-sixteenths of a knight's fee in Vaudreuil shortly after the conquest.

[2] Delisle, *Ech.,* no. 789. A Guillaume de Dameneville, knight, attended the Exchequer in 1248.

Eu camp du Chief Bois que l'en apele du Londel,[1] III verg. XXXI perches et demie—Ballies a Arnoulf de Chief Ville por XXIIII s. l'acre et a letres et obliga I acre de terre en la paroisse de Quatremares.[2]

Ce sont
les parties

Item, la quarte partie que—le Roy a en II acres de terre lesqueles I prevost tient a meteerie.

Eu camp des Marlieres, I verge XXII perches et demie.

Eu camp de l'Espine Berte, I vergee et demie, XV perches.

Eu camp de la Parelle, demie acre et XVI perches—Ballies sont a Jehan le Prevost por XXVIII s.; c'est assavoir por la metie —le Roy.

fol. 219v

Eu camp de la Fosse du Perier, II acres LX perches—Ballies a a Thomas et a Lorenz por XXIIII s. l'acre.

Eu camp de la gastine que l'en apele des VII acres, IX acres I verg. XXXI perches—Ballies a Thomas, a Andreu, et a Robert Escaude, chascune acre por XXIIII s., et a letres.

Eu camp des Roes, sus la voie, II acres III verg. X perches— Ballies a Ernoulf de Chief Ville, l'acre por XXVII s. et a letres sicomme est desus dit.

Eu camp Travesein IIII acres, XV perches—Ballies a Thomas Laur[ent][1] por XXIIII s. chascune acre.

Hucusque
sunt terre

Dameneville

Item, est ileques I jardin, vaut XXX s.

Item, est ileques l'erbage, contient entor IIII acres, vaut XX s. —Ballie a Guillaume Dameneville, chevalier, sicomme desus est dit.

La seignorie
le—Roy

Anvers Soarville[2] eu camp Louveis, V verges et XXXIII perches.

Eu camp de la Haguete, III acres et demie et XXVIII perches.

Eu camp de la Boissiere, III acres I vergie et XII perches.

Eu camp du Valet de Daubeu,[3] I acre et demie et XXXII perches.

Eu camp de VII acres, VI acres et XXV perches.

fol. 220

Item, eu Camp Vie de Montoire, LI perche et III quartiers.

---

[1] Le Londel, Eure, a. and c. Louviers, cne. Quatremare.
[2] Quatremare, Eure, a. and c. Louviers.

---

[1] Is this the Thomas *and* Lorenz of the first item on this folio?
[2] Surville, Eure, a. and c. Louviers.
[3] Daubeuf-la-Campagne, Eure, a. Louviers, c. Le Neubourg.

Eu camp du Puiz que l'en apele la Verge, I vergie, III perches.

La somme XVI acres III verges et XXIIII perches.[1]

Ices terres desus dites sont ballies a Thomas Pincon, a Ricart Convenant, a Robert le Couturier, chascune acre por XXVII s., et ont letres.

La somme XXII lb. XVI s.

Item, XIII acres a meteerie desqueles le—Roy a la metie a Soarville, de laquele ce sunt les parties, valent XIII lb.:

Eu camp Loveis, V verg. et XXXIII perches, de la metie Thomas le Bolengier. Iceli prist la partie le—Roy por XX s., c'est assavoir por chascune acre.

Eu camp d'Esketomare[2] as III buissons, demie acre et IIII perches d'icele metie—Iceli prist por icel pris la partie—le Roy—

Eu camp de la Boissiere de la metie Robert du Gardin, I acre et demie et XVI perches—Iceli les prist por XXXII s. a la Saint Michiel.

Item, en iceli camp de la metie Renout Baudoin, I acre et demie, XVI perches—Iceli meesmes prist iceles por XXXII s. a celi terme.

Eu camp du Valet de la metie Ode Sadoc, II acres—Iceli les prist por XL s. a la Saint Michiel.

Item, en iceli camp de la metie Rogier Covenant, I acre—Iceli la prist por XX s. a la Saint Michiel.

Item, en icel camp de la metie Ode du Parrey, I acre—Iceli la prist por XX s. a celi terme.

Eu camp de VII acres de la metie Pierres Sadoc, V verg.—Iceli les prist por XXV s.

Eu camp Semice du Parrier de la metie Adan de Brutemare, demie acre et VII perches, valent X s.

Eu camp sus la Mare Close de la metie Thomas le Bolengier, LXXVI perches.—Ballies a iceli Thomas au pris de XX s. l'acre.

Eu camp au Castelain de la metie Avice la Bastarde, V verges et XIII perches—Icele les prist por XXVI s. VI d.

Eu camp du Puis en la courte piece de la metie Thomas le

---

[1] Here again we have 40 *perches* to the virgate.

[2] Hectomare, Eure, a. Louviers, c. Le Neubourg.

Bolengier demie acre, IX perches—Ballies a iceli Thomas a cel pris.

Eu camp du Puiz en la grant piece d'icele metie, I acre, VII perches meinz. Ballies a iceli Thomas a celi pris.

Les ventes et les rel. ileques, XL s.

Item, chascune des acres devant dites la metie doit I geline de rente.

La some LXXVII lb. IIII s. II d.

La some des chose ballies et a ballier CVIII lb. XIIII s. IIII d.

La ferme Audefuble—IIII lb. X s.

Les terres ileques, V acres III verges et demie, V perches— Ballies a Pierres Picart et a Robert de Vraville, clerc, por XXIIII s.

III capons, et demie galline, XXX oeus.

Le cens ileques, X s.

La some VII lb. XVIII d. et ont letres.

La ferme de la terre de Surtoville[1] IIII.XX lb.

Les terres arables LX acres, valent LXX lb.

Eu camp de la Grant Mare, IIII acres, l'acre XXVI s.

Eu camp joste Fontenelles, III acres, l'acre XXII s.

Eu camp de Keve Rue, VIII acres, l'acre XXVIII s.

Sus le cortil Robert le Porchier, V verges, l'acre XXVI s.

En la couture de la Rue Dame Osane, III acres, l'acre XXVIII s.

Sus le camp Richart de Liliori en la voie de Killebue, II acres, chascune acre XXVI s.

Au Perier Tyol, II acres, l'acre XXVI s.

Eu camp de la Rue Gombart, III acres, l'acre XXVI s.

Item, ileques I acre, vaut XX s.

Eu camp Sorel, III acres, l'acre XXIIII s.

Eu camp des Tesnieres,[2] V verges, l'acre XXIIII s.

Eu camp de la Marete, III acres, l'acre XXIIII s.

Item, ileques sus la voie Daubeu,[3] II acres et demie, l'acre XXIIII s.

---

[1] Surtauville, Eure, a. and c. Louviers.

[2] Or "Cesnieres."

[3] Daubeuf-la-Campagne, Eure, a. Louviers, c. Le Neubourg.

Le fieu Ricart Potier, VII acres, l'acre XXV s.

En la couture du mostier, IIII acres, I verg., l'acre XXVIII s.

Ioste la meson Robert de Paris une masure, contient entor V verges, por tout XXXV s.

fol. 222

Ioste le mostier l'autre masure, I acre, por tout XXVIII s.

Eu camp au Beicu, V verges, por tout XXX s. L'autre de XXXV s.

Eu camp au Deus Lons, II acres et demie, l'acre XXVI s.

En camp de Chief Ville ioste la meson Renout, II acres, XXVIII s. l'acre-Jehan Lebret prist chascune acre por XXXI s.

A la croiz Raoul, I acre, c'est assavoir en l'angle de la forest demie acre, vaut X s., l'autre demie vaut XII s.

Eu camp de la Longue Raie, III verges, l'acre XXIIII s.

A la voie de Daubeu, I acre et demie, l'acre XXVI s.

Ici commencent les terres qui sont apelées les freques.

Juques ici durent les terres

Au Parruquey, demie acre.

A la mare, III verg.

Eu camp Sorel, demie acre.

Item, ileques ioste la voie, V verges.

Eu camp des Escritures et a la fosse du Tremblei, I acre et demie.

Eu camp de la Fontenelle, III acres.

Eu camp Germain Gondart, I acre.

Eu camp au Beicu, V verges.

Chascune acre est estimée a XV s.

fol. 222v

Le cens ileques, XIII lb. XIIII s.

Capons, XXVI. Gelines IIII.XX et XVIII, o les gelines VIII s., o les chapons IIII d.

Item, XLIIII boiss. d'avoine.

Item, VII.C.L oeus.

Por XXV corvées, C s.

Por herces, X s.

Por les ventes et les rel., C s.

La somme IIII.XX.XVIII lb. VII s. X d.

La ferme de la terre Loqueri, XLII s.

Les terres III acres, XIII perches meinz—Lorenz le Quarteniers prist tout por LXIX s. quite au—Roy.

La ferme de la terre de Lymare[1]—comtée par le ballif de Gisorz o la
ferme de Gallion.[2]

fol. 223
Comté par
sey

    Le cens, LV s.

    Capons, XXII; gelines III; oeus VIII.XX et VIII, et o les oeus
    IIII d.

    Item, X oues, III boiss. de forment et XIX boiss. d'avoine.

    Les terres, XXII acres III verg. VIII perches, valent XXII
    lb. X s.

    II corvées qui valent III s.

    Les ventes, les rel., et les services V s.

        La somme XXVII lb. IX s. III d.

    Item, eu camp du Codreel, IIII acres de terre, valent VI lb.

    Item, anvers Quatremares,[3] L s. de rente. Item, II capons. Icestes
    sont comtées par le ballif de Gisorz o la ferme de Gallon.

    Item, anvers Quatremares est I acre de terre qui fu Phelippe de
    Herefort, de batart devint au—Roy par Gefroy Lebigaut.

fol. 223v

              Veci la Serganterie du Noef Bourc[1]

La ferme de la terre au Bende Troussebout,[2] Guillaume d'Auge, et
Guillaume de la Mare,[3] VIII.XX et XV lb.

    Anvers Torville,[4] le cens, XXII lb. et X s.

    Item, I mui de forment, II boiss. meinz, vaut le setier XIIII s.

    L'avoine ileques XLIX setiers, vaut le setier VI s. De cen si
    enchient IX boiss. por le gardin Pate.

        Les terres, LXII acres, dequei les parties sont cestes—a
        esté estimée l'acre a XX s.

    Eu camp du Motoi, II acres I verg. XIIII perches, l'acre

---

[1] Limare, Eure, a. Louviers, c. Le Neubourg.

[2] *Cart. Nor.*, no. 363. This was one of the tenements surrendered by Cadoc, former
castellan of Gaillon, in return for being freed from prison in 1227.

[3] Quatremare, Eure, a. and c. Louviers.

---

[1] Le Neubourg, Eure, a. Louviers.

[2] Troussebout (?), Eure, a. Louviers, c. Amfreville, cne. la Harengère.

[3] Stapleton, I, 94 *ff.* Guillaume de la Mare was an important financial agent of Henry
II in Normandy. In 1180 he held the *bailliage* of Auge and the viscounties of St. Mère
Eglise and Conteville. *ibid.*, 199. In 1195 he had the bailliage of Pont-Audemer. He was a
regular member of the court in the latter part of Henry's reign. *cf.* Delisle-Berger, II, 192,
261, 277, 289, etc.

[4] Tourville-la-Campagne, Eure, a. Louviers, c. Amfreville.

XXXVIII s. Nichole et Guillaume Hermer pristrent chascune acre por XXXIX s.—La somme IIII lb. IX s. VII d.

Eu camp de II acres sont II acres et I verg., l'acre XXX s.—Robert et Nichole H[er]m[er] ont pris l'acre por XXXVI s.—Some IIII lb. XII d.

fol. 224

Anvers Hermefosse II acres et demie, XXIIII perches, l'acre XXVIII s. Thomas Loroour, Hue le Mercier, et Guillaume Boufi pristrent l'acre por XXX s.—La somme LXXIX s. VI d.

Eu Val de Sain Oein,[1] V verges, l'acre XXX s.—Symon Compaignon et Guillaume de Bardoville por XXXII s. l'acre—Some XL s.

A la Croute, VI acres et demie et XXXI perche, l'acre XXX s.—Guillaume Blondel prist chascune acre por XXXIII s.—Some XI lb. X d.

En l'angle, XIII acres et II perches, l'acre XX s.—Symon Compaignon et Bardoville tout pristrent por XXXII s. l'acre. Some XX lb. X[2]

Souz le mostier, V acres et XXXVI perches, l'acre XXXVI s.—Robert Lavole prist chascune acre por XXXVIII s.—Some IX lb. XVIII s. VI d.[3]

En la couture que l'en apele le camp le—Roy, ioste la Grant Couture, VII verges, estimée l'acre a XXXVI s.—Richart Loreor et Ricart du Pin ont pris por XXXVI s. l'acre, en tele maniere que en iceles VII verges mistrent IIII s. d'encherissement por tout et non pas por chascune acre—Some LXVII s.

En la couture des XV acres sont XIIII acres, estimée l'acre a XXX s.—Durant Morin, I acre, por XXXII s. Raoul Pignie en mie le camp, I acre, XXXII s. Robert Barbatre, I acre, XXXII s.

Torne le foillet et trouveras le bail du remanant.

fol. 224v

Item, en icele couture—Nichole le Noble, I acre por XXXII s.

Item, en icele couture—Thomas Loreor et son frere, II acres et demie verg. por XXXII s. Some LXVIII s.

---

[1] Probably near Saint-Ouen-de-Pontcheuil, Eure, a. Louviers, c. Amfreville.

[2] The page has been cut here, but the top of a "V" can be seen at the edge. The entry probably read "XX lb. XVI s."

[3] If the revenue is compared with the area in this and earlier entries on fols. 223v and 224, it will be apparent that the virgate of 40 *perches* is being used.

Item, en icele couture—Jehan dit le Roy, III verg. et demie a
celi pris. S[umm]a XXVIII s.

Item, en icele couture—Rogier le Carver et Ricart le Mercier,
I acre a celi pris, Thomas Loror l'encheri de XII d.—Some
XXXIII s.

Item, en icele couture—Thomas Loror, por III verg. et demie,
XVI s.—S[umm]a XXVIII s.

Item, en icele couture—Phelippe Baudoin, demie acre a celi pris.

Item, ileques—Robert Baudoin, I acre a celi pris.

Item, ileques—Hue dict le Roy, demie acre a celi pris.

Item, ileques—Symon le Mercier, demie acre a celi pris.

Item, ileques—Ricart Loreor, demie acre por XVIII s.

Item, ileques—Jehan Goytre, le remanant, c'est assavoir II
acres et demie vergee por XXXII s. l'acre.

D'icele
ferme

Eu Gadimatre, VI acres et LX perches, estimée chascune
acre a XXXVI s.

Robert le Suor I acre, XXXVI s.

Durant le Prevost I acre, XXXVI s.

Pierres le Conte et Guillaume Biaupere I acre et demie, XXXVI
s. l'acre.

Durant Ivelin, demie acre, XX s.

Item, iceli tout autant por XIX s. VI d.

Rad. Symon, I acre, XXXVII s.

Rad. Andreu, III verg. et demie por XXXVI s. l'acre.

fol. 225

Au Faudeis V acres et VII perches, estimée chascune
acre a XXXVI s.

Robert le Suor, II acres et demie verg. por XXXVI s. l'acre—
S[umm]a LXXVI s. VI d.

Guillaume du Parray, I acre—XXXVI s.

Durant Yvelin, I acre—XXXVIII s.

Guillaume Socon, III verg. XXVII perches, por XXXVII s.
l'acre—S[umm]a XXIII s. X d.

Item, eu camp de l'angle, I acre et demie, I verg. et VI perches
que Richier et Gautier les Talloors tenoient a metie—Iceulz
icen meismes pristrent la partie le—Roy por XLVI s.—La
tierce partie a Pasques et les II parties a la Saint Michiel et
doivent rendre desus II capons de l'anciane rente.

Eu camp Piquenel, IIII acres et LIIII perches, l'acre XX s.
Toutein du Hamel et Aubin son filz, II acres por XXII s.

l'acre—S[umm]a XLIIII s. Michiel Vavassor les autres II et LIIII perches por XXIIII s. l'acre. Some LVI s. II d.[1]

La terre d'iceli qui fu pendu, LXIIII perches, estimées a XV s. Thomas Loreor, Hue le Mercier, et Guillaume Boufi pristrent por XI s.

fol. 225v
Jusques ici
durent
les devant
dites terres

Le gardin Pate, VI s.—Duran Motel[1] prist le gardin, et IX boiss. d'avoine lesquelz sa meson devoit, tout por XII s., mes il paiera les autres rentes lesquelz la meson devoit devant.

Eu camp Hericie, II acres et X perches, XXIIII s.—Ricart et Guillaume de la Vielle Haie, por l'acre XXX s.—Some LXI s. X d.

Item, X acres et LXVI perches de parreiz, XL s.

Gautier le Talloor, demie acre vers le bosc Bancelin, por III s.

Durant Morel,[1] II acres sus sa terre a celi pris.

Richier de Solengen, I acre apres la terre Durant vers le bois, VI s.

Symon de Sologen, II acres apres la terre Durant por XII s.

Item, demie acre por III s. III d.

Durant de Sologen I acre eu buc de sa terre—Le remanant est ballie.

Le jardin de Sologen,[2] I acre, vaut XL s.

Item, l'autre jardin joste l'iglise, vaut XL s.—Ballie por XXX s.

Item, VI.C oeus, IIII s. VI d.

Item, LXV gelines et o chascune I d.

Item, VII.XX et XI capons, et o chascun I d.

fol. 226

Item, sont ileques III homes desquelz chascun doit III foiz en l'an aler entre Rille et Sainne et faire cen que le seignor voudra.

Robert H[er]m[er] qui estoit I d'icelz prist ses services por XVIII d. por tout.

Le campart de XIII acres vaut XXXVI s.

L'erbage du bosc de Sologen vaut VI setiers d'avoine.

Lande ileques valent XXV s. par an et tienent I acre et demie.

---

[1] Entries on this folio show 40 *perches* to the virgate.

---

[1] Perhaps these two Durants are the same. Careless copying might easily make an "r" into a "t."

[2] Le Soulanger, Eure, a. Louviers, c. Amfreville, cne. Tourville.

Item, sont ileques les corvées des carues; chascune carue quant-cumbien il ait chevaus doit XII d. a chascune sesonne, c'est assavoir en ybernage et in iachia. Qui n'aura fors I cheval ne paera fors IIII d. en chascune sesone—Ices corvées sont ballies as homes de Torville por XII d. de chascune carue en chascune seson.

Por carues et por herces, XL s.

La masure Gefroy Lambert ne doit pas carue.

Item, chascune herce doit II corvées par II sesons, c'est assavoir en ybernage et en marz et rent chascune herce IIII d.—Les corvées ensement sont ballies por IIII d., chascune herce en chascune seson.

fol. 226v

Uns sont qui ne doivent corvées d'erce comme le fieu Durant de Sologen, le fieu Gefroy le Pastor et uns autre qui sont franz de ancianeté.

> Somme des choses ballies et a ballier en la ferme de Torville, XII.XX lb. X s. VI d.
> Et creist de LXV lb. X s. VI d.

Les ventes, les reliez et une serganterie ileques estimée a VI lb. Nous creons que ele vaille XX lb.

En la dite serganterie sont XI setiers et IX boiss. et demie.

Anvers Linderon, VII acres et IIII perches, valent VII lb. Guillaume Basset prist tout por VIII lb. X s.

Anvers Puillie,[1] VI acres I verg. et VII perches, IIII lb. X s. Gautier le Pic et Guillaume Blandin ont pris chascune acre por[2] VIII s.
Some VIII lb. XVI s.

Anvers Croville[3] la moute vaut C s.

fol. 227

Anvers Crestot,[1] XIII lb. par les parties deden escriptes.
Les terres, XI acres III verg. XV perches et demie.
Le cens, XIX s.
Por I esprevier, XII d.
Une oue.
Poucins, XII, et XVI d.

---

[1] La Pyle, Eure, a. Louviers, c. Amfreville.
[2] To obtain the sum given below we must assume that an "XX" was omitted here.
[3] Crosville-la-Vielle, Eure, a. Louviers, c. Neubourg.

[1] Crestot, Eure, a. Louviers, c. Le Neubourg.

Capons, XIIII, I geline et XVII d.

Oeus IX.XX et XVII d.

Troiz corvées, valent X s.

Lucas Coquere et Viel de Crestot ont pris iceste por XVIII lb., la terce partie a Pasques et la terce a la Saint Michiel.[2]

Anvers Ivile,[3] XII lb., par ces parties.

Avoine, VII setiers.

Capons, XXX. Gelines, VII. Une oue.

Item, III.C.L oeus, II aigniaulz et XVII d.

Le cens, XXXVII s. a la Saint Michiel et XV mansoiz a Noel.

Eu camp Gibot, I acre et I verg., XXX s.

Item, XL s., lesquelz G. chevalier doit.

La moute seiche, qui vaut XLV s.

Les ventes et les rel.

Gefroy du Quesne prist por XIII lb. III s. IX d.[2]

fol. 227v

La somme des choses desus dites VIII.XX.XVII lb. VII d.

Ices choses devant dites lesqueles sont ballies valent VIII. XX.XVIII lb. VI s. VI d.

Le fermier a le remanant.

Comtée
par sey

La ferme de la terre qui fu Esmauri de Boissoi XIX lb.

Les terres, LXV acres et XIX perches, desqueles XXV acres sont estimées, c'est assavoir l'acre a XXV s.—du remanant a de certes est estimée l'acre a VIII s.

Le cens en deniers, XXXIX s.

Item, sont XX gelines et II capons, I livre de poivre.

Jehan dict le Vemerres, chevalier, prist por XLIII lb. IIII s. et creist de XXIIII lb. IIII s.—Iceli est tenu a nous en arrerages de II anz ou de III d C s. par an donnez as II soers por lor vivre.

fol. 228
Comtée
par sey

La ferme Ernaut de Torville[1] VI lb. X s.

Le campart, XII lb.—Icest campart est en IX quarten-[ies] et demie: en quarten[ie] sont VII acres et demie, lesqueles tienent ices:

---

[2] Both these entries are written in the margin, and, to judge by the state of the ink and the pen, at a different time from the description of the farms.

[3] Iville, Eure, a. Louviers, c. Le Neubourg.

---

[1] *cf.* note, fol. 78.

Gervaise de Osmontville, V acres.

Richart Reice, .V acres.

Vincent Berost et Parisi, VIII acres et demie.

Durant le Telier, VII acres et demie.

Rad. de la Prée, VII acres et demie—Icest Guerout prist sa
partie, c'est assavoir IIII acres, I quartier meinz por IIII s.
l'acre.

Rad. Morant, II acres.

Godefrey Lovel, II acres, I verg.

Ogier du Four, I acre et demie verg.

Rad. Basset, III verg.

Gillebert Annot, I verg.

Robert Renoart et ses parchonniers, VII acres et demie.

Iceulz iceli meismes, IIII acres, I verg. meinz.

Godefroy des Hales et Henri le Prevost, IIII acres, I verg.
meinz.

Item, sont II quarten[ies] et demie franche, desqueles II doivent
X s.

[Le cens]² et demie doit III s.

fol. 228v

Le cens, XXXVIII s., qui est colli en IX quarten[ies] et demie,
desquelz IX doivent c'est assavoir chascun II s.—demie qua-
tener[ie] doit V s., et les II et demie doivent XIII s.

La meson Ogier du Four, IIII s.

Item, XXX oeus et II d. et V capons.

Les ventes et les reliez.

La somme des premieres parties XV lb. XIX [*sic*] X d.
Et creist de IX lb. IX s. V d.

La valor des porprestures de la forest du Bort XXXI lb.
V s. VI d.

La somme de toutes les choses devant dites selonc le bail
—au ballif, M.V.C.IIII.XX.XII lb. XVIII s.
VIII d. sanz la ferme de Lymare.

Somme selonc cen que eles sont estimées des Jureors
XVI.C.IIII.XX.X lb. XVII s. VIII d.

fol. 229

La ferme des porprestures de la forest du Bort vaut XXXI lb. V s. VI d.

Ricart le Teulier et Robin son frere, V acres et demie por XL s.

---

² This is an error which the scribe forgot to erase. He began "le cens" and then realized
that he still had to account for the half *quartenie* mentioned in the line above.

Robin le Teulier,[1] II acres, XXVI s.

Guillaume Martin demie acre et demie perche, III s. VI d.

Perres le Formager,[2] V acres et demie perche, XLII s.

Cristofre le Charon, I acre, IX s. X d., laquele Bochet tient.

Estiene de Lerie, II verg., II s.

Martin de Bonnaire, IIII acres, XVI s.

Perronnelle la Caquierresse, I verg. et demie, XVIII d.

Aaliz la fame Henri le Teulier, III verg., III s.

Jehan le Bouvier, demie acre, IIII s.

Guillaume le Carpentier, II acres, VIII s.

Ricart du Val,[3] I acre et demie, VI s.

Guillaume le Fevre, VI verges, XV s.

Gefroy le Coc, demie acre, II s.

Nichole et Guillaume Laignel, IX verg., IX s.

Michiel le Bouchier, demie acre, XVIII d.

Guillaume Pouquedieu et son frere, IX acres, LXIIII s.

Aden le Rouz,[4] VI verg., III s.

Ricart Raier, II acres et demie verg., VIII s. VI d.

fol. 229v

Gefrey Bigaut, I acre, IIII s.

Gefroy Langleiz, demie acre et XI perches, II s. VI d.

Rogier le Bolengier, IIII verg. et demie, XII s.

Henri Langleiz, I acre, VIII s. VI d.[1]

Guillaume Sonefort, demie acre, XII s.

Thommas Lepotier, XII acres, VI lb.

Pierres Bigaut, VI acres, XXIIII s.

Kamelin Langleiz, II acres, XVI s.

Nichole Rossel,[2] demie acre, IIII s.

Jehan le Porcher, demie acre et X perches, VI s.

Renaut Poilehaste, I masure, IX d.

Danaise, I acre, IIII s.

Perronnele la fille Nichole, III verg. et demie, VI s.

---

[1] *Cart. Nor.*, no. 1144. Gamelin and Robert "Tegulator" received several pieces of land in Bort, *c.* 1230.

[2] *ibid.* The wife of "Petrus Le Formager" testifies that her husband was granted 2½ acres in Bort. *c.* 1230.

[3] *ibid.* "Ricardus de Valle" and Raoul de Cliquebeuf took 3 virgates and "tria quarteria" at the same time.

[4] *ibid.* "Adam *Rufus*" was granted 6 virgates in Bort, *c.* 1230.

[1] *Cart. Nor.*, no. 1144. "Henricus Anglicus" was granted one acre in Bort, *c.* 1230.

[2] *ibid.* "Nicholaus Rossellus" was granted one virgate in Bort, *c.* 1230.

Pierres Bicaut, demie acre et XXVIII perches, XVII d.

Jehan Dyonis, II acres por I setier d'avoine.

Nichole Maquerel, IIII acres, XVI s.

Adan Langleiz, III acres et demie, XX s. VI d.

Nichole[3] et Raoul Lesuor, demie acre, VI s.

Raoul Leprevost, vergie et demie, VI d.

Asceline de Craville, I verg., XII d.

Thomas du Jardin, I acre, IIII s.

Les heirs Guillaume de Kally, I acre, II s.

Jehan Juliane, VII verg., IIII s.

Jehan Goitte, I acre, II s.

Raoul Tybout, V verg., III s.

Nichole du Parc et Pierres le Suor, demie acre, XII d.

Raoul du Mesnil et Ricart, III verg., IIII s.

Iceli Ricart por le clos Moart, II s.

Robert Coipel, IX acres, IX s.

Rogier de Preaulz, VI acres, VI s.

Ricart Mahieu, demie acre, XII d.

Rad. le Grant, I acre, XII d.

Symon Mahieu, demie acre, XII d.

Rad. Leporchier, demie acre, XII d.

Jehan Lepiquart, demie acre, XII d.

Crestian le Suor demie acre, XII d.

Rogier du Puiz, demie acre, XII d.

Jehan Dalyssi, I vergee III d.

Pierres d'Angerville, XI acres, XXII s.

Nichole Lebouchier, demie acre, XII d.

Le filz Germain Lebouchier, II acres, III s. IX d.

Jehan Gonceline, III acres et demie, III s. VIII d.

Crestian Conem, demie acre, XII d.

Gillebert Beleit, demie acre, XII d., et por le tiers de l'acre XVIII d.

Beneete la fame Thomas, I acre, XII d.

Pierres le Comtoor,[1] II s.

Hurtevent, III verg., III s.

Les heirs Gefroy le Cairon, demie acre, II s. VI d.

---

[3] Probably Nichole du Parc, cf. fol. 230.

---

[1] Cart. Nor., no. 629. A "Petrus Computator" had land at Pont-de-l'Arche, and witnessed a charter of a burgess of that town in 1259.

Robert Boutel,[2] I acre, II s.
Renout Lefevre, demie acre, XII d.
Ricart Lemercier, I acre, II s.
Guillaume Mansois, demie acre, XII d.
Thomas le Potier de Montoire, XIX d.

Somme XXXII lb. XIII s. V d. et en tel maniere semonte l'autre somme de XXVIII s. I d.

fol. 231

Les porprestures de la forest du Bort anvers Montoire,[1] II.C et IX
acres et demie par mesure, de cen chient por les voies et les desfautes
VII acres et demie—Et en tel maniere demorent II.C et II acres.

De ces choses ballies sont d'ancianement par Galtier de Tornam et Odart
le Panetier[2] LVI acres et demie, X perches et demie qui sont con-
tenues es parties desus dites.

Item, X acres remanent en pastures.

Item, as hommes de la Haye de Male Herbe,[3] XL acres, l'acre X s.
eu chief du bosc en un tenant.

Item, as hommes de Montoire et de Craville,[4] IIII.XX.XV acres et
LXIX perches et demie, desqueles le priour aura XV acres et le
prestre de Montoire II acres. D'iceles IIII.XX.XV acres, XX acres
por le pris de chascune acre V s., le remanant por VII s. chascune
acre.

Somme d'ices parties, c'est assavoir des hommes de la
Haie de Male Herbe jusques ici, LI lb. VII s. X d.
La crescence de ceste viscomté du Pont de l'Arche
II. C. XXII lb. XVIII s. V d. sanz les LI lb. VII s.
X d. por les porprestures et sanz Lymare.

---

[2] Or "Boucel."

---

[1] Montaure, Eure, a. Louviers, c. Pont-de-l'Arche.

[2] *Cart. Nor.*, no. 1144. An inquest was held *c.* 1230 on essarts in Bort which had
been made by master "Galterus de Tornam . . . de tempore Odardi panetarii." The two
seem to have accepted small bribes in return for granting permission to make essarts.
Odart was apparently castellan of Bort, and master Gautier may have been his clerk,
or a "mensurator."

H.F., XXIV, 114. Gautier de "Tornam" had some authority in Poitou, *c.* 1242, when the
expedition against the count of La Marche was planned.

Eude Rigaud, p. 776. Master Gautier was rich enough (from his bribes?) to buy an
estate for 450 l.

[3] La Haye-Malherbe, Eure, a. and c. Louviers.

[4] Crasville, Eure, a. and c. Louviers.

FACSIMILES

(reduced to 75%)

Ici commenche la .. Vicomté de Roem ..

c̃ La Sergantrie de Roem .. —

c̃ Le Vivier de souz Sainte Katerine . xij lb̃ . q̃ baillie
— A larcheuesque de Roem p̃ . xlv lb̃ . — ⁊ creist̃ de
xxxij lb̃ .

q̃ La Noue de Roem   viij̇xx . lb̃ .

q̃ La tire as foulons . xx lb̃ . — Le q̃ant̃ ⁊ la ville la tient̃ ;

c̃ La tre au comte de Leucestre . xl . lb̃)

côte Fr̃ — Le cay de Sainte emont . vij lb̃ p̃tuel .

c̃ Le molin tenant q̃min . c s̃ — p̃et — comte p̃ soi a passé .

q̃ Por le sel de Roem vendu p̃ tout lan en fieu . lxvi s̃ .

c̃ La tenture a alait . ix lb̃ du cens p̃et .

c̃ Amis Roem en men̄us cens . cx lb̃ p̃et .

c̃ Une nef d'Yslande j̇ empire de mirtres ou x lb̃ p̃et .

c̃ Les hales as courriers . ij lb̃ p̃ tout .

q̃ La hale a gros drapiers p̃ la merie de la hale . cxij lb̃ x s̃ .

c̃ Lautre p̃tie d'icele hale . iiij̇xx xlvi lb̃ .

1.   fol.3

La ferme de la tre de villers · xl f.

le cens ileques · xlvij f.

It · xxxv chapons valet ylvij f · vj d.

It · mil . ocus valet · vuj f . ix d.

Lasōme luj f · uj d.

Les apprestmes de romare valet · xj lb · nos nauōs les pues dcue
z̃ ladiesme z comte par ſrij

La cuiterie de romare · xv lb.

Guils mirōme · i . Acre de tre saĝle tenaur fmen tient z dic iuj ſ.

Gefry louchart ileques · i · acre valt iuj ſ.

Robt charue · i · verge · ix d.

Jceste ĝrāchie coust de · xj lb · iuj ſ · vj d.

Lasome de tote la crisconce de Rouy · iij · Sxluj lb xbf ·
uj d.

Lanoine de lafonde · xluj · gnyij p̃ tout · xxxv lb · gte ī p Srij.

La ferme de lacre boge alis a maneual̃ vaut · viij · lb ·

En camp des molems · xj · acr̃ lacre · xb · f ·

Es baulz sous la court · iiij · acr̃ lacre · xx · f ·

Amu̅s lamare au bois · iiij · acr̃ acch pris ·

Juxte Amu̅s lamarnerie au regn̅ · iiij · acr̃ lacre · xx · f ·

Amu̅s la mare blacre · ij · acr̃ acch pris ·

Amu̅s cellui · iij · acr̃ acch pris ·

En camp heliot du mesnill̃ · b · bges vaut lacre · xx · f ·

En camp ballellies · j · acr̃ e demi lacre · xx · f ·

Deuant la meson creslion · iiij · acr̃ lacre · xij · f ·

Amu̅s les crabliaus · j · acr̃ e demie lacre · xbiij · f ·

En val erd · vij · berg̃ lacre · xbiij · f ·

Amu̅s les crdillez demie acre · x · f ·

Amu̅s les mares · j · acr̃ · xbj · f ·

3. fol.106

La ferme de la tre de dandet̄ al o̅mij d̄rubec·   l· ℔

En la coure donat· vuij acꝛ ꞇ dem̅ vaut lacre· xij f·

Au maneir de drubec· xxuj acꝛ acch priſ·

Les pꝛeꝫ· ꝉ acre ꞇ dem̅ pꝛout· xxx f·

It̄ ileques· ꝉ pꝛece de boſt· v· acꝛ vaut lacre· xij f· pꝛ
meſ· vj· acꝛ

Par meſ· xxxv· acꝛ· l· pcħ·

It̄ ileques· xij boiſſ de formet̄ vale̅t̄· xxx f·   ꞇ· xvj
boiſſ feront le ſetier·

ℓe cens en deniis· xij· ℔ v· f· vj· ꝺ·

It̄· lx gelines ꞇ lvuj ꝺ·

It̄· xj capons ꞇ· ij ꝺ·

It̄· vj· oeus ꞇ o· x· oeus ꝉ ꝺ·

ℓe ꝃalm̅ ileques· xxx ℔·

4.   fol.181v

APPENDIX

ECONOMIC CONDITIONS IN THE COUNTY OF BEAUMONT-LE-ROGER, 1261-1313

WHEN Robert II of Artois fell at Courtrai before the low-born Flemish rebels, his subjects had reason for more than conventional expressions of grief. The unexpected death of the count caused a disputed succession, one of the worst curses which could be inflicted on any population in the Middle Ages. The two possible heirs were the count's daughter Mahaut, and his grandson, Robert. If Robert's father, son of Robert II, had lived, there could have been no dispute, but his premature death raised the difficult problem of representation, a great stumbling-block in all regions of feudal law. On the whole, custom favored the child of the last ruler, in preference to the more remote heir of the next generation, and this tendency had been strengthened by acts of Robert II in favor of Mahaut.[1] On the other hand, the nearest heir was a woman, and many of the nobles of Artois preferred a man. Mahaut had the double advantage of being of age and in possession, but as soon as young Robert reached his majority he began to protest and continued protesting for the rest of his life. A decision of Parlement against him in 1309 silenced him momentarily, but he took advantage of the troubled times following the death of Philip the Fair to stage an armed rebellion. When the rebellion collapsed he returned to the law-courts and again lost his case, in 1318. This time he remained quiet for a longer period, but his claims were revived in the reign of Philip of Valois.

The quarrel over Artois was terribly embarrassing to the kings of France. Both claimants were of the blood-royal, descendants of Louis VIII; both were able and persistent leaders with hosts of powerful friends. Artois was in an extremely sensitive area, on the borders of Flanders, which was in an almost constant state of rebellion against the king. Trouble in Artois made it difficult to retain control of Flanders, and it was an essential rule of French royal policy to keep Flanders from becoming independent. Robert's grievances could be used by the leagues of nobles which threatened royal power on the accession of Louis X. Robert's supporters made the most of the great scandal which smeared the royal family in 1314 — the scandal of the adulterous daughters-in-law of Philip the Fair. Two of the accused princesses were daughters of Mahaut, and Mahaut herself was charged with using sorcery, love-potions, and poison in an effort to save her children from the consequences of their sins. Every French king of this period — Philip the Fair, Louis X, and Philip V — had strong reasons for wishing a quick and permanent solution of the question of the Artois succession.

From the beginning of the quarrel it was evident that the king and his advisers wanted Mahaut to have Artois. This meant that Robert had to be satisfied elsewhere, and at the king's expense. Philip the Fair hit upon the solution which was finally adopted, after a decade of bickering. Robert was to have the county of Beaumont-le-Roger in Normandy, with the services of some of the great Norman nobles (notably the Harcourts), high justice over thousands of peasants, and domains worth 5000 *livres tournois* a year. The grant was made in 1310,[2] but the surveying of the lands did not begin until 1313[3] and Robert did not have full possession of the county until 26 March 1319.[4] Some of the delay was certainly due to technical difficulties — it was not a light or easy matter to carve so great an estate out of the royal domain — but much more must have been caused by Robert's unwillingness to accept the loss of Artois as final. It is significant that he received full possession of the revenues of Beaumont only after the decision of 1318 which confirmed Mahaut's position as countess of Artois, and only after a formal reconciliation with Mahaut had been arranged by Philip V.

The dispute over the Artois succession naturally produced a great mass of records, many of which are still in the French archives. One of the most interesting of these is the survey of the lands and revenues finally assigned to Robert which was made by Philippe le Convers, king's clerk, and Pierre de Hangest, *bailli* of Rouen. The names of these two commissioners indicate the importance of the work. Philippe was one of the most active of the royal clerks, frequently entrusted with important missions,[5] while Pierre de Hangest was for many years *bailli* in some of the most important provinces of the realm.[6] Their survey, now Ms. français 8764 of the Bibliothèque Nationale, is one of the most detailed descriptions of the domains of a great lord ever made, and is full of information about economic conditions in Normandy in the early years of the fourteenth century. Fortunately, this information can be compared with that derived from earlier records — the lists of fiefs drawn up under Henry II and Philip Augustus, farms of the royal domain published in Delisle's *Cartulaire Normand*, and the 'etat du domaine royal' in the *bailliage* of Rouen of 1261.[7] Thus we have rather detailed descriptions of the same district from both the thirteenth and early fourteenth centuries and this gives us an almost unique opportunity to study the changes wrought during a critical period. France experienced some rude shocks during those years, war, inflation, sudden and heavy taxation, and it is interesting to see what effect they had on the economy of a prosperous agricultural region.

Two general observations must be made before a detailed comparison of records from different periods can be attempted. In the first place, as we have seen, the king was anxious to appease Robert and his commissioners were aware of this attitude. They may therefore have been inclined to underestimate the value of certain revenues assigned to the count,[8] in order to gain his goodwill and his acceptance of the award. In earlier records the *baillis* were trying to demonstrate the efficiency of their administration by farming the domain at the highest possible rate. This led, in some cases, to exaggerated reports of the value of certain revenues.[9] Thus, decreases in the value of some parts of the domain may be more apparent than real. In the second place, the records are never strictly comparable in all their details. The records of the thirteenth century deal with large units of land, fiefs and farms, and list most payments as lump sums, while the fourteenth-century survey is more concerned with a multitude of small payments made by individual tenants. Thus lands mentioned in early records cannot always be identified, while the long lists of rents given by the fourteenth-century commissioners do not always correspond with the brief descriptions in the farms made by the royal officials of the thirteenth century. This is another reason for being suspicious of wide changes in prices and values; apparent discrepancies may be due solely to incomplete or erroneous identifications of items in one list with those in the other.

In spite of the limiting effects of these observations, we can still learn much from a comparison of the two periods. In the first place, it is clear that the basic structure of Norman administration has not changed greatly in the years between St Louis and Philip the Fair. The *bailliage*, the viscounty and the sergeanty are still the main administrative units, though there has been some shifting of names and boundaries. Thus Verneuil, which had been a separate *bailliage* until the end of the thirteenth century, is now merely a viscounty of Gisors, and the viscounty of Bernay has become the viscounty of Orbec. There has been some change in the sergeanties of the viscounty of Orbec — Le Sap takes the place of Gacé, Moyaux that of Cormeilles, Folleville that of Lieurey, while a new sergeanty emerges at Chambrais. On the whole these are minor changes compared to the sweeping readjustments which took place in the early years of the reign of St Louis. More important is the fact that the parish, completely ignored in royal records of the thirteenth century, is prominent in the later document. While the sergeanty is still the basic accounting unit, lands, rents, fiefs and woods are grouped by parishes within each sergeanty and names of individuals are repeated whenever they hold land or owe payments in more than one parish. This was probably done in order to facilitate collection of revenues by the new administrative personnel of the count. On the other hand, the unity of the parish is disregarded when parish boundaries fail to coincide with those of sergeanties; in several cases part of a parish is described in one sergeanty and the remainder in another.[10]

Information for the survey was gathered, as the commissioners themselves state,[11] from the records of the *bailliage* of Rouen and the testimony of good men. The records gave the location of each part of the domain, and its value in cases where income had been fixed by perpetual leases. For most of the domain, however, income fluctuated from year to year, and values had to be established by the old Norman device of the sworn inquest. Hundreds of juries were impaneled to estimate the average value of lands, rents, woods, and fiefs. Juries usually had at least six members, and groups of ten or twelve were not uncommon, so that a respectable part of the men of the county took part in this work. The most interesting use of a jury took place at the very beginning of the survey, when the commissioners wanted to know what was meant by the king's order that four-fifths of the grant was to be valued according to the 'ancienne assiete' of Normandy. They turned to a group of twenty Norman notables who had been summoned to Parlement to give advice on another matter and asked them to define the custom.[12] These men were sworn to 'dire verité et loial conseil' and their answer had an important influence on the results of the survey.

The decision to grant four-fifths of the county according to the 'ancienne assiete' gave great advantages to Robert of Artois. According to the verdict of the twenty 'ancienne assiete de terre eu dit duchée se fesoit et devoit estre fete —

la tierce partie en grains, la tierce partie en demaines et en rentes et l'autre tierce partie en homages et en seigneuries.'[13] If the sum of the payments in kind did not reach one-third of the total then the deficit was to be increased by fifty percent and met from other sources. That is, to use the example given by the jury, if 20 l. of income in grain were lacking 'l'en prendroit des autres emolumens pour les dites XX. l. jusques à la quantité de XXX. l. . . . '[14] Moreover, payments in kind were to be valued at a fixed scale which seems to have been considerably below market values, not only of the early fourteenth century, but even of the reign of St Louis. For example, wheat was to be valued at 10 s. a *setier*, oats at 5 s. a *setier*, and eggs at ten for a penny.[15] Corresponding values in 1261 were 14 to 16 s. for wheat, 6 s. for oats and 1 d. for ten eggs.[16] Contemporary Norman documents value wheat at 15 s. a *setier*, oats at 6 s. a *setier*, and eggs at eight for a penny.[17] In short, Robert had a triple protection against fluctuations in the currency which might lessen the value of his domains. One-third of his income was to be in kind, and the value of payments in kind was set at the lowest possible level. If enough payments in kind could not be found, then he was to receive a fifty percent bonus in other revenues. As a matter of fact, there was a deficiency in payments of grain, fowl and eggs, and Robert received almost 500 l.t. of other revenues, above the 5000 l.t. promised him, in order to compensate for the loss of these particularly desirable items.[18]

The jury of Norman notables laid down other rules for valuing the domains given to the count.[19] The patronages of churches assigned to him were valued at five percent of the annual income of the church. Fiefs held directly of the count were also valued at five percent of their annual income, rear-fiefs at only one percent. Since the chief income from fiefs came from wardships, it is evident that the jurors estimated that there would be a wardship about once every generation. Rights of high justice were valued at 12 d. a hearth, and *fouage* (originally a payment to ensure a stable currency[20]) at 4 d. a hearth. The tax of one-third the value of sales of private woods held of the lord (*tiers*) was included in the 'ancienne assiete' because it was 'une ancienne redevance,' but *danger*, a ten percent surtax on these sales added in the reign of St Louis, was not included because it was 'un nouvel usage . . . qui n'est pas deu de droit commun.' This is an interesting distinction and supports the theory that *tiers* originated in customs of the Angevin period while *danger* was a recent and unpopular innovation.[21] The jurors also insisted that, in estimating the revenue which might be produced by *tiers*, deductions be made for the amount of wood which the lord and his men would cut every year for their own use. The commissioners eventually decided that this deduction reduced the potential value of *tiers* by one-half.[22] Thus in estimating the income which woods held of the count might produce they first asked a local jury the average annual value of sales, and then took one-sixth of this figure as the average annual income to the count. For example, M. Jehan de Gaillon held 73 acres of wood, worth 7 l. 6 s. 'de rente par an'; this was worth 1 l. 4 s. 4 d. to the count.[23]

These rules of assessment were, on the whole, favorable to Robert of Artois. Philip the Fair also favored his cousin when he ordered the commissioners to take lands only in Beaumont, Orbec, and neighboring sergeanties.[24] A compact lordship could be administered much more efficiently and economically than one which was composed of widely scattered territories. The king's orders were followed closely; the most valuable parts of the county were located in the three sergeanties of Beaumont, Orbec, and Bernay, and none of the outlying possessions were very far from these centers.

The commissioners classified the things given to Robert under six heads: lands and rents, churches, fiefs, rear-fiefs, woods owing *tiers*, and profits of justice and *fouage*.[25] Three of these categories need only brief discussion. Few churches were included in the grant to Robert and none of them was very valuable, so that the total revenue under this head was only 18 l. 5 s. The rear-fiefs were numerous, but yielded only small sums to the count, a total of 45 l. 2 s. 9 d. We have already seen the way in which woods owing *tiers* were valued. There were many of these woods, some quite large, but the estimated revenues from *tiers* was only 223 l. 17 s. a year.

The fiefs which were to be held directly of the count were a much more important part of the grant. The average annual income from them was estimated at 769 l. 17 s., about one-seventh of the total. Equally important was the fact that, by subordinating these fiefs to Robert of Artois, he was given a new clientele to replace that which he had lost in Artois. The social and political relationships thus established would strengthen Robert's position as one of the great lords of the realm.

On the other hand, the commissioners did not concern themselves greatly with the military service nominally owed by the vassals. If it happened to be mentioned in the records or by the jurors they wrote it down, but they made no effort in many cases to discover what service was owed. Most frequently mentioned was castle-guard, which perhaps still had some value, and we can see remnants of the old grouping of fiefs around a castle, such as Beaumont, which was the defensive center of a district.[26] Occasionally forty days' service or twenty days' service in the army are mentioned, or the fact that a vassal had 'un membre entier,' 'un membre de hauberc' or 'un quart d'un membre de hauberc.'[27] But the vague expressions 'un fie' or 'une partie d'un noble fie' occur frequently,[28] without any specific requirement of service. It is also significant that in only one case is it suggested that a vassal owes more than one knight's service, although several baronies were included in the county.[29] The old Norman system of specific amounts of military service, based on multiples of the knight's fee, had broken down many years before,[30] and no one thought of reviving it.

It is interesting to note that very few of the fiefs mentioned in our record can be traced back to the time of Philip Augustus or Henry II. There are cases in which the same fief continued to be held by men of the same name, but they are the exceptions. For example, around Beaumont the Harcourts, the Thibervilles, the Bigars, and the Houtevilles still hold fiefs which were in their families under Philip Augustus, but thirteen other fiefs cannot be traced in the earlier records and a fourteenth has been acquired by the Harcourts.[31] Scholars familiar with genealogies of Norman families could probably find more examples of continuity, especially through the female line, but there still must have been very consider-able changes in the old land-holding class. Confiscations for adherence to the English kings, deaths without heirs, and exchanges of property removed many of the old families, and grants by the king or great lords introduced many new ones. The same phenomenon may be found in other regions in the later Middle Ages. The land-holding class remains powerful for centuries, but individual estates frequently pass from one family to another, and new families rise to wealth as old ones decline.

Rights of high justice, low justice, and *fouage* formed an important part of the grant to Robert. As we have seen, high and low justice were each valued at 12 d. per hearth per year, while *fouage* was worth 4 d. per hearth per year.[32] Using this formula, the commissioners found that high justice in the domains granted the count was worth 1300 l.t. a year, *fouage* 423 l.t., and low justice 133 l.t. — a total of 1856 l.t. for the three rights, or almost exactly one-third of the revenues granted the count. Justice and *fouage* together accounted for more than half the revenue in six of the eleven sergeanties from which the count was to draw his income. They also had more than a purely monetary value; they distinguished Robert of Artois from the great mass of lords who were never granted such rights. Even though he had to exercise his right of justice under the watchful eye of royal officials, still he was the immediate superior and lord of thousands of inhabitants of central Normandy.

How many thousands? — this is not easy to answer. Since the grant was made in the early years of the fourteenth century, when the *feu* had not yet become a mere unit of accounting, we can be fairly sure that the number of *feus* is reason-ably close to the actual number of households. Also, since grants of high justice in this region had been rare, we can assume that the number of households in a sergeanty or village subject to the count's high justice represents almost the entire population of the sergeanty or village. But how many people should be counted to a household? The coefficient 4 or 5 is often used, but Professor J. C. Russell has given strong reasons for adopting a smaller figure, about 3.5.[33] It is true that most of his evidence comes from England, but Normandy was more like England than any other region for which we have data. However, since Russell admits that the coefficient was probably a little higher just before the Black Death, I have taken 3.5 as the minimum number per household and 4 as the maximum. Since the count had high justice over 26,004 *feus*, this would mean that he was lord of at least 91,000 subjects and perhaps of 104,000.

The boundaries of a mediaeval parish do not necessarily coincide with those of a modern commune, but it is interesting to compare the figures for the early fourteenth century with those given in the *Dictionnaire des Communes*. As may be seen from the table below,[34] there is a rather remarkable stability in the popu-lation of this area. None of the mediaeval towns or villages has become a large city, although some have experienced a modest growth. But if Orbec, Bernay and Le Neubourg have increased in population, Beaumont, La Neuve Lire, Glos and Le Sap have decreased. One is left with the impression that the population in 1310 was not greatly inferior to that of today, and that it may actually have been denser in some of the less fertile agricultural areas.

Fol. of MS. B	Commune	Number of *feus* in 1313	Estimated population in 1313		Population in 1936
			min.	max.	
14	Barc	151	529	604	468
14	Beaumont-le-Roger	538	1883	2152	2070
36v	Bernay	1100	3550	4400	7700
59	Bois-Normand-près-Lyre	80	280	320	403
48	Cisai-S. Aubin	80	280	320	265
48	Chaumont	244	854	976	244
17	Combon	280	980	1120	400
48	Croisilles	80	280	320	233
14	Epreville-près-le-Neubourg	148	518	592	264
14–17	Feuguerolles et Nassandres	146	511	584	1038
36v	Friardel	100	350	400	246
14	Goupillières	197	690	788	534
57	Glos-la-Ferrière	360	1260	1440	554
17	Neubourg(Le)	227	795	908	2362
59	Neuve Lyre(La)	400	1400	1600	736
36v	Orbec	308	1078	1232	2837
48	Orgeres	140	490	560	281
48	S. Evroult-de-Montfort	162	567	648	424
36v	S. Germain-la-Campagne	260	910	1040	733
36v	S. Mards-de-Fresne	200	700	800	370
48	Sap (Le)	550	1925	2200	1061
14	Thiberville	102	354	404	1029
59	Vielle-Lyre (La)	240	840	960	507

The last, and largest block of revenues given the count came from the domains, that is, forests, *prévôtés*, lands and rents. From these sources he was expected to draw 2560 l.t., or very nearly half of the income of the county. But this sum was very unequally distributed among the different categories. The forests were supposed to yield 1575 l.t., almost exactly three-fifths of the total sum, and the forest of Beaumont alone was to produce 1300 l.t. a year. These figures might have been much higher, for a jury originally valued the forest of Beaumont at 1800 l.t. a year. Robert of Artois protested vigorously, saying that at this price 'il seroit outrageusement decue,' but even his officials were willing to admit that the forest was worth 1000 l.t. a year. A new inquest was ordered and the king's agents this time valued the forest at 1600 l.t. a year, so that the final figure of 1300 l.t. represented a compromise between the king and the count.[35]

These facts indicate the economic importance of the Norman forests. There is evidence to show that clearing of forest land, increased population, and greater use of wood had made forest products more valuable as early as the reign of St Louis.[36] Since there were important metallurgical industries in the county of Beaumont, wood may have been especially valuable in this region. 'Forges grossieres' are mentioned at Orbec and at Glos. They were especially numerous in the latter town, where there was a 'mestre des ferons' responsible for collecting rents from 200 forges.[37] On the whole, Robert of Artois probably strengthened his economic position by accepting a large amount of forest land. There was always a market for the wood, and prices could rise as money depreciated in value.

Rents from arable land were often fixed by custom or long-term leases, but, save for a few rights of usage, the count could exploit his forests as he wished.

The remaining parts of the domain present a rather surprising picture. In the thirteenth century arable land, *cens et rentes*, mills and the *prévôtés* had produced a large part of the royal revenue from the district of Beaumont; in the fourteenth century these sources seem much less important. There are several reasons for this change. Most of the grant to Robert of Artois was made under the rules of the 'ancienne assiete,' which emphasized other kinds of income. The royal domain had been diminished by grants of lands and rents to officials and friends of the king. Other parts of the domain had been granted on perpetual leases (*fieffermes*) which now yielded less than the real value of the properties. This last fact, however, should not be overemphasized. Perpetual leases were less permanent than the name implies and many were surrendered shortly after they were made. For example, Les Moutiers-Hubert was granted as a *fiefferme* in November 1311 but returned to the king in time to be given to Robert of Artois.[38] Some of the *fieffermes* made in the reign of St Louis survived,[39] but these were already taken into account in the survey of 1261 and so do not help to explain the decrease in the value of the domain after that date. We must conclude that there had been a general decrease in the value of lands and rents during the reign of Philip the Fair, in spite of the inflationary influence of a fluctuating currency and heavy expenditures for war.

If we study individual items, this conclusion is strengthened. We can be most certain about the revenues from mills, since every mill had a monopoly in its district and should have done about the same amount of business every year. Yet of eight mills which can be identified both in the survey of 1261 and in the grant to Robert of Artois, all but one have decreased in value. The four mills of Beaumont were valued at 500 l.t. a year under St Louis and at only 224 l.t. under Philip the Fair; the mill of Canapville dropped from 56 l.t. to 22 l. 16 s., a tanning mill from 60 s. to 30 s. and the mill of St Ouen from 7 l. 10 s. to 1 l. 14 s.[40] It is true that in all these cases, except the tanning mill, the yearly revenue is given in *setiers* of grain, which are then valued at the conventional prices of the 'ancienne assiete,' but even if we use a higher price the revenues are worth less than those reported for 1261. Perhaps the commissioners favored the count by undervaluing mills granted to him, but contemporary leases of mills by the *bailli* of Rouen also show decreases in value. We have records of nine such leases in 1310 and 1312; in four cases the mill is worth less than in 1261, in three the rent is about the same and in only two has there been an increase.[41] Moreover, there were two complaints that the farmers could make no profit from their mills, and in both cases the *bailli* permitted a large reduction in the promised payments.[42]

If we look at the *prévôtés* we again find evidence of declining revenues. The *prévôté* of Beaumont was worth 1200 l.t. a year in 1261 and only 795 l.t. when it was granted to Robert of Artois.[43] Here again, about one-third of the income comes from grain conventionally valued, but, even if we increase the price of the grain by fifty percent, the *prévôté* is still worth much less than under St Louis. We can find a decrease in almost every part of the revenue of the *prévôté*: the product of the 'denier et maaille' has dropped from 120 l.t. to 72 l.t., that of 'havage' from 33 l.t. to 9 l. 12 s.t., 'seiche moute' from 11 l.t. to 7 l. 12 s.t., and the fisheries of the Rille from 40 l.t. to 31 l. 10 s.t. The *prévôtés* of Glos and La Neuve Lire show similar decreases. Here we can follow the process in detail, thanks to the accounts and extracts from the accounts of the *bailli* of Verneuil which are preserved in the Archives Nationales and the Bibliothèque Nationale.[44] Income from Lire and Glos increased until 1271, when it leveled off at fairly high sums. During the period 1271–1282 the *prévôté* of Lire yielded from 249 l. to 270 l. a year, and the *prévôté* of Glos from 180 l. to 210 l. In 1285 there was a sharp drop, perhaps caused by the troubles of the crusade of Aragon. Lire and Glos in that year were each valued at only 159 l. When the two *prévôtés* were given to Robert of Artois, Lire was worth 160 l. a year and Glos only 133 l. a year. Here again, the decrease is observable in other places in the region. The extracts of accounts already mentioned give the following figures.[45]

	Easter 1252	Easter 1272	Easter 1285
Prévôte of Falaise		283£ 6 s.	248£
Prévôté of Chateau Vire		240£	200£
Prévôté of Exmes	166£	175£	66£ 13 s.
Prévôté of Verneuil	425£	450£	325£
Prévôté of Bonsmoulins*	140£ = 98l 6 s. 8 d.	83£ 6 s.	80£

* In 1252 half of the income of Bonsmoulins was collected at Easter and half at Michaelmas. In the other years the normal practice of this region was followed; one-third of the payments were made at Easter and two-thirds at Michaelmas.

Since a large part of the income from the *prévôtés* was derived from business transactions we have here an indication of declining economic activity.

It is more difficult to trace decreases in the value of land, since the commissioners of 1313 usually list the *cens et rentes* owed by individuals without connecting these payments with specific amounts of land. One fact, however, is immediately evident. There has been a great increase in the number of vavassories, for example around Pontchardon and Les Moutiers-Hubert.[46] These vavassories pay only sixpence or a shilling an acre, far less than the real value of the land. Most of them do not appear in earlier documents and it is hard to understand why such grants were ever made. Perhaps the possessors of these vavassories paid large lump sums to the *bailli* in return for grants of land on favorable terms, but there is no evidence of such payments in the records which survive. In any case, the large number of these vavassories seriously decreased the income from the domain.

If we turn to land which was leased for short terms we find that there was some decline in value, especially when payments were made in grain. Thus at Les Moutiers-Hubert a meadow which was worth 20 s. a year in 1261 is valued at only 16 s. in 1313, and a field which was farmed at 3 s. an acre in 1261 pays only four bushels of oats (or 1 s. 6 d.) an acre in 1313.[47] A great deal of land in this region is leased in 1313 for only 2 s. 6 d. an acre, a much lower price than that which prevailed in 1261.[48] These payments are in grain, but even if we value the grain at more than the conventional price the land is still very cheap. It must be said that near Beaumont land was worth about as much in 1313 as in 1261,[49] but it is significant that in no place has land increased in value. This offers a contrast to the period from 1204 to 1270,[50] when land increased steadily in value.

In conclusion, we can say that this study of the establishment of the county of Beaumont-le-Roger suggests two problems for future investigation. In the first place, when royal officials or favored members of the nobility secured grants of royal estates, did they always seek safeguards against fluctuations in the value of money? Robert of Artois protected himself by receiving much of his income from forests or in kind, and by undervaluing payments in kind. If this were common practice it would explain why many landholders remained relatively well-to-do during the troubles of the fourteenth and fifteenth centuries. In the second place, is there evidence of economic stagnation, not to say depression, in the early fourteenth century in other regions of France? Certainly, around Beaumont, the boom of the thirteenth century had ended and there is some proof that an economic recession was beginning. If this was true elsewhere, then we can understand the violent protests against royal taxation in the reign of Philip the Fair and the failure of the king to bring the campaigns against Flanders to a satisfactory solution. Most historians will admit that the second half of the fourteenth century was not a period of prosperity and that economic troubles aggravated political and social difficulties. It would be interesting to discover that economic troubles began early in the reign of Philip the Fair.

PRINCETON UNIVERSITY

[1] P. Lehugeur, *Histoire de Philippe le Long*, (Paris, 1897), i, 61.

[2] Lehugeur, i, 61 ff., 166 ff.

[3] B. N., MS. français 8764 (hereafter cited as B), fol. 1.

[4] B, fol. 2, fol. 61v.

[5] Master Philippe de Villepereux, often called Philippe le Convers, was canon of Tournai, archdeacon of Brie, and finally (in 1314) archdeacon of Auge. He began his career in the royal service as a collector of war subsidies in 1297–1299, but he soon became a specialist in forest administration. His accounts in this capacity are listed in R. Mignon, *Inventaire d'anciens comptes royaux* (Paris, 1899), nos. 364, 1193, 1203, 1436, 2245, 2246, 2247, 2248 and p. 359. He was *maître des eaux et forêts* in 1309 at the latest, and he authorized most of the royal letters dealing with forest affairs, for example, *A.N.*, JJ42A, fol. 74; JJ44, fol. 8v; JJ45, foi. 81; JJ47, fols. 31, 96; JJ48, fol. 80v. He was a member of the Norman Exchequer in 1309–1310 and in 1314; see Mignon, nos. 2248 and p. 359. He had lands in the Norman viscounty of Pont de l'Arche which were enlarged by several grants from Philip the Fair, *A.N.*, JJ45, fols. 81, 84; JJ48, fol. 51; JJ49, fols. 71, 86; JJ50, fol. 58. Our Philippe le Convers is probably the one named as an executor of the will of Philip the Fair, but the Philippe le Convers who served as *maître des requêtes* under Philip V is almost certainly a nephew, see *A.N.*, JJ56, fols. 195v, 208; A. Guillois, *Recherches sur les maîtres des requêtes de l'hotel* (Paris, 1909), pp. 219–220; Ch. V. Langlois in *Notices et extraits*, XL, 40.

[6] *H.F.*, XXIV, preface; Pierre de Hangest was *bailli* of Amiens in 1299, of Gisors from 1300 to 1301, of Rouen from 1303 to 1320 and from 1322 to 1326, of the Cotentin from 1320 to 1322. He was a brother of Guillaume de Hangest, one of the treasurers of Philip the Fair.

[7] The lists of fiefs are published in *H.F.*, XXIII, and the *Cartulaire Normand* in the *Mémoires de la Société des Antiquaires de Normandie*, 2nd series, Vol. VI. The 'état du domaine royal' is in J. R. Strayer, *The Royal Domain in the Bailliage of Rouen* (Princeton, 1936).

[8] B, fol. 1v.

[9] Strayer, *Royal Domain*, pp. 5, 13.

[10] B, fols. 8, 53v, Châtel-la-Lune and Beaumontel are listed in both the sergeanty of Beaumont and in that of Ouche.

[11] B, fol. 2v. The survey was made 'o l'avis des comptes de la baillie de Roen et par les relations des prodeshommes du pays.'

[12] B, fol. 1. 'Nous eusson appele et fet assembler en une chambre delez le palais de Paris . . . la greignour partie des anciens hommes sages et pourveus de la coustume de Normendie . . . qui au parlement estoient venus por avoir conseil sur une autre cause . . . .'

[13] B, fol. 1v.

[14] *Ibid.*

[15] *Ibid.* A.N., J623, no. 101, gives a list of similar conventional valuations in Poitou.

[16] Strayer, *Royal Domain*, pp. 24, 25, 26.

[17] A.N., JJ47, fol. 64; JJ48, fol. 109; JJ49, fol. 30v; B.N., ms. Moreau 215, fol. 83.

[18] B, fol. 61.

[19] B, fols. 1, 1v.

[20] J. R. Strayer, *The Administration of Normandy under St Louis* (Cambridge, 1932), p. 46.

[21] Borrelli de Serres, *Recherches sur divers services publiques* (Paris, 1895), I, 396 ff.; Strayer, *Administration*, pp. 76–79.

[22] B, fols. 1v, 2v.

[23] B, fol. 13v.

[24] B, fol. 1.

[25] B, fol. 2v.

[26] B, fols. 12, 12v, 13, 38v, 51v. Tenants of 22 fiefs owe castle-guard at Beaumont.

[27] B, fols. 12, 12v, 38v.

[28] *Ibid.*

[29] B, fol. 46v, the lord of Gacé owes two knights; *H.F.*, XXIII, 710, under Philip Augustus he owed three knights.

[30] Strayer, *Administration*, pp. 67, 68.

[31] B, fols. 12, 12v; *H.F.*, XXIII, 710.

[32] B, fol. 1v.

[33] J. C. Russell, *British Medieval Population* (Albuquerque, N. M., 1948), pp. 22 ff., 26, 30, and Russell, 'Late Medieval Population Patterns,' Speculum, XX (1945), 162–163.

[34] See the table on p. 283.

[35] B, fol. 11v.

[36] Strayer, *Administration*, pp. 43–44, 77.

[37] B, fols. 10v, 17v, 55.

[38] A.N., JJ49, fol. 30v; Strayer, *Royal Domain*, p. 21.

[39] Especially in the sergeanty of Ouche (fol. 50v) where we find eight farms 'des forfetures d'Angleterre' which go back to the first years of the reign of St Louis.

[40] B, fols. 10v, 24, 32, 50v; Strayer, *Royal Domain*, pp. 76, 78, 155, 143, 172.

[41] A.N., JJ45, fol. 110v; JJ47, fol. 53. B.N., ms. français 25993, no. 193. Strayer, *Royal Domain*, pp. 104, 218, 224, 208, 205, 186, 202.

[42] A.N., JJ47, fol. 53, the farm of the mills of Vaudreuil falls from 144 l.t. to 120 l.t.; JJ52, fol. 22, the farm of the mill of 'Hastenc' falls from 55 l.t. to 30 l.t.

[43] Strayer, *Royal Domain*, p. 75; B, fols. 3v–11.

[44] Strayer, *Royal Domain*, pp. 75–76; B, fols. 10, 10v.

[45] A.N., J775, J780; B.N., ms. lat. 9018, p. 24; B, fols. 54v, 58.

[46] A.N., J775, J780.

[47] B, fols. 25, 18.

[48] B, fol. 24v; Strayer, *Royal Domain*, p. 155.

[49] B, fols. 24, 24v; Strayer, *Royal Domain*, p. 24.

[50] B, fol. 3v; Strayer, *Royal Domain*, pp. 78, 79.

[51] Strayer, *Royal Domain*, p. 24.

ECONOMIC CONDITIONS IN UPPER NORMANDY

AT THE END

OF THE REIGN OF PHILIP THE FAIR

Some years ago I published an article suggesting that income from the royal domain in Normandy began to decrease during the reign of Philip the Fair and that this decrease indicated the start of the economic depression of the fourteenth century. This conclusion was based on a comparison of the annual income from mills, *prévôtés* (mainly tolls, market-rights and other income from commerce) and arable land in the latter part of the reign of St. Louis, with the same kinds of income in 1313, when a survey was made of the lands that were to be given to Robert of Artois as part of his new county of Beaumont-le-Roger [1].

Thanks to the publication of the *Comptes Royaux* by our regretted colleague, Robert Fawtier [2], and of the *Cartulaire d'Enguerran de Marigny* by Jean Favier [3], it is now possible to review and refine the conclusions of my earlier study. The documents concerning Marigny give annual values of certain lands, and rights annexed to land, for various dates running from 1308 to 1310. In the *Comptes Royaux* we have an account of the viscount of Auge for Michaelmas, 1312. These dates are so close to that of the survey of the county of Beaumont-le-Roger (1313) that we can assume the general price level remained about the same during the period covered by all our documents. We can also assume a fairly stable currency ; « good money » had been restored in 1306 and the slight overvaluation of certain coins in 1311-1312 was not great enough to affect long-term leases. It is true that the « good money » of 1306 did not contain quite as much silver as the currency of St. Louis, but, given the increase in the price of silver, coins of the period 1308-1313 should have had about the

---

1. *Economic Conditions in the County of Beaumont-le-Roger, 1261-1313*, see p.[253-263]
2. *Recueil des historiens de la France, Documents financiers*, t. III. *Comptes Royaux (1285-1314)*, 3 vol., Paris, 1953-1956.
3. *Collection de documents inédits sur l'histoire de France*, série in-8°, vol. 2, *Cartulaire et actes d'Enguerran de Marigny*, Paris, 1965.

same purchasing power as those of the 1260's[4]. Thus a change in the income from a mill or a farm between 1261 and 1312 represents a real increase or decrease and not simply an adjustment to an altered currency. On the other hand, prices and estimated annual incomes given in documents running from 1298 to 1304 must be looked on with some suspicion, since this was a period in which the currency was seriously overvalued.

One further problem : all our figures came from official documents and therefore may be distorted by the tendency of officials to use conventional values or to undervalue property given to a royal favorite. Both these tendencies are apparent and are openly admitted in the grant to Robert of Artois ; for example, grain is valued at a conventional price much below the market price[5]. Certainly some conventional prices are given in the documents examined in this essay but there is reason to believe that in most cases we have the true annual value, or at least something fairly close to the average annual value. A viscount was supposed to collect as much money as he could from his viscounty. He would not have endeared himself to his superiors by accepting low returns from the farms of lands and rents of the royal domain. The Exchequer set up elaborate rules requiring public bidding for all farms[6] and we can see these rules being enforced even for farms that brought in only a few pounds a year[7]. Many of our documents describe exchanges of holdings between the king and ecclesiastical or secular lords. In such cases the tendency would have been for each party to overvalue, not undervalue, the lands and rents that he was surrendering. Most reassuring of all, the prices given in our documents fall within the same range, whether they come from farms, exchanges, gifts, or sales on the open market. If we find that a certain price curve declines in almost all our sources, we can be reasonably sure that the decline is real.

The first such decline is in the expected income from arable land. The best example is the farm of Menneval, where, in 1310,

---

4. Borrelli de SERRES, *Les variations monétaires sous Philippe le Bel*, in *Gazette numismatique française*, 1902, p. 245-425, (also tirage à part, Châlon-sur-Saône, 1902). See especially, p. 342-367.

5. *Economic Conditions in Beaumont-le-Roger*, p.[256]. Another striking example of conventional valuation comes from Châtillon-sur-Indre, Arch. nat., J 623 n° 10 (no date but late 13th c.) where a jury reported that by ancient custom wheat was to be valued at 5 s. a setier, rye at 4 s., barley at 3 s. and oats at 2 s. 6 d. Whatever measure was being used, these are very low prices.

6. *Ordonnances*, t. I, p. 461 (Easter 1306). Most of these rules had long been observed.

7. To lease the walls and ditch near the Porte Beauvoisine (Rouen), and half the gate itself, the *bailli* swore in good men to appraise the value. They reported that these things were worth 3 l. t. a year. The *bailli* asked for bids, received one for 3 l., then asked for higher bids. When none came in, he finally executed the lease, 6 August, 1290. *Rec. Hist. G. et F*, t. XXIV, *preuves*, n° 225.

45 acres were farmed for 12 s.t. an acre[8]. In the 1260's 24 acres at Menneval were valued at 20 s. an acre, 11 at 15 s., 5 at 12 s., 2 1/2 at 6 s. and the remainder (all small pieces of land) at 16 or 18 s. an acre[9]. Elsewhere we cannot match acre for acre, but almost all farms of land in the viscounty of Auge decreased or remained stable in value between the 1260's and 1312. Thus the land of Guillaume Bardouf, worth 21 l. 17 s. a year under St. Louis, had been given out as a perpetual farm (*fiefferme*) for 16 l. by 1312[10]. The lands of Agatha Troussebot, without the mills, were farmed for 125 l. 17 s. 8 d. in the earlier period and for 113 l. 10 s. under Philip the Fair[11]. The farm of Equemauville plus one of two mills was valued at either 74 or 76 l. in the *Etat du domaine royal ;* the farm of Equemauville with one mill brought in 57 l. in 1312[12]. At Coquainvilliers the drop in income came early ; it was farmed for 72 l. in 1259, for 65 l. in 1271, and farmed again for 65 l. at some date after 1271[13]. Lands farmed to Henry the priest of Vandreuil were estimated to be worth 16 l. 16 s. and were granted to him in the 1260's for at least 15 l. 11 s. and perhaps as much as 21 l. 12 s. In 1314 « la terre qui fut à Herri le Prestre » brought in 12 l. 11 s.[14].

There are several other cases of a decrease in the yield of a farm ; there are others in which the farm has been rearranged so that it is hard to tell whether we are dealing with the same unit. For example, the land of Robert Formentin at Grandouet was estimated at 56 l. under St. Louis and was farmed for 60 l. in 1312. But Robert also had land at Manerbe, not valued, but clearly worth 3 or 4 l. a year ; if this was included in the farm of 1312 then the yield remained constant[15]. Or, to take another very difficult case, the three farms of Thomas Basset, Hue Boutevilain and Henri de Gurneville were apparently worth only 55 l. 16 s. 1 d. in the 1260's, while they yielded 72 l. 5 s. in 1312. But in the earlier record these three farms were combined with the farm of Darnétal at Drubec and the woods of all four farms were treated as a separate unit. The parson of Clarbec paid 140 l. for the four farms plus an unspecified amount for the woods. Now if we subtract the value of Drubec (68 l. 10 s. 2 d.) from 140 l. we get 71 l. 9 s. 10 d., almost the same as the 72 l. 5 s. of 1312. The slight difference is more than made up by a wood at Drumare, not included in the 140 l., which was worth at

---

8. Arch. nat., JJ 47, f° 64 v° - 65 v°, n° 48.
9. J.R. STRAYER, *The Royal Domain in the Bailliage of Rouen*, Princeton, 1936, p. 131-132. This survey was begun in 1261 and was virtually complete by 1266. Most of the information describes conditions in 1260, 1261, or 1262. For the sake of convenience, I shall refer to the document as the survey of 1261.
10. *Royal Domain*, p. 262 ; *Comptes Royaux*, n° 17539[19].
11. *Royal Domain*, p. 217 ; *Comptes Royaux*, n°s 17539[20], 17539[21].
12. *Royal Domain*, p. 218-219 ; *Comptes Royaux*, n° 17447.
13. *Royal Domain*, p. 200-202 ; *Comptes Royaux*, n° 17362.
14. *Royal Domain*, p. 225 ; Arch. nat., JJ 50, f° 58, n° 90.
15. *Royal Domain*, p. 214-215 ; *Comptes Royaux*, n° 17369.

least 16 s. [16]. If other woods were also included in the 1312 figure then we would have a clear decline in value by that date instead of the apparent increase. Similar calculations may be made for the farm of the lands of Robert d'Angerville at La Thillaye. Here there was apparently a slight increase (from 202 l. to 213 l.) but if we add in two small farms, one of which is explicitly mentioned as a separate farm in the 1312 total, we find that we have at least 213 l. income for the earlier period and perhaps a little more [17].

This is not to say that no land increased in value. Land at Les Planets rose from 11 s. an acre to 12 s. an acre [18]. The land of Hue de Roies was farmed for 18 l. 2 s. in the 1260's and for 19 l. 4 s. in 1312 [19]. Some very small farms rose a shilling or two in value [20]. But, in spite of uncertainties in identification it is clear that between 1261 and 1312 there had been none of the tremendous increases in the value of individual farms that marked the period between 1238 and 1261 [21].

One final statistic must be offered with caution. In an earlier work I found that the mean annual value of an acre as given in the survey of the *bailliage* of Rouen in 1261 was 16 s. [22]. The mean annual value of land mentioned in the cartulary of Marigny was 12 s. an acre. The comparison is not entirely fair, for much of Marigny's land was in the *bailliage* of Gisors, a region for which I have no thirteenth century figures, and some of it was clearly in areas that had once been forest or waste. Nevertheless, as the case of Menneval shows, the decline was as great in the viscounty of Bernay (for which we do have good thirteenth century evidence) as it was elsewhere, and an overall drop of 25 % is too great to be explained by pure chance.

Another sign of economic decline, the decrease in the annual value of mills, may be discussed more briefly, since much of the evidence was presented in my article on Beaumont-le-Roger [23]. A brief table will show the changes. The left-hand column refers to pages in *The Royal Domain in the Bailliage of Rouen* (c. 1261), the right-hand column gives the entries in vol. II of the *Comptes Royaux* that come from the account of the viscount of Auge in 1312, or entries in the registers of Philip IV.

---

16. *Royal Domain*, p. 197-199 ; *Comptes Royaux*, n° 17388.
17. *Royal Domain*, p. 185-189 ; *Comptes Royaux*, n° 17384.
18. *Royal Domain*, p. 86 ; *Cartulaire de Marigny*, p. 104.
19. *Royal Domain*, p. 200 ; *Comptes Royaux*, n° 17390.
20. For example, land of Rogier Leprevost rose from 50 s. to 85 s. and the land of Robert de Bloville, from 35 s. to 36 s. 6 d., see *Royal Domain*, p. 202, and *Comptes Royaux*, n° 17367 and 17390.
21. *Royal Domain*, p. 5, 13-15.
22. *Ibid.*, p. 24.
23. *Economic Conditions in Beaumont*, p.[260].

TABLE I

p. 208 « Le molin de Gibellenc », 40 l.

n⁰ 17376 « Du moulin Gibellent », feefarmed, 42 l.

p. 196 Mill of Pont l'Evêque, 40 l., « de cen est deue la disme », net is 36 l.

n⁰ 17377 Mill of Pont l'Evêque, feefarmed, 33 l.

p. 205 « Le molin de Kalunde », 80 l.

n⁰ 17378 « Du moulin de Calompne », feefarmed, 52 l.

p. 186 « Le molin Telliart o la moute seiche et l. verg. de pré, por tout XVI l. »

n⁰ 17379 « Du moulin Teillart fé », 12 l.

p. 208 « Le molin de Wacul », 32 l.

n⁰ 17399 « Du moulin de Vacul », 33 l. 9 s.

p. 204 « Vers les Autielz, demie molin », 24 l.

n⁰ 17401 « Du moulin des Aautiex », 26 l. 2 s. 3 d. (Is this still just half a mill ?)

p. 178 « Le molin de la porte et du vivier o la moute seiche », 20 l. « Le molin foulerez o le prael » 7 l. (Both these in the farm of Angerville.)

nᵒ 17451 « Du moulin fouleor et du moulin de la Port à Angerville », feefarmed, 18 l.

p. 202 « Le molin de Herouessart por la partie le Roi, 8 l., et 1 setier de forment de 16 s. »

n⁰ 17458 « Du moulin de Herouxart », feefarmed, 6 l.

p. 132 « Le molin au ble o la seiche moute de Maneval », 34 l.
p. 138 « 2 moulins foulerez », 30 l.

JJ 47, fol 65, n⁰ 48 (1310), mill of Menneval, 30 l. fulling mill, 8 l.

p. 84 three mills at Montfort-sur-Risle, 160 l.

JJ 49, fol. 102 v⁰, n⁰ 230 (1314), mills of Montfort-sur-Risle, 130 l.

To summarize, in eight cases, the annual income from the mill had declined, sometimes sharply, in three cases it has risen slightly. The practice of giving perpetual farms (fieffarms) may account for some of the declines (although in one case there was a rise), but it may also reflect difficulties in finding men who would lease mills for a short term. And may I remind the reader that two farmers who took mills at high rents under Philip the Fair found that they had made a bad bargain[24]. The mills of Vaudreuil with the fisheries and the port had been valued in 1261 at least 114 l. 5 s. Under Philip the Fair the mills and their appartenances were feefarmed for 144 l. a year. The farmer complained that the lease had been made during the period when royal money was overvalued and that a new mill, built with royal permission in this neighborhood, was injuring his business. The farm was reduced to 120 l. a year, a slight increase over the 1261 valuation, but probably still too high considering the competition from the new mill[25]. In the other case the mill of the Busc de Hastingues had been farmed for 55 l. a year under Philip. The farmer complained that he had been deceveid about the value of the mill and the *bailli*, after investigation, agreed. Louis X cut the payment to 30 l. a year[26]. The fact that the government was willing to make such sharp reductions suggests that it would not have been easy to find other farmers, and that leasing royal mills was no longer as attractive an investment as it had been in the days of Saint Louis.

Little needs to be said about loss of income from *prévôtés*, since they were discussed at some length in my article on Beaumont. To summarize this information briefly, income from the *prévôtés* of Beaumont, Bonsmoulins, Breteuil, Exmes, Falaise, Verneuil, Vire and the Lire-Rugles-Glos group declined during the last two decades of the thirteenth century, and in the cases of Beaumont, Lire and Glos, the decline was continuing as late as 1310. The following tables show changes in income from these *prévôtés* from 1271 or 1272 to 1310.

TABLE II [28]

Beaumont 1261 1 200 l.   1310 795 l. plus 100 to 150 l. for
                                                 undervalued grain.

TABLE III [29]

	Breteuil	Exmes	Falaise	Moulins-Bonsmoulins	Verneuil	Vire
1271	560 l.			250 l.	725 l.	
1272			850 l.	250 l.	900 l. ?[30]	480 l.

---

24. *Economic Conditions in Beaumont*, p.[260].

25. *Royal Domain*, p. 224. If « la costume ileques » and the fair of St. Denis (both of which follow the entry about the mills) were added in, we would have 144 l. in 1261. Arch. nat., JJ 47, f° 53, n° 83, the leases under Philip the Fair definitely included the fisheries and the port, and also rights of justice (1309-1310).

26. *Ibid.*, JJ 52, f° 22, n° 44 (1315).

27. *Economic Conditions in Beaumont*, p.[260-261].

28. *Ibid.*, p. 284 ; *Royal Domain*, p. 75.

29. Arch. nat. J 775, J 780. Entries for 1292, 1297 and 1299 are printed in the *Comptes Royaux*, t. I, p. 338-339, 343, 350-351, 357.

30. J 775, n° 6, the entry for Easter 1272 is not clear, but the Michaelmas payment was definitely 450 l.

Year						
1273	580 l.			250 l.	800 l. [31]	
1274	580 l.			250 l.	750 l.	
1275	620 l.			250 l.	725 l.[32]	480 l.
1276	620 l.	240 l.	725 l.	250 l.	700 l. ? [33]	480 l.
1277	625 l.	240 l.	725 l.	250 l.	725 l.	500 l.
1278		240 l.	750 l.		800 l.	500 l.
1279	600 l.	240 l.	750 l.	200 l.	800 l.	440 l.
1280	568 l.	240 l.	720 l.	200 l.	600 l.	440 l.
1281	600 l.	200 l.	745 l.	240 l.	650 l.	410 l.
1282	650 l.	240 l.	720 l.	220 l.	800 l. ? [34]	440 l.
1292	600 l.	210 l.	720 l.		800 l. ? [34]	380 l.
1297		230 l.				400 l.
1299	550 l.				725 l. [35]	
1302	550 l.				600 to 700 l. [36]	

Note that the highest yields all came in the reign of Philip III and also that the last three years (1297, 1299 and 1302) all came in the period of « feeble money », that is, a period of a grossly overvalued currency. Granting that the French economy of the late thirteenth century was much more resistant to inflationary pressures than our own, one would still expect some increase in prices and therefore some increase in taxes on commerce, which formed a considerable part of the revenues of prévôtés.

TABLE IV [37]

	Lire	Rugles	Clos
1272	270 l.	80 l.	200 l.
1273	250 l.	80 l.	200 l.
1274	250 l.	95 l.	200 l.
1275	270 l.	95 l.	210 l.
1276	270 l.	95 l.	210 l.
1277	270 l.	95 l.	210 l.
1278	270 l.	100 l.	210 l.

31. Arch. nat., J 780, n° 4, the Easter payment is 350 l. and the Michaelmas payment is 450 l.

32. J 780, n° 4, 350 l. at Michaelmas and 375 l. at Easter.

33. J 775, n° 9, only the Michaelmas payment of 350 l. is given. The Easter payment may have been 375 l., as in the previous year.

34. J 780, n°ˢ 7-8, only the Michaelmas payments are given for these years, but it looks as if payments were at that time equally divided between the terms.

35. Comptes Royaux, n° 7185, only the Easter payment is given.

36. Ibid., n° 15610, the entry is not entirely legible. It is 3 l. 10 s.; my guess is that it was 312 l. 10 s. for the term or 625 l. for the year, but it could have been 337 l. 10 s. or 675 l. a year. Verneuil regularly paid in multiples of 25 l.

37. Arch. nat., J 775, 780 ; Comptes Royaux, t. I, p. 343, 353-354, 357, t. II, p. 130 ; B.N., français 8764, f° 10, 10 v°.

1279	240 l.	100 l.	210 l.
1280	240 l.	100 l.	210 l. [38]
1281	163 l.	140 l.	160 l.
1282	270 l.	110 l.	180 l.
1292	220 l.	125 l.	150 l.
1297	175 l.	130 l.	130 l.
1299	175 l. [39]	130 l. [39]	150 l.
1302	175 l.	130 l. ? [40]	158 l. 10 s.
1310	160 l.		133 l.

Lire and Glos followed the same pattern of decline that we have seen elsewhere. Rugles, on the contrary, rose fairly steadily. It was given to the heirs of Jean Le Veneur in 1308 in exchange for their holdings at Longchamps [41], and if we add up items that presumably were part of the *prévôté* the total value would still be 130 l. or a little more. One important item was « le denier et le maille de blé, de fer, de la coustume qui vient à la ville et des acenses du minerei et pour la tornoierie », 38 l. a year [42]. Glos-la-Ferrière was a well-known iron-working center ; it had always been closely associated with Rugles ; it is possible that the sharp drop in income from Glos and the increase at Rugles was due to a shift of some metal workers from Glos to Rugles. But in spite of this redistribution, the three *prévôtés* taken together were yielding 100 l. less a year in 1297 and 1299 than in the 1270's.

Our records are unfortunately incomplete for the two largest *prévôtés*, Caen and Rouen. For Caen there is a perceptible rise in yearly income, 2000 l. in 1272, 2100 l. in 1278, 2275 l. in 1281, 2200 l. in 1282 and 2208 l. in 1292 [43]. The high point in 1281 is

---

38. Arch. nat. J 775, n° 11. The three *prévôtés* of Lire, Rugles and Glos at times were paid for at three terms, with one ferm a little higher than the others, and sometimes at two terms, 2/3 at one term and 1/3 at the other. (See n. 40.) In 1280 we have for Glos 70 l. at Easter (= Candlemas ?) and 80 l. at Michaelmas (= All Saints ?). I suspect that there was a payment of 60 l. at Ascension, which would give the 210 l. that Glos had been paying since 1275.

39. The 16th c. clerk who made these extracts for the Chambre des Comptes wrote a very poor hand, and made a number of errors. J 780, n° 11 (for 1299) is especially bad. Because « molendino » appeared in the preceding entry, he inserted « molendino » before « prepositure Lire ». The figures show, however, that the payment of 116 l. 13 s. 4 d. was the normal payment of 2/3 of the farm of the *prévôté*, of Lire. For Rugles, Fawtier read 96 l. 13 s. 4 d. (*Comptes Royaux*, n° 7188) and I read 86 l. 13 s. 4 d. I think my reading is correct, for it makes the annual payment for Rugles 130 l., the same as the year before and (probably) the same as in 1302.

40. *Comptes Royaux*, n°ᵒˢ 15615 and 15616, Rugles pays 40 l. « pro tertio Candelose », and 50 l. « pro tertio Ascensionis ». This is another case of three unequal payments ; if the final payment were 40 l., the total, 130 l., would conform to the payments for 1297 and 1299.

41. *Cartulaire de Marigny*, p. 54-55.

42. *Ibid.*, p. 54.

43. Arch. nat., J 775, n°ᵒˢ 6, 10, 11, 12 , J 780, n° 8 (entry for 1292 printed in *Comptes Royaux*, n° 6738).

typical, and several other *prévôtés* which reached a high point in 1281 or 1282 declined in value only after 1292, so that Caen may or may not be an exception to the general trend. The Viscounty of the Water at Rouen was the equivalent of a *prévôté*[44], but it was so large and its income was collected in so many different ways that it is difficult to make exact comparisons. The Viscounty could be farmed as a whole, divided into several farms, farmed only in part, or administered entirely by royal officials. We cannot use the survey of 1261 as a base line, because it gives no values for dues on wine, which were the most important part of the revenue of the Viscounty. We should also remember that prices for wine changed much more rapidly and sharply than those for most other commodities. Nevertheless, it is clear that the Viscounty of the Water followed the pattern of the smaller *prévôtés*. During the thirteenth century yearly income from the Viscounty increased ; after 1300 the trend was downward.

TABLE V

Yearly Income from the Viscounty of the Water at Rouen[45].

1230   2900 l. at Michaelmas, or 5800 l. a year.
1238   2950 l. at Easter, or 5900 l. a year.
1301   7062 l. at Easter, 1385 l. at Michaelmas, 8447 l. for the year*.
1304   3890 l. at Easter, 1373 l. at Michaelmas, 5261 l. for the year*.
1305   Farmed for 8000 l., plus 188 l. not farmed, 8188 l. for the year*.
1311   Farmed for 6000 l., plus 30 l. for a small farm, 6301 l. for the year.
1316   Farmed for 6050 l. for the year.
1317   Royal officers collected 4372 l. for the year.
1318   Farmed for 4762 l. for the year.

* Years of overvalued currency.

It is possible to trace the yield of one important component of the income from the Viscounty from 1261 to 1317. This is the group of dues called « menues boistes », perhaps collections from outlying ports[46]. In 1261 « menue boiste » was said to be worth

---

44. The basic study is Ch. de BEAUREPAIRE, *De la Vicomté de l'Eau de Rouen*, Paris and Rouen, 1856. See especially chapter 3, on the farms of the viscounty and chapter 6 on the revenues.

45. *Ibid.*, p. 66-70, and 422-459 for all the fourteenth century entries. For the years 1230 and 1238 see Rec. Hist. G. et F., t. XXIV, *preuves*, n° 89, and, t. XXI, p. 255.

46. Du Cange suggests that « boista » was a duty on grain and was connected with « boistellus » a variant of « boissellus ». In his French dictionary he says « boiste » is a « péage ». But while « minuta boista » is used in early accounts, by 1317 it has become « minuta pissida », which can only mean boxes, probably boxes in which small payments were collected. Beaurepaire, p. 29, a farmer of the Viscounty in 1452 claimed the right to establish a collector and a « boite » at the port of Jumièges.

1500 l. a year [47]. In 1301 it yielded 783 l., in 1304 only 707 l. and in 1317 it had gone up to 973 l. [48]. The fluctuations after 1300 are less important than the unusually sharp drop from 1261 to 1301.

There remains only the abnormal case of Honfleur. Valued at 9 l. a year in 1261, it yielded 28 l. in 1312 [49]. Honfleur had had a small part in the building and supplying of a navy during the period of war and tension with England [50], and this may have stimulated economic activity in the port. It is also possible that the king had bought up rights of some lord in the region. In any case, the fourfold increase in annual yield cannot be matched anywhere else in the viscounty of Auge.

To sum up this part of the discussion, nine *prévôtés* declined in value (Beaumont, Breteuil, Falaise, Moulins-Bonsmoulins, Glos, Lire, Rouen, Verneuil and Vire), one declined less than ten percent (Exmes), two increased in value (Caen slightly, Rugles markedly), and one small *prévôté*, Honfleur rose sharply. The king was getting less from his Norman *prévôtés* after 1300 than he had in the decades just before 1300.

So far, then, the evidence seems to be consistent. An economic depression had affected both agriculture and commerce. Income from leases of land, from leases of mills and from dues on buying, selling and transporting goods had declined. This decline had taken place in spite of the stimulus of war expenditures and monetary inflation. The economy of Normandy was in an unhealthy condition.

Two pieces of evidence could be cited against this conclusion. In the first place, according to the account of 1312, the viscount of Auge owed 4937 l. for the Michaelmas term of 1312, while the estimated yearly value of the domain of the viscounty in the 1260's was only 2748 l. [51]. This apparently huge increase in yield, however, is deceptive. We must first substract 1269 l. carried over from the Easter account [52], and then about 1350 l. for income from sales of woods, *tiers et danger*, amercements, the viscount's seal and other intermittent and unpredictable sources of income [52]. Such items were deliberately omitted from the survey of 1261, which was concerned only with regular annual income. Finally, we must remember that more than half the income of the

---

47. *Royal Domain*, p. 38.
48. BEAUREPAIRE, p. 424, 427, 429, 432, 452-454.
49. *Royal Domain*, p. 219 ; *Comptes Royaux*, n° 17372.
50. *Comptes Royaux*, n°ˢ 24761, 25916.
51. *Comptes Royaux*, n° 17503 (this should be n° 17505) ; *Royal Domain*, p. 14.
52. *Comptes Royaux*, n° 17359 [15].
53. *Ibid.*, n°ˢ 17472-17504. This estimate may be a little low. It is evident that a mistake was made in adding up *tiers et danger* from small woods ; the total given in n° 17479 is less than the total of n°ˢ 17480-17490 (even if n° 17482 which was cancelled is omitted). At n° 17505 (erroneously printed as n° 17503) there is a partial total of 1385 l. which may well be the total for this casual income.

viscounty was received at Michaelmas. At that term some farmers paid half the money they owed, but many paid two-thirds, and some paid all of their annual rent. It is impossible to give exact figures, but a rough estimate would be that income from the domain, as defined in the survey of 1261, had increased by about 670 l. by 1312.

Faulty as these calculations may be, an increase of 25 % is too large to be explained away by errors in definition and in arithmetic. The only possible explanation is that the royal domain had increased in size, even though individual portions of the domain had decreased in value. Given the ceaseless activity of the government in buying, confiscating, exchanging, selling and giving away real estate, it would not be surprising to find that at a particular moment in a relatively small district the king had acquired more than he had lost. Over the long run the size of the royal domain tended to decrease, but this tendency was not very evident in Normandy in the early years of the fourteenth century. The Journals of the Treasury suggest that all the Norman viscounts were collecting large sums of money from the domain in 1301 [54].

There is specific evidence to support the hypothesis that the royal domain in the viscounty of Auge had increased rather than decreased between 1261 and 1312. The king had kept almost all the large farms in his hands and some on the large farms had increased in size. For example, the farm of the land of the lady of Darnetal at Criqueville had been greatly expanded to include a holding at Drubec [55]. Some recently forfeited lands were specifically mentioned in the account of 1312 [56], and there are about 20 other entries, not duplicated in the survey of 1261, that may refer to earlier forfeitures [57]. Finally, in 1312, income from lands held in wardship was included, as it had not been in the earlier document, and this alone accounted for 105 l. a year [58]. Altogether, items than can clearly be identified as temporary or permanent additions to the royal domain after 1261 amount to about 350 l., more than half the difference between the estimated yield of 1261 and the approximate income for 1312. The remaining 320 l. could

---

54. J. VIARD, *Les journaux du Trésor de Philippe le Bel*, Paris 1940, n⁰ˢ 4635, 5372, 2548, 3468, 4635, 5374. See J.R. STRAYER, *Viscounts and Viguiers under Philip the Fair*, in *Speculum*, XXXVIII (1963), p. 243-244.

55. *Comptes Royaux*, n⁰ˢ 17360, 17361, and 17375, farms of the lands of the lady of Darnétal yield at least 225 l. in 1312. *Royal Domain*, p. 179, the only farm named for the lady in 1261 was at Criqueville and was valued at 40 l. a year. Perhaps some of the lands of Raoul de Tilli, lord of Darnétal and Drubec (*Royal Domain*, p. 175, 198) had been added to the farm of the lady's lands, but no one unit of the farm of Raoul de Tilli would give us even approximately the income listed for 1312.

56. *Comptes Royaux*, n⁰ˢ 17459-17464.

57. *Ibid.*, n⁰ˢ 17442, 17443, lands of Mons. Nicholas Malesmains at Le Vieux Bourg and Cresseveuille, worth 34 l. 10 s. a year.

58. *Ibid.*, n⁰ˢ 17466-17471.

easily have come from additions to existing farms, and especially from adding in small woods and waste land that had not been mentioned in 1261. This apparently was done in the case of the Basset farm [59], and in two farms in neighboring viscounties. Income from the farm of Menneval increased from 160 l. in 1261 to 234 l. in 1311, even thought the value of land per acre went down [60]. But the farm of 1311 included 110 acres of woods, which were not mentioned in the survey of 1261, and by 1311 wooded land was very valuable [61]. The farm of Les Moutiers-Hubert, valued at 356 l. in 1261 was bid up to 390 l. in 1311, but once more a new item appears, 110 acres of « fades terres [62] ». Unfortunately, the account of 1312 does not give enough detail to show all such additions, but, since it included many items not listed in 1261 it may well have included woods and waste not previously accounted for.

At least we can say that the income from the royal domain in the viscounty of Auge did not increase during the reign of Philip the Fair at the spectacular rate at which it had increased during the middle years of the thirteenth century. The increase, if any, was slight, and it seems more likely that relative stability hab been attained by adding new holdings to make up for decreasing income from old holdings. If we had more complete figures for the reign of Saint Louis we might even find some decrease in overall income, but cessation of growth and the beginnings of stagnation are enough to show a change in the economic climate.

The other body of evidence that suggests improvement rather than depression in economic conditions in Normandy comes from prices of grain. If rents per acre of land were declining, if the mills that ground grain were yielding less revenue, if income from *prévôtés* (a large part of which came from imposts on the transportation and the sale of grain) were decreasing, then one would expect a corresponding decrease in the value of grain. Instead, we get a rather inconsistent pattern, lower values in the *bailliage* of Verneuil-Gisors, constant or slightly higher values in the *bailliage* of Rouen, and some tendency for the price of oats to rise relative the price of wheat. Many of these discrepancies can be explained by differences in the size of the measures that were used. For example, the measure of Vernon was about one-fourth smaller than that of Rouen [63] while the measure used at Les Andelys was only about 3 per cent smaller [64]. The first difference was great enough

59. See above, p.[267], and note 16.
60. *Royal Domain*, p. 131-132 ; Arch. nat., JJ 47, f° 64 v°, n° 98. For the decrease in the value of land per acre see above, p.[267], and notes 8 and 9.
61. *Economic Conditions in Beaumont*, p.[259].
62. *Royal Domain*, p. 152-154 ; A.N., JJ 49, f° 30 v°, n° 65.
63. *Comptes Royaux*, n° 24603, 10 setiers and 2 bushels of Vernon equal 7 1/2 setiers and 2 bushels of Rouen.
64. *Ibid.*, n°⁵ 24601, 24602, 98 muis and 5 1/2 setiers of Les Andelys equal 95 muis and 7 1/2 setiers of Rouen.

to affect all prices ; the second would be noticeable only where large quantities of grain were sold. We also know that the measure of Bonneville-sur-Touques was so large that prices there were higher than anywhere else in the *bailliage* of *Rouen* both in 1261 and in 1312 [65]. We must also remember that the value assigned to a rent in grain that was to be collected year after year would not be the same as the market value of the grain in any particular year.

In the survey of 1261 wheat was valued at 12 to 16 s. a setier (omitting the exceptional case of Bonneville) and oats at 4 s., 6 s. or 8 s. a setier [66]. In Marigny's cartulary (1308-1311) the setier of wheat in the *bailliage* of *Gisors* was valued at 10 or 11 s. of Paris, that is, at about 12 s. tournois (the usual Norman currency) [67]. In the *bailliage* of Rouen wheat was valued at 15, 17, and 20 s.t. a setier [68]. Oats were 5 s. 4 d. par. a setier (about 6 s. 4 d.t.) near Gisors, 6 s. 3 d.t. by the small measure of Les Andelys near Rouen, and 8 s.t., 12 s.t. and even 14 s.t. in places that used larger measures [69]. In the account of 1312, the setier of wheat is 20 to 24 s.t. in the region of Bonneville [70]. In the farm of Menneval (viscounty of Bernay) wheat had been 12 s. a setier and oats 4 s. a setier in 1261, in 1310 they were valued at 15 s. and 6 s. respectively [71]. On the other hand, near Rouen the setier of oats had been valued at 6 s. in 1261 and was worth only 5 s. 8 d. according to a document of 1314 [72].

These few scattered examples prove very little, but they certainly argue against the hypothesis of a long-term decline in the price of grain. They do not, however, demonstrate any overall increase in prices. The highest prices came from an area where prices had always been high. The apparent increase in the price of oats relative to the price of wheat had already been anticipated in the actual farms (as opposed to the estimated values) made in the 1260's. Thus oats valued at 6 s. a setier were farmed for 7 s., oats valued at 5 s. a setier were farmed for 7 s. 6 d. a setier, and on two occasions oats were farmed for 8 s. a setier [73]. In two cases the farm paid for both wheat and oats increased, but the increase was greater for oats. In the first case, wheat valued at 10 s. a setier was farmed for 12 s., an increase of 20 % ; oats

65. *Royal Domain*, p. 106 ; *Comptes Royaux*, n⁰ˢ 17400, 17424, 17430.
66. *Royal Domain*, p. 25, 45, 52, 58-59, 121-122, 178, 218-219. (Here and elsewhere I take « blé » to mean wheat, though I am aware that it could mean grain in general. But in Normandy prices for « blé » are always in the range for prices of wheat.)
67. *Cartulaire de Marigny*, p. 34, 53, 61, 124.
68. *Ibid.*, p. 82, 102, 103.
69. *Ibid.*, p. 124, 103, 84, 102, 105, 69.
70. *Comptes Royaux*, n⁰ˢ 17391, 17400, 17424.
71. *Royal Domain*, p. 132 ; Arch. nat., JJ 47, f° 64 v°, n° 48.
72. *Royal Domain*, p. 44 ; Arch. nat., JJ 49, f° 70, n° 163.
73. *Royal Domain*, p. 45, 218, 51-52, 219.

valued at 4 s. a setier were farmed for 6 s., an increase of 33 1/3 % [74]. In the second case wheat rose from 13 s. 4 d. a setier to 14 s. (5 %) while oats rose from 4 s. a setier to 5 s. a setier (25 %) [75].

In short, the scanty data on grain values seem to support the earlier conclusion about the domain as a whole. During the thirteenth century the estimated (and probably the actual) value of grain rose sharply [76] ; after 1300 the estimated value leveled off and may even have declined in some regions such as the *bailliage* of Gisors-Verneuil. Remembering that, thanks to the return to « good money » in 1306, all our prices are expressed in money of almost constant value, these are surprising results. In the case of grain, particularly, the estimated values may give a truer indication of the economic climate than a series of actual market prices. There must have been great fluctuations in market prices, as there were all through the fourteenth century, but men buying, leasing or exchanging land had to take a long-term view, and this view was not optimistic. Overall, they expected no greater income from sales of grain than their predecessors had enjoyed. We have seen the same attitude in regard to land, mills, and *prévôtés*. Lack of confidence in the future, doubts about growth in income and production — these are signs of an economic depression. It can scarcely be doubted that such a depression had begun in Normandy by the end of the thirteenth century.

---

74. *Royal Domain*, p. 58-59.
75. *Ibid.*, p. 121-122. While there can be no direct comparison between grain prices in Normandy and in Touraine, it is interesting to note that when grain was bought for the army in 1304 in the *bailliage* of Tours, prices for oats were very high in relation to prices for wheat. *Comptes Royaux*, n°ˢ 27134 to 27167, wheat was bought for 9 to 10 s. a setier while oats were 6 to 7 s. a setier.
76. *Royal Domain*, p. 25-26 ; L. DELISLE, *Etudes sur la classe agricole en Normandie*, Evreux, 1851, p. 589 ff.

INDEX
THE ROYAL DOMAIN
IN THE BAILLIAGE OF ROUEN

INDEX OF NAMES AND PLACES
IN THE APPENDIX

SUBJECT INDEX

All ordinary words are given in their modern French form. For example the entry for "froment" includes the O.F. form "forment" and the English "wheat"; "oeufs" includes O.F. "oeus", "oes", and English "eggs", etc. Capons, hens and eggs appear so frequently and usually in such close association with each other that they have been put under a single heading. "Corvée" and "preere" are used interchangeably; it seemed better to list all such services under the heading "corvée" in order to give a true picture of the frequency of boon labor. Unusual and doubtful words are given in the original spelling. This index covers both the original text and the Appendix.